THE OLD-FASHIONED COOKBOOK

By Jan McBride Carlton

Illustrations by Alice and Martin Provensen

Weathervane Books

New York

Acknowledgments

Many individuals and organizations were of invaluable help to me in preparing this cookbook. In particular I would like to thank the following friends and relatives who contributed so much of their time and support: Mae Barnes, Crist Brown, Dottie Butts, J. Robert Carlton, Jr., Nell Clarke, Ruth Ellen Church, Virginia Cottrell, Sally Dawson, Ann Siegel Drucker, Esther Easton, Marion Ecker, Bob Finley, Josephine Fisher, Elinor Fox, Edna Gaul, Judy Greenwalt, Kay Helmick, Nancy Hitch, Ann Honey, Barbara Horman, Mary Jamerson, Gay Montague Jewett, Doris G. Johnson, Martha Johnston, Virginia and Elmer Keller, Eileen Kiess, Francia Koehn, Mary Lou Laursen, Marjory Lichtenberg, Ruth Lier, Joanne Locke, the late Pearl McBride, Robert L. McBride, Marillyn McCulloch, Joseph Morrow, Roseanne Parr, Judy Ponton, Inger Rice, Virginia Richards, Ann and Michael Rostafinski, Edward Saxe, Reba Stagg, Joan Stoy, Chris Stroman, Ann Tyler, Kathy Vandenberg, Gretchen Van Ert, Bebe West, and Jo Anne Will.

I am especially indebted to my late grandmother, Elizabeth Stienz Keller, my late great-aunt, Effie Johnson Harvey, and the late Pauline Carlton, who preserved my husband's favorite recipes that have been handed down from generation to generation.

I am also indebted to the following who most kindly provided me with their kitchen-tested recipes: the American Institute of Baking, Betty Crocker Kitchens, Campbell Soup Company, Carlton House Resort Inn, General Foods Corporation, H. J. Heinz Company, Hershey Foods Corporation, Kraft Foods, the National Broiler Council, the National Dairy Council, the National Duckling Council, the Nestle Company, the Pillsbury Company, and the Quaker Oats Company.

In addition, I wish to thank the American Dairy Association, the American Meat Institute, the Chocolate Information Council, Hunt Wesson Foods, the National Live Stock and Meat Board, the National Marine Fisheries Services, the National Turkey Federation, the Pan American Coffee Institute, and the United States Department of Agriculture for their advice and expertise.

I am also grateful to Chiquita Brands, Inc., ITT Gwaltney, Inc., John Morrell & Company, Sunkist Growers, Inc., the Wheat Flour Institute, and Wilson & Company for their very valuable information and guidance.

And finally my thanks to various state departments of commerce and agriculture, local chambers of commerce, newspaper food editors, historical societies, utility companies, and certain restaurants throughout the country for their generous support.

J. McB. C.

CHIVE.

Copyright © MCMLXXV by Jan McBride Carlton.
Illustrations copyright © MCMLXXV by Alice and Martin Provensen.
All rights reserved.
This edition is published by Weathervane Books, distributed by Crown Publishers, Inc., by arrangement with Holt, Rinehart and Winston.
a b c d e f g h
WEATHERVANE 1979 EDITION
Book design by Jos. Trautwein
Printed in the United States of America

Library of Congress Cataloging in Publication Data
Main entry under title:
The Old-fashioned cookbook.
  Includes index.
  1. Cookery, American.   I. Carlton,
Jan McBride, 1936-
TX715.043   1975b   641.5′973   78-31898
ISBN 0-517-27794-8

CONTENTS

For
Pussycat

With special thanks to Chris, Esther, Marge, and Marion.

And my gratitude

to Albert as well for his part in making

this book a reality.

INTRODUCTION

In a little over two hundred years the United States has developed from thirteen sparsely populated colonies into a country of vast proportions and complexities. Ours is a nation of immigrants from every corner of the globe who brought with them the customs and cuisines of their homeland.

America's constantly evolving culinary traditions are among the most varied in the world because they derive from so many sources. First was the indigenous food cultivated and prepared by the American Indians, then an adaptation of the cooking styles of the Dutch and English settlers, the addition of the hearty ethnic dishes of the northern European pioneers, and, later, the absorption of the wide-ranging culinary styles of the succeeding waves of immigrants. Even now the expansion of our cuisine continues, thanks to the advances made in modern technology.

Across the country a great deal of pride is still taken in preserving the culinary traditions of our "melting pot" heritage. As a home economist it has been my privilege and pleasure to travel extensively throughout the country over the years. During those trips I became fascinated by the wealth of local specialty dishes and the way they varied from region to region. In an attempt to record and preserve the wide range of American food customs I began a collection of old cookbooks, many of which date back to the 1800s. I collected recipes from garden-club, community, and church-group cookbooks and even recorded family favorites of friends whom I encountered along the way. Many of the recipes had been handed down from generation to generation; some were carefully written down, while others were passed along by word of mouth. Out of what became a mammoth collection I have selected those recipes that I feel represent the true diversity of American cooking.

Reading old cookbooks as history can be entertaining but not very practical for the modern cook in her up-to-date kitchen. The pioneer woman often spent all day in the kitchen preparing stocks, plucking fowls, baking pies, and canning preserves. Today's woman has too many outside demands on her time. It is for this reason that I have adapted these time-honored recipes for the fast-paced living of today. My goal, however, has been to retain authenticity and flavor while using time-saving techniques. When practical, the original ingredients have been maintained, but in some cases substitutions were made, since the foods available in supermarkets today are very different from those available to our forebears. While the preparation methods of these recipes have been updated and simplified, the results still have that special down-home goodness and flavor that I hope will delight you, your family, and your friends. *Bon appétit!*

JAN McBRIDE CARLTON

BASIC INFORMATION

Margarine may be substituted for butter unless otherwise specified.

Flour is all-purpose unless otherwise indicated.

Sour cream denotes the commercial product.

Herbs and spices are ground unless otherwise indicated.

Canned soups are to be used undiluted.

When whipping cream, chill cream, bowl, and beaters thoroughly before using.

Have egg whites at room temperature when whipping.

Use very cold water or iced water when testing candy temperatures.

When sauterne is called for, use the dry white domestic table wine known as sauterne rather than the sweeter French variety.

If fish or shellfish are purchased frozen, thaw and then proceed as recipe directs.

Preheat oven for 10 to 15 minutes before baking.

Insert meat thermometer into thickest part of meat, away from fat and bone. Keep dial as far away from heat source as possible.

To heatproof the handle of a pot or skillet to be used in the oven, cover the handle loosely with two or three thicknesses of slightly crushed aluminum foil.

Packaged commercial stuffing may be substituted for Grandma's Bread Stuffing (see index).

A commercial cooked salad dressing may be substituted in recipes calling for Tangy Cooked Salad Dressing (see index) or mayonnaise.

Undiluted evaporated milk may be substituted for light cream or half and half.

Commercial packaged pie-crust mix may be substituted for Pastry for Double-Crust Pie (see index).

To *sauté,* cook in melted butter over low heat. When directions call for *browning* meats, use moderate heat.

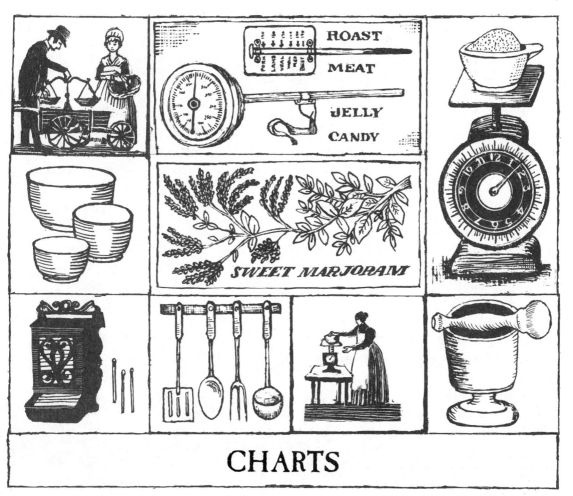

CHARTS

EMERGENCY SUBSTITUTIONS

Follow recipes exactly when possible. In emergencies you may have to substitute one of the following.

	IF YOU DON'T HAVE	USE
BAKING POWDER	1 teaspoon baking powder	1 teaspoon cream of tartar plus 1 teaspoon baking soda
BUTTER*	1 cup butter	1 cup margarine or $7/8$ to 1 cup hydrogenated fat or lard plus ½ teaspoon salt
CHOCOLATE*	1 square (1 ounce) chocolate	3 tablespoons cocoa powder plus 1 tablespoon fat
CORNSTARCH[1]	1 tablespoon cornstarch	2 tablespoons flour (approximate)
FLOUR		
For thickening*	1 teaspoon flour	½ teaspoon cornstarch or 2 teaspoons quick-cooking tapioca
For baking*	1 cup all-purpose flour 1 cup cake flour	1 cup plus 2 tablespoons cake flour $7/8$ cup all-purpose flour
HERBS	1 tablespoon fresh	1 teaspoon dried
MILK		
Sour or buttermilk*	1 cup sour or buttermilk	1 cup milk plus 1 tablespoon lemon juice or vinegar
Fresh, whole[1]	1 cup fresh whole milk	½ cup evaporated milk plus ½ cup water
SUGARS AND SYRUPS		
Honey*	1 cup honey	1¼ cups sugar plus ¼ cup liquid
Corn syrup*	1½ cups corn syrup	1 cup sugar plus ¼ cup water
Cinnamon sugar	¼ cup cinnamon sugar	¼ cup granulated sugar plus 1 teaspoon cinnamon
YEAST*	1 cake compressed yeast	1 package or 5 teaspoons active dry yeast

[1]. SOURCE: Author

* *Handbook of Food Preparation* (Sixth Edition, 1971). Published by American Home Economics Association, 2010 Massachusetts Avenue, N.W., Washington, D.C.

FOOD EQUIVALENTS

BEANS, DRIED
Kidney or Lima*	1 pound	2½ cups uncooked; 5½ cups cooked
Navy*	1 pound	2⅓ cups uncooked; 5½ cups cooked

BREAD, LOAF
	1 pound loaf	12 to 16 regular slices
Bread crumbs, soft[1]	1 slice	½ cup soft crumbs
Bread crumbs, dry[1]	1 slice	⅓ cup fine dry bread crumbs

BROTH, CHICKEN OR BEEF
	1 cup	1 bouillon cube or 1 envelope powdered broth base dissolved in 1 cup boiling water

BUTTERS, FATS, OILS
Butter or margarine*	1 pound	2 cups
Hydrogenated shortening*	1 pound	2⅓ cups
Butter or margarine, whipped*	1 pound	3 cups
Oils*	1 pint or 1 pound	2 cups
Suet, chopped medium-fine*	1 pound	3¾ cups

CEREALS
Cornmeal
white*	1 cup	4 cups cooked
	1 pound	3 to 3½ cups
yellow*	1 pound	3 cups; 16⅔ cups cooked
Farina*	1 pound	3 cups; 16⅔ cups cooked
Grits*	1 pound	3 cups; 10 cups cooked
Hominy, whole*	1 pound	2½ cups; 16⅔ cups cooked
Oats, rolled*	1 pound	6¼ cups; 8 cups cooked

Rice
long-grain*	1 pound	2½ cups; about 8 cups cooked
precooked*	½ pound	2 cups

CHEESE
Cheddar, American, Swiss, mozzarella*	1 pound	4 cups grated
Cottage*	1 pound	2 cups
Cream*	8 ounces	1 cup
	3 ounces	6 tablespoons (about ⅓ cup)
Parmesan*	3 ounces	1 cup grated or shredded

CHOCOLATE
Chips*	6 ounces	1 cup
Unsweetened (bitter)*	1 ounce	1 square

*[1]Source information for this chart is found on page 14.

COCONUT, SHREDDED OR FLAKED	3½- to 4-ounce can	1¼ to 1⅓ cups
COFFEE, GROUND[1]	1 pound	80 tablespoons
CREAM,		
Light	½ pint	1 cup
Half and half*	1 pint	2 cups
Heavy or whipping*	½ pint	1 cup; 2 cups whipped
EGGS		
Whole[1]	5–7	1 cup (approximate)
Whites, large[1]	1 cup	8 to 10 whites (approximate)
Yolks, large[1]	1 cup	12 to 14 (approximate)
	1 yolk	1 tablespoon
FLOURS		
All-purpose, sifted*	1 pound	4 cups
All-purpose, unsifted, spooned*	1 pound	3½ cups
Cake, sifted*	1 pound	4⅔ cups (approximate)
Cake, unsifted, spooned*	1 pound	4 cups (approximate)
Self-rising, sifted*	1 pound	4 cups
Whole-wheat*	1 pound	3⅓ cups
Rye, light, sifted*	1 pound	5 cups (approximate)
Rye, dark, sifted*	1 pound	3½ cups (approximate)
FRUITS, CANNED		
Apples, sliced*	20 ounces	2½ cups
Apricots		
whole*	1 pound	8 to 12
halved*	1 pound	2½ cups
Blueberries*	14 ounces	1½ cups
Cherries, red tart, pitted*	1 pound	2 cups (approximate)
Cranberry juice*	1 quart	4 cups
Cranberry sauce*	1 pound	1⅔ cups
Fruit juices (grapefruit, orange, pineapple)*	46 ounces	5¾ cups
Fruit salad or cocktail*	17 ounces	2 cups
Grapefruit, sections*	1 pound	2 cups
Peaches		
halves*	1 pound	6 to 10 halves
sliced*	1 pound	2 cups

Pears, halves*	1 pound	6 to 10 halves
Pineapple		
chunks and tidbits*	29 ounces	3¾ cups
crushed*	29 ounces	3¾ cups
sliced*	20 ounces	10 slices

FRUITS, DRIED

Apricots		
dried*	1 pound	3 cups
cooked*	1 pound	6 cups
Currants*	1 pound	3¼ cups
Dates		
whole*	1 pound	60
pitted, cut	1 pound	2½ cups
Figs		
whole*	1 pound	44
cut fine*	1 pound	2⅔ cups
Prunes		
whole with pits*	1 pound	2½ cups
cooked*	1 pound	4 to 4½ cups
pitted*	1 pound	2¼ cups
pitted and cooked*	1 pound	4 to 4½ cups
Raisins, seedless		
whole*	1 pound	2¾ cups
chopped*	1 pound	2 cups

FRUITS, FRESH AND FROZEN

Apples, fresh, whole*	1 pound	3 medium; 3 cups cored and sliced
Apricots, fresh*	1 pound	8 to 12; 2½ cups sliced or halved
Avocado	1 pound	2½ cups cubed
Bananas, whole*	1 pound	3 to 4 medium; 2 to 2½ cups sliced; 1⅓ cups mashed
Blueberries		
fresh*	1 pound	2 cups
frozen*	10 ounces	1½ cups
Cherries, sour pitted		
fresh*	1 pound	2⅓ cups
frozen*	20 ounces	2½ cups
Cranberries, fresh*	1 pound	3½ to 4 cups
Grapes, seedless, fresh*	1 pound	2½ cups
Lemons		
fresh*	1 medium	3 tablespoons juice (approximate); 2 teaspoons grated peel
frozen juice (concentrate)*	6 fluid ounces	¾ cup
Limes, fresh*	1 medium	2 tablespoons juice; 2 teaspoons grated peel

Oranges
    fresh* — 1 medium — ⅓ to ½ cup juice (approximate); 2 to 3 tablespoons grated peel
    frozen orange juice (concentrate)* — 6 fluid ounces — ¾ cup

Peaches, fresh* — 1 pound — 4 medium; 2 cups peeled and sliced
Pears, fresh* — 1 pound — 4 medium; 2 cups sliced

Pineapple
    fresh* — 2 pounds — 3 cups cubed
    frozen, chunks* — 13½ ounces — 1½ cups

Rhubarb
    fresh* — 1 pound — 4 to 8 stalks; 2 cups cut up and cooked
    frozen, sliced* — 12 ounces — 1½ cups

Strawberries
    fresh, whole* — 1 pint — 2 cups
    frozen, whole* — 1 pound — 1⅓ cups
    frozen, sliced — 10 ounces — 1 cup

GELATIN, UNFLAVORED* — 1 ounce — 1 envelope or 1 tablespoon

MACARONI, SPAGHETTI, NOODLES — 8 ounces — 4 cups cooked

MILK
    Whole, skim, buttermilk* — 1 quart — 4 cups
    Evaporated* — 13 ounces — 1 cup plus 5 tablespoons; 2½ cups plus 2 tablespoons reconstituted

NUTS

		In shells	Shelled
Almonds*	1 pound	1 to 1½ cups	3¼ cups
Peanuts[1]	1 pound	2 to 2½ cups	4 cups
Pecans*	1 pound	2¼ cups	3½ to 4 cups
Walnuts, English*	1 pound	2 cups	3½ cups

SUGARS
    Brown, light* — 1 pound — 2¼ cups (packed)
    Confectioners', unsifted* — 1 pound — 4½ cups (approximate)
    Granulated[1] — 1 pound — 2 to 2¼ cups (approximate)
    Superfine[1] — 1 pound — 2⅓ cups (approximate)

SYRUPS
    Corn syrup* — 16 fluid ounces — 2 cups
    Honey* — 1 pound — 1⅓ cups
    Maple syrup* — 12 fluid ounces — 1½ cups
    Molasses, cane* — 12 fluid ounces — 1½ cups
    Sorghum* — 1 pound — 1⅓ cups

VEGETABLES, FRESH, FROZEN, AND CANNED

Asparagus spears

fresh*	1 pound	16 to 20 pieces; 2 cups cooked
frozen*	10 ounces	2 cups
canned*	10 ounces	2 cups

Green or Wax Beans

fresh*	1 pound	3 cups; 2½ cups cooked
frozen*	9 ounces	1½ cups
canned*	15½ ounces	1¾ cups

Lima Beans

fresh*	1 pound	2 cups; 1⅔ to 2 cups cooked
frozen*	10 ounces	1¾ cups
canned*	1 pound	2 cups

Beets

canned*	16 or 17 ounces	2 cups
fresh (no tops)*	1 pound	2 cups; 2 cups cooked

Broccoli spears

fresh*	1 pound	2 cups cooked
frozen*	10 ounces	1½ cups cooked

Cabbage

fresh, shredded*	1 pound	3½ to 4½ cups; 2 cups cooked

Carrots

fresh (no tops)*	1 pound	3 cups; 2½ cups shredded or diced, cooked
canned*	1 pound	2 cups

Cauliflower

fresh*	1 pound	1½ cups; 1½ cups cooked
frozen*	10 ounces	1½ cups cooked

Corn	12 ounces	3 cups, cut

Mushrooms

fresh, sliced*	1 pound (36 medium)	2 to 3 cups sliced
dried	3 ounces	1 pound fresh
canned*	4 ounces	⅔ cup

Okra

fresh*	1 pound	2¼ cups cooked
frozen*	10 ounces	1¼ cups
canned*	15½ ounces	1¾ cups

Onions

fresh*	1 pound	3 large; 2 to 2½ cups chopped
frozen, chopped*	12 ounces	3 cups
canned*	16 to 17 ounces	2 cups

Peas

fresh in pod*	1 pound	1 cup shelled; 1 cup cooked
frozen*	10 ounces	2 cups; 2 cups cooked
canned*	1 pound	2 cups

Potatoes, white
fresh*	1 pound	3 medium; 2¼ cups cooked; 1¾ cups mashed
frozen, french-fries or puffs*	9 ounces	3 to 4 servings
canned, whole*	16 to 17 ounces	8 to 12

Spinach
fresh*	1 pound	4 cups; 1½ cups cooked
frozen*	10 ounces	1½ cups cooked
canned*	15 ounces	2 cups

Sweet potatoes
fresh*	1 pound	3 medium
frozen*	12 ounces	3 to 4
canned*	16 to 17 ounces	1¾ to 2 cups

Tomatoes
fresh*	1 pound	3 or 4 small

[1]. SOURCE: Author

* *Handbook of Food Preparation* (Sixth Edition, 1971). Published by American Home Economics Association, 2010 Massachusetts Avenue, N.W., Washington, D.C.

OVEN TEMPERATURE GUIDE

Oven Temperature*	°F.	°C.
Very slow	250°F. to 275°F.	121°C. to 135°C.
Slow	300°F. to 325°F.	149°C. to 163°C.
Moderate	350°F. to 375°F.	177°C. to 190°C.
Hot	400°F. to 425°F.	204°C. to 218°C.
Very hot	450°F. to 475°F.	232°C. to 246°C.
Extremely hot	500°F. to 525°F.	260°C. to 274°C.

*SOURCE: *Handbook of Food Preparation* (Sixth Edition, 1971). Published by American Home Economics Association, 2010 Massachusetts Avenue, N.W., Washington, D.C.

DEEP-FAT FRYING TEMPERATURES

Food	Fry at		One-inch bread cube dropped in hot fat will brown in:
	°F.	°C.	
Chicken	350°	177°	65 seconds
Doughnuts, fish, fritters, oysters, soft-shell crabs, scallops	350° to 365°	177° to 185°	60 to 65 seconds
Croquettes	375°	190°	40 seconds
French-fried potatoes, vegetables, onions	385° to 395°	196° to 201°	20 seconds

GUIDE TO CANDY AND SYRUP TEMPERATURES

ITEM	TEMPERATURE AT SEA LEVEL*		TEST FOR DONENESS
	F°	C°	
Syrup	230° to 234°	110° to 112°	Thread stage: syrup spins a thread 2 inches long when dropped from spoon.
Fudge, Panocha, Fondant	234° to 240°	112° to 115°	Soft-ball stage: syrup forms a soft ball in very cold water that will flatten when removed from water.
Caramels	244° to 248°	118° to 120°	Firm-ball stage: forms a firm ball when dropped into very cold water that will not flatten.
Divinity	250° to 266°	121° to 130°	Hard-ball stage: forms a ball hard enough to hold its shape in cold water.
Butterscotch, Taffy, Popcorn balls	270° to 290°	132° to 143°	Soft-crack stage: separates into hard brittle threads when dropped into very cold water.
Brittles	300° to 310°	149° to 154°	Hard-crack stage: separates into very brittle strings that crack in cold water.

*As elevations increase 500 feet, cook syrups 1° F. lower than above temperatures. When centigrade temperatures are used, cook syrup to 1° C. lower for each 900 feet elevation.

GUIDE TO HIGH-ALTITUDE CAKE BAKING

Recipes in this book are designed for baking at sea level and need not be altered for baking at elevations up to 3,000 feet. For altitudes above 3,000 feet, adjust as follows:

ALTITUDE	*REDUCE*		*INCREASE*
	Baking Powder	Sugar	Liquid
3,000 to 5,000 feet	⅛ teaspoon per teaspoon called for	1 tablespoon per cup called for	1 to 2 tablespoons per cup called for
5,000 to 7,000 feet	⅛ to ¼ teaspoon per teaspoon called for	2 tablespoons per cup called for	2 to 4 tablespoons per cup called for
7,000 feet	¼ teaspoon per teaspoon called for	2 to 3 tablespoons per cup called for	3 to 4 tablespoons per cup called for

NOTE: Rich cakes sometimes need to have shortening reduced by 1 or 2 tablespoons for each cup called for.

EQUIVALENT   WEIGHTS   AND   MEASURES

1 teaspoon = 4.9 milliliters
3 teaspoons = 1 tablespoon
4 tablespoons = ¼ cup
5⅓ tablespoons = ⅓ cup
8 tablespoons = ½ cup
16 tablespoons = 1 cup
1 cup = 8 fluid ounces or ½ pint or 2 gills
2 cups = 1 pint
1 pint = 2 cups or 16 fluid ounces
2 pints = 1 quart or 4 cups
1 quart = 4 cups
4 quarts = 1 gallon or 16 cups
8 quarts = 1 peck
  (dry measure)
4 pecks = 1 bushel
  (dry measure)

1 fluid ounce = 2 tablespoons
1 ounce = 28.35 grams
1 pound = 16 ounces or 453.60 grams
1 gram = 0.035 ounces
1 kilogram = 2.205 pounds
1 liter = 35 fluid ounces, 1.056 quarts, or
  1,000 milliliters
1 jigger = 3 tablespoons or 1½ fluid ounces
1 wineglass = ¼ cup
1 Imperial quart (Great Britain) = 40 fluid
  ounces or 5 cups
1 Imperial pint (Great Britain) = 20 fluid
  ounces or 2½ cups

HERBS AND SPICES

NAME	DESCRIPTION	USES
Allspice *Pimenta officinalis*	Miniature-sized fruit from a West Indian tree, named for its flavor which resembles a blend of cinnamon, cloves, and nutmeg.	*Whole*—pickling, preparation of meats, gravies, and fish. *Ground*—relishes, desserts, fruit preserves, puddings, and baked goods.
Anise *Pimpinella anisum*	An annual native to the Mediterranean region produces this licorice-flavored seed.	Used in vegetable soups, with sausages and roast pork, and in baked goods, particularly coffeecakes and cookies.
Balm, Lemon *Melissa officinalis*	A perennial of the mint family which grows to a height of two feet and bears purplish-white flowers.	The lemon-scented leaves are used as a seasoning as well as in herb tea, fruit cups, or salads.
Basil, Sweet *Ocimum basilicum*	Herb of the mint family.	Good in stews, salads, soups, and sauces. Add to any tomato-base sauce.
Bay Leaves *Folia laurus nobilis*	The aromatic leaf of the laurel tree.	Used in pickling, stews, spiced vinegars, and soups. Excellent with fish and tomato dishes.
Capers *Capparis spinosa*	The unopened bud of the prickly plant of the caper bush.	Use sparingly in tomato and seafood salads. Especially good with crabmeat and lobster.
Caraway Seed *Carum carvi*	Dried fruit of a hardy biennial of the parsley family.	A flavoring for rye bread, cakes, biscuits, cheese, applesauce, and cookies.
Cardamom *Elettaria cardamomum maton*	Tall perennial of the ginger family.	*Whole*—pickling spices. *Ground*—breads, coffeecakes, and pastries.
Cayenne *Capsicum frutescens*	Finely ground red peppers.	Excellent with meats, fish, and sauces.
Celery Seed *Apium graveolens*	Dried fruit of a biennial herb of the parsley family.	Used in soups, stews, and pickling, and with fish and salads.

CHERVIL
Anthriscus cerefolium

Small, low-growing annual of the parsley family.

Mainly used in fines herbes, chervil can be used alone with egg dishes, lamb, veal, and pork, and fish.

CHIVES
Allium schoenoprasum

A perennial of the lily family.

Use in any recipe requiring a mild onion flavor.

CINNAMON
Cinnamomum zeylanicum

Pungent bark of cinnamon (laurel) tree.

Stick—pickling and preserving. Used in beverages. *Ground*—baked goods.

CLOVES
Caryophyllus aromaticus

Dried nail-shaped flower bud of the clove tree.

Whole—studding pork and ham. Pickled fruits and syrups. *Ground*—chocolate puddings, baked goods, stews, and soups.

CORIANDER SEED
Coriandrum sativum

Annual herb of the parsley family.

Whole—in mixed pickles, soups, cakes, cookies, and stuffings. *Ground*—sausages and pork. An important ingredient in curry powder.

DILL SEED
Anethum graveolens

An herb of the parsley family with small feathery leaves and yellow flowers.

Used for pickling, sauerkraut, salads, fish and meat sauces, gravies, and spiced vinegars.

FENNEL
Foeniculum vulgare

Tiny seedlike fruit with flavor similar to anise.

Flavoring of fish sauces, soups, and sweet pickles.

GARLIC
Allium sativum

The pungent bulb of a perennial plant of the lily family.

Used for garlic butter and bread and in meat sauces and marinades.

GINGER
Zingiber officinale

A pungent rootstock.

Whole and cracked—flavors syrups and pickling vinegar. *Ground*—gingerbread, desserts, and Oriental meat dishes.

HORSERADISH
Armoracia lapathifolia

The root of a plant of the mustard family.

Grated—beef, oyster, and shrimp recipes, sauces and dips.

LEEK
Allium porrum

An onionlike vegetable of the lily family.

Used in vichyssoise and other soups and salads.

MACE
Myristica moschata

Dried outer covering of the fruit of the nutmeg tree. Orange-red in color.

Essential in fine pound cakes; valuable in all chocolate dishes. Used in oyster stews.

MARJORAM
Marjorana hortensis

Herb of the mint family.

Leaf—with lamb and as garnish. *Dried herb*—for meats, liverwurst, some cheeses, vegetables, soups, and sauces.

MINT
Mentha

Perennials cultivated for their aromatic leaves.

Sprigs used in beverages. Chopped leaves used in mint sauce for roast lamb, stuffing for fish, or a garnish for vegetables.

MUSTARD SEED
Brassica alba

Three mustards—white, yellow, and black or brown.

Whole—may be used in pickling and garnishing salads. *Dry*—flavors meats, sauces, and gravies.

NUTMEG
Myristica fragrans

Glossy brown, oily seed from the nutmeg tree.

Used in baked goods and flavoring for meat products. Also used in soups, sauces, preserves, eggnog, and puddings.

OREGANO
Origanum vulgare virens

A perennial of the mint family, it is closely related to marjoram and is often called "wild marjoram."

An excellent seasoning for pork dishes. Good for omelets, gravies, beef stew, lamb, and any tomato dish.

PAPRIKA
Capsicum annuum

There are many varieties—some are mild and sweet and others very hot.

Used extensively in Creole cooking, egg dishes, potato salads, salad dressings, and as a garnish.

PEPPER
Piper nigrum

Prepared from the small berry of a woody evergreen climbing vine.

Both black and white pepper are used in almost any type of food.

ROSEMARY
Rosemarinus officinalis

Small, spiky evergreen shrub of the mint family.

Fish and meat stocks, lamb dishes, potatoes, and other vegetables.

SAFFRON
Crocus sativus

Said to be the world's most expensive spice, saffron is made from the dried stamen of the crocus plant.

An essential ingredient of Spanish and Mexican dishes.

SAGE
Salvia officinalis

Leaf of a low-growing evergreen shrub of the mint family.

Used in meat and poultry stuffings. Also in pork products.

SESAME SEED
Sesamum indicum

Tiny honey-colored seed of an annual herb. Also called benne.

Sprinkle on bread and rolls and crackers and biscuits. Also good on buttered noodles.

SHALLOT
Allium ascalonicum

A perennial bulb of the lily family like garlic in shape but milder in flavor.

Chopped shallots are used in chicken, fish and vegetable soups, meat, and fish stews.

TARRAGON
Artemisia dracunculus

The peculiar bittersweet flavor is produced by a small perennial plant of the sunflower family.

Use in soups, salads, stews, sauces, and vinegar. Good with chicken and lobster.

THYME
Thymus vulgaris

Garden herb of the mint family.

Flavors clam and fish chowders, meats, sausages, poultry dressings, some fish sauces, and fresh tomatoes.

VANILLA
Vanilla planifolia

The dried pod of a climbing plant of the orchid family.

Extract—ice cream, custards, cakes, sauces, puddings, eggnogs.

BLENDED SPICES

CURRY POWDER
There is considerable variation in curry-powder blends. As a general rule it contains a blend of six or more of the following ingredients: cumin, coriander, fenugreek, turmeric, ginger, pepper, dill, mace, cardamom, and cloves.

FINES HERBES
Combination of three or more herbs ground fine and carefully blended. Herbs that may be used are parsley, chervil, tarragon, chives, sage, savory, and basil.

ITALIAN HERB SEASONING
Oregano, marjoram, thyme, savory, basil, rosemary, and sage generally make up this seasoning spice. Excellent used on fresh green salads and may also be used, mixed with water, as a meat marinade.

PICKLING SPICE
A combination of cinnamon, bay leaves, coriander, mustard, ginger, allspice, cloves, dill, chili peppers, pepper, mace, and cardamom may be found in pickling spices.

POULTRY SEASONING
Sage, onion, thyme, and marjoram are usually combined in poultry-seasoning blends.

PUMPKIN-PIE SPICE
Usually consists of cinnamon, ginger, nutmeg, allspice, mace, and cloves.

SALAD HERBS
Basil, tarragon, and thyme make up this seasoning.

SALAD SEASONING
Usually consists of sesame seed, poppy seed, onion, garlic, and celery seed.

HORS D'OEUVRES AND APPETIZERS

SHRIMP NOËL
About 90 hors d'oeuvres

3 *pounds medium-sized raw shrimp*
2 *quarts water*
½ *cup salt*
4 *large bunches curly endive*
1 *plastic foam cone, 2½ feet high*
1 *plastic foam square, 12 x 12 x 1 inch*
1 *small box round wooden picks*
Cocktail sauce

Place shrimp in boiling salted water. Cover and simmer for 3 to 5 minutes, or until shrimp are pink. Drain. Peel shrimp, leaving the last section of the shell and tail on. Devein, rinse with cold water, and chill. Separate and wash endive. Chill.

Place cone in center of foam square and draw a circle around base of cone. Cut out circle and insert cone. Cover base and cone with overlapping leaves of endive, fastening with wooden pick halves. Start at the outside edge of base and work up. Cover cone fully with greens to resemble a Christmas tree. Attach shrimp to tree with wooden picks. Serve with cocktail sauce.

ANGELS ON HORSEBACK
About 30 hors d'oeuvres

This old English dish was traditionally served at the end of the meal as a savory, but it also makes a delicious hors d'oeuvre. It consists of oysters wrapped in bacon and broiled until the bacon is crisp.

1 *pint fresh oysters or 1 (12-ounce) can, fresh or frozen*
2 *tablespoons chopped parsley*
½ *teaspoon salt*
Paprika
Pepper
10 *slices bacon, cut in thirds*

Thaw oysters, if frozen, and drain. Sprinkle with parsley and seasonings. Wrap each oyster in a piece of bacon and secure with wooden picks. Place oysters on broiler pan and broil 4 inches from heat source for 8 to 10 minutes. Turn carefully and broil 4 to 6 minutes longer, or until bacon is crisp.

CAVIAR CROWN
About 2 cups spread

Most people assume that the only caviar is the black sturgeon caviar, but there is a world of delicious things you can do with the less expensive types such as red salmon caviar and the poor cousin of the black sturgeon, whitefish caviar. I have used these caviars in the following recipe, which is pretty, practical, and tasty.

1 *(4-ounce) jar salmon caviar*
1 *(3½-ounce) jar whitefish caviar*
2 *(8-ounce) packages cream cheese, softened*
2 *tablespoons lemon juice*
2 *tablespoons chopped green onion*
1 *teaspoon Worcestershire sauce*
Parsley
Assorted party breads or Melba toast

Drain caviars. Cream cheese and seasonings. Place cheese mixture in center of a serving plate and shape in a circle about 7 inches in diameter and 1 inch thick. Cover a 4-inch circle in the center with salmon caviar. Cover remaining 1½ inches on top and the sides with whitefish caviar. Garnish base of cheese mixture with parsley. (A ring of overlapping slices of tiny stuffed olives or a ribbon of cream cheese put through a pastry tube may be substituted for parsley.) Serve with party breads or Melba toast.

NOTE: *For large parties, fix several small crowns, using half recipe for each one. Divide cheese mixture in half and make two cheese circles about 3½ inches in diameter and 1 inch thick. Cover a 2-inch circle in center of each with salmon caviar and remaining outside edges with whitefish caviar. Proceed as directed above.*

CRAB DABS

30 hors d'oeuvres

Sweet, tender Dungeness crab, caught along the Pacific coast from Alaska to San Francisco, was named for a village on the Juan de Fuca Strait in northwestern Washington.

    1 *(12-ounce) can Dungeness crabmeat or lump crabmeat, fresh or frozen*
    2 *(6½- or 7½-ounce) cans crabmeat*
    ⅓ *cup fine soft bread crumbs*
    2 *tablespoons dry sherry*
    1 *teaspoon chopped chives*
    1 *teaspoon hot dry mustard*
    ¼ *teaspoon salt*
    10 *slices bacon, cut in thirds*

Drain crabmeat, pick over carefully to remove any remaining shell or cartilage, and chop. Combine all ingredients except bacon and mix thoroughly. Chill for 30 minutes. Shape equal amounts of crab mixture into small rolls. Wrap one bacon piece around each roll, secure with wooden pick, and place on broiler pan. Broil about 4 inches from heat source for 8 to 10 minutes. Turn carefully, and broil for 4 to 5 minutes longer, or until bacon is crisp.

EMBASSY FROSTED PÂTÉ

About 12 servings

I'm not sure that this has actually been served at an embassy, but it is elegant enough to be.

    1½ *cups finely ground cooked chicken*
    1 *cup finely chopped toasted almonds*
    ¼ *cup chopped green onion or chives*
    3 *tablespoons finely chopped preserved or crystallized ginger*
    1½ *tablespoons soy sauce*
    1 *tablespoon garlic-flavored wine vinegar*
    ½ *to 1 teaspoon Worcestershire sauce*
    ½ *cup mayonnaise*
    Salt and pepper to taste
    1 *to 1½ cups sour cream*
    Parsley sprigs for garnish

Combine all ingredients, except sour cream, in bowl and blend thoroughly. Cover and refrigerate for 24 hours. Shape into crescent, oval, or circle. Frost completely with sour cream and garnish with parsley sprigs. Serve with crackers.

NOTE: *This can be made in advance, chilled for 24 hours, and frozen, unfrosted, for 2 to 3 weeks.*

TUNA PUFFS

About 4 dozen hors d'oeuvres

    2 *(6½- or 7-ounce) cans tuna fish*
    1 *cup finely chopped celery*
    ½ *cup mayonnaise*
    2 *tablespoons chopped onion*
    2 *tablespoons chopped sweet pickle*
    Salt to taste
    Miniature Cream Puffs (see index)

Drain and flake tuna fish. Combine all ingredients except puff shells and blend thoroughly. Cut tops from puff shells and fill each with 2 teaspoonfuls of mixture.

LOBSTER

LIVER SAUSAGE PÂTÉ IN ASPIC
About 3 cups

Created by a Parisian chef, liver sausage pâté requires some skill to create, but the finished appearance and taste is worth the work!

     1 *pound liver sausage*
     2 *(3-ounce) packages cream cheese*
     1 *teaspoon minced onion*
    ¼ *cup brandy (optional)*
     1 *envelope unflavored gelatin*
     1 *cup beef consommé*
        Cream cheese, pitted ripe olives, party rye bread, or Melba toast

Place a 3- to 3½-cup metal mold or bowl in freezing compartment of refrigerator to chill. Combine liver sausage, cream cheese, onion, and brandy. Blend well and chill. Soak gelatin in ¼ cup cold consommé. Bring remaining consommé to a boil and remove from heat. Add gelatin mixture and stir until dissolved. Reserve ⅓ cup consommé and keep at room temperature.

Cool remaining consommé until syrupy. Glaze inside of chilled mold with a thin, even layer of gelatin. (It may be easier to brush on several thin coatings.) Chill until gelatin is firm. Fill mold with liver sausage mixture and pour reserved consommé over sausage. Chill thoroughly. Unmold and chill again until firm.

To serve, arrange on serving tray and garnish with cream cheese put through pastry tube and slices of ripe olive. Serve with thinly sliced party rye bread or Melba toast.

SPICY LOBSTER BOATS
32 hors d'oeuvres

     1 *pound cooked lobster meat*
    ⅔ *cup mayonnaise*
     1 *tablespoon chili sauce*
     1 *teaspoon chopped green pepper*
     1 *teaspoon grated onion*
     1 *teaspoon chopped pimiento*
    16 *hard-cooked eggs*
        Chopped parsley

Pick over lobster meat carefully to remove any remaining shell or cartilage and chop. Combine mayonnaise, chili sauce, green pepper, onion, pimiento, and lobster. Cut eggs in half lengthwise, remove yolks and reserve for other purposes. Fill each egg white with 1 tablespoon of the lobster mixture, sprinkle with parsley, and chill.

PORK TENDERLOIN SERVED IN THE FRENCH MANNER
40 to 50 appetizers

     2 *pounds pork tenderloin (1 to 1 ½ inches in diameter)*
    1½ *teaspoons salt*
     1 *cup red wine*
     1 *teaspoon onion salt*
    ½ *teaspoon fines herbes*
     1 *clove garlic, halved lengthwise*
        Thinly sliced French bread
        Mustard Sauce (see next column)

Sprinkle surface of meat evenly with salt and place in shallow baking pan. Bake in slow oven (325°F.) for about 1¼ hours, or until tender. In a saucepan, combine red wine, onion salt, fines herbes, and garlic. Bring to a boil, then reduce heat and simmer for 1 minute. Spread French bread with Mustard Sauce. Top with thinly sliced meat and pour hot wine sauce over.

MUSTARD SAUCE   1 cup

1 *cup mayonnaise*

1 *tablespoon honey*

1 *tablespoon finely chopped parsley*

2 *teaspoons prepared mustard*

1 *teaspoon curry powder*

½ *teaspoon paprika*

Combine first 3 ingredients, then stir in remaining ingredients.

EMPANADITAS

32 hors d'oeuvres

Popular at Christmastime in Mexico and the Southwest, empanadas are pastry turnovers filled with meat, fruit, or nuts. They can be served as an entrée or in miniature form as hors d'oeuvres called Empanaditas.

¾ *pound ground beef, chuck or round steak*

½ *cup finely chopped onion*

1 *teaspoon butter*

1 *tablespoon flour*

1½ *teaspoons chili powder*

1 *teaspoon salt*

½ *teaspoon cinnamon*

¼ *teaspoon oregano*

1 *(8-ounce) can tomato sauce*

¼ *cup chopped seedless raisins*

2 *recipes Pastry for Double-Crust Pie (see index)*

Sauté beef and onion in butter until meat is crumbly, stirring frequently. Drain off excess fat and blend in flour, chili powder, salt, cinnamon, and oregano. Add tomato sauce and raisins. Cook, stirring constantly, until thickened. Cool.

Roll out pastry ⅛ inch thick on lightly floured board. Cut into 3½- or 4-inch circles. Spoon about 1 tablespoon of filling on each pastry circle to one side of center. Moisten pastry edges and fold in half. Press edges together and flute with tines of fork. Make 2 or 3 small slits on top of each empanadita.

Place on ungreased baking sheet and bake in hot oven (425° F.) for 12 to 15 minutes, or until pastry is done and lightly browned. Empanaditas may be made in advance, placed on baking sheet, covered with plastic wrap, and stored in refrigerator. Allow 3 to 4 minutes extra baking time if refrigerated.

MINIATURE PIROSHKI

32 appetizers

A Russian and Polish favorite, piroshkis are miniature meat loaves accented with pungent dill and baked in a crust.

¾ *pound ground beef, chuck or round steak*

⅓ *cup finely chopped onion*

1 *teaspoon butter*

2 *cups finely chopped fresh mushrooms (about 6 ounces)*

1 *tablespoon flour*

1 *teaspoon salt*

½ *cup sour cream*

2 *tablespoons chopped parsley*

2 *teaspoons dried dill weed*

2 *teaspoons Worcestershire sauce*

2 *recipes Pastry for Double-Crust Pie (see index)*

Sauté beef and onion in butter until meat is crumbly. Add mushrooms and cook until tender, stirring often. Drain off fat. Stir in flour and salt. Add sour cream, parsley, dill weed, and Worcestershire sauce. Simmer, stirring constantly, until thickened. Cool.

Roll out pastry ⅛ inch thick on lightly floured board. Cut into 3½- or 4-inch circles. Center about 1 tablespoon of filling on each circle and moisten edges. Bring edges up over filling, press together, and flute or crimp.

Bake on an ungreased baking sheet in hot oven (425° F.) for 12 to 15 minutes, or until crust is done and lightly browned. Miniature piroshkis may be made in advance, placed on baking sheet, covered with plastic wrap, and refrigerated. Allow 3 to 4 minutes' extra baking time if refrigerated prior to baking.

TINY MEAT TARTS

2 dozen tarts

> *Pastry for Double-Crust Pie (see index)*
>
> *Beef, Ham, or Frankfurter Filling (see below)*

Prepare pie crust as directed and roll out ⅛ inch thick on lightly floured board. Line small patty pans (*sandbakkel* pans) with pie crust and prick crust with tines of fork. Bake in hot oven (425° F.) for 8 to 10 minutes, or until done. Cool and fill with desired filling.

SPICY BEEF FILLING   about 2½ cups

> 1 *pound ground beef*
> ½ *cup chopped onion*
> 1 *tablespoon cooking oil*
> 1 *tablespoon red wine vinegar*
> 1 *(8-ounce) can tomato sauce*
> ½ *cup seedless raisins, chopped*
> ½ *teaspoon cinnamon*
> ¼ *teaspoon allspice*
> ½ *teaspoon salt*
> ⅛ *teaspoon pepper*

Sauté beef and onion in oil until beef is crumbly and browned. Stir in remaining ingredients and heat thoroughly. Chill.

HAM AND CHEESE FILLING   3½ cups

> 2 *cups finely chopped cooked ham*
> ½ *cup shredded Cheddar cheese*
> ½ *cup mayonnaise or Tangy Cooked Salad Dressing (see index)*
> ¼ *cup finely chopped onion*
> ¼ *cup drained sweet pickle relish*
> 4 *teaspoons prepared mustard*

Combine ingredients.

FRANKFURTER FILLING

Substitute chopped frankfurters for ham and omit onion.

STEAK TARTARE

20 to 25 hors d'oeuvre servings

A colorful legend accompanies this hearty dish. According to the tale, Steak Tartare originated during the raids of Genghis Khan on neighboring Asian tribes. Raw yak meat, the food staple of the raiders, was carried on the backs of ponies and was tenderized by the animals' bouncing gait. After a raid, the Tartars would dine on a quickly prepared feast of raw meat and fermented mare's milk, a meal thought to insure their virility. Throughout the years, Steak Tartare has been touted as an aphrodisiac.

> 2 *pounds top-quality beef, fillet, sirloin, or round steak, ground fine three times*
> 2 *egg yolks, lightly beaten*
> ½ *onion, grated*
> 8 *anchovy fillets, finely chopped*
> 1½ *tablespoons lemon juice*
> 1 *tablespoon capers (optional)*
> 2 *teaspoons Worcestershire sauce*
> ½ *clove garlic, mashed*
> 1 *teaspoon salt*
> ¼ *teaspoon hot dry mustard*
> *Dash of hot pepper sauce*
> *Buttered party rye bread, hot buttered toast squares, or Melba toast*
> *Chopped chives, chopped parsley, capers, or anchovy fillets*
> *Watercress*

Combine first 11 ingredients. Pat down in bowl or mold lined with plastic wrap. Chill for 1 to 2 hours. Turn out onto serving platter and surround with breads or crackers and small bowls of chives, parsley, capers, or anchovy fillets. Garnish with watercress.

QUICK PINEAPPLE SAUSAGE TIDBITS
About 90 tidbits

3 *(1-pound) packages link pork sausage*

2 *(1-pound 4-ounce) cans unsweetened pineapple chunks*

½ *cup brown sugar, firmly packed*

Cut sausage links in half. Drain pineapple and reserve juice. Skewer one half link and a pineapple chunk on a wooden pick. Repeat until all links and pineapple chunks are used. Place in a 9 × 13-inch baking dish. Combine brown sugar and pineapple juice in a small bowl and pour over tidbits. Bake in hot oven (400° F.) for 20 minutes, or until lightly browned and thoroughly heated.

WESTERN-STYLE BEEF JERKY
About ½ pound

A favorite way to preserve meat in pioneer days was to dry it in the sun or smoke it over a fire, Indian-fashion, making a jerky.

1 *pound top round or beef flank steak*

½ *cup soy sauce*

Salt or garlic salt

Black pepper

Trim fat from meat and chill in freezer for 1 to 2 hours. Using a very sharp knife, cut meat into ¼-inch strips across the grain. Coat meat with soy sauce and arrange one layer of strips in shallow baking dish. Sprinkle with salt or garlic salt, and pepper. Repeat layers until all beef is used. Cover meat with foil or plastic wrap. Place a heavy weight on top. Refrigerate for several hours or overnight.

Drain meat strips and dry on paper toweling. Arrange strips on rack on shallow 15 × 10 × 1-inch baking pan. Bake in very slow oven (250° F.) for 4 hours, or until dry, chewy, and somewhat leathery but not crisp. A lower oven

temperature is more desirable. If your oven will maintain an even temperature of 150° F., bake for 8 to 10 hours. Cool. Store in plastic bag or airtight container and refrigerate until used.

BOURBON FRANKS
About 120 to 150 pieces

These frankfurters, simmered in a bourbon sauce, are delicious. The alcohol evaporates in the cooking process, but it lends a distinctive flavor to the sauce.

½ *cup chopped onion*

½ *cup chopped green pepper*

¼ *cup butter*

4 *(8-ounce) cans tomato sauce*

1 *cup plus 2 tablespoons brown sugar*

1 *(12-ounce) can tomato paste*

1 *cup bourbon whisky*

4 *teaspoons Worcestershire sauce*

4 *teaspoons wine vinegar*

4 *teaspoons prepared mustard*

1 *teaspoon minced garlic*

¼ *to ½ teaspoon salt*

¼ *teaspoon pepper*

4 *to 5 drops Tabasco sauce*

3 *to 4 pounds frankfurters, cut in 1-inch pieces*

Sauté onion and green pepper in butter until soft and add remaining ingredients except frankfurters. Bring to a boil, then reduce heat. Add frankfurters and simmer for 1 hour. Transfer to heated chafing dish and provide wooden picks.

NOTE: *May be prepared a day in advance, refrigerated, and reheated.*

BRANDIED MEAT BALLS
About 40 meat balls
Of all the recipes included in the book, this is
my favorite.

  2 *pounds ground beef*
  ¾ *cup milk*
  ½ *cup bread crumbs*
  1 *tablespoon Worcestershire sauce*
1½ *teaspoons salt*
  1 *teaspoon garlic powder*
  ¼ *teaspoon nutmeg*
  ¼ *teaspoon ground ginger*
  ⅛ *teaspoon ground pepper*
  2 *drops hot pepper sauce*
  2 *tablespoons melted shortening or oil*
   Brandied Peach Sauce (see below)
  1 *tablespoon cornstarch (if needed)*
  1 *tablespoon cold water (if needed)*

Blend first 10 ingredients together in bowl.
Shape mixture into 1½- to 2-inch balls. In
large skillet or electric fry pan, brown meat
balls in hot shortening. Remove with slotted
spoon, set aside, and keep warm. Lower heat,
blend Brandied Peach Sauce into meat drippings, and simmer for 10 minutes. Add meat
balls to sauce and coat thoroughly. Cover and
simmer for 45 minutes to 1 hour. If necessary,
blend cornstarch with cold water to form
paste, add to sauce, stirring constantly, and
cook over low heat until thickened. Transfer
to chafing dish for buffet service.

BRANDIED PEACH SAUCE   About 3 cups
  1 *(1-pound 2-ounce) jar peach preserves*
  ¾ *cup light brown sugar, firmly packed*
  ½ *cup brandy*
  ½ *cup peach brandy*
  ¼ *teaspoon nutmeg*

Combine ingredients in bowl.

ORIENTAL MOCK DRUMSTICKS
24 drumsticks
24 *chicken wings*
  1 *cup cornstarch*
  ½ *cup milk*
  2 *eggs, beaten well*
  ¼ *teaspoon garlic salt*
  ⅛ *teaspoon poultry seasoning*
  4 *cups cooking oil*
  ¾ *cup sugar*
  ½ *cup white vinegar*
  ⅔ *cup catsup*
  ⅓ *cup water*
  ¾ *teaspoon soy sauce*

Remove heavy section of wings with single
bone for mock drumsticks (save remaining
parts for other uses). Combine next 5 ingredients in bowl. Dip wings in cornstarch mixture and drain. Fry a few at a time in deep hot
oil (375° F.) for 5 minutes, or until batter is
cooked. Drain on paper toweling. When all
wings have been fried, combine remaining ingredients in 13 × 9 × 2-inch baking pan. Add
chicken pieces and turn once. Cover and refrigerate for 30 minutes to 1 hour. Turn
chicken pieces in sauce and bake in moderate
oven (350° F.) for 25 to 35 minutes. Transfer
chicken pieces and sauce to heated chafing
dish and serve.

HAM AND CHEESE BALL

One ball, about 3½-inch diameter (1⅔ cups)

  1 *(8-ounce) package cream cheese, softened*
  1 *tablespoon prepared horseradish*
  1 *tablespoon prepared mustard*
  1 *teaspoon grated onion*
  1 *cup finely chopped cooked ham*
 ⅓ *cup finely chopped nuts*
   Assorted crackers and vegetables

Blend first 4 ingredients until smooth and stir in ham. Chill until mixture can be shaped into ball, about 1 hour. Roll ball in nuts. Wrap in foil and chill until serving time. Serve with assorted crackers, sliced cucumber or carrots, or celery stalks.

CHEESE STRAWS

About 5 dozen Cheese Straws

An old Southern favorite, Cheese Straws, rounds, or balls make a big hit as a party treat.

 1¼ *cups flour*
  ½ *teaspoon salt*
   Dash of white pepper
   Dash of cayenne pepper
  ¼ *cup butter, softened*
  1 *cup (4 ounces) finely shredded sharp Cheddar cheese*

Combine first 4 ingredients. Beat butter until light and fluffy and add cheese gradually, beating well after each addition. Stir in flour mixture and blend thoroughly. Shape into a round flat patty and roll out ⅛ inch thick between sheets of heavy waxed paper. With plain or fluted pastry wheel cut strips ½ inch wide and 3 to 4 inches long. Place ½ inch apart on ungreased baking sheet. Bake in hot oven (400° F.) for 8 to 10 minutes, or until done and a light gold color. (Watch carefully, as this rich pastry will burn quickly.) Transfer straws to wire rack to cool.

VARIATIONS

  Sesame Seed Rounds: Cut dough into 1- or 2-inch rounds with plain or scalloped cookie cutters. Sprinkle tops with sesame seeds, pressing down lightly, before baking.

  Cheese-Nut Balls: Cut dough into small balls. Press top down with finger and insert half a walnut into the indentation. Bake for approximately 15 minutes.

PARTY CHEESE BALL

One ball, 6 inches in diameter

Cheese has been a staple of the American diet ever since the days of the Pilgrims. Cheese balls, in many flavor combinations, came into vogue during the 1940s and are still a favorite standby of many hostesses.

 1½ *pounds grated Cheddar cheese*
  1 *(8-ounce) package cream cheese, softened*
  1 *cup crumbled blue cheese*
 10 *to 12 slices bacon, cooked and crumbled*
  ¼ *cup dry sherry*
  1 *tablespoon Worcestershire sauce*
  1 *cup finely chopped walnuts*
   Parsley or pimiento strips
   Crackers

Combine first 6 ingredients in bowl and mix well. Shape into a large ball and roll in nuts. Refrigerate for several hours. Decorate with sprigs of parsley or pimiento strips and serve with crackers.

SILD AGURK SNITTER (Norse Herring Cucumber Canapés)

About 24 canapés

> 1 *large cucumber*
> 2 *teaspoons salt*
> 3 *cups ice water*
> 2 *tablespoons butter*
> 1 *(8-ounce) loaf party rye bread, sliced*
> 1 *(12-ounce) jar herring in sour cream*
> *Paprika*

Wash unpeeled cucumber and score with a sharp-tined fork lengthwise from end to end. Cut crosswise into very thin slices and place in a bowl. Combine salt and ice water and pour over cucumbers. Let stand for 30 minutes, or until crisp. Drain slices on absorbent paper. Butter bread. Overlap 2 slices of cucumber on each bread slice and top with 1 large or 2 small pieces of herring. Sprinkle with paprika.

DEVILED EGGS

24 to 28 deviled egg halves

Deviled Eggs were a mainstay of Midwestern box socials or Fourth-of-July picnics during the nineteenth century when most rural families kept hens.

> 14 *hard-cooked eggs, peeled and chilled*
> ½ *cup Tangy Cooked Salad Dressing (see index) or mayonnaise*
> 1½ *teaspoons Worcestershire sauce*
> 1 *teaspoon prepared mustard*
> ½ *teaspoon salt*
> ¼ *teaspoon pepper*
> 3 *or 4 drops hot pepper sauce*
> 2 *green onions, finely chopped*
> 2 *tablespoons well-drained pickle relish*
> ½ *teaspoon celery seed*
> *Paprika (optional)*

Cut eggs in half lengthwise, remove yolks, and reserve whites. Sieve or mash yolks until smooth. Combine yolks, dressing or mayonnaise, Worcestershire sauce, mustard, salt, pepper, and hot pepper sauce and beat at medium speed until smooth. Stir in onion, pickle relish, and celery seed. Spoon mixture into cavities of egg whites. Sprinkle tops with paprika.

Garnishes for Deviled Eggs: Dash of paprika, parsley sprigs, ripe olive wedges, green pepper or pimiento diamonds, red or black caviar, tiny sardines or shrimps, smoked oysters, chunks of crabmeat.

NOTE: *Prepare 1 or 2 extra eggs. If any break during cooking, the extra yolks make a more generous filling for the remaining egg whites.*

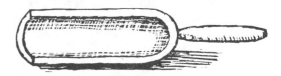

JAN'S CHICKEN LIVER MAGNIFICO

4 servings

I have adapted this recipe from one given me by photographer Edward Saxe and serve it to special guests.

> 1 *pound chicken livers*
> ½ *to ¾ cup flour*
> 4 *to 6 tablespoons butter*
> *Salt and pepper to taste*
> ¼ *to ⅓ cup brandy or dry sherry (or a combination)*

Dredge chicken livers in flour, then sauté in butter for 2 to 3 minutes on each side (do not overcook—chicken livers should be crisp on the outside and slightly pink inside). Sprinkle liberally with salt and pepper. Just before serving, add brandy or sherry and blend thoroughly. Serve hot with scrambled eggs, buttered noodles, or rice.

HOT MARDI GRAS SPREAD
3 cups

    1 *(8-ounce) package cream cheese, at
      room temperature*
    1 *cup sour cream*
    1 *(3-ounce) package dried chipped beef,
      finely chopped*
    ½ *cup chopped green pepper*
    ½ *cup stuffed or pitted black olives, sliced*
    2 *tablespoons dry sherry*
    1 *teaspoon Worcestershire sauce*
    ½ *teaspoon garlic powder*
    2 *or 3 dashes hot pepper sauce*
    ⅛ *teaspoon pepper*
    ½ *cup finely chopped pecans*
    Crackers or Melba toast

Beat cream cheese and ½ cup sour cream until smooth. Stir in remaining ingredients except pecans and crackers. Spoon into 1½-quart casserole and sprinkle nuts over top. Bake in slow oven (325° F.) for 30 minutes. Serve with crackers or Melba toast.

HAWAIIAN CHEESE SPREAD
3½ cups

    2 *(8-ounce) packages cream cheese, at
      room temperature*
    1 *(8½-ounce) can crushed pineapple, well
      drained*
    2 *tablespoons finely chopped onion*
    1 *teaspoon celery salt*
    ⅛ *teaspoon garlic powder*
    ⅛ *teaspoon onion powder*
    1 *cup chopped pecans*
    ¼ *cup chopped green pepper*
    Additional chopped pecans (optional)
    Crackers or toast points

Beat cream cheese until smooth. Add pineapple, onion, celery salt, garlic and onion powders and continue beating. Stir in pecans and green pepper. Chill thoroughly. Spoon into attractive serving bowl and sprinkle with additional pecans. Serve on crackers or toast points.

GUACAMOLE
About 2¼ cups

Even those who turn up their noses at avocados will dip into Guacamole, the zesty, fresh avocado mixture so popular in the Southwest.

    2 *medium-sized ripe avocados*
    1 *medium tomato, peeled, finely chopped,
      and drained*
    1 *to 2 small canned green chili peppers,
      finely chopped and mashed (optional)*
    1 *tablespoon lemon juice*
    2 *teaspoons grated onion*
    ½ *teaspoon salt*
    ¼ *teaspoon freshly ground pepper*
    ¼ *teaspoon chili powder*
    ¼ *cup mayonnaise*

Cut avocados in half, peel, and remove seeds. Mash and sieve avocado and tomato or whiz in blender. Turn into bowl and stir in remaining ingredients except mayonnaise. Spread mayonnaise over top of mixture to prevent discoloration. Cover bowl with plastic wrap and chill. At serving time fold mayonnaise into avocado mixture and turn into serving bowl.

TEXAS HOT CHEESE DIP

1¾ cups

 1 *pound fresh pork sausage meat*

 1 *(7½-ounce) can green chili sauce or tomato and green chili sauce*

 2 *(8-ounce) packages pasteurized process cheese spread, cut in small pieces*

 ½ *teaspoon garlic powder (optional)*

 Crisp corn chips or fried tortilla quarters

Cut sausage into small chunks and sauté in heavy skillet, stirring with a fork to crumble. Cook until lightly browned, stirring constantly, and drain thoroughly. Lower heat and stir in sauce, cheese, and garlic powder. Cover and heat just until cheese melts, stirring frequently. Pour into chafing dish or fondue pot and serve with crisp corn chips or crisp fried tortillas.

NOTE: *The dip may be made ahead of time, refrigerated, and then reheated at serving time.*

MEXICAN BEAN AND BACON DIP

4 cups

 2 *(1-pound 6-ounce) cans baked beans*

 2 *cups grated Cheddar cheese*

 3 *tablespoons Worcestershire sauce*

 1½ *teaspoons minced onion*

 1 *teaspoon chili powder*

 ½ *teaspoon minced garlic*

 ½ *teaspoon cumin*

 4 *drops hot pepper sauce*

 1 *cup crisp crumbled bacon (8 to 10 slices)*

 Corn chips or tostadas

Purée beans in blender and combine with all other ingredients, except bacon and chips, in saucepan. Cook over low heat, stirring constantly, until thoroughly heated. Stir in bacon. Transfer to chafing dish and serve with corn chips or tostadas.

CURRY CREAM DIP

2½ cups

 2 *cups sour cream*

 ½ *cup crumbled blue cheese*

 2 *tablespoons chili sauce*

 1 *teaspoon curry powder*

 ½ *teaspoon minced garlic*

 3 *drops Worcestershire sauce*

 Cooked ham, cut into ½-inch cubes

 Hard salami, thinly sliced

Combine first 6 ingredients thoroughly in electric mixer or blender. Spoon into serving bowl. Arrange on tray with ham, salami, and wooden picks.

GREEK DIP

2½ cups

Yogurt dip is a good choice for calorie-conscious guests.

 2 *cups peeled, finely chopped cucumber*

 2 *tablespoons olive oil*

 2 *tablespoons chopped green onion*

 ½ *teaspoon garlic salt*

 ¼ *teaspoon salt*

 ¼ *teaspoon dill weed*

 ⅛ *teaspoon pepper*

 1 *cup plain or natural yogurt*

 ¼ *cup chopped walnuts*

 Melba toast or raw vegetables

Drain cucumber well in sieve and press out excess liquid. Carefully stir olive oil, green onion, salts, dill weed, and pepper into yogurt (mixture will be soupy). Stir in cucumber and walnuts. Chill thoroughly. Serve with Melba toast or raw vegetables.

WHITE HOUSE SHRIMP

8 appetizer servings

Adapted from an appetizer served at the White House, these shrimp are easy to prepare and sure to win 'votes at any party.

SHRIMP

2 *quarts water*

1 *stalk celery with leaves, washed*

1 *medium onion, chopped*

1 *bay leaf*

1½ *teaspoons salt*

2 *pounds raw shrimp*

SAUCE

1 *cup olive or salad oil*

½ *cup chili sauce*

½ *cup finely chopped celery*

2 *green onions, finely chopped*

3 *tablespoons lemon juice*

2 *tablespoons chopped chives*

2 *tablespoons horseradish*

1 *tablespoon prepared mustard*

½ *teaspoon paprika*

½ *teaspoon salt*

1 *to 2 dashes hot pepper sauce*

Watercress

Melba toast or Parmesan Rye Chips (see next column)

Combine first 5 ingredients in Dutch oven. Cover and bring to a boil. Add shrimp and bring to a second boil. Cook shrimp for 4 minutes, remove from heat, and uncover. Cool shrimp in liquid. When cool, remove shrimp from liquid and shell, devein, and chill.

In a large non-metallic bowl, combine sauce ingredients. Add shrimp and coat thoroughly. Cover bowl and refrigerate for 10 to 12 hours before serving. Serve chilled in a large bowl and garnish with watercress. Serve with Melba toast or Parmesan Rye Chips.

Parmesan Rye Chips: Brush party rye bread with melted butter and sprinkle with grated or shredded Parmesan cheese. Arrange on baking sheet, place in very slow oven (275° F.) until toasted and crisp.

SEAFOOD APPETIZER CRÊPES

24 crêpes

¾ *cup sifted flour*

¼ *teaspoon salt*

2 *eggs, beaten*

1 *cup milk*

Softened cream cheese or sour cream

Favorite fish or seafood: smoked fish or oysters, tiny sardines, red or black caviar

Parsley, watercress, pimiento, green pepper for garnish

To prepare crêpes, sift flour and salt into mixing bowl. Combine eggs and milk and slowly add to dry ingredients. Beat just until batter is smooth. Pour 1 tablespoonful of batter onto hot, greased 7-inch fry pan or griddle. Fry until brown on underside, turn, and cook second side. Spread crêpes with softened cream cheese or sour cream. Top with favorite smoked fish, sardines, smoked oysters, or red or black caviar. Roll or fold as desired. Serve crêpes warm or cooled. Garnish as desired.

TIME-SAVER HINT: *Crêpes may be made ahead of time and refrigerated when cool. To reheat, arrange on baking sheet, cover with aluminum foil, and bake in slow oven (300° F.) for 3 to 5 minutes.*

CEVICHE, MEXICAN-STYLE
12 appetizer servings

Ceviche is an interesting appetizer of Mexico and the Southwest. Raw fish is marinated in lime or lemon juice, and the action of the citric acid "cooks" the fish, turning it slightly white and toning down any fishy taste.

    2 *pounds red snapper, bay scallops, or firm fish fillets*
    1 *cup lime juice or lime and lemon juice combined*
    2 *tablespoons cider or white wine vinegar*
    2 *cups peeled, seeded, diced tomatoes*
 1½ *cups thinly sliced red or white onion*
    1 *canned green chili, seeded and chopped*
    ½ *cup halved pimiento-stuffed olives*
    ¼ *cup olive or salad oil*
 1½ *teaspoons salt*
    ½ *teaspoon oregano*
    1 *avocado, peeled and sliced (optional)*

Cut fish into small bite-sized pieces and place in a non-metallic bowl. Add lime or lime and lemon juice and vinegar and mix well. Cover with plastic wrap and refrigerate for 2 hours. Add remaining ingredients, except avocado, and mix carefully. Cover and refrigerate overnight. Drain. Serve in attractive bowl garnished with avocado slices.

OYSTERS CASINO
4 to 6 servings

   24 *oysters on the half shell*
   12 *slices bacon, cut crosswise into 4 pieces*
    1 *(8-ounce) can tomato sauce*
    2 *tablespoons lemon juice*
    2 *teaspoons sugar*
    ½ *teaspoon salt*
    ½ *teaspoon pepper*
    ¼ *teaspoon hot pepper sauce (approximate)*
    1 *cup finely shredded American or Cheddar cheese*
    Parsley sprigs

Arrange oysters in pan of rock salt. Partially cook bacon. Combine tomato sauce, lemon juice, sugar, salt, pepper, and hot pepper sauce. Spoon an equal amount of tomato mixture over oysters. Top each with 2 pieces of bacon. Sprinkle with cheese. Bake in a very hot oven (450° F.) for 7 to 8 minutes, or until oysters are done and edges curl. Serve on the half shell, garnished with sprigs of parsley.

OYSTERS ROCKEFELLER
6 servings

   36 *oysters on the half shell*
    2 *cups spinach, cooked and drained*
    ¼ *cup chopped onion*
    2 *tablespoons minced parsley*
    ½ *teaspoon celery salt*
    ½ *teaspoon salt*
    6 *drops hot pepper sauce*
    ⅓ *cup butter*
    ½ *cup fine dry bread crumbs*
    Lemon slices (for garnish)

Put oysters in their shells on a bed of rock salt so they will remain upright and not lose their juice. Combine spinach, onion, and parsley and chop very fine, or put through food grinder. Add salts and hot pepper sauce, mixing well. Cook in butter over low heat for 4 to 5 minutes, stirring as needed. Fold in bread crumbs and spread about 1 tablespoon on each oyster. Bake in hot oven (400° F.) for 10 minutes, or until lightly browned. Garnish with lemon slices.

NOTE: *2 (12-ounce) cans fresh select oysters may be substituted. Drain oysters, arrange in small baking shells or spread over bottom of shallow buttered baking dish, and top with spinach mixture.*

CRAB-STUFFED MUSHROOMS
6 servings

  1 *pound blue crabmeat or 3 (6½- or 7½-ounce) cans*
 24 *fresh mushrooms, approximately 1½ inches in diameter*
  2 *tablespoons butter*
  1 *egg, beaten*
  2 *tablespoons chopped parsley*
  ½ *teaspoon salt*
  ¼ *teaspoon finely chopped garlic*
     Dash of white pepper
  2 *tablespoons grated Parmesan cheese*

Drain crabmeat and pick over carefully to remove any remaining shell or cartilage. Wipe mushrooms with a damp cloth, remove stems, and chop stems to measure ½ cup. Sauté stems in butter for 5 minutes. Combine all ingredients except cheese and mushroom caps. Stuff each mushroom cap with about 2 tablespoonfuls of crab mixture. Sprinkle with cheese. Place mushrooms in a greased 15 × 10 × 1-inch baking pan. Bake in moderate oven (375° F.) for 12 to 15 minutes, or until lightly browned.

NOTE: *Omit the salt when using canned crabmeat.*

CRAB IMPERIAL
6 appetizer servings

A specialty of the Carlton House Resort Inn in Orlando, Florida, Crab Imperial is an impressive first course to serve on very special occasions.

  1 *pound lump crabmeat or 2 (6-ounce) packages frozen*
  ¼ *cup finely chopped onion*
  ¼ *cup butter*
  1 *cup sliced fresh mushrooms*
  ½ *cup Chablis (or other dry white wine)*
  ¼ *teaspoon salt*
     Dash of pepper
  ⅓ *to ½ cup Hollandaise Sauce (see index)*
     Toast points

Thaw and drain crabmeat if frozen. Pick over carefully to remove any remaining shell or cartilage. Sauté onion in butter until tender but not brown. Add mushrooms and cook for 2 to 3 minutes. Add wine and simmer until liquid has almost evaporated. Add crabmeat, salt, and pepper and heat thoroughly. Remove from heat and carefully stir in Hollandaise Sauce. Serve on toast points.

SHRIMP IN BEER (Krevetten in Biere)

10 to 12 appetizers or 6 buffet servings

  2 *pounds shrimp*
  3 *tablespoons chopped onion*
 ¼ *cup oil*
  2 *tablespoons flour*
 ¾ *teaspoon salt*
  1 *cup beer or ale*
  3 *tablespoons lemon juice*
 ¼ *teaspoon hot pepper sauce*
 ¼ *teaspoon thyme*
  1 *small bay leaf*
  2 *teaspoons chopped parsley*

Peel, devein, and rinse shrimp in cold water. Sauté onion in oil until tender. Add shrimp and cook, stirring frequently, for 3 to 5 minutes, or until shrimp are pink. Blend in flour and salt. Add beer, lemon juice, and hot pepper sauce and cook until thickened, stirring constantly. Add thyme and bay leaf and cook over low heat for 5 minutes longer, stirring occasionally. Remove bay leaf. Sprinkle with parsley. Serve hot as an appetizer or entrée.

BAKED HEARTS OF PALM WITH MORNAY SAUCE

4 to 6 appetizer servings

A specialty of the Carlton House Resort Inn in Orlando, Florida, Baked Hearts of Palm is a delicacy fit for royalty. Canned hearts of palm are available in most gourmet-food shops.

  1 *(14-ounce) can hearts of palm, drained*
  1 *tablespoon butter*
  1 *tablespoon flour*
 ½ *teaspoon salt*
Dash of pepper
  1 *cup milk*
  1 *egg yolk, beaten*
  2 *tablespoons heavy cream*
  1 *to 1½ tablespoons grated Parmesan cheese*
Parsley sprigs

Cut hearts of palm in quarters and arrange in 4 or 6 small buttered casseroles or shells. Melt butter in small, heavy saucepan and stir in flour, salt, and pepper. Add milk and cook until thickened, stirring constantly. Combine egg yolk and cream. Stir egg mixture and half the cheese into hot sauce and cook for 1 minute, stirring constantly. Divide sauce evenly over hearts of palm and sprinkle with remaining cheese. Broil 3 to 4 inches from heat source for 5 to 7 minutes, or until hot and lightly browned. Garnish with parsley.

MARINATED BRUSSELS SPROUTS

12 appetizer servings (40 to 50 pieces)

Your guests will enjoy the dill flavor of these Brussels sprouts.

  8 *cups (2 quarts) Brussels sprouts or 2 (10-ounce) packages frozen*
1⅓ *cups Italian dressing (approximate)*
  3 *tablespoons wine vinegar*
  2 *tablespoons thinly sliced green onion*
  1 *teaspoon dill weed*

Cook Brussels sprouts in enough unsalted boiling water to cover for 10 to 15 minutes, or until barely tender. Drain and put in a container with tight-fitting cover. Combine remaining ingredients and pour over Brussels sprouts. Cover tightly and shake gently to coat all sprouts with marinade. Refrigerate for 24 hours, shaking occasionally. Turn into small serving bowl.

QUICHE À LA JEANETTE

6 dinner servings, 8 luncheon servings

  8 *slices bacon*
  ½ *cup sliced fresh mushrooms*
  ¼ *cup chopped onion*
  ¼ *cup chopped green pepper*
  3 *tablespoons butter*
1½ *cups (6 ounces) shredded Swiss cheese*
  1 *cup cubed cooked ham*
   Unbaked (10-inch) Pie Shell (see index) with high fluted edge
  3 *eggs*
  2 *cups milk*
  1 *tablespoon flour*
  1 *teaspoon salt*
  ⅛ *teaspoon nutmeg*

Pan-fry bacon until crisp, drain, and crumble when cool. Sauté mushrooms, onion, and green pepper in 2 tablespoons butter until tender but not brown. Alternate layers of cheese, ham, bacon, and vegetable mixture in pie shell. Combine remaining ingredients, beating slightly, and strain over filling. Pour remaining 1 tablespoon butter over top. Bake in moderate oven (375° F.) for 35 to 40 minutes, or until set. A silver knife inserted in center of pie will come out clean when pie is done.

NOTE: *Pie shell may be prepared ahead of time and refrigerated or frozen. Allow time for shell to come to room temperature before filling.*

STUFFED MUSHROOMS ITALIENNE

4 servings (16 hors d'oeuvres)

16 *large fresh mushrooms*
  6 *ounces sweet Italian sausage*
  1 *clove garlic, minced*
  3 *tablespoons olive oil*
  2 *tablespoons minced parsley*
  ¼ *cup shredded or grated Parmesan cheese*
  2 *tablespoons sweet vermouth (optional)*
  ¼ *cup water*

Wipe mushrooms with a damp cloth, remove stems, and chop stems fine. Remove casing from sausage and add to stems with garlic and 1 tablespoon oil. Sauté in heavy skillet until lightly browned. Stir in 1 tablespoon oil, parsley, cheese, and vermouth. Fill mushroom caps with mixture, rounding tops. Place in shallow baking pan, add remaining 1 tablespoon oil and water to pan. Bake in moderate oven (350° F.) for 20 minutes. Serve hot as an appetizer or as an hors d'oeuvre.

SOUPS

CHILLED CURRIED
ASPARAGUS SOUP

6 to 8 servings

2 *(10¾-ounce) cans cream of asparagus*
  soup
1 *cup milk*
3 *tablespoons crumbled crisp bacon*
1 *teaspoon curry powder*
¼ *teaspoon pepper (or to taste)*
3 *dashes hot pepper sauce*
½ *teaspoon Worcestershire sauce*
½ *cup sour cream*
Paprika

Slowly combine soup and milk, stirring or beating until smooth and lump-free. Stir in bacon, curry powder, pepper, hot pepper sauce, and Worcestershire sauce. Chill thoroughly. To serve, spoon into soup bowls and garnish with sour cream and paprika.

GAZPACHO

4 to 6 servings (about 3½ cups)

Here is my version of the popular Spanish icy salad soup.

2 *cups tomato juice*
2 *tablespoons olive oil*
2 *tablespoons red wine vinegar*
1 *chicken bouillon cube*
½ *teaspoon garlic salt*
¼ *teaspoon salt*
⅛ *teaspoon pepper*
2 *or 3 dashes hot pepper sauce*
1 *fresh ripe tomato, peeled and cubed*
1 *cup peeled, diced cucumber*
¼ *cup 1-inch green pepper squares*
¼ *medium onion, sliced*
Chopped tomatoes, cucumbers, green
  peppers, and croutons

Combine in blender 1 cup tomato juice and next 7 ingredients. Whiz at medium speed for a few seconds. Add tomato, cucumber, green pepper, and onion. Whiz at medium speed until tomato is chopped moderately fine. Add remaining 1 cup tomato juice. Pour into covered container and chill for several hours or overnight. To serve, spoon gazpacho into bowls packed in crushed ice. Pass bowls of finely chopped tomato, cucumber, green pepper, and croutons.

CREOLE PEANUT BUTTER SOUP

6 servings

Although Thomas Jefferson recorded peanut crops in his plantation ledger in the eighteenth century, peanut cultivation was not widespread until the next century. Peanut soup, a specialty of Southern cooks, is presented here in a modern interpretation.

3 *tablespoons finely chopped onion*
½ *cup finely chopped celery*
2 *tablespoons butter*
3 *tablespoons flour*
4 *cups chicken stock*
1⅓ *cups creamy peanut butter*
1 *cup half and half*
Watercress sprigs (optional)

In heavy saucepan sauté onion and celery in butter until tender but not brown. Stir in flour and cook until bubbly. Add chicken stock, stirring constantly, until thickened. Add peanut butter and stir until smooth. Stir in half and half and heat through. Serve hot or chill thoroughly and set in crushed ice. Garnish with watercress.

NOTE: *If a smoother, thinner soup is desired, whiz briefly in blender before serving.*

STRAWBERRY SOUP

6 to 8 servings (about 4 cups)

Strawberry Soup can be served as a first course or as a dessert. It is one of the specialties of the Carlton House Inn in Orlando, Florida.

1 *pint (2 cups) fresh strawberries*

1 *cup sour cream*

1 *cup half and half or light cream*

¼ *cup sugar*

2 *tablespoons brandy*

½ *teaspoon vanilla extract*

Sliced strawberries (garnish)

Mint sprigs

Wash and hull strawberries. Place strawberries and next 5 ingredients in blender and whiz 30 to 45 seconds, or until smooth. Serve in chilled cups and garnish with sliced strawberries and mint sprigs.

HEARTY GREEN PEA SOUP

8 servings (about 2 quarts)

1 *pound (2½ cups) dried green or yellow split peas*

8 *cups cold water*

2 *pounds ham shanks*

1 *cup sliced onion*

½ *teaspoon salt*

¼ *teaspoon garlic salt*

½ *teaspoon marjoram or sweet basil*

½ *teaspoon leaf thyme*

¼ *teaspoon coarsely ground pepper*

1 *cup sliced celery*

2 *carrots, peeled and diced*

Plain or herb croutons or crumbled crisp bacon for garnish (optional)

Combine split peas and water in a large saucepan, bring to a boil, and boil for 3 minutes. Remove from heat and let stand for 30 minutes. Add ham shanks, onion, salt, garlic salt, herbs, and pepper. Cover and cook over low heat for 2 to 2½ hours, or until peas are soft and soup thickens. Add celery and carrots and cook for 30 to 40 minutes longer, or until tender. Dice the meat from the ham shanks and return meat to soup. Reheat. Serve plain or garnish soup bowls with plain or herb croutons or crumbled crisp bacon.

SENATE BEAN SOUP

6 to 8 servings (about 2 quarts)

"Uncle Joe" Cannon, Speaker of the U.S. House of Representatives in 1904, made Senate Bean Soup famous when he bellowed, "From now on, hot or cold, rain, snow or shine, I want it on the menu every day!"

1 *pound (2½ cups) navy beans*

3 *to 4 quarts cold water*

1 *meaty ham bone or 2 pounds ham shanks*

3 *quarts hot water*

1 *cup mashed potatoes*

1½ *cups finely chopped onion*

1¼ *cups finely chopped celery*

2 *cloves garlic, minced*

3 *tablespoons minced parsley*

Salt and pepper to taste

Pour beans into colander or sieve, rinse with hot water, and turn into large pan or bowl. Cover with cold water and let stand overnight. Drain beans and turn into large pan with close-fitting lid. Add ham bone or shanks and hot water.

Cover and simmer for 2 hours. Stir in mashed potatoes and cook over low heat until beans are almost tender, about 30 minutes. Add onion, celery, garlic, and parsley and continue simmering for 1 hour, or until beans are tender. Remove ham bone from soup, dice meat, and return to soup. Add salt and pepper to taste. If soup is thicker than desired, stir in a small amount of hot water.

CARLTON'S VEGETABLE SOUP

15 to 20 servings

  2 *to 3 pounds beef chuck, cut in 1-inch cubes*
  2 *tablespoons shortening*
  8 *cups water (approximate)*
  2 *(1-pound 12-ounce) cans tomatoes*
  1 *soup bone*
  1 *tablespoon salt*
  1 *teaspoon basil*
  ½ *teaspoon pepper*
  2 *bay leaves, crushed*
  1 *teaspoon sugar*
  3 *to 4 medium onions, chopped*
  3 *to 4 carrots, thinly sliced*
1¾ *cups fresh Lima beans or 1 (10-ounce) package frozen*
  1 *(5½-ounce) can cut okra, drained*
  1 *(5½-ounce) can whole-kernel corn, drained*
  2 *medium turnips, peeled and diced*
  2 *medium parsnips, peeled and diced*
  3 *medium potatoes, peeled and diced*
  2 *cups fresh shelled peas or 1 (10-ounce) package frozen*

In a 5-quart kettle, brown meat in shortening and remove. Add 6 cups water, tomatoes, soup bone, salt, basil, pepper, and bay leaves and bring to boil. Lower heat and simmer for 1 hour. Add sugar, meat, and all vegetables except potatoes and peas. Continue simmering over low heat for 1 hour longer. Add potatoes and peas and continue cooking for 30 minutes, or until meat and vegetables are tender. Add remaining 2 cups water, if necessary.

SEAFOOD BISQUE

6 servings

  ¼ *cup finely chopped onion*
  ¼ *cup finely chopped celery*
  ¼ *cup butter*
  2 *tablespoons flour*
  1 *teaspoon salt*
  ¼ *teaspoon paprika*
    Dash of white pepper
  4 *cups milk or 2 cups milk and 2 cups half and half*
  2 *cups Pacific pink or other shrimp, cooked and chopped, or king or Dungeness crabmeat, cooked and flaked*

Sauté onion and celery in butter until tender. Stir in flour and seasonings. Add liquid gradually and cook until thick, stirring constantly. Fold in seafood. Heat through and serve at once.

ICED TOMATO BISQUE
6 to 8 servings

   1 *(8-ounce) package cream cheese, softened*
   1 *teaspoon lemon juice*
  ½ *teaspoon minced chives*
  ¼ *teaspoon sugar*
  ¼ *teaspoon salt*
   1 *(10¾-ounce) can tomato soup*
   1 *cup finely shredded baby Gouda or Cheddar cheese*
  ½ *cup heavy cream, whipped*
   Watercress

Combine the first 5 ingredients and beat until smooth. Blend in tomato soup. Stir in cheese and chill thoroughly. Fold in whipped cream and refrigerate for 1 to 3 hours before serving. Spoon into chilled bowls surrounded by crushed ice. Garnish with watercress.

CREAM OF CRAB SOUP
6 servings

   1 *pound Chesapeake blue crabmeat*
  ¼ *cup chopped onion*
  ¼ *cup butter*
   2 *tablespoons flour*
   1 *teaspoon salt*
  ¼ *teaspoon celery salt*
   Dash of pepper
   3 *or 4 dashes hot pepper sauce*
   4 *cups milk or 2 cups milk and 2 cups half and half*
   1 *cup rich chicken stock*
   Chopped parsley (garnish)

Pick over crabmeat, removing any shell or cartilage. Sauté onion in butter until tender but not brown. Blend in flour and seasonings.

Add milk and chicken stock gradually and cook until thickened, stirring constantly. Fold in crabmeat carefully and heat through. Garnish with parsley.

FAMILY-STYLE CREAM OF TOMATO SOUP
4 to 6 servings

   3 *cups (5 to 6 medium) fresh tomatoes or 1 (1-pound) can*
  ½ *cup chopped onion*
   2 *whole cloves*
   1 *teaspoon salt*
   1 *teaspoon sugar*
  ⅛ *teaspoon white pepper*
   3 *tablespoons butter*
   2 *tablespoons flour*
 1½ *cups milk*
   1 *cup half and half*
   Croutons (optional)
   Whipped cream (optional)

Peel, core, and chop fresh tomatoes and combine with next 5 ingredients in saucepan. Cover and simmer over moderate heat until tomatoes are just tender. Remove cloves. If a smooth soup is desired, whiz in blender until smooth. Blend butter and flour, add milk and half and half, and cook, stirring constantly, until mixture is thickened and smooth. Add hot tomato mixture gradually, stirring constantly. Serve at once topped with croutons or whipped cream.

CREAM OF FRESH MUSHROOM SOUP

6 servings (about 5 cups)

½ *pound fresh mushrooms, washed and finely chopped*

2 *teaspoons chopped onion*

¼ *cup butter*

⅓ *cup flour*

3½ *cups rich chicken broth or 2 (13¾-ounce) cans*

½ *cup water*

½ *teaspoon salt (or to taste)*

Dash of white pepper

1 *cup half and half*

Sauté the mushrooms and onion in butter for 3 to 4 minutes, stirring constantly. Stir in flour and cook just until bubbly. Add chicken broth, water, salt, and pepper and cook, stirring constantly, until mixture thickens. Add half and half and heat through, stirring constantly.

ALASKA CLAM AND CORN CHOWDER

6 servings

2 *(7-ounce) cans minced clams*

3 *slices bacon, chopped*

1 *cup chopped onion*

2 *cups diced raw potato*

1½ *cups whole-kernel corn, drained*

3 *cups milk*

2 *tablespoons flour*

1 *tablespoon butter*

1 *teaspoon celery salt*

1 *teaspoon salt*

Dash of pepper

½ *cup coarse cracker crumbs (optional)*

Drain clams and combine clam liquor with enough water to measure 1 cup. Pan-fry bacon until crisp. Add onion and sauté until tender but not brown. Add potatoes and combined clam liquor and water. Cover and simmer gently until potatoes are tender, about 15 minutes. Add corn and milk. Blend flour and butter and stir into soup. Cook slowly until mixture thickens slightly, stirring constantly. Add seasonings and clams, simmering for 5 minutes. Top with cracker crumbs. Serve hot.

WESTERN CREAM OF CORN SOUP

4 to 6 servings (about 6 cups)

When the pioneers prepared corn soup they had to use chewy dried corn. Modern technology allows us to have fresh or canned corn year round.

8 *slices bacon, diced*

¼ *cup finely chopped onion*

¼ *cup flour*

4 *cups milk*

1 *(1-pound 1-ounce) can cream-style corn*

1 *teaspoon salt*

¼ *teaspoon pepper*

¼ *teaspoon celery salt*

Pan-fry bacon until almost crisp, remove, and keep warm. Sauté onion in drippings until tender but not brown. Stir in flour. Add milk and cook, stirring constantly, until smooth and thick. Stir in corn and bring to a boil. Add seasonings and bacon.

HEARTY BEEF VEGETABLE SOUP

6 to 8 servings

  3 *pounds meaty beef shank*

  6 *cups hot water*

  1 *tablespoon salt*

 ⅛ *teaspoon leaf thyme*

  6 *whole peppercorns*

  1 *bay leaf*

  1 *(10-ounce) package frozen Lima beans or 1 (9-ounce) package frozen peas, defrosted*

  1 *(1-pound) can tomatoes*

  1 *cup coarsely chopped onion*

  1 *cup sliced celery*

  1 *cup sliced carrots*

  1 *cup diced potatoes*

  1 *(12-ounce) can whole-kernel corn, drained*

Combine beef shank and next 6 ingredients in a 6-quart Dutch oven or saucepan. Cover and simmer for 3 to 3½ hours, or until meat on bones is very tender. Remove beef shank, peppercorns, and bay leaf. Remove meat from bones, cut into chunks, and return to soup. Add remaining ingredients, cover, and simmer for 30 to 40 minutes, or until vegetables are tender.

NOTE: *Sliced turnips, cabbage, green pepper, green beans, and okra may be substituted for any of the vegetables suggested above.*

OLD-FASHIONED CHICKEN SOUP

6 to 8 servings

  1 *(5- to 6-pound) stewing chicken, whole or cut in serving pieces*

  1 *to 2 teaspoons salt*

  6 *cups water*

  1 *large onion, sliced*

  2 *cups coarsely chopped celery*

  3 *carrots, cut in 2-inch pieces*

  1 *bay leaf, crumbled*

 ¼ *teaspoon peppercorns (optional)*

Place chicken in a 5-quart saucepan with salt and water. Add onion, 1 cup celery, and half the carrots. Simmer for 1 hour, then skim fat from soup. Remove chicken and cut meat into bite-sized pieces. Add remaining celery, carrots, chicken, and seasonings to stock. Continue cooking over low heat for 1 hour longer.

QUICK OYSTER PICKUP

2 servings

Oyster stew, highly prized and easy to prepare, is a delicious treat for Sunday-night supper.

  1 *(12-ounce) can oysters, fresh or frozen*

  1 *(1¾-ounce) package cream of leek soup mix*

  1 *cup milk*

  1 *tablespoon chopped parsley*

Thaw oysters, if frozen, drain, and reserve liquor. Add enough water to oyster liquor to measure 2 cups. Combine with soup mix and bring to a boil, stirring constantly. Reduce heat and simmer for 10 minutes. Add milk and heat, stirring occasionally. Add oysters and heat 3 to 5 minutes longer, or until edges of oysters begin to curl. Sprinkle with parsley.

HOLIDAY OYSTER STEW
6 servings

  2 *(12-ounce) cans oysters, fresh or frozen*
  2 *slices bacon, chopped*
 ⅓ *cup chopped onion*
  1 *(10½-ounce) can cream of potato soup*
  4 *cups oyster liquor and half and half, combined*
1¼ *teaspoons salt*
    Dash of white pepper
    Chopped parsley

Thaw oysters, if frozen, drain, and reserve liquor. Pan-fry bacon until crisp and remove from drippings. Add onion to drippings and cook until tender. Add potato soup, oyster liquor, half and half, and seasonings. Heat, stirring occasionally. Add bacon and oysters and cook for 3 to 5 minutes longer, or until edges of oysters begin to curl. Sprinkle with parsley.

HEARTY FISH CHOWDER
8 servings (10 cups chowder)

  2 *pounds pollack, cod, or other thick fish fillets*
  2 *cups sliced carrots*
  2 *cups cubed raw potatoes*
  2 *cups sliced onion*
  2 *teaspoons salt*
  1 *teaspoon dill weed*
  2 *whole cloves*
  1 *small bay leaf*
 ¼ *cup butter*
  2 *cups boiling water*
 ½ *cup dry white wine or milk*
  1 *cup half and half*
  2 *tablespoons flour*
  2 *tablespoons chopped parsley*

Slice fillets into 1½-inch pieces and refrigerate. Combine carrots, potatoes, onion, salt, dill weed, cloves, bay leaf, and butter in 6-quart Dutch oven. Add boiling water and cover tightly. Bake in a moderate oven (375° F.) for 40 minutes, or until vegetables are tender. Add fish and wine. Cover and bake for an additional 20 minutes, or until fish flakes easily when tested with a fork. Combine half and half and flour, blend until smooth, and add to chowder. Cook, stirring, until hot and slightly thickened. Sprinkle with parsley.

TOM TURKEY CHOWDER
8 to 10 servings

  1 *cup thinly sliced onion*
  2 *tablespoons chopped green pepper (optional)*
 ¼ *cup butter*
  2 *cups diced raw potatoes*
1¼ *cups thinly sliced celery*
  1 *cup water*
  2 *teaspoons salt*
  2 *chicken bouillon cubes*
  3 *cups milk*
  3 *cups diced, cooked turkey*
  1 *(1-pound 1-ounce) can cream-style corn*
 ½ *teaspoon leaf thyme*
  2 *tablespoons diced pimiento (optional)*
 ¼ *cup chopped parsley*
    French bread or assorted crackers

Sauté onion and green pepper in butter until tender but not brown. Add next 5 ingredients, cover, and simmer until potatoes and celery are tender, about 15 minutes. Stir in milk, turkey, corn, thyme, and pimiento and heat through. Just before serving, sprinkle with parsley. Serve with hot buttered French bread or assorted crackers.

SAVORY BEEF-BARLEY SOUP

6 to 8 servings

Early settlers brought barley seeds with them to New England, where they grew barley for use in the making of soups, cereals, bread, and beer.

  1 *pound beef (chuck, round, or stew meat), cut in 1-inch cubes*
  1 *knuckle beef bone*
  2 *tablespoons shortening or oil*
  8 *cups water*
  2 *tablespoons barley*
  1 *tablespoon Worcestershire sauce*
  1 *tablespoon salt*
  ½ *teaspoon basil*
  ½ *teaspoon minced garlic*
  ¼ *teaspoon coarsely ground pepper*
  ¼ *teaspoon rosemary*
  ¼ *teaspoon chopped bay leaves*
  ⅛ *teaspoon oregano*
  3 *drops hot pepper sauce*
  1 *cup canned tomatoes*
  3 *celery stalks plus leaves, cut up*
  ½ *cup canned whole-kernel corn, drained*
  ½ *cup fresh cut green beans*

Brown beef cubes and bone in shortening or oil in a large pot. Add 6 cups water and barley. Simmer for 1 hour. Skim off excess fat and add seasonings. Continue simmering for 2 hours longer. Add vegetables and remaining 2 cups water. Cook for 1 hour longer.

BAY.

GUMBO

Gumbo, a thickened soup or stew served over hot cooked rice, is the crowning achievement of Creole cooking. Many varieties of fish and sea-food, as well as ham and chicken, are used in preparing a tasty gumbo. Okra is usually an essential ingredient, although it is often omitted in New Orleans. Filé powder is added for thickening just before serving. Flour has been used in place of filé in the following recipes because filé powder is often unavailable.

GULFPORT GUMBO SPECIAL

6 to 8 servings (9 cups)

  2 *pounds raw shrimp*
  2 *(10-ounce) cans frozen oysters, undrained*
1½ *cups chopped onion*
1½ *cups sliced celery*
  1 *cup chopped green pepper*
  1 *clove garlic, finely chopped*
  ⅓ *cup cooking oil*
  ⅓ *cup flour*
  1 *(1-pound 12-ounce) can tomatoes, undrained*
1½ *cups chicken broth or 1 (13¾-ounce) can*
  1 *tablespoon Worcestershire sauce*
2½ *teaspoons salt*
  ¼ *teaspoon pepper*
  1 *bay leaf*
  2 *to 3 dashes hot pepper sauce*
  1 *(10-ounce) package frozen sliced okra, partially thawed and broken apart*
  6 *to 8 servings hot cooked seasoned rice*

Peel, devein, and wash shrimp. Thaw oysters. Sauté onion, celery, green pepper, and garlic in oil in large Dutch oven until tender but not brown. Blend in flour. Add tomatoes, chicken broth, Worcestershire sauce, salt, pepper, and bay leaf. Add hot pepper sauce, cover, and simmer gently for 30 minutes, stirring occasionally. Uncover. Add shrimp, oysters, and okra. Simmer for 15 to 20 minutes, or until shrimp and okra are tender and mixture is consistency desired. Remove bay leaf and serve over hot rice.

PONTCHARTRAIN FISH GUMBO
6 servings

    1 *pound red snapper or other thick fish fillets*
    ¼ *cup oil or butter*
    1 *cup chopped onion*
    1 *cup thinly sliced celery*
    ¾ *cup chopped green pepper*
    1 *tablespoon finely chopped parsley*
    1 *clove garlic, minced*
    1 *tablespoon flour*
    1½ *teaspoons chili powder*
    1½ *teaspoons salt*
    1 *teaspoon paprika*
    Dash of cayenne pepper
    1 *(1-pound) can tomato wedges*
    1 *(8-ounce) can tomato sauce*
    ½ *cup water*
    1 *(10-ounce) package frozen okra, defrosted*
    6 *servings hot cooked seasoned rice*

Remove skin from fillets and cut fillets into 1½-inch chunks. Heat oil or butter in large skillet or Dutch oven. Add onion, celery, green pepper, parsley, and garlic. Cook slowly until vegetables are tender but not brown, stirring often. Combine flour, chili powder, salt, paprika, and cayenne. Stir into vegetables. Add tomato wedges, tomato sauce, and water. Simmer, mixing in fish and okra carefully.

Cover and cook slowly for 10 to 15 minutes, or until fish flakes easily when tested with a fork and okra is done. Serve with hot cooked seasoned rice.

CATFISH GUMBO
6 servings

    1 *pound skinned catfish fillets or other fillets*
    ½ *cup chopped celery*
    ½ *cup chopped green pepper*
    ½ *cup chopped onion*
    1 *clove garlic, finely chopped*
    ¼ *cup oil*
    2 *cups beef broth*
    1 *(1-pound) can tomatoes*
    1 *(10-ounce) package frozen okra, sliced*
    2 *teaspoons salt*
    ¼ *teaspoon pepper*
    ¼ *teaspoon thyme*
    1 *bay leaf*
    Dash of hot pepper sauce
    1½ *cups hot cooked rice*

Cut fish into 1-inch pieces. Sauté celery, green pepper, onion, and garlic in oil until tender. Add beef broth, tomatoes, okra, and seasonings. Cover and simmer for 30 minutes. Add fish. Cover and simmer for 15 minutes longer, or until fish flakes easily when tested with a fork. Remove bay leaf. Place ¼ cup rice in each of 6 soup bowls. Fill with gumbo.

MINESTRONE

6 to 8 generous servings

- ½ *cup dried navy or red kidney beans*
- 3 *slices bacon, very finely chopped*
- ½ *cup finely chopped ham*
- 1 *cup chopped onion*
- 1 *tablespoon olive or cooking oil*
- 1 *clove garlic, minced*
- 1 *teaspoon basil*
- 1 *sprig parsley, finely chopped*
- 2½ *quarts (10 cups) liquid*
- 2 *chicken or beef bouillon cubes*
- 1 *cup chopped fresh or canned tomatoes*
- 1 *cup diced carrots*
- 1 *cup diced potato*
- 1 *cup finely shredded cabbage*
- ½ *cup diced celery*
- 1 *medium zucchini, diced*
- ¼ *cup tomato paste*
- 1 *cup elbow macaroni or spaghetti, broken into 1-inch lengths*
- *Salt and pepper to taste*
- *Shredded or grated Parmesan cheese*

Cover beans with cold water, cover, and let stand overnight. Drain, cover beans with water, and cook slowly until tender. Drain, reserve water, and set beans aside. Combine bacon and next 6 ingredients in large Dutch oven or kettle. Cook over low heat until lightly browned, stirring often. Add liquid (bean water and water as needed) and next 8 ingredients, mixing thoroughly. Cover and bring to a boil. Lower heat and cook slowly for 45 to 60 minutes. Add beans and macaroni or spaghetti, cover, and cook for 10 to 12 minutes, or until tender. Add salt and pepper to taste. Serve at once topped with cheese.

MULLIGATAWNY

8 servings

Created in India and Anglicized by the British, Mulligatawny soup derives its name from a corruption of the Tamil *milagutanni,* meaning "pepper water."

- 1½ *cups peeled, cored, and chopped raw apple*
- 1 *cup thinly sliced onion*
- 1 *cup thinly sliced carrots*
- 1 *small clove garlic, minced*
- ¼ *cup butter*
- 3 *tablespoons flour*
- 1 *to 1½ teaspoons curry powder (or to taste)*
- 1 *teaspoon salt*
- 1 *(1-pound) can tomato wedges*
- 1 *cup rich chicken broth*
- ½ *cup half and half*
- 2 *cups cooked chicken or turkey, finely diced*

In a soup kettle, sauté apple, onion, carrots, and garlic in butter until tender, stirring often. Stir in flour, curry powder, and salt. Mix in tomatoes and chicken broth. Cover and cook slowly for 45 to 50 minutes, or until vegetables are tender and the flavors blended. If a smooth soup is desired, whiz in blender. Return to soup kettle, stir in half and half and chicken or turkey. Reheat and serve.

VICHYSSOISE

6 to 8 servings

Vichyssoise, an American adaptation of a French country soup, is the invention of Louis Diat, who created it to celebrate the opening of the roof garden at the old Ritz Carlton Hotel in New York.

4 *leeks or 1 cup chopped onion*

3 *tablespoons butter*

3 *cups thinly sliced potatoes*

1 *cup rich chicken broth*

1 *teaspoon salt*

Dash of white pepper

1 *bay leaf*

3 *cups half and half or 1 cup milk and 2 cups half and half*

1 *cup cream*

1 *tablespoon finely chopped chives or finely chopped parsley (optional)*

Watercress (optional)

Slice white and very light-green parts of leeks very thinly. Sauté leeks or onion in butter until tender but not brown. Add potatoes, chicken broth, salt, pepper, and bay leaf. Simmer, covered, until potatoes are very tender, about 30 minutes. Remove bay leaf. Whiz mixture in blender, a little at a time, until smooth or put through a food mill. Return to saucepan and stir in half and half or milk and half and half. Stir in cream just before serving. Serve hot or thoroughly chilled. Garnish each serving with chives or parsley and a sprig of watercress.

FRENCH ONION SOUP

8 servings

2 *pounds yellow onions, very thinly sliced*

¼ *cup butter*

3 *tablespoons flour*

6 *cups beef broth*

1 *cup dry white wine or water*

Salt and pepper to taste

8 *slices French bread, toasted*

1 *cup grated Swiss cheese*

Sauté onions in butter, for 10 to 15 minutes, or until onions are golden. Stir in flour. Add broth and wine. Add salt and pepper to taste. Cover and simmer for 45 minutes. Place a toast slice in each individual heatproof soup bowl. Ladle soup over toast. When toast rises to top, spoon cheese over toast. Place in very hot oven (450° F.) 2 to 3 minutes.

CANADIAN POTATO CHEESE SOUP

6 servings

1½ *cups thinly sliced onion*

¼ *cup butter*

3 *cups thinly sliced potatoes*

1 *cup hot water*

2 *teaspoons salt*

Dash of white pepper

4 *chicken bouillon cubes*

3 *cups milk*

1 *cup half and half*

2 *cups (½ pound) shredded sharp American cheese*

2 *tablespoons minced parsley*

Sauté onion in butter until tender. Add potatoes, water, salt, pepper, and 1 bouillon cube. Cook, covered, until potatoes are tender, about 20 minutes. Add 2 cups milk. Whiz potato mixture and liquid in blender a little at a time. Return to saucepan, add remaining 3 bouillon cubes, 1 cup milk, half and half, and cheese, stirring until melted. Serve hot topped with parsley.

FISH AND SEAFOOD

SALMON

Once the Atlantic salmon rushed in profusion up the Hudson River to spawn, but dams and pollution have caused them practically to disappear. Today, Maine is the only place where they are found. Pacific salmon of Oregon and Washington have fared much better. Several years ago Chinook and Coho salmon were transplanted from the West Coast into Lake Michigan and have thrived. Whether smoked, poached, broiled, or baked, served hot or cold, salmon is delicious eating.

GLAZED WHOLE SALMON

8 to 12 servings (approximate)

  1 *(3- to 4-pound) salmon, with head and tail intact*

  Court Bouillon (see next column)

  Seasoned Aspic Glaze (see next column)

  Garnishes: cucumbers, olives, radishes, thinly sliced carrots, pimiento, or fresh dill

  Clear Glaze (see next column)

Rinse salmon with cold water and dry. Place on rack in a 20-inch fish steamer or poaching pan. Pour in cooled Court Bouillon. Cover and simmer for 20 to 30 minutes, or until fish flakes when tested with a fork. Remove fish immediately, leaving head and tail intact. Carefully remove skin and gray fatty flesh. Cool fish and then chill thoroughly.

Prepare Seasoned Aspic Glaze. To glaze fish, paint cooled (but not thickened) Seasoned Aspic Glaze evenly over entire fish with a very soft pastry brush or spoon over fish slowly, a small amount at a time. Chill. Continue glazing and chilling until you have built up an even layer about ⅛ inch thick over entire fish. Arrange a border of cucumber slices around edge of fish and decorate top with thinly sliced radishes, sliced stuffed or pitted ripe olives, pimiento, carrots, and fresh dill (use tiny vegetable cutters to cut vegetables into attractive shapes). Chill again.

Spoon slightly thickened Clear Glaze over the entire fish and chill thoroughly. Garnish as desired and chill until serving time. Serve with mayonnaise, mustard, sour cream, or favorite fish sauce.

COURT BOUILLON   about 6 cups

  2 *quarts water*

  2 *cups sliced celery*

  1½ *cups sliced onion*

  1 *cup thinly sliced carrots*

  ½ *cup vinegar*

  2 *tablespoons salt*

  8 *peppercorns*

  4 *lemon slices*

  3 *parsley sprigs*

  2 *bay leaves*

  ½ *teaspoon leaf thyme*

Combine ingredients in 4-quart saucepan. Simmer for 45 minutes, strain, and cool.

SEASONED ASPIC GLAZE   2½ cups

  2 *envelopes gelatin*

  ½ *cup cold water*

  2 *cups boiling rich chicken broth*

  2 *tablespoons lemon juice*

Soften gelatin in cold water. Add gelatin to broth and stir until dissolved. Stir in lemon juice. Chill until slightly thickened.

CLEAR GLAZE   About 1 cup

  1 *envelope gelatin*

  ¼ *cup cold water*

  ¾ *cup boiling water*

Soften gelatin in cold water. Dissolve in boiling water. Chill until slightly thickened.

BROILED SALMON STEAKS WITH HERB SAUCE

6 servings

¼ *cup butter*
¼ *cup dry white wine*
1 *tablespoon chopped parsley*
¼ *teaspoon fines herbes*
1 *clove garlic, sliced*
6 *salmon steaks (about 2 pounds)*
1 *teaspoon salt*

Combine butter, wine, parsley, herbs, and garlic and heat slowly until butter is melted. Let stand for 15 minutes. Sprinkle steaks with salt. Place fish on a greased broiler pan and brush with sauce. Broil about 3 inches from heat source for 4 to 6 minutes on each side, basting with sauce several times.

NORTHWESTERN SALMON PIE

6 servings

1 *(1-pound) can salmon*
Milk
1 *cup soft bread crumbs*
3 *eggs, beaten slightly*
1 *cup diced celery*
¼ *cup chopped onion*
2 *tablespoons butter*
2 *tablespoons chopped parsley*
1 *tablespoon lemon juice*
¾ *teaspoon salt*
Unbaked (9-inch) Pie Shell (see index)

Drain salmon, reserve liquid, and bone, skin, and flake. Add milk to salmon liquid to measure 1 cup. Combine with bread crumbs and eggs and set aside. Sauté celery and onion in butter until celery is tender. Add cooked vegetables, salmon, parsley, lemon juice, and salt to egg mixture, blending thoroughly.

Pour into prepared pastry shell and bake in a hot oven (400° F.) for 25 to 30 minutes, or until crust is done and mixture set. Let stand for 8 to 10 minutes before cutting into wedges.

COQUILLES ST. JACQUES

4 servings

1 *pound bay or sea scallops*
½ *cup water*
½ *cup dry white wine*
½ *teaspoon salt*
Dash of white pepper
1 *cup sliced fresh mushrooms*
¼ *cup sliced green onion*
¼ *cup butter*
3 *tablespoons flour*
¾ *cup half and half*
½ *cup shredded Swiss cheese*
1¼ *cups coarsely crushed and buttered corn-flake crumbs or 1 ½ cups hot mashed potatoes*

Rinse scallops in cold water (if scallops are large, cut in halves or quarters). Combine scallops, water, wine, salt, and pepper in saucepan and simmer for 4 to 5 minutes, or until scallops are tender. Remove scallops from pan and reserve cooking liquid. Simmer liquid until it is reduced to ¾ cup.

Sauté mushrooms and green onion in butter until tender and stir in flour. Add reserved cooking liquid and half and half and cook until thickened, stirring constantly. Fold in scallops and ¼ cup cheese. Spoon scallop mixture into 4 large baking shells or individual 10-ounce baking dishes. Sprinkle with remaining cheese. Edge dishes with crumbs or spoon hot mashed potatoes around edge. Bake in moderate oven (375° F.) for 15 minutes, or until crumbs or potatoes are lightly browned.

GULF SHORE POMPANO EN PAPILLOTE

6 servings

 6 *pompano fillets (about 2 pounds)*
 2 *cups boiling water*
 ¼ *cup lemon juice*
 1 *teaspoon salt*
 ¼ *teaspoon leaf thyme*
 1 *small bay leaf*
 ½ *cup fresh mushrooms, sliced*
 ¼ *cup sliced stuffed olives (optional)*
 ½ *pound shrimp, cooked, peeled, and deveined, halved lengthwise*
 Onion Sauce (see below)
 1 *tablespoon minced parsley*

Wash, drain, and arrange fillets, skin side down, on lightly oiled baking pan. Combine water, lemon juice, salt, thyme, and bay leaf and pour over fillets. Cover pan securely with aluminum foil and bake in moderate oven (350° F.) for 20 minutes, or until fish flakes easily when tested with a fork. Remove fillets carefully with a wide spatula and drain. Arrange each fillet on a sheet of aluminum foil 1¼ inches larger all around than fish. Arrange mushrooms, olives, and shrimp on each fillet and spoon over an equal amount of Onion Sauce. Slip each fillet on foil into a paper bag large enough to allow fish to lie flat and close bag tightly. Place on baking sheet and bake in hot oven (400° F.) for 15 minutes. To serve, cut a cross in top of each package and fold back corners. Sprinkle with parsley.

ONION SAUCE About 2 cups

 6 *slices bacon, cut crosswise into ½-inch slices*
 ½ *cup sliced green onion*
 ¼ *cup flour*
 ½ *teaspoon salt*
 ¼ *teaspoon paprika*
 2 *cups half and half or milk*

Pan-fry bacon until crisp and lightly browned, drain on absorbent paper, and reserve 3 tablespoons drippings. Sauté onion in drippings until tender but not brown. Stir in flour and seasonings. Add half and half or milk and cook over low heat until thickened, stirring constantly. Fold in bacon.

MASGOUF FISH (Iraqi Broiled Fish)

4 to 6 servings

One of the best fish dishes I have ever eaten was served to me recently by a charming businessman from Iraq who borrowed my kitchen for his preparation. I added saffron rice, a green salad, and an all-American lemon meringue pie to round out the menu.

 1 *(3- to 4-pound) rockfish (bluefish, sea bass, whitefish or lake trout may be substituted)*
 Vegetable oil
 1 *large tomato, diced*
 1 *medium onion, peeled and diced*
 1 *cup diced celery*
 2 *cloves garlic, minced*
 Parsley sprigs
 1 *tablespoon curry powder*
 1 *tablespoon white vinegar*
 ½ *to 1 teaspoon salt (or to taste)*
 ⅛ *to ¼ teaspoon pepper*
 2 *tablespoons lemon juice*

Rub outside of fish with vegetable oil. Place in 9 × 13-inch baking dish and set aside. Combine tomato, onion, celery, garlic, parsley, curry powder, vinegar, salt, and pepper. Spoon over fish. Bake in a moderate oven (350° F.) for 30 to 40 minutes, or until fish is browned and flakes easily when tested with a fork. Sprinkle lemon juice over fish just before serving. Garnish with additional parsley sprigs.

CODFISH, POLLACK, and HALIBUT

New England is the home of the cod, and Massachusetts has officially acknowledged its importance. Since 1784 a painted wooden codfish, four feet eleven inches long, has hung in the Old Boston State House as a memorial to the role codfishing played in maintaining the welfare of the Commonwealth. In areas where game was scarce the Cape Cod Turkey, a whole stuffed baked codfish with sumptuous trimmings, was substituted on important occasions.

OLD-FASHIONED CODFISH CAKES WITH EGG SAUCE

12 cakes

> ½ *pound salt codfish*
> 1½ *cups diced raw potato*
> 2 *tablespoons milk*
> 1 *tablespoon butter*
> 2 *tablespoons finely chopped onion*
> 2 *eggs*
> ¼ *teaspoon dry mustard*
> *Dash of pepper*
> *Cooking oil*
> *Egg Sauce (see index)*

Cover fish with cold water and refrigerate in a covered container for 12 hours. Drain, rinse, and flake or chop very fine. Cook potatoes in unsalted water to cover until tender, about 20 minutes, drain, and beat or mash until smooth. Add milk, butter, onion, eggs, mustard, and pepper. Beat with an electric mixer at medium speed for 5 minutes, or until soft and very fluffy. Beat in flaked codfish. Using ¼ cup for each codfish cake, spoon mixture into skillet containing ⅛-inch hot oil. Cook over medium heat, turning once, until browned, about 5 to 7 minutes total cooking time. Serve hot with Egg Sauce.

SEA ISLAND RED SNAPPER WITH CAPER SAUCE

6 to 8 servings

> 1 *(3- to 4-pound) red snapper*
> 1 *teaspoon salt*
> ½ *teaspoon garlic salt*
> ⅓ *cup chopped onion*
> ⅓ *cup butter*
> ⅓ *cup chopped blanched almonds*
> 3 *cups bread cubes*
> 1 *cup peeled, diced cucumber*
> 1 *tablespoon drained capers*
> ⅛ *teaspoon pepper*
> ⅛ *teaspoon ground cloves*
> 2 *tablespoons melted fat or oil*
> *Caper Sauce (see index)*

Clean, wash, and dry fish. Sprinkle cavity with ½ teaspoon salt and garlic salt. Sauté onion in butter until tender but not brown. Add almonds and brown lightly, stirring constantly. Add bread cubes, cucumber, capers, remaining ½ teaspoon salt, pepper, and cloves and toss lightly. Stuff fish loosely and secure with small metal skewers or wooden picks. Place fish on greased baking pan and brush with fat or oil. Cover fish fins and tail loosely with foil. Bake in moderate oven (350° F.) for 45 to 60 minutes, or until fish flakes easily when tested with a fork. Baste occasionally with fat. Serve with Caper Sauce.

HALIBUT POT ROAST
6 servings

  3 *pounds chunk halibut, salmon, or other firm fish*
⅓ *cup water*
  1 *clove garlic, minced*
⅓ *cup butter, melted*
  2 *teaspoons salt*
¼ *teaspoon pepper*
12 *carrots, peeled and sliced*
  6 *potatoes, peeled and sliced*
  2 *cups sliced celery*

Center fish in large, greased baking pan. Combine water and garlic and pour over. Brush fish with butter and sprinkle with salt and pepper. Cover with foil and bake in moderate oven (350° F.) for 20 minutes. Arrange vegetables around fish and brush with butter. Recover and bake for 40 to 45 minutes, or until vegetables are tender and fish flakes easily when tested with a fork. Transfer fish and vegetables to heated platter. Serve with pan drippings, if desired.

BAKED PIKE
6 servings

  1 *(3- or 4-pound) whole fish (northern pike, muskellunge, pickerel, striped sea bass, or red snapper), fresh or frozen*
⅓ *cup melted butter*
Salt and pepper
Bread Stuffing (see next column)

Clean, wash, and dry fish. Brush cavity of fish with butter and sprinkle with salt and pepper. Place on well-greased 18 × 13-inch baking pan and stuff loosely. Brush fish with remaining butter. Bake in moderate oven (350° F.) for 45 to 60 minutes, or until fish flakes easily when tested with a fork. Transfer to serving platter.

BREAD STUFFING 3 cups
½ *cup chopped celery*
¼ *cup chopped onion*
¼ *cup butter, melted*
  4 *cups dry bread cubes*
  1 *egg, beaten*
½ *teaspoon sage*
½ *teaspoon salt*
¼ *teaspoon thyme*
Dash of pepper

Sauté celery and onion in butter until tender. Combine with remaining ingredients and blend thoroughly.

BAKED POLLACK WITH CRANBERRY-ORANGE SAUCE
6 servings

  2 *pounds pollack or other fish fillets*
  1 *cup sliced celery*
⅓ *cup chopped onion*
  6 *tablespoons butter*
  4 *cups soft bread cubes*
½ *cup chopped pecans*
1¼ *teaspoons salt*
  1 *teaspoon grated orange rind*
¼ *cup orange juice*
Cranberry-Orange Sauce (see index)

Cut fillets into 6 portions. Sauté celery and onion in 4 tablespoons butter until tender but not brown. Stir in bread cubes, pecans, ¼ teaspoon salt, orange rind, and orange juice. Turn stuffing into greased 12 × 8 × 2-inch baking dish. Arrange fish in a single layer over stuffing. Melt remaining 2 tablespoons butter and drizzle over fish. Sprinkle with remaining 1 teaspoon salt. Bake in a moderate oven (350° F.) for 25 to 30 minutes, or until fish flakes easily when tested with a fork. Serve with Cranberry-Orange Sauce.

THE JOHN DORY

36 to 40 pastries

FILLING

1½ *pounds ocean perch, whiting, or other fish fillets*

1½ *teaspoons salt*

Hot water

2 *cups chopped celery*

1 *cup chopped onion*

¼ *cup butter*

1 *cup shredded raw potato*

1 *(10-ounce) can tomatoes, undrained*

1 *teaspoon oregano*

¼ *teaspoon pepper*

¼ *cup grated Romano cheese*

CRUST

6 *tablespoons shortening*

6 *cups self-rising flour*

2 *cups cold water (approximate)*

Oil for deep frying

Simmer fish and ¾ teaspoon salt in hot water to cover for 10 minutes. Drain, chill, remove skin, and flake. Sauté celery and onion in butter until tender, 7 to 10 minutes. Add potato and cook for 5 minutes. Add tomatoes, oregano, remaining ¾ teaspoon salt, and pepper. Cook slowly, stirring constantly, for 10 minutes. Cool and then chill. Fold in flaked fish and cheese.

Prepare crust while fish mixture is chilling. Cut shortening into flour. Add enough cold water to make a stiff dough. Divide crust into 4 equal portions. Roll out one portion at a time on a lightly floured surface, rolling dough very thin. Cut into 4½- or 5-inch squares. Place 2 tablespoons of fish mixture on each square slightly to one side of center. Moisten edges with water, fold in half, and seal. Fry in hot oil (375° F.) about 2 minutes, or until browned, turning once. Remove from oil and drain. Serve hot or cold.

BOUILLABAISSE MARSEILLAISE

8 servings (10 cups)

While Greeks call it *psaro*, Italians call it *zuppa di pesce*, Belgians *waterzooie*, Frenchmen *bouillabaisse*, and Americans *fish stew*. The English author William Makepeace Thackeray, stymied for a definition, described it as "a soup or broth, or brew, or hotchpotch."

2 *pounds red snapper, mullet, or redfish fillets*

1 *pound raw shrimp*

1 *cup coarsely chopped onion*

1 *clove garlic, finely chopped*

½ *cup butter or olive oil*

3 *tablespoons flour*

1 *cup coarsely chopped fresh tomato*

2 *cups fish stock or water*

1 *cup tomato juice*

½ *cup dry sherry*

½ *lemon, sliced*

2 *teaspoons salt*

⅛ *teaspoon cayenne pepper*

⅛ *teaspoon leaf thyme*

3 *whole allspice*

1 *small bay leaf*

Pinch of saffron (optional)

1 *pint shucked oysters or 1 (10-ounce) can frozen, undrained*

French bread

Skin fillets and cut in slices or large chunks. Peel, devein, and wash shrimp. Sauté onion and garlic in butter or olive oil in Dutch oven until tender. Blend in flour. Add next 11 ingredients and mix thoroughly. Simmer gently for 30 minutes, or until flavors are well blended. Add fish, shrimp and oysters. Simmer gently for 15 to 20 minutes, or until shrimp is tender and fish flakes easily when tested with a fork. Serve with crusty French bread.

QUICK FISH STEW WITH DUMPLINGS
6 to 8 servings

  2 *pounds pollack or other fish fillets*
1½ *cups sliced onion*
  ¼ *cup butter*
  1 *(10-ounce) package frozen mixed vegetables, partially defrosted*
  1 *(4-ounce) can sliced mushrooms, undrained*
  2 *(10½-ounce) cans cream of celery soup*
Milk
  1 *teaspoon salt*
  ½ *teaspoon leaf thyme*
  4 *strips bacon, diced*
  ½ *(18-ounce) package corn-muffin mix*

Cut fish into 1-inch pieces. In a 6-quart Dutch oven with heatproof handles sauté onion in butter until tender but not brown, stirring often. Stir in frozen vegetables. Add mushrooms, soup, 1 cup milk, salt, and thyme. Heat, stirring, until hot. Fold in fish. Cover and bake in a hot oven (400° F.) for 15 minutes, or until hot and bubbly.

Fry bacon until crisp and drain on paper toweling. Prepare muffin mix according to package directions, reducing milk by half. Stir in crisp bacon and drop 6 to 8 mounds of batter into hot fish mixture. Return to oven. Bake for 20 minutes, or until fish flakes easily when tested with a fork.

ALASKAN FISHERMAN STEW
6 servings

  2 *pounds rockfish, lingcod, Pacific Ocean perch, salmon, halibut, or other firm fish*
1½ *cups sliced celery*
  ½ *cup chopped onion*
  1 *clove garlic, minced*
  ¼ *cup butter*
  1 *(1-pound 12-ounce) can tomatoes, undrained*
  1 *(8-ounce) can tomato sauce*
  2 *teaspoons salt*
  ½ *teaspoon paprika*
  ½ *teaspoon chili powder*
  ¼ *teaspoon pepper*
  1 *(8-ounce) package spaghetti*
  2 *cups boiling water*
  ¼ *cup grated or shredded Parmesan cheese*

Cut fish into 1-inch chunks. Sauté celery, onion, and garlic in butter until tender. Add tomatoes, tomato sauce, and seasonings. Simmer, covered, for 20 minutes. Mix in spaghetti and water. Cover and cook slowly for 10 minutes. Add fish, cover, and simmer for 10 minutes. Serve with cheese sprinkled over top.

LAKE MICHIGAN DOMERS (Baked Whitefish in Foil)

4 servings

During the nineteenth century, steamboats with domes on top were used as fishing boats on the Great Lakes. The only food the fishermen carried were packages of vegetables wrapped in parchment. After a long day of fishing, they would cook their meal in the only place available—atop the domes.

1½   *pounds whitefish or other fillets*
¼   *cup butter*
¼   *cup flour*
1½   *teaspoons salt*
1   *cup milk*
2   *tablespoons lemon juice*
¼   *teaspoon paprika*
⅛   *teaspoon pepper*
Topping Combinations (see below)
Chopped parsley

Cut fish into 4 serving portions. Cut 4 14-inch lengths of heavy-duty aluminum foil and grease. Melt butter and stir in flour and 1 teaspoon salt. Add milk all at once and cook, stirring constantly, until thick. Stir in lemon juice and paprika. Place one portion of fish in the center of each foil piece. Sprinkle fish with remaining ½ teaspoon salt and pepper. Arrange the desired Topping Combination on fish and spoon an equal amount of sauce over each. Bring the foil up over the fish and close all edges with tight double folds. Place foil bags on baking sheet or shallow baking pan. Bake in hot oven (425° F.) for 40 minutes. To serve, place bags on plates and snip foil with scissors to form a crisscross in the center of bag, turning edges back. Sprinkle with chopped parsley. Eat directly from foil.

TOPPING COMBINATIONS

1. ¼ pound peeled and cleaned shrimp and ¼ pound mushroom caps sautéed in butter.

2. 1 onion, sliced, and 4 carrots, cut in thin strips.
3. 1 cup *each* chopped celery and green pepper, ½ cup chopped onion, and 4 large tomato slices.
4. 1½ cups fresh shelled peas or 1 (10-ounce) package frozen and 8 tiny onions.

STRIPED BASS WITH APPLE-ONION STUFFING

6 servings

3 or 4 *pounds striped bass or other fish, fresh or frozen*
1½   *teaspoons salt*
Apple-Onion Stuffing (see below)
2   *tablespoons melted fat or oil*
Lemon wedges

Clean, wash, and dry fish. Sprinkle inside with salt and stuff loosely. Close opening with small skewers or wooden picks. Place fish on greased 16 × 10-inch baking pan. Brush with fat. Bake in a moderate oven (350° F.) for 40 to 60 minutes, or until fish flakes easily when tested with a fork. Remove skewers. Transfer to serving platter and serve with lemon wedges.

APPLE-ONION STUFFING   1 quart

1   *cup chopped onion*
2   *tablespoons butter*
3   *cups peeled, chopped apple*
½   *cup chopped celery*
⅓   *cup chopped parsley*
3   *tablespoons lemon juice*
½   *teaspoon salt*
¼   *teaspoon thyme*

Sauté onion in butter until tender. Combine with remaining ingredients and mix thoroughly.

LEMON

BAKED WHITEFISH WITH LEMON RICE STUFFING

6 servings

   1 *(3- to 4-pound) whitefish (or lake trout or bluefish) with head and tail intact*

1½ *teaspoons salt*

    Lemon Rice Stuffing (see below)

   2 *tablespoons melted fat or oil*

Clean, wash, and dry fish. Sprinkle inside and out with salt. Stuff fish loosely and secure with small metal skewers or wooden picks. Place fish on a greased, heatproof 16 × 10-inch platter. Brush with fat or oil. Bake in a moderate oven (350° F.) for 40 to 60 minutes, or until fish flakes easily when tested with a fork. Baste fish with fat occasionally during cooking.

LEMON RICE STUFFING

1½ *cups cooked long-grain rice*

 ¾ *cup chopped celery*

 ½ *cup chopped onion*

 ¼ *cup melted fat or oil*

 2 *tablespoons grated lemon peel*

 1 *teaspoon paprika*

 1 *teaspoon salt*

   Dash of thyme

 ⅓ *cup sour cream*

 ¼ *cup diced peeled lemon*

Sauté celery and onion in fat until tender. Combine with grated lemon, paprika, salt, and thyme and stir into rice. Add sour cream and diced lemon peel, tossing lightly.

CIOPPINO

6 to 8 servings

Cioppino is a spicy fish stew. As the story goes, the name originated from the cry of the fishermen of San Francisco's wharf area to their compatriots returning in boats laden with fish. "Chip-in-o," they appealed, and contributions of fish and shellfish were added to the steaming pots of stew they were preparing. Serve Cioppino in deep soup bowls accompanied by wine and hot, crusty sourdough bread.

1½ *pounds halibut, lingcod, rockfish, or sea bass*

 2 *cups sliced onion*

 2 *cloves garlic, finely minced*

 ¼ *cup cooking or olive oil*

 1 *(1-pound 12-ounce) can tomatoes, undrained*

 1 *(8-ounce) can tomato sauce*

 1 *cup water*

 ¼ *cup chopped parsley*

 2 *teaspoons salt*

 1 *teaspoon basil*

 ½ *teaspoon oregano*

 ¼ *teaspoon pepper*

 1 *dozen clams in shell, washed*

 1 *cup cooked, peeled Pacific pink shrimp (or other shrimp)*

Cut fish into 1½-inch chunks. Sauté onion and garlic in oil until onion is tender but not brown. Add tomatoes, tomato sauce, water, parsley, salt, basil, oregano, and pepper. Cover and simmer gently for 30 minutes. Add fish chunks, cover, and simmer 10 to 20 minutes longer. Add clams in shells and shrimp. Cover and cook 10 minutes longer, or until fish flakes easily when tested with a fork.

SMOKED WHITEFISH CASSEROLE

12 servings

Smoked fish, especially the delicate whitefish, is a specialty of the area around the Great Lakes.

2 *pounds smoked whitefish or other smoked fish*

4 *hard-cooked eggs*

6 *tablespoons butter*

¼ *cup flour*

¼ *teaspoon salt*

¼ *teaspoon white pepper*

3½ *cups milk*

1 *(7-ounce) package macaroni, cooked and drained (about 4 cups)*

1 *cup shredded sharp Cheddar cheese*

½ *cup sliced fresh mushrooms or 1 (4-ounce) can sliced mushrooms, undrained*

¼ *cup sliced ripe olives*

¼ *cup chopped pimiento*

1 *cup soft bread crumbs*

12 *pitted ripe olives (garnish)*

Remove skin and bones from fish and flake. Slice eggs, reserving 12 slices for garnish, and chop remaining eggs. Melt ¼ cup butter in saucepan, stirring constantly, and blend in flour and seasonings. Add milk gradually and cook, stirring constantly, until thick. Combine all ingredients except egg slices, crumbs, butter, and olives. Place in a greased 3-quart casserole. Melt remaining 2 tablespoons butter, combine with crumbs, and sprinkle over casserole. Bake in a moderate oven (350° F.) for 45 to 60 minutes. Garnish with olives and egg slices.

NOTE: *This casserole may be prepared a day ahead and refrigerated. Allow about 30 minutes additional baking time.*

SHAD

Baked shad is reputed to have been one of George Washington's favorite dishes. When shad "run" each spring, both the fish and roe are still considered delicacies. Found exclusively in Atlantic waters until 1871, shad were transported cross-country and released into the Pacific and today are one of the most common fish of the Northwest.

BROILED SHAD

6 servings

2 *pounds shad fillets*

¼ *cup butter, melted*

2 *tablespoons horseradish*

2 *tablespoons lemon juice*

2 *teaspoons prepared mustard*

1 *teaspoon salt*

¼ *teaspoon pepper*

Paprika

Cut fillets into serving pieces. Combine butter, horseradish, lemon juice, mustard, salt, and pepper. Place fish, skin side up, on a greased broiler pan. Brush with sauce. Broil about 3 inches from heat source for 4 to 5 minutes on each side, basting occasionally with the sauce. Sprinkle with paprika and serve.

SHAD ROE WITH BACON
6 servings

  6 *pairs shad roe (about 2 pounds)*
¼ *cup flour*
  1 *teaspoon salt*
⅛ *teaspoon pepper*
½ *cup butter*
  6 *slices buttered toast*
    Minced parsley
  6 *slices bacon, cooked and drained*
    Lemon wedges (optional)

Separate the pairs of roe carefully so as not to break the membrane. Place roe in saucepan, cover with hot water, and simmer for 4 to 5 minutes. Drain. Combine next 3 ingredients. Lightly dust each pair of roe with flour mixture. Melt 3 tablespoons butter, add roe, and cook over moderately low heat until browned on both sides. Place each portion of roe on a slice of hot buttered toast. Melt remaining butter and pour an equal amount over each portion. Sprinkle with parsley. Serve with crisp bacon and lemon wedges.

VARIATION
My Husband's Method: Place shad roe on square of wax paper large enough to cover completely. Sprinkle with lemon juice, salt, and pepper. Dot with butter or cover with bacon slices. Fold paper over roe, as you would wrap a sandwich, and tuck ends under. Place in lightly greased frying pan. Pan-fry at medium to low heat until as brown as desired. Turn over, wax paper and all, to brown both sides.

SMELTS
Smelts are a particular favorite in the area around the Great Lakes. Originally found in New England waters, they were transplanted from Maine to the Great Lakes region in 1912 to provide food for larger species of fish. In the early spring, just as the ice breaks, the smelts leave the lakes to spawn in streams, and people from nearby communities turn out to see the sight and catch the fish.

SMELTS, ITALIAN STYLE
6 servings

  2 *cups sliced onion*
  2 *cloves garlic, minced*
¼ *cup melted fat or oil*
  1 *(1-pound 12-ounce) can Italian tomatoes, undrained*
  1 *(6-ounce) can tomato paste*
1½ *teaspoons oregano*
1½ *teaspoons salt*
  1 *teaspoon sugar*
¼ *teaspoon pepper*
¼ *cup chopped parsley*
  2 *pounds Pacific smelts*
  1 *cup shredded mozzarella cheese*
¼ *cup shredded Parmesan cheese*

Sauté onion and garlic in fat or oil until onion is tender but not brown. Mix in tomatoes, tomato paste, oregano, 1 teaspoon salt, sugar, and pepper. Cover and simmer for 30 minutes, or until slightly thickened, stirring often. Stir in parsley. Pour sauce into 2- or 3-quart stove-to-table baking dish. Arrange smelts in a single layer on sauce down center of baking dish. Sprinkle with remaining ½ teaspoon salt and cheeses. Bake in a hot oven (400° F.) for 15 to 20 minutes, or until fish flakes easily when tested with a fork.

FRIED SMELTS WITH HERB BUTTER

6 servings

  2 *pounds smelts*
½ *cup butter*
  1 *tablespoon finely chopped parsley*
  1 *tablespoon finely chopped chives*
  1 *tablespoon lime juice*
⅛ *teaspoon hot pepper sauce*
  Freshly ground pepper
1½ *teaspoons salt*
  1 *cup fine corn-flake crumbs*
  Fat for frying

Wash and dry smelts. Cream butter until smooth and fluffy and beat in parsley, chives, lime juice, hot pepper sauce, pepper, and ½ teaspoon salt. Sprinkle fish with remaining 1 teaspoon salt. Roll in crumbs to coat thoroughly. Fry fish in hot fat for 2 to 3 minutes on each side. Spoon herb butter over and serve.

FRENCH QUARTER CATFISH WITH BÉARNAISE SAUCE

6 servings

  6 *(12-ounce) catfish*
¾ *cup French dressing*
  2 *cups fine dry bread crumbs*
  1 *tablespoon butter, melted*
1½ *teaspoons fines herbes*
1½ *teaspoons paprika*
  1 *tablespoon minced onion*
¾ *teaspoon salt*
½ *teaspoon celery salt*
  Lemon slices (optional)
  Béarnaise Sauce (see index)

Clean, wash, and dry fish. Brush inside and out with French dressing and arrange in shallow dish. Cover and refrigerate for 1 to 2 hours, basting with dressing several times. Combine crumbs, butter, fines herbes, paprika, onion, salt, and celery salt. Roll fish in crumbs and arrange in greased shallow baking pan. Bake in moderate oven (350° F.) for 30 to 35 minutes, or until fish flakes easily when tested with a fork. Garnish with lemon slices and serve with Béarnaise Sauce.

CRISPY FRIED CATFISH

6 servings

  6 *(12-ounce) catfish or other small fish*
¼ *cup evaporated milk*
1½ *teaspoons salt*
  Dash of pepper
½ *cup flour*
¼ *cup yellow cornmeal*
  1 *teaspoon paprika*
  3 *to 4 tablespoons fat*

Clean, wash, and dry fish. Combine milk, salt, and pepper. Mix together flour, cornmeal, and paprika. Dip fish in milk mixture and dredge in flour mixture. Fry in hot fat for 4 to 5 minutes on each side. Drain on absorbent paper. Serve with hush puppies.

TROUT

A fierce fighter when hooked on a fishing line, rainbow trout makes truly delectable eating. The cold mountain-stream waters make them extra firm and tender. When cooked outdoors, small trout, such as brook, brown, and spotted, are usually pan-fried quickly, but the rainbows may be laid open on a grill and cooked with bacon for natural basting.

RAINBOW TROUT WITH MUSHROOM-HERB STUFFING

6 servings

- 6 *rainbow trout*
- 2 *teaspoons salt*
- 4 *cups soft bread cubes*
- ⅔ *cup butter, melted*
- 1 *cup sliced fresh mushrooms*
- ⅔ *cup sliced green onion*
- ¼ *cup chopped parsley*
- 2 *tablespoons chopped pimiento*
- 4 *teaspoons lemon juice*
- ½ *teaspoon marjoram*

Clean, wash, and dry fish. Sprinkle inside and out with 1½ teaspoons salt. Sauté bread cubes in ½ cup butter until lightly browned, stirring frequently. Add mushrooms and onion and cook until mushrooms are tender. Stir in remaining ½ teaspoon salt, parsley, pimiento, lemon juice, and marjoram and toss lightly. Stuff fish, skewer with wooden picks, and arrange in single layer in a greased baking pan. Brush with remaining melted butter. Bake in a moderate oven (350° F.) for 25 to 30 minutes, or until fish flakes easily when tested with a fork. Serve plain or with a fish sauce.

STUFFED LAKE TROUT

6 to 8 servings

- 1 *cup diced celery*
- ½ *cup chopped onion*
- ½ *cup butter*
- ½ *cup chopped blanched almonds*
- 4 *cups diced bread cubes*
- 2 *eggs, beaten*
- ½ *cup tomato juice*
- 1 *teaspoon salt*
- ½ *teaspoon seasoned salt*
- ½ *teaspoon pepper*
- 1 *(4- to 5-pound) lake trout, head and tail removed, boned or filleted for stuffing*

Sauté celery and onion in butter until butter is lightly brown. Drain off butter, add ¼ cup almonds, and set aside for basting fish. Combine cooked celery, onion, bread cubes, eggs, tomato juice, salt, seasoned salt, and pepper and mix lightly. Place fish in shallow baking pan and stuff, sprinkling stuffing with remaining ¼ cup almonds. Add ¼ inch water to bottom of pan. Bake in hot oven (400° F.) for 45 minutes, or until fish flakes easily when tested with a fork. Baste fish every 10 minutes with butter and almond mixture.

BOILED LOBSTER

6 servings

  ⅓ *cup salt*
1½ *gallons water*
  6 *live lobsters (1 pound each)*
    Melted butter

Add salt to water, cover, and bring to a boil. Plunge lobsters in head first. Cover and simmer for 15 minutes, depending on size of lobsters. Drain, crack claws, and serve with melted butter.

GRILLED SPINY LOBSTER TAILS

6 servings

  6 *spiny lobster tails (8 ounces each)*
¼ *cup butter, melted*
  2 *tablespoons lemon juice*
½ *teaspoon salt*
    Melted butter

Using scissors to cut through the under shell, cut lobster in half lengthwise and remove center portion of shell. Cut 6 12-inch squares of heavy-duty aluminum foil and place a lobster tail on each. Combine butter, lemon juice, and salt and baste lobster meat. Bring the foil up over the lobster and close all edges with double folds. Place packages on a grill, shell side down, about 5 inches from hot coals and cook for 20 minutes. Remove lobster tails from the foil. Place on grill, flesh side down, and cook 2 to 3 minutes longer, or until lightly browned. Serve with melted butter.

NOTE: *Frozen lobster tails may be used for this recipe. Thaw and proceed as directed above.*

DELMONICO'S LOBSTER NEWBURG

6 to 8 servings (5½ cups)

  ⅓ *cup butter*
  3 *tablespoons flour*
  1 *teaspoon salt*
  ⅛ *teaspoon white pepper*
Dash of cayenne pepper
  1 *or 2 dashes nutmeg*
  4 *cups half and half*
  3 *egg yolks, beaten*
  2 *cups diced cooked lobster*
½ *cup dry sherry*
  2 *teaspoons lemon juice*
  6 *to 8 patty shells or 12 to 16 biscuits or toast points or hot seasoned rice, as desired*

Melt 3 tablespoons butter and blend in flour and seasonings. Gradually stir in half and half and cook, stirring constantly, until thickened. Beat a small amount of hot sauce into egg yolks. Add egg-yolk mixture to remaining sauce in a fine stream and cook until thickened and smooth, stirring constantly. Melt remaining butter, add lobster, and heat through. Stir sherry into sauce and heat for 2 or 3 minutes. Stir lobster and lemon juice into sauce and heat. Serve in heated patty shells, on hot biscuits, toast points, or on hot seasoned cooked rice.

LOBSTER

OVEN-ROASTED OYSTERS IN SHELLS

6 servings

3 *dozen oysters in shell*
⅓ *cup butter, melted*

Clean oysters thoroughly and place on baking sheet. Roast in very hot oven (450° F.) for 15 minutes, or until shells begin to open. Serve in shell with melted butter.

CRISPY FRIED OYSTERS

6 servings

1 *quart fresh oysters*
½ *to ¾ cup flour*
4 *to 6 tablespoons melted butter*
Salt and pepper to taste
Pinch of cayenne pepper (optional)
Parsley sprigs

Dredge oysters in flour. Pan-fry in butter for 3 to 4 minutes on each side, or until crust is golden brown and crisp. Sprinkle liberally with salt and pepper and add cayenne. Garnish with parsley sprigs.

HANGTOWN FRY, WESTERN STYLE

6 servings

The miners of California gold-rush days considered Hangtown Fry a meal fit for a king. Legend suggests a rich miner swaggered into Hangtown, so named for the hanging of five men from the same tree in one day, demanding the best meal money could buy. He was served a monstrous portion of fried eggs, bacon, and oysters. Thereafter, ordering a Hangtown Fry was the status symbol of the day.

1 *pint fresh oysters or 1 (12-ounce) can*
3 *slices bacon, cut in 1-inch pieces*
8 *eggs*
¼ *cup water*
½ *teaspoon salt*
Dash of pepper
½ *cup dry bread or cracker crumbs*
⅓ *cup flour*
3 *tablespoons milk*
2 *tablespoons butter*
2 *teaspoons minced parsley*
Lemon wedges

Drain oyster thoroughly. Pan-fry bacon in 10-inch fry pan until crisp and drain. Pour off bacon drippings and reserve. Combine eggs, water, salt, and pepper, beat slightly, and set aside. Combine crumbs and flour. Dip oysters in milk and roll in crumb mixture. Heat butter and reserved bacon drippings in fry pan and pan-fry oysters for 2 or 3 minutes on each side, or until lightly browned. Sprinkle bacon pieces over oysters.

Pour egg mixture over bacon and oysters and cook over low heat. Gently lift edge of omelet with spatula to allow uncooked egg to flow to bottom of pan. Cook just until eggs are set. Sprinkle with parsley and serve with lemon wedges.

BAYOU JAMBALAYA

6 servings

"Jambalaya and a crawfish pie and fillet gumbo . . ." —from the song "Jambalaya"

Jambalaya, a meal-in-a-dish, can be made with chopped ham, chicken, crabmeat, oysters, or sausage and the usual Creole vegetables, rice, herbs, and sometimes filé powder for thickening. It is the subject of much discussion whether Jambalaya is a Cajun dish or a true Creole one. Both claim it proudly as part of their cuisine.

  1 *pound raw shrimp*
  6 *slices bacon, cut crosswise into ¾-inch pieces*
  1 *cup sliced onion*
  ¾ *cup sliced celery*
  ½ *cup coarsely chopped green pepper*
  1 *clove garlic, finely chopped*
  1 *(1-pound) can tomatoes*
1½ *cups water*
  1 *cup raw rice*
  2 *teaspoons salt*
  ½ *teaspoon leaf thyme*
  ⅛ *teaspoon paprika*
  1 *small bay leaf*
  2 *to 3 dashes hot pepper sauce*
  1 *pint fresh oysters, shucked, or 1 (10-ounce) can frozen, undrained*

Peel, devein, and wash shrimp. Pan-fry bacon until crisp in Dutch oven. Remove bacon bits with a slotted spoon and drain on paper toweling. Add onion, celery, green pepper, and garlic to bacon drippings and sauté until vegetables are almost tender but not brown. Mix in tomatoes, water, rice, and seasonings. Cover and simmer gently for 20 minutes. Add shrimp, oysters, and bacon bits. Cover and cook for 15 to 20 minutes longer, or until rice is of desired tenderness, stirring occasionally. Remove bay leaf.

HERBED SHRIMP IN BUTTER

4 to 6 servings

  1 *pound cooked, peeled, and deveined shrimp*
  ½ *cup butter*
  3 *green onions, finely chopped*
  ⅛ *teaspoon nutmeg*
  ⅛ *teaspoon salt*
  ⅛ *teaspoon white pepper*
  Dash of cayenne pepper (optional)
  ⅓ *cup buttered fine dry bread crumbs*

Arrange shrimp in 4 or 6 baking shells or small ramekins. Beat butter until light and creamy and stir in onion, and seasonings. Spoon an equal amount of butter mixture into each baking shell and divide crumbs evenly. Broil 4 inches from heat for 5 to 8 minutes, or until shrimp are hot and crumbs lightly browned.

SHRIMP NEW ORLEANS

6 servings

  1 *pound raw shrimp*
  ¾ *cup toasted dry bread crumbs*
  ¼ *cup chopped green onion and tops*
  ½ *cup chopped parsley*
  ¾ *teaspoon crushed tarragon*
  ¼ *teaspoon crushed garlic*
  ¼ *teaspoon nutmeg*
  ¼ *teaspoon salt*
  Dash of pepper
  ½ *cup butter, melted*
  ¼ *cup sherry*

Peel, devein, and wash shrimp. Combine remaining ingredients and mix well. Mix in shrimp and toss lightly. Place about ⅔ cup in each of 6 greased individual baking shells or ramekins. Bake in hot oven (400° F.) for 10 to 15 minutes.

SHRIMP CURRY WITH PARSLEY RICE

6 servings

> 1 *pound cooked, peeled, and deveined shrimp*
> 2 *tablespoons lemon juice*
> ½ *cup chopped onion*
> ½ *cup thinly sliced celery*
> ⅓ *cup butter*
> ¼ *cup flour*
> 1½ *to 2 teaspoons curry powder*
> ¾ *teaspoon salt*
> ½ *teaspoon sugar*
> 2 *cups milk*
> 1 *cup half and half*
> ½ *cup seedless raisins*
> 1 *chicken bouillon cube*
> ½ *cup sliced blanched almonds*
> 3 *tablespoons minced parsley*
> 6 *servings hot cooked seasoned rice*
> *Pickled watermelon rind or chutney and coconut (optional)*

If large, cut shrimp in half lengthwise. Drizzle lemon juice over shrimp, cover, and refrigerate for 15 to 20 minutes. Sauté onion and celery in ¼ cup butter until onion is tender. Stir in flour, curry powder, salt, and sugar. Add milk, half and half, raisins, and bouillon cube and cook, stirring constantly, until thickened. Add shrimp and heat through. Keep warm in chafing dish. Lightly toast almonds in remaining butter. Fold parsley into rice and serve with curry shrimp mixture. Sprinkle almonds over shrimp and accompany with pickled watermelon rind or chutney and coconut.

ELEGANT CRAB

6 servings

> 1 *cup sliced celery*
> ¼ *cup butter*
> ½ *cup sliced fresh mushrooms or 1 (4-ounce) can, drained*
> ¼ *cup sliced green onion*
> 3 *tablespoons flour*
> ¼ *teaspoon salt*
> *Dash of white pepper*
> 1 *cup milk*
> ½ *cup half and half*
> ¼ *cup sherry (optional)*
> ½ *teaspoon Worcestershire sauce*
> 2 *cups Dungeness or other crabmeat, flaked*
> 2 *tablespoons diced pimiento*
> 6 *servings hot cooked seasoned rice*
> 1 *ripe avocado, peeled and sliced (optional)*

Sauté celery in butter until tender. Add mushrooms and onion and cook until onion is tender. Blend in flour, salt, and pepper. Stir in milk and half and half and cook, stirring constantly, until thickened. Gently fold in sherry, Worcestershire sauce, crabmeat, and pimiento. Place over low heat and bring to serving temperature, stirring often. Serve on rice and garnish with avocado slices.

OLD SALEM CRABMEAT IN PATTY SHELLS
6 servings (6 cups crabmeat mixture)

1 *pound crabmeat or 2 (6½- or 7½-ounce) cans, drained*

1 *cup thinly sliced celery*

¼ *cup butter*

¼ *cup sliced green onion*

2 *cups sliced fresh mushrooms*

¼ *teaspoon crushed chervil*

2 *(10-ounce) cans frozen cream of shrimp soup, thawed*

½ *cup half and half or milk (or a combination)*

¼ *cup diced pimiento*

6 *patty shells or 12 biscuits or toast points*

Pick over crabmeat carefully, removing any remaining shell or cartilage. Sauté celery in butter until tender. Add onion, mushrooms, and chervil and cook until mushrooms are tender and lightly browned. Blend soup and half and half or milk, add to vegetables, and heat. Fold in crabmeat and pimiento and heat through. Serve in heated patty shells or over hot biscuits or buttered toast points.

FRIED SOFT-SHELLED CRABS
6 servings

12 *to 18 soft-shelled crabs*

Salt and pepper to taste

1 *to 1½ cups flour (optional)*

Butter

Wash crabs and pat dry. Season with salt and pepper. Dredge lightly with flour. Cook in just enough butter to prevent sticking until light brown, about 5 minutes on each side.

VARIATIONS

Deep-Fat-Fried: Fry crabs in deep hot fat (375° F.) for 2 to 3 minutes, or until brown. Dry on paper toweling.

Soft-Shelled Crab Amandine: Sauté ½ cup slivered or sliced almonds in 2 tablespoons butter until just brown. Remove almonds and pan-fry crabs in almond butter. Just before serving, return almonds to the skillet.

PALMETTO DEVILED CRAB
8 servings

1 *pound crabmeat or 2 (6½- or 7½-ounce) cans, drained*

½ *cup commercial cooked salad dressing*

½ *teaspoon salt*

1 *tablespoon Worcestershire sauce*

4 *teaspoons lemon juice*

2 *teaspoons prepared mustard*

½ *teaspoon horseradish*

4 *dashes hot pepper sauce*

2 *hard-cooked eggs, coarsely chopped*

2 *tablespoons chopped parsley*

2 *cups soft bread cubes*

2 *tablespoons butter, melted*

Pick over crabmeat thoroughly and remove any remaining shell or cartilage. Blend dressing, salt, Worcestershire sauce, lemon juice, mustard, horseradish, and hot pepper sauce. Combine crabmeat, eggs, and parsley and fold in dressing mixture. Spoon an equal amount into 8 buttered ramekins or individual casseroles. Combine bread cubes and butter and sprinkle over crab mixture. Bake in hot oven (400° F.) for 10 to 12 minutes, or until mixture is hot and cubes are lightly browned.

MARYLAND FRIED CLAMS
6 servings

1 *quart soft-shelled clams, shucked*
2 *eggs*
2 *tablespoons milk*
2 *teaspoons salt*
Dash of pepper
3 *cups fine dry bread crumbs*
Fat for deep frying
Tartar Sauce (see index)

Drain clams. Combine eggs, milk, salt, and pepper and beat slightly. Dip clams in egg mixture, drain slightly, and roll in crumbs. Fry in basket in deep hot fat (350° F.) for 1 to 2 minutes, or until done. Shake basket gently during frying to prevent clams from sticking together. Drain well on paper toweling. Serve hot with Tartar Sauce.

FRIED SOFT-SHELLED CLAMS
6 servings

1 *quart soft-shelled clams, shucked*
1 *egg, beaten*
1 *tablespoon milk*
1 *teaspoon salt*
Dash of pepper
1 *cup dry bread or cracker crumbs or cornmeal*
Fat for deep frying

Drain clams and pick over for any remaining bits of shell. Combine next 4 ingredients. Dip clams in egg mixture, drain, and roll in crumbs or cornmeal. Deep-fry clams, a few at a time, in hot fat (375° F.) for 1½ to 3 minutes, or until brown. Drain on paper toweling and serve hot.

NEW ENGLAND CLAMBAKE
18 to 24 servings

18 *to 24 dozen steamer clams*
36 *to 48 small onions, peeled*
18 *to 24 medium baking potatoes*
18 *to 24 ears corn in the husks*
18 *to 24 live lobsters (1 pound each)*
Rockweed (optional)
Lemon wedges
Butter, melted

Wash clams thoroughly. Parboil onions and potatoes for 15 minutes and drain. Remove silk from corn ears and replace husks. Cut 36 to 48 pieces of cheesecloth and 36 to 48 pieces of heavy-duty aluminum foil, 18 × 36 inches each. Place 2 pieces of cheesecloth on top of 2 pieces of foil. Center 2 onions, 1 potato, 1 ear of corn, 1 lobster, 1 dozen clams, and rockweed on cheesecloth. Tie opposite corners of cheesecloth together. Pour 1 cup water over the package. Bring foil up over and close all edges with tight folds. Arrange packages on grill about 4 inches from hot coals. Cover with a hood or aluminum foil. Cook for 45 to 60 minutes, or until onions and potatoes are tender. Serve with lemon wedges and melted butter.

CHESAPEAKE BAY CLAMBAKE
Follow preceding recipe for New England Clambake and use soft-shelled clams. Substitute live blue crabs for lobsters and omit rockweed.

POULTRY, GAME, AND STUFFINGS

BAKED CHICKEN WITH ORANGE SAUCE

6 to 8 servings

  2 *(2½- to 3-pound) frying chickens, cut into serving pieces*

  2 *teaspoons curry powder*

1½ *teaspoons salt*

  3 *tablespoons butter, melted*

1¾ *cups orange juice*

  ⅓ *cup light brown sugar, firmly packed*

  2 *tablespoons prepared mustard*

  2 *tablespoons cornstarch*

  ¼ *cup cold water*

  ½ *cup seedless grapes, halved lengthwise*

  2 *to 4 tablespoons toasted slivered almonds (optional)*

  6 *to 8 servings hot seasoned rice*

Wash chicken pieces and pat dry. Combine curry powder and salt and rub chicken pieces thoroughly with mixture. Pour melted butter into large, shallow baking pan and add chicken pieces, skin side down. Combine 1 cup orange juice, brown sugar, and mustard in saucepan and cook, stirring constantly, until sugar dissolves. Pour over chicken pieces.

Bake in moderate oven (375° F.) for 30 minutes, basting chicken with pan juices two or three times. Turn chicken pieces, spoon sauce over chicken, and continue baking for 15 to 18 minutes, or until chicken is tender. Arrange pieces in serving dish, cover, and keep warm. Mix cornstarch with cold water in saucepan. Stir in remaining ¾ cup orange juice and pan drippings. Cook until thickened. Fold in grapes. Pour sauce over chicken pieces. Sprinkle almonds over top. Serve with rice.

ORANGE

OVEN-BAKED HERB CHICKEN

4 to 6 servings

  ⅔ *cup flour*

  1 *teaspoon salt*

  1 *teaspoon paprika*

  ½ *teaspoon rosemary*

  ½ *teaspoon chervil*

  ½ *teaspoon marjoram*

  ⅛ *teaspoon pepper*

  ⅔ *cup butter*

  1 *(3-pound) chicken, cut into serving pieces*

Combine the first 7 ingredients. Melt butter and pour half into a 15 × 10 × 1-inch baking dish. Dip each piece of chicken in remaining butter, drain, and roll in flour mixture. Place in baking dish, skin side up. Sprinkle with any remaining flour mixture and drizzle any remaining butter over top. Cover securely with aluminum foil. Bake in hot oven (400° F.) for 20 minutes. Remove foil and continue baking for 10 to 15 minutes longer, or until chicken is brown and tender.

VARIATION

Crunchy Oven-Fried Herb Chicken: Omit flour and mix herbs with melted butter. Roll chicken pieces in herb butter, drain, and roll in ¾ cup fine corn-flake crumbs.

CHEESE BAKED CHICKEN
6 servings

> ½ *cup butter*
>
> ½ *cup grated Parmesan cheese*
>
> ½ *cup fine cracker crumbs*
>
> ½ *teaspoon salt*
>
> 1 *egg*
>
> ¼ *cup milk*
>
> 3 *pounds chicken pieces*

Melt butter in 13 × 9 × 2-inch baking pan in hot oven (400° F.). Combine cheese, crumbs, and salt. Beat egg and milk together slightly. Dip chicken pieces in egg mixture, drain, and coat with cheese and crumb mixture. Place chicken pieces in pan, skin side down, and turn once to coat with melted butter. Bake in hot oven (400 ° F.) for 25 minutes, turn, and bake 25 minutes longer, or until chicken is brown and tender.

SOUTHERN-FRIED CHICKEN, VIRGINIA STYLE
12 servings

Many Virginians use only bacon drippings for frying chicken. It gives a very special flavor.

> 1 *cup flour*
>
> 1 *tablespoon salt*
>
> 1 *tablespoon paprika*
>
> 1½ *teaspoons poultry seasoning*
>
> ¾ *teaspoon pepper*
>
> 3 *(3-pound) frying chickens, cut into serving pieces*
>
> 1½ *cups shortening, cooking oil, or bacon drippings (or a combination)*

Combine first 5 ingredients in a paper bag. Place 3 or 4 chicken pieces in bag at a time and shake to coat well with seasoned flour. In a large skillet melt fat, add chicken pieces, and cook over moderate heat until browned and crisp on both sides (do not crowd chicken pieces in skillet). Transfer chicken to two 13 × 9 × 2-inch baking pans and cover securely with aluminum foil. Bake in moderate oven (350° F.) for 40 minutes. Uncover and continue baking for 20 minutes longer, or until chicken is tender and crisp.

CREAMY CHICKEN AND BROCCOLI BAKE
8 servings

An adaptation of Chicken Divan, a dish said to have originated many years ago at the Divan Parisien, a New York restaurant, this is a superb casserole to prepare for a crowd.

> 8 *chicken breasts, boned and halved*
>
> 1 *cup flour*
>
> ¼ *cup shortening*
>
> *Sherry Sauce (see next column)*
>
> 1 *pound fresh broccoli, cut into spears and partially cooked and drained*
>
> ⅓ *cup slivered almonds*
>
> ¼ *cup grated Parmesan cheese*
>
> *Paprika*

Dredge chicken breasts in flour. In a heavy skillet or electric fry pan melt shortening and brown chicken thoroughly on all sides. Transfer chicken breasts to 9 × 13-inch baking dish and bake in moderate oven (350° F.) for 40 minutes. Prepare sauce while chicken is baking. When chicken is done, arrange broccoli spears between chicken breasts and pour sauce over top. Sprinkle with almonds, cheese, and paprika. Return to oven and bake for 15 to 20 minutes longer, or until chicken and broccoli are tender and sauce is bubbly.

Sherry Sauce   4¾ cups

¾ *cup butter*

¾ *cup flour*

2 *teaspoons salt*

¼ *teaspoon coarsely ground black pepper*

4 *cups milk*

2 *teaspoons Worcestershire sauce*

2 *to 4 drops hot pepper sauce*

½ *cup dry sherry*

¼ *cup commercial cooked salad dressing*

Melt butter in a heavy saucepan. Stir in flour, salt, and pepper. Add milk and cook, stirring constantly, until thickened and bubbly. Remove from heat and stir in Worcestershire and hot pepper sauces. Blend in sherry and dressing.

QUICK CHICKEN PROVOLONE
6 servings

Chicken Parmigiana, usually topped by mozzarella cheese, is given a new and interesting flavor by the use of Provolone.

2 *tablespoons butter*

6 *chicken breasts, boned and halved*

1 *(10 ¾-ounce) can tomato soup*

½ *cup chili sauce*

1 *tablespoon Worcestershire sauce*

1 *teaspoon salt*

½ *teaspoon minced garlic*

⅛ *teaspoon oregano*

⅛ *teaspoon coarsely ground black pepper*

1 *teaspoon dried chives*

2 *bay leaves*

6 *slices Provolone cheese, cut in half*

In a heavy skillet or electric fry pan melt butter and brown chicken thoroughly on all sides, remove from pan, and keep warm. Reduce heat and add remaining ingredients, except the cheese, mixing well. Add chicken pieces to sauce, coating thoroughly. Cover and cook over low heat for 25 minutes, or until chicken is tender. Top each chicken piece with a cheese slice, cover pan, and allow cheese to melt off the heat.

BRUNSWICK STEW
8 servings

The citizens of Brunswick County, Virginia, and those of Brunswick, Georgia, both claim to have created Brunswick Stew, although some say it was named in honor of the Duke of Brunswick. Originally made with squirrel, it is still favored today by Southerners.

3 *tablespoons bacon drippings or butter*

2 *(2½- to 3-pound) chickens or 1 (4½- to 5-pound) rabbit, cut into serving pieces*

3 *quarts hot water*

2 *teaspoons salt (or to taste)*

¼ *teaspoon pepper*

1 *small red pepper pod, crushed*

½ *pound lean ham, diced*

4 *cups peeled, diced tomatoes*

3 *medium potatoes, peeled and diced*

2 *cups fresh or defrosted frozen Lima beans*

1½ *cups sliced onion*

2 *cups fresh corn, cut from cob, defrosted frozen, or canned whole-kernel*

1 *cup sliced fresh or frozen okra (optional)*

Melt bacon drippings or butter in large heavy Dutch oven and brown chicken or rabbit evenly on all sides. Add water, salt, pepper, and pepper pod, cover, and simmer for 2 hours. Add ham, cover, and continue cooking for 30 minutes, or until meat is tender. Remove chicken or rabbit, cut meat from bones, and set aside. Add tomatoes, potatoes, beans, and onion to stock. Simmer, covered, until vegetables are almost tender, then add meat, corn, and okra. Heat for 10 minutes and serve immediately in flat soup plates.

FARM-STYLE CHICKEN FRICASSEE

6 servings

Fricassee has been a popular dish in rural America since pioneer days. The long slow cooking turns an old hen into a delicacy.

¾ *cup flour*

2 *teaspoons paprika*

1½ *teaspoons salt*

¼ *teaspoon pepper*

¼ *teaspoon poultry seasoning (optional)*

1 *(4- to 5-pound) stewing chicken, cut into serving pieces*

3 *tablespoons butter*

3 *tablespoons shortening*

1 *cup water*

1 *cup milk*

Combine the first 5 ingredients. Set aside 2 tablespoons seasoned flour to thicken gravy. Dredge chicken pieces in remaining flour. In a heavy skillet brown chicken on all sides in butter and shortening. Add water, cover, and simmer for 50 to 60 minutes, or until chicken is tender, shifting pieces as necessary to cook evenly.

Transfer chicken to heated platter. Skim off excess fat from gravy. Blend reserved flour into pan drippings. Add milk gradually and cook, stirring, until gravy is smooth and thickened. Pour gravy over the chicken or serve separately.

COUNTRY CAPTAIN CHICKEN

6 servings

Rather than of early American origin, as the title denotes, Country Captain is a dish from India, and "captain" is thought to be a corruption of the word "capon."

⅓ *cup flour*

1 *teaspoon salt*

½ *teaspoon leaf thyme (optional)*

¼ *teaspoon pepper*

1 *(3- to 3½-pound) frying chicken, cut into serving pieces*

⅓ *cup butter*

1 *(8¼-ounce) can tomatoes*

1 *medium onion, finely chopped*

½ *cup fresh mushrooms, sliced, or 1 (4-ounce) can mushroom stems and pieces, drained*

1 *small clove garlic, thinly sliced (optional)*

¼ *cup seedless raisins or currants*

1 *cup water*

½ *cup coarsely chopped green pepper*

¼ *cup peach brandy (optional)*

6 *servings hot cooked seasoned rice*

¼ *cup toasted slivered almonds or broken pecan halves*

Combine first 4 ingredients. Dredge chicken pieces in flour mixture. In heavy skillet or Dutch oven brown chicken evenly on all sides in butter. Sprinkle any leftover flour mixture over chicken. Combine tomatoes, onion, mushrooms, garlic, raisins or currants, and water and pour over chicken. Cover and simmer for 45 to 55 minutes, or until chicken is tender. Add green pepper and peach brandy 10 minutes before end of cooking time. Serve chicken on top of rice, sprinkled with nuts.

NELL'S CHICKEN AND DUMPLINGS

6 servings

Nell, who has been running the Carlton family for fifteen years, created this dish. Don't be surprised if everyone asks for seconds. They always do when Nell makes it.

    1 *(5-pound) stewing chicken, cut into serving pieces*
    4 *cups water*
    3 *stalks celery with leaves, cleaned and cut into 1-inch chunks*
    1 *carrot, peeled and sliced*
    ½ *cup coarsely chopped onion*
    2 *teaspoons salt*
    ¼ *teaspoon pepper*
    ⅓ *cup flour*
    1 *cup milk*
    Biscuit Dumplings (see next column)
    2 *teaspoons minced parsley*

Combine first 7 ingredients in a large Dutch oven with close-fitting cover and bring to a boil. Reduce heat and simmer for 2½ hours, or until chicken is very tender. Skim fat from broth. Remove chicken pieces and keep warm. Strain broth, measure, and add enough water to make 3 cups liquid. In covered jar shake flour and ½ cup milk together until smooth. Stir in remaining ½ cup milk. Return broth to Dutch oven and bring to a boil. Stir in flour-milk mixture and cook until thickened slightly, stirring constantly. Simmer for 3 to 5 min-utes. Return chicken pieces to gravy and cover. Prepare dumplings. Drop dumpling mixture by tablespoonfuls into gently bubbling gravy. Cover pan at once and cook 20 to 25 minutes, or until dumplings are cooked through. Just before serving, sprinkle with parsley.

BISCUIT DUMPLINGS   6 servings

    ¼ *cup shortening*
    2 *cups self-rising flour*
    ⅓ *cup milk (approximate)*

Cut shortening into flour. Stir in milk, blending with a fork just until dry ingredients are moistened. Drop by rounded tablespoonfuls into broth. If preferred, knead on floured surface 10 to 12 strokes, roll ½ inch thick and into a 6 × 4-inch rectangle. Cut into 2-inch squares.

OLD DOMINION CREAMED CHICKEN

4 to 6 servings

    4 *tablespoons flour*
    4 *tablespoons butter*
    2 *cups milk*
    2 *chicken bouillon cubes*
    ⅛ *teaspoon pepper*
    3 *cups cooked, cubed chicken or turkey*
    1 *(10-ounce) package frozen peas*
    Baking Powder Biscuits (see index)

Combine flour and butter and cook over low heat until butter melts. Slowly add milk, bouillon cubes, and pepper. Cook over low heat until thick. Add chicken and peas and cook until peas are softened and chicken hot. Serve over biscuits.

ARROZ CON POLLO (Mexican Rice and Chicken)
6 to 8 servings

Arroz con Pollo, flavored with herbs and tomatoes, is a popular entrée in Southwestern and Mexican homes.

> 1 *(3-pound) frying chicken, cut into serving pieces*
> 1½ *teaspoons salt*
> ¼ *cup olive oil*
> 2 *tablespoons butter*
> 2 *cups long-grain rice*
> 2 *cups chicken broth (approximate)*
> 1 *cup coarsely chopped onion*
> 1 *clove garlic, minced*
> ½ *teaspoon oregano*
> ¼ *teaspoon pepper*
> ¼ *teaspoon paprika*
> ⅛ *teaspoon saffron (optional)*
> 1 *chili pepper, crushed (optional)*
> 1 *(1-pound 12-ounce) can tomatoes*
> ¼ *cup diced pimiento*
> ¼ *cup sliced pitted black olives*
> 1 *(9-ounce) package frozen artichoke hearts, defrosted*

Season chicken pieces with ¾ teaspoon salt and brown evenly on all sides in oil and butter. Remove from pan. Add rice to pan and cook, stirring, until rice turns golden. Stir in chicken broth, onion, garlic, remaining ¾ teaspoon salt, oregano, pepper, paprika, and saffron.

Cover and cook over low heat for 20 minutes. Stir in chili pepper and tomatoes and top with chicken pieces. Cover and cook for 30 minutes, or until chicken is almost tender. Sprinkle pimiento and black olives over mixture and add artichoke hearts. Add more chicken broth or water, if needed. Cover and cook for 10 to 15 minutes longer, or until chicken and artichokes are tender and rice is quite dry.

NOTE: *1 (10-ounce) package frozen peas, defrosted, may be substituted for the artichokes.*

CURRIED CHICKEN
6 servings

> 2 *tablespoons butter*
> 1 *cup chopped onion*
> 1 *small clove garlic, minced*
> 2 *tablespoons flour*
> 1 *tablespoon curry powder (or to taste)*
> ½ *teaspoon dry mustard*
> ½ *teaspoon ginger*
> 1 *teaspoon salt*
> 1 *tablespoon brown sugar*
> 1½ *cups water*
> 1 *(8-ounce) can tomato sauce*
> 1 *cup peeled, chopped apple*
> 2 *chicken or beef bouillon cubes, crumbled*
> 3 *cups diced cooked chicken*
> 6 *servings hot cooked seasoned rice*
> *Condiments: chopped sweet pickle relish, watermelon pickle, kumquats, peanuts, toasted slivered almonds*

Melt butter in chafing dish over direct high flame or in an electric skillet over moderate heat. Sauté onion and garlic until onion is tender but not brown. Blend in flour, spices, salt, and sugar. Add water, tomato sauce, apple, and bouillon cubes. Simmer, covered, to blend flavors for 20 to 25 minutes. Add chicken and heat. Serve with the rice and condiments.

ROCK CORNISH HENS

The Romans introduced Cornish hens into England in 43 A.D. *During the 1950s an American crossbred the Cornish hens with White Plymouth Rock chickens to develop Rock Cornish hens, a meaty, tender delicacy usually marketed at six weeks when the hens weigh around a pound each.*

ROCK CORNISH HENS WITH CRANBERRY-ORANGE SAUCE

4 to 6 servings

   4 *to 6 Rock Cornish hens*
1½ *cups Grandma's Bread Stuffing with Herbs (see index)*
   ½ *cup chopped onion*
   1 *apple, peeled, cored, and chopped*
   3 *tablespoons chopped fresh cranberries*
   ½ *cup pecan halves*
   ¾ *cup butter, melted*
   1 *(1-pound) can whole-berry cranberry sauce*
   ¾ *cup orange marmalade*

Wash the hens and dry with paper toweling. Prepare stuffing. Stir in onion, apple, cranberries, pecans, and ½ cup butter. Stuff hens loosely. Close openings with small metal skewers and string. Arrange in baking pan and brush with remaining ¼ cup butter. Bake in moderate oven (350° F.) for 30 minutes, basting occasionally with drippings or additional melted butter. Combine cranberry sauce and marmalade and heat. Spoon sauce over hens and bake an additional 30 minutes.

ROCK CORNISH HENS VÉRONIQUE

6 servings

   6 *Rock Cornish hens*
1½ *teaspoons salt*
   ⅓ *cup butter, melted*
   ¼ *cup sugar*
   ½ *cup orange juice*
   ¼ *cup water*
   ⅓ *cup dry white wine*
1½ *tablespoons cornstarch*
   ½ *teaspoon grated orange or lemon peel*
   ½ *cup seedless grapes, halved lengthwise*

Wash game hens and pat dry with paper toweling. Sprinkle cavities, using 1 teaspoon salt in all. Tie legs to tail and skewer neck skin to back. Place hens on rack in 15 × 10 × 1 1- or 2-inch baking pan. Cover pan securely with foil. Bake in moderate oven (375° F.) for 30 minutes. Uncover and continue baking for 30 minutes longer, or until brown and tender, basting with melted butter several times.

To prepare Véronique sauce, melt sugar in small heavy saucepan over low heat, stirring constantly, until sugar is lightly caramelized. Remove from heat and stir in orange juice and water. Return to heat and stir until sugar melts. Combine wine, cornstarch, remaining ½ teaspoon salt, and grated orange or lemon peel. Stir into caramelized sugar and cook, stirring, until mixture boils. Fold in grapes and reheat. Spoon over Rock Cornish hens or serve separately.

ROYAL STREET CHICKEN LIVERS AND MUSHROOMS

6 servings

  1½ *pounds chicken livers*

   ⅓ *cup finely chopped onion*

  1½ *teaspoons salt*

   ⅛ *teaspoon white pepper*

   ½ *cup butter*

  1½ *cups sliced fresh mushrooms*

   2 *tablespoons flour*

  1¾ *cups half and half*

   3 *tablespoons cognac (optional)*

   6 *patty shells, noodle baskets, or toast points*

   6 *crisp bacon curls*

    Watercress sprigs (optional)

In a heavy skillet or Dutch oven, combine chicken livers, onion, salt, and pepper and sauté in butter for 3 or 4 minutes, turning livers as needed to cook evenly. Add mushrooms and continue cooking for 3 or 4 minutes, or until livers are done. Remove livers from pan and keep warm. Stir in flour, add half and half slowly, and cook, stirring constantly, until sauce is thickened. Stir in chicken livers and reheat. Add cognac. Serve in warmed patty shells or noodle baskets or on hot buttered toast points. Garnish with crisp bacon curls and watercress sprigs.

    NOTE: *This may be served in a chafing dish for a buffet table.*

STUFFED ROAST CAPON

6 to 8 servings

   1 *(6-pound) oven-ready capon*

   1 *teaspoon salt*

   2 *cups chopped onion*

  ½ *cup butter*

   3 *cups coarse cracker crumbs*

  ¼ *cup chopped parsley*

   1 *cup chopped chestnuts or pecans*

  ¼ *teaspoon pepper*

  ⅛ *teaspoon nutmeg*

   1 *cup milk*

   2 *eggs, beaten*

  ¾ *cup chopped celery*

  ¾ *cup thinly sliced carrots*

   1 *cup chicken broth*

    Cooking oil

   3 *tablespoons flour*

Wash capon and dry with paper toweling. Sprinkle body and neck cavities with ½ teaspoon salt. In a heavy skillet, sauté 1½ cups onion in butter until tender. Remove from heat. In a mixing bowl, combine crumbs, parsley, nuts, ¼ teaspoon salt, pepper, and nutmeg. Add onion mixture, milk, and eggs and mix lightly. Fill neck and body cavities loosely with stuffing. Skewer neck skin to back and close opening with skewers and string.

    Combine remaining ½ cup onion, celery, carrots, and ¼ cup chicken broth in bottom of shallow baking pan. Place capon, breast side up, on vegetables and brush skin with oil. Bake in moderate oven (350° F.) for 1½ to 2 hours,

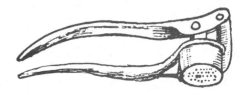

or until tender. Turn once on each side of breast during last 45 minutes. Baste occasionally with pan juices during roasting. Add additional broth to pan during roasting, if needed.

Transfer capon to heated platter and keep warm. Pour vegetables and pan drippings in baking pan into a 2-cup measurer. Add any remaining broth and water or milk as needed to fill cup. Combine flour and remaining ¼ teaspoon salt in saucepan. Stir in liquids gradually, stirring constantly. Cook, stirring, until thickened. Serve in a gravy boat.

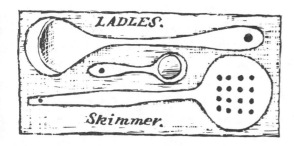

ROAST CAPON IN A BAG
6 to 8 servings

> 2 *cups sliced fresh mushrooms*
> ½ *cup butter, melted*
> 2 *cups Grandma's Bread Stuffing with Herbs (see index)*
> ¼ *teaspoon sage*
> ¼ *teaspoon poultry seasoning*
> ½ *cup walnuts*
> 1 *(4- to 6-pound) capon*
> 1 *teaspoon salt*

Sauté mushrooms in butter until soft. Combine with stuffing, seasonings, and walnuts and set aside. Wash capon and remove or singe any pinfeathers. Remove large pieces of fat from cavity and place in a cold skillet. Melt fat over low heat and set aside. Rub inside of capon with salt and fill with stuffing. Fasten with skewers. Rub outside of capon with rendered fat. Place in large brown bag on a rack in roasting pan. Bake in moderate oven (350° F.) for 3½ hours.

ROAST TURKEY WITH VIRGINIA OR CHESTNUT STUFFING
20 to 32 servings

The native wild turkey found by early colonists on the eastern shores of the United States had only a passing resemblance to today's plump specimen. It was usually a tough old bird with mostly dark meat that required long hours of cooking.

> 1 *(12- to 16-pound) turkey*
> *Melted butter or shortening*
> *Virginia or Chestnut Stuffing (see index)*

Remove giblets and neck from body cavity. Rinse turkey and pat dry with paper toweling. Fill neck cavity loosely with stuffing. Do not pack, as stuffing expands during roasting. Fold neck skin over dressing in cavity opening and fasten securely to back with skewers. Stuff body cavity loosely and tie drumsticks to tail with heavy string.

Place turkey on rack in shallow roasting pan. Brush entire bird with melted butter or shortening. Repeat process often during roasting. Place in slow oven (325° F.) until done, about 4½ to 5 hours. (Allow 20 to 25 minutes per pound for roasting.) Place a tent of aluminum foil loosely over breast of turkey when it starts to brown. Cut string holding legs when two-thirds done. Remove turkey from oven when done and cover tightly with aluminum foil. Let rest for 20 to 25 minutes for easier carving. Arrange turkey on heated platter, garnish, and serve.

TURKEY TETRAZZINI
8 servings

Luisa Tetrazzini, the Italian opera star of the early 1900s, has lent her name to this dish, which is decidedly American in character.

1 *(7- or 8-ounce) package spaghetti*

½ *pound fresh mushrooms, sliced*

½ *medium green pepper, seeded and cut into diamonds*

⅓ *cup butter*

½ *cup flour*

2 *teaspoons salt*

¼ *teaspoon white pepper*

4 *cups milk or 2 cups milk and 2 cups half and half*

½ *cup shredded Swiss cheese*

2 *cups cooked turkey or chicken, cut into ¾-inch cubes*

1 *pimiento, chopped*

⅓ *cup grated or shredded Parmesan cheese*

Cook spaghetti according to package directions, drain thoroughly, and set aside. Sauté mushrooms and green pepper in butter until tender, stirring constantly. Stir in flour and seasonings. Add milk or milk and half and half gradually and simmer until thickened, stirring constantly. Combine with Swiss cheese, turkey, spaghetti, and pimiento and mix carefully. Turn into shallow 2-quart baking dish. Sprinkle Parmesan cheese over top. Bake in slow oven (325° F.) for 40 to 45 minutes, or until hot and bubbly.

TURKEY CASSEROLE
8 to 10 servings

4 *cups cooked turkey, cut into ½-inch cubes*

3 *cups herb croutons*

1 *onion, chopped (about ½ cup)*

1 *tablespoon Worcestershire sauce*

1 *tablespoon minced parsley*

1 *(10¾-ounce) can cream of mushroom soup*

1 *(10¾-ounce) can cream of chicken soup*

Mushroom Sauce (see below)

Combine all ingredients except Mushroom Sauce. Spoon evenly into 13 × 9 × 2-inch baking dish. Cover securely with foil. Bake in moderate oven (350° F.) for 50 minutes. Remove foil and spoon sauce over turkey mixture. Return to oven and bake 10 minutes longer, or until hot and bubbly.

MUSHROOM SAUCE   2½ cups

2 *(10¾-ounce) cans cream of mushroom soup*

1 *tablespoon Worcestershire sauce*

1 *tablespoon minced parsley*

¼ *teaspoon poultry seasoning*

⅛ *teaspoon black pepper*

1 *or 2 drops hot pepper sauce*

Combine all the ingredients and heat.

DUCK

Domestic ducks derive from the wild Mallard or Muscovy duck, both native to the Americas. However, today's ducklings are the descendants of White Pekin ducks brought to the United States from China in 1873.

JELLY-GLAZED DUCKLING
4 servings

   1 *(4½- to 5-pound) duckling*
  ½ *teaspoon salt*
  Dash of pepper
  ½ *cup chopped onion*
  ¼ *cup butter*
  ⅔ *cup brown rice, cooked*
   1 *cup sliced celery*
  ½ *cup seedless raisins*
  ½ *cup coarsely chopped walnuts*
   1 *(10-ounce) jar crab-apple jelly*
  ¼ *cup red wine vinegar*
  ¼ *teaspoon cloves*
  ¼ *teaspoon nutmeg*
  Glazed Apple Halves (see next column)

Wash, drain, and dry duckling. Sprinkle body and neck cavities with salt and pepper. Sauté onion in butter until tender but not brown. Add rice, celery, raisins, and walnuts and mix lightly. Fill neck and body cavities loosely with stuffing. Skewer neck skin to back. Cover opening of body cavity with aluminum foil and tie legs together loosely. Place duckling on rack in shallow roasting pan. Bake in slow oven (325° F.) for 2 to 2½ hours, or until drumstick meat is very tender.

To make glaze, combine jelly, vinegar, and spices in saucepan. Place over low heat, bring to boil, and boil for 2 to 3 minutes. Brush duckling with glaze several times during last 30 minutes of cooking. Serve any remaining glaze separately.

GLAZED APPLE HALVES 4 servings

   4 *tart apples, peeled and cored*
  Salt
   1 *(10-ounce) jar crab-apple jelly*
  ¾ *cup warm water*
  ½ *cup sugar*
   4 *whole cloves*
  Few drops red food coloring (optional)

Cut apples in half. Let stand in lightly salted cold water until syrup is made. Melt crab-apple jelly in heavy saucepan over very low heat. Stir in water, sugar, and cloves. Bring to a boil and boil for 1 to 2 minutes. Add enough food coloring to make syrup a light red color. Cook apple halves in gently simmering syrup until tender but not mushy. Baste apples with syrup constantly to cook evenly. Serve hot or cold with Jelly-Glazed Duckling.

BARBECUED DUCKLING QUARTERS
4 servings

   1 *(4½- to 5-pound) duckling, quartered*
  ½ *teaspoon salt*
  Melted butter or oil
  Tangy Barbecue Sauce (see index)

Wash and dry duck quarters and sprinkle with salt. Place on grill, skin side up, over low glowing coals. Baste with butter or oil as needed. Cook until lightly browned, turn, and cook until skin is browned and crisp. Turn again and continue cooking until meat is tender, about 1 to 1½ hours' total cooking time. Baste with Tangy Barbecue Sauce during last 30 minutes of cooking. Serve with remaining sauce.

SHINNECOCK ORANGE DUCKLING

4 servings

   1 *(4½- to 5-pound) duckling*

  ½ *teaspoon salt*

   1 *onion, quartered*

   2 *stalks celery, cut into large chunks*

   1 *bay leaf*

  ½ *cup orange juice*

   2 *tablespoons lemon juice*

  ½ *cup thick orange marmalade*

   1 *tablespoon cornstarch*

  ⅓ *cup orange liqueur (Cointreau or Grand Marnier)*

   2 *to 3 tablespoons coarsely shredded orange peel*

    Orange slices for garnish (optional)

    Watercress or mint for garnish (optional)

Wash the duckling and dry well with paper towels inside and out. Sprinkle the cavities with salt and insert onion, celery, and bay leaf. Skewer neck skin to back and tie legs together loosely. Place on rack in shallow roasting pan and bake in slow oven (325° F.) for 2 to 2½ hours, or until meat on drumstick is tender.

To prepare sauce, blend orange juice, lemon juice, orange marmalade, and cornstarch and cook, stirring constantly, until thickened. Add orange liqueur and reheat. Drizzle a small amount of sauce over duck during last 20 to 30 minutes of baking. Remove duck from oven and sprinkle with orange peel. Garnish with orange slices and a few sprigs of watercress or mint. Pass remaining sauce separately.

NOTE: *An equal amount of orange juice may be substituted for the orange liqueur, if desired.*

ORANGE

PHEASANT JUBILEE

8 to 10 servings

Pheasant are still abundant in the cornfields of Iowa. When I lived there, I usually gave one or two game dinners a year. After much experimentation, I developed this recipe, which works equally well with pheasant or quail.

   8 *to 10 pheasant breasts, boned and halved*

   1 *cup flour*

  ½ *cup butter, melted*

   1 *(10¾-ounce) can cream of mushroom soup*

   1 *(10¾-ounce) can cream of chicken soup*

   1 *cup dry sherry*

   1 *teaspoon Worcestershire sauce*

  ½ *teaspoon salt*

  ½ *teaspoon basil*

  ½ *teaspoon poultry seasoning*

   2 *bay leaves, crushed*

Dredge pheasant in flour. Brown in butter until golden and crisp on both sides. Remove and drain excess drippings. Place in 9 × 13-inch baking dish and set aside. Combine remaining ingredients in bowl and blend well. Pour over pheasant and cover tightly with foil. Bake in slow oven (325° F.) for 2 hours, or until tender.

NOTE: *Whole quail or boned, halved chicken breasts may be substituted for pheasant. Quail and pheasant taste better if they are soaked for 24 hours in salted water after they're cleaned.*

QUAIL WITH GRAPES

6 servings

   6 *quail*

   Salt

   2 *cups seedless grapes*

   ½ *cup cognac*

   ¼ *teaspoon ground pepper*

   5 *tablespoons Clarified Butter (see below)*

   2 *cups Quick Brown Sauce (see below)*

Cover quail with salted water and let stand for 24 hours. Marinate grapes in cognac for 24 hours.

Drain quail and dry with paper toweling. Season with ½ teaspoon salt and pepper. In a large heavy skillet pan-fry quail in Clarified Butter until golden brown on all sides. Transfer to large baking dish or roaster and bake in moderate oven (350° F.) for 30 minutes.

Drain grapes thoroughly and reserve cognac marinade. Remove excess drippings from skillet and add cognac. Bring cognac to a boil over high heat. Reduce heat and gradually add Quick Brown Sauce, blending well. Continue cooking over low heat, stirring constantly, for 5 minutes. Adjust seasoning, if necessary. Remove from heat and add grapes. Arrange quail on heated platter and serve with sauce.

CLARIFIED BUTTER   5 tablespoons

   Melt ½ cup butter in top of double boiler over hot water. Pour off clear layer and discard milky sediment.

QUICK BROWN SAUCE   About 2¼ cups

   6 *tablespoons butter, melted*

   ½ *cup flour*

   2 *(10½-ounce) cans beef bouillon*

Blend butter and flour together in small saucepan to form a paste. Cook over low heat until golden brown (do not burn). Remove from heat and gradually add bouillon, blending well. Continue cooking over low heat, stirring constantly, until mixture thickens.

ROASTED QUAIL IN WINE SAUCE

4 servings

   1 *to 1½ cups plus 2 tablespoons flour*

   1 *teaspoon salt*

   ½ *teaspoon pepper*

   4 *quail*

   6 *tablespoons butter*

   1 *medium onion, thinly sliced*

   1 *cup sliced fresh mushrooms*

   1 *bay leaf*

   1 *cup dry red wine*

Combine 1 to 1½ cups flour, salt, and pepper on a sheet of waxed paper and dredge quail thoroughly. Brown quail in 4 tablespoons butter in a large skillet. Remove and set aside. Add onion to drippings and sauté until transparent but not brown. Add mushrooms and bay leaf and sauté until mushrooms are soft. Remove bay leaf and add wine to sauce, blending well. Place quail in roaster, spoon sauce over, and cover.

Bake in moderate oven (350° F.) for 1 to 1½ hours, or until tender. Remove quail to heated serving platter. In saucepan blend 2 tablespoons flour with 2 tablespoons butter to form paste. Gradually add to pan juices, blending thoroughly. Cook over medium heat, stirring constantly, until wine sauce becomes thickened. Pour into gravy boat and serve with quail.

WILD DUCK BREASTS WITH ORANGE SAUCE

3 to 4 servings

   ½ *cup olive oil*
   ¼ *cup dry white wine*
   2 *onions, thinly sliced*
   3 *sprigs parsley, chopped*
   ½ *teaspoon Worcestershire sauce*
   ½ *teaspoon salt*
   ¼ *teaspoon pepper*
   4 *wild duck breasts*
   ¼ to ½ *cup butter*
   Orange Sauce (see below)
   1 *orange, thinly sliced*

Combine oil, wine, onion, parsley, Worcestershire sauce, salt, and pepper in a large bowl and marinate duck breasts in mixture for several hours. Remove and drain. In large heavy skillet sauté duck breasts in butter for 20 to 30 minutes, or until tender. While duck is cooking, prepare sauce. Arrange duck on a heated serving platter. Spoon hot Orange Sauce over and garnish with orange slices.

ORANGE SAUCE   1½ cups

   3 *tablespoons sugar*
   1 *tablespoon cornstarch*
   1 *cup orange juice*
   2 *tablespoons curaçao or Grand Marnier*
   1 *tablespoon grated orange peel*

In a saucepan, blend sugar and cornstarch with a small amount of orange juice to form a paste. Gradually blend in remaining orange juice and cook over medium heat, stirring constantly, until mixture begins to boil and thickens. Remove from heat, add liqueur and grated orange peel.

WILD DUCK WITH GIN MARMALADE

4 servings

   2 *wild ducks, picked and cleaned*
   2 *quarts water*
   1 *tablespoon salt*
   2 *onions, peeled*
   2 *apples, quartered*
   1 *cup gin*
   2 *(12-ounce) jars orange marmalade*

Put ducks, water, and salt in 4-quart kettle, bring to a boil, and boil 5 to 7 minutes. Remove ducks and stuff with onion and apple. Place ducks in roaster, breast side up. Pour gin over ducks and coat each duck liberally with marmalade. Cover and roast in slow oven (325° F.) for 2 hours, or until tender.

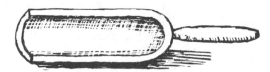

RABBIT, COUNTRY STYLE

4 to 6 servings

  1½ *cups plus 2 tablespoons flour*
   1 *teaspoon salt*
   ½ *teaspoon pepper*
   1 *rabbit, cut into serving pieces*
   6 *tablespoons butter, melted, or 4 tablespoons bacon drippings and 2 tablespoons butter*
   1 *onion, thinly sliced*
   1 *carrot, thinly sliced*
   1 *cup sliced fresh mushrooms*
   ½ *teaspoon rosemary*
   ½ *teaspoon thyme*
   1 *bay leaf, crushed*
   1 *cup rich chicken broth*
   1 *cup dry white wine*

Combine 1½ cups flour, salt, and pepper on sheet of waxed paper and dredge rabbit pieces. Brown rabbit in large skillet in 4 tablespoons butter or bacon drippings over medium heat. Transfer to a 9 × 9-inch baking dish and set aside.

Add onion, carrot, mushrooms, rosemary, thyme, and bay leaf to drippings. Sauté over low heat until vegetables are tender. Blend chicken broth and wine into mixture. Cook over low heat for 3 to 5 minutes, stirring constantly. Pour over meat, cover with aluminum foil, and bake in slow oven (325° F.) for 1 hour, or until meat is tender.

Transfer meat to a heated serving platter. Combine 2 tablespoons butter and 2 tablespoons flour to form paste, add small amount of sauce, and blend thoroughly. Gradually add to sauce. Cook over moderate heat, stirring constantly, until thickened. Serve with rabbit.

SQUIRREL FRICASSEE

4 servings

  1½ *cups flour*
   1 *teaspoon salt*
  ½ *teaspoon pepper*
   2 *squirrels, cut into serving pieces*
   3 *tablespoons bacon drippings*
   2 *cups chicken broth*
    Salt and pepper to taste

Combine flour, salt, and pepper on a sheet of waxed paper and dredge squirrel pieces. Brown in a large skillet in bacon drippings over low heat. Add broth and simmer for 1 hour, or until tender. Add salt and pepper to taste, if necessary. Serve with biscuits or dumplings.

VIRGINIA STUFFING FOR TURKEY

12 cups stuffing (stuffing for a 12-pound turkey). Allow 1 cup stuffing for each pound of poultry.

   4 *cups warm water*
    Giblets from 1 turkey, capon, or chicken
  ¾ *cup diced celery*
   1 *carrot, peeled and sliced*
   1 *small onion, sliced*
   1 *tablespoon plus 1½ teaspoons salt*
   2 *cups thinly sliced celery*
   2 *cups chopped onion*
  ½ *pound fresh mushrooms, thinly sliced*
   1 *cup butter*
   1 *cup long-grain rice*
   4 *cups cubed corn bread*
   2 *cups cubed day-old whole-wheat bread*
   1 *cup chopped pecans*
   1 *tablespoon poultry seasoning*
  ½ *teaspoon pepper*

Combine first 5 ingredients and 1 tablespoon salt in saucepan, cover, and simmer gently until gizzard is tender. Drain, discard vegetables, and reserve stock. Chop giblets, cutting meat from neck, and set aside for use in gravy. Sauté sliced celery, chopped onion, and mushrooms in ½ cup butter until onion is tender but not brown, stirring often. Set aside.

Brown rice in remaining ½ cup butter, stirring constantly. Add reserved giblet stock and enough water to measure 3 cups liquid and simmer for 10 minutes. Combine celery-onion-mushroom mixture, rice and stock, breads, pecans, poultry seasoning, 1½ teaspoons salt, and pepper in a large bowl and blend thoroughly. Use for stuffing turkey.

GRANDMA'S BREAD STUFFING
About 5½ cups stuffing

1½ *cups diced celery*
1 *cup coarsely chopped onion*
¾ *cup butter*
8 *cups day-old white bread cubes*
⅔ *cup hot chicken broth or water*
2 *eggs, beaten slightly*
1 *teaspoon salt*
1 *tablespoon poultry seasoning*
⅛ *teaspoon black pepper*

Sauté celery and onion in butter until tender. While vegetables are cooking, turn bread cubes into large bowl, moisten with hot liquid, and cover bowl. When vegetables are tender, add to bread. Stir in eggs and add seasonings, tossing lightly. Use for stuffing turkey, capon, roast chicken, duck, or goose. Stuffing may be baked separately in a casserole in moderate oven (375° F.) for 25 to 30 minutes.

VARIATIONS

Apple Stuffing: Substitute raisin bread for white bread. Reduce celery to 1 cup, butter and onion to ⅓ cup each, and omit pepper. Add 2 cups peeled, chopped apple and 1 tablespoon sugar to celery-onion mixture and cook until tender. Yield: about 5 cups.

Chestnut Stuffing: Wash ½ pound of chestnuts and cut gashes in the flat side of each. Bake in very hot oven (450° F.) for 20 minutes. Remove shells and skins. Cook in water to cover for 20 minutes, or until tender. Drain, chop, and fold into Grandma's Bread Stuffing. Yield: about 5½ to 6 cups.

Giblet Stuffing: Fold ¾ to 1 cup of chopped cooked giblets into dressing.

Stuffing with Herbs: Substitute ½ teaspoon basil and ½ teaspoon *fines herbes* for the poultry seasoning.

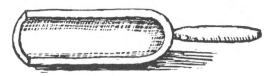

OYSTER STUFFING
About 4 cups stuffing

The following will yield sufficient stuffing for a 4-pound ready-to-cook bird. If additional stuffing is needed, double, triple, quadruple, or quintuple the recipe.

1 *pint oysters or 1 (12-ounce) can oysters, fresh or frozen*
½ *cup chopped celery*
½ *cup chopped onion*
¼ *cup melted fat or oil*
6 *cups soft bread cubes*
1 *egg, beaten*
1 *tablespoon chopped parsley*
1 *tablespoon salt*
1 *tablespoon poultry seasoning*
Dash of pepper

Drain oysters and chop coarsely. Sauté celery and onion in fat until tender, stirring occasionally. Combine all ingredients and mix thoroughly.

PLANTATION CORN-BREAD STUFFING
About 4 cups stuffing

1 *cup chopped celery*
1 *cup chopped onion*
¼ *cup butter*
4 *cups toasted corn-bread cubes*
½ *cup chicken broth*
1 *teaspoon poultry seasoning*
1 *teaspoon sage*
¼ *to ½ teaspoon mace*

Sauté celery and onion in butter until tender. Combine with remaining ingredients and mix thoroughly.

MEATS

HORSE RADISH

GARLIC.

MUSTARD

BEEF

American cattle are the descendants of cattle imported from northern Europe by the early colonists and the Texas longhorn, which originated in Mexico. The most famous of the early cattle pastures is Boston Common, laid out in 1634 for "the feeding of cattell" and "trayning of soldiers." John Pyncheon, who lived in Springfield, Massachusetts, in the late 1600s, is credited with being America's first meat processor.

BEEF TENDERLOIN SUPREME

4 to 6 servings

    1½ *pounds (4 to 6 slices) beef tenderloin (filet mignon)*
        Melted butter
     1 *pound fresh mushrooms, sliced*
     ½ *cup chopped green pepper*
     ½ *cup chopped onion*
    1½ *tablespoons flour*
    1½ *cups beef broth or 1 (10½-ounce) can consommé*
     1 *cup red Burgundy wine*
    1½ *teaspoons wine vinegar*
     1 *teaspoon Worcestershire sauce*
     1 *teaspoon salt*
     ¼ *teaspoon sweet basil*
     ⅛ *teaspoon coarsely ground pepper*
     ⅛ *teaspoon leaf thyme*
     1 *bay leaf*
     2 *tablespoons chili sauce*
     1 *tablespoon finely chopped fresh parsley*

Arrange meat slices on preheated broiler pan and brush with melted butter. Broil 3 to 4 inches from heat source, turning once and brushing with additional butter. Total broiling time, 10 to 15 minutes for rare, 20 to 25 minutes for medium rare, and 30 to 35 minutes for medium.

While meat is broiling, sauté mushrooms, green pepper, and onion in ⅓ cup melted butter until soft. Remove vegetables with slotted spoon and set aside.

Blend flour into drippings, add broth or consommé and wine gradually, stirring constantly, until mixture thickens slightly and begins to simmer. Add remaining ingredients except chili sauce and parsley. Cover and simmer for 10 to 15 minutes. Add chili sauce and reserved vegetables and heat through. To serve, spoon sauce over meat and sprinkle with parsley.

BRANDIED TENDERLOIN FLAMBÉ

8 to 10 servings (2 to 3 servings per pound)

     1 *(3- to 4-pound) beef tenderloin, whole*
     5 *cloves garlic, halved*
    1½ *cups brandy*
     ¼ *cup butter, melted*
        Brandied Peaches (see following page)

Make small slits in tenderloin and insert garlic pieces. Place meat in shallow glass baking dish and add 1 cup brandy. Cover and refrigerate for several hours, turning frequently. Transfer meat to rack in shallow roasting pan. Insert meat thermometer in center. Roast, uncovered, in hot oven (425° F.) for 45 minutes to 1 hour (thermometer registers 140° for rare or 160° for medium).

Combine remaining ½ cup brandy and butter in saucepan and keep warm. Baste meat frequently with brandy mixture during roasting. Let meat stand for 10 to 12 minutes before carving. For a spectacular effect, arrange Brandied Peaches around meat on heated platter. Pour additional warmed brandy over meat and peaches and ignite.

BRANDIED PEACHES

    2 *(1-pound 13-ounce) cans peach halves*
   ½ *cup peach brandy*
   ¼ *cup plus 2 tablespoons brown sugar*

Drain peach halves and reserve syrup. Combine peach brandy, ½ cup reserved syrup, and sugar. Pour mixture over peach halves and marinate for 4 hours or overnight. Bake in moderate oven (350° F.) for 30 minutes. If baking with roast, reduce baking time to 20 minutes.

BEEF STROGANOFF

6 servings

Named for a family of Russian merchant noblemen, Stroganoff is a charming marriage of Russian and French cuisine.

    2 *pounds fillet of beef, sirloin or tenderloin steak*
    2 *cups coarsely chopped Bermuda onion*
    1 *clove garlic, minced*
   ½ *cup butter*
    3 *tablespoons flour*
   ¾ *teaspoon salt*
  1½ *cups beef broth or 1 (10½-ounce) can consommé*
    2 *teaspoons prepared mustard*
     Dash of freshly ground pepper
   ½ *cup sour cream*
    6 *servings hot cooked seasoned rice*

Trim meat of all fat and gristle and cut into strips ¼ inch thick and 2 inches long. Sauté onion and garlic in ¼ cup butter until onion is golden. Stir in flour and ¼ teaspoon salt. Add beef broth or consommé and mustard and cook, stirring constantly, until thickened.

Pan-fry steak quickly in remaining ¼ cup butter to desired degree of doneness. Sprinkle with remaining ½ teaspoon salt and pepper. Stir sour cream into gravy mixture. Arrange meat on rice and spoon sauce over meat.

NOB HILL STEW

6 servings

    2 *pounds round steak or sirloin tip, sliced thin and cut into 4-inch pieces*
    8 *tablespoons butter, melted*
     Salt and pepper
    1 *pound fresh whole mushrooms, washed*
  1½ *cups beef broth or 1 (10½-ounce) can consommé*
    5 *tablespoons dry sherry*
  1½ *teaspoons minced garlic*
    1 *tablespoon Worcestershire sauce*
    1 *tablespoon minced parsley*
    2 *tablespoons flour*
    2 *tablespoons water*

In large skillet, brown meat on both sides in 2 tablespoons butter. Season to taste. Remove meat and set aside. Add mushrooms to remaining 6 tablespoons butter, coat well, and simmer for 10 minutes. Add broth or consommé, 2 tablespoons sherry, garlic, Worcestershire sauce, and parsley. Add meat, coat with sauce, and continue cooking over low heat for 35 to 45 minutes. Remove meat and keep warm.

Mix flour and water to make thin paste and blend into meat sauce, stirring constantly until thickened. Add remaining 3 tablespoons sherry and meat 3 minutes before serving. Serve sauce over meat.

COMPANY BRAISED BEEF
8 servings

  ¼ *cup chopped onion*
  ½ *cup chopped green pepper*
  2 *tablespoons butter, melted*
  3 *pounds boneless chuck steak, cut 1 ½ to 2 inches thick*
  1 *(1-pound 14-ounce) can tomatoes*
  1 *(8-ounce) can tomato sauce*
  3 *tablespoons Worcestershire sauce*
  2 *teaspoons minced garlic*
  1 *teaspoon basil*
  1 *teaspoon salt*
  4 *drops hot pepper sauce*
  ¼ *teaspoon coarsely ground pepper*
  ¼ *teaspoon rosemary*
  2 *bay leaves, crumbled*
  ½ *to 1 cup water (if necessary)*

In a large skillet, sauté onion and green pepper in butter until soft. Drain and set aside. Brown meat on both sides in drippings. Mix tomatoes, tomato sauce, seasonings, and onion-pepper mixture in bowl. Spoon over meat. Cover and simmer over low heat for 2½ to 3 hours, or until meat is tender. Add water during cooking if sauce becomes too thick.

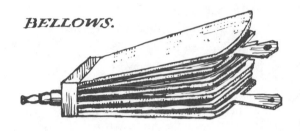

BELLOWS.

CHALET SWISS STEAK
6 servings

Swiss steak is traditionally tenderized by being pounded with flour and braised.

  2 *pounds round steak, cut 1 to 1 ½ inches thick*
  ⅓ *cup flour*
1½ *teaspoons salt*
  1 *teaspoon paprika*
  ½ *teaspoon sugar*
  ¼ *teaspoon pepper*
  2 *tablespoons shortening*
  1 *cup thickly sliced onion*
  1 *clove garlic, minced*
  1 *(8-ounce) can tomato sauce*
  ⅓ *cup red wine or cider vinegar*
  4 *whole cloves*
  1 *bay leaf*
      Water
  6 *servings hot buttered noodles (optional)*

Pound into both sides of steak as much flour as it will hold, using a meat hammer or the back edge of a heavy knife. Combine remaining flour, salt, paprika, sugar, and pepper. Brown steak evenly on both sides in hot shortening in skillet with close-fitting lid. Sprinkle each side of steak with half the flour-seasoning mixture. Add onion, garlic, tomato sauce, vinegar, cloves, and bay leaf. Cover and cook slowly for 2 to 2½ hours, or until meat is tender. Add water as needed to keep moisture in bottom of pan. Serve plain or with noodles.

BURGUNDY SWISS STEAK
8 servings

- 1 *cup fresh sliced mushrooms*
- ¼ *cup chopped onion*
- 4 *tablespoons butter, melted*
- 3 *pounds boneless chuck steak, cut 1½ to 2 inches thick*
- 1½ *cups beef broth or 1 (10½-ounce) can consommé*
- 3 *tablespoons red Burgundy wine*
- 1 *tablespoon Worcestershire sauce*
- 1 *teaspoon dried chives*
- ½ *teaspoon salt*
- ⅛ *teaspoon coarsely ground pepper*
- ½ *to 1 cup water (if necessary)*
- 2 *cups shelled peas or 1 (10-ounce) package frozen*
- *Gravy (see below)*

Sauté mushrooms and onion in butter until soft, drain, and set aside. Brown meat on both sides in pan drippings. Mix stock, wine, Worcestershire sauce, chives, salt, and pepper with onion and mushrooms and add to meat. Cover and simmer for 2½ to 3 hours, or until meat is tender. Add water if sauce becomes too thick. Stir in fresh peas for last 30 minutes of cooking (15 minutes, if frozen). Transfer meat to a heated platter and keep warm. Reserve sauce and prepare gravy.

GRAVY ⅔ to 1 cup
- 2 *tablespoons flour*
- *Water*
- 2 *tablespoons red Burgundy wine*

Blend flour and small amount of cold water together to form paste. Add additional cold water to measure ⅔ cup and stir into reserved sauce. Add wine and cook over medium heat until slightly thickened. Spoon gravy over meat.

MARINATED FLANK STEAKS
6 to 8 servings

- ¼ *cup wine vinegar*
- ½ *cup cooking oil*
- 1 *tablespoon Worcestershire sauce*
- ½ *teaspoon minced garlic*
- 3 *drops hot pepper sauce*
- 1 *teaspoon salad herbs*
- 1 *teaspoon salt*
- ½ *teaspoon coarsely ground pepper*
- 2 *(1½- to 1¾-pound) flank steaks*
- 1 *cup fresh sliced mushrooms*
- *Water*
- 2 *tablespoons flour*

Combine first 6 ingredients, ½ teaspoon salt, and ¼ teaspoon pepper in a jar and shake well. Place flank steaks in baking dish and cover completely with marinade. Refrigerate for several hours or overnight, turning two or three times. Brown meat evenly on both sides in small amount of marinade. Remove and set aside. Sauté mushrooms in drippings (add more marinade, if necessary) until soft, remove, and set aside. Add 1½ cups water, return meat to sauce, and continue cooking over low heat for 1½ to 2 hours.

In measuring cup, blend flour and enough cold water to make ¼ cup paste. Mix into meat sauce. Add remaining ½ teaspoon salt and ¼ teaspoon pepper. Cook, stirring constantly, over low heat until thickened. Add mushrooms. Serve sauce spooned over meat.

PEPPER STEAK POTPOURRI

4 to 6 servings

> 1½ *pounds round steak, cut into 1½ ×*
> *½-inch strips*
>
> ¼ *cup shortening or oil*
>
> 1 *clove garlic, minced*
>
> 2 *cups canned tomatoes*
>
> 1¼ *cups water*
>
> 1 *cup diced green pepper*
>
> 1 *cup diced onion*
>
> ½ *cup diced celery*
>
> 2 *tablespoons plus 1 teaspoon cornstarch*
>
> 6 *tablespoons soy sauce*
>
> 1 *teaspoon Worcestershire sauce*
>
> ¼ *teaspoon coarsely ground pepper*
>
> ¼ *teaspoon minced garlic*
>
> 4 *to 6 servings hot cooked seasoned rice*

In large skillet, brown meat in shortening. Add garlic clove, tomatoes, and 1 cup water and simmer over low heat for 30 minutes. Add diced vegetables and cook for 15 minutes. Blend cornstarch with ¼ cup water to form a paste. Add to meat-vegetable mixture. Add soy sauce, Worcestershire sauce, pepper, and ¼ teaspoon garlic and heat through. Spoon over mounds of cooked rice.

RARE ROASTED CHUCK STEAK

8 to 10 servings

Although chuck is usually braised, a well-marbleized chuck steak that has been marinated is a steak-pleaser that is sure to draw applause.

> 1 *thick quality-grade beef chuck steak*
> *(about 6 pounds)*
>
> *Steak Marinade (see next column)*
>
> *Salt and pepper to taste*
>
> *Rémoulade Sauce (see index)*

Place steak in plastic bag, pour marinade in, and close tightly. Refrigerate for 24 hours, turning several times. Drain steak and season with salt and pepper. Place on rack in shallow roasting pan. Insert meat thermometer in center of steak and roast in moderate oven (375° F.) until thermometer reads 140° for rare, about 1½ hours.

Brush with marinade once or twice during roasting. Bone, if desired, before serving. Slice very thin, diagonally across the grain of the meat. Serve with Rémoulade Sauce.

STEAK MARINADE

Combine ⅔ cup *each* salad oil and wine or cider vinegar, 2 cloves garlic, minced, 2 teaspoons salt, and ½ teaspoon *each* basil and pepper. Blend thoroughly and pour over steak.

ROYAL BEEF ROLLS

6 to 8 servings

> 1 *(6-ounce) package long-grain and wild*
> *rice*
>
> 1 *cup fresh sliced mushrooms*
>
> ½ *cup chopped onion*
>
> 2 *to 3 tablespoons butter, melted*
>
> 3 *pounds boneless round steak, ½ inch*
> *thick*
>
> 3 *to 4 tablespoons shortening*
>
> *Gravy (see next column)*

Cook rice according to package directions. Sauté mushrooms and onion in butter until soft and drain. Mix with cooked rice and set aside. Cut steak into 4 × 6-inch serving pieces. Spoon rice onto steak pieces, roll, and fasten with wooden picks or metal skewers. Brown steak rolls in shortening over medium heat. Pour off drippings and reserve. Place in 9 × 13-inch baking dish. Prepare gravy and pour over meat. Bake, uncovered, in moderate oven (350° F.) for 30 minutes.

GRAVY 2½ cups

   5 *tablespoons flour*

   Reserved meat drippings

1½ *cups beef broth or 1 (10½-ounce) can consommé*

   1 *cup water*

   3 *beef bouillon cubes*

   ½ *cup red Burgundy wine*

   1 *teaspoon minced garlic*

   ⅛ *teaspoon pepper*

Blend flour into meat drippings to form paste. Gradually add remaining ingredients. Cook over low heat, stirring constantly, until gravy thickens.

BEEF ITALIANO

4 to 6 servings

1½ *cups fresh sliced mushrooms*

   ½ *cup chopped green pepper*

   3 *to 4 tablespoons butter, melted*

1½ *pounds round steak, cut into 1½ × ½-inch strips*

   1 *(1-pound 14-ounce) can tomatoes*

   1 *(8-ounce) can tomato sauce*

   1 *pound white onions, peeled, or 1 (16-ounce) jar whole onions, drained*

   3 *tablespoons Worcestershire sauce*

   1 *tablespoon minced garlic*

   1 *teaspoon basil*

   4 *drops hot pepper sauce*

   1 *teaspoon salt*

   ¼ *teaspoon coarsely ground black pepper*

   ¼ *teaspoon oregano*

   2 *bay leaves, crumbled*

   3 *tablespoons grated Parmesan cheese*

   ½ *to 1 cup water (if necessary)*

   4 *to 6 servings hot buttered noodles*

Sauté mushrooms and green pepper in butter until soft. Remove with a slotted spoon and set aside. Brown meat on both sides in drippings. Combine tomatoes, tomato sauce, onions, seasonings, and Parmesan cheese in bowl and spoon over meat. Reduce heat, cover, and simmer for 2½ to 3 hours, or until meat is tender. Add water as needed if sauce becomes too thick. Serve over noodles.

GINGER BEEF

6 servings

   ¾ *cup soy sauce*

   ¼ *cup water*

   ¼ *cup lime juice*

   ¼ *cup brown sugar, firmly packed*

   2 *pounds round steak, cut into 1½ × ½-inch strips*

   2 *tablespoons shortening or oil*

   ¼ *teaspoon ground ginger*

   ½ *teaspoon minced garlic*

1½ *tablespoons cornstarch*

   1 *large green pepper, cut into 2-inch pieces*

Blend soy sauce, water, lime juice, and sugar in large bowl. Add meat, cover, and marinate for at least 8 hours. Drain meat and reserve marinade. Brown meat evenly in shortening. Add ginger and garlic to marinade. Mix 2 tablespoons marinade with cornstarch to make paste. Blend paste into marinade and cook over low heat, stirring constantly, until thickened. Return meat to marinade and add green pepper just before serving. Spoon over cooked fluffy rice or chow-mein noodles.

ROLLED BEEF WITH PIMIENTO

8 servings

Elegant enough to serve at a dinner party yet economical to prepare, this festive dish is sure to delight your guests.

- 2 *(1 ½-pound) boneless round steaks, cut ½ to ¾ inch thick*
- 2 *teaspoons salt*
- 1 *teaspoon coarsely ground pepper*
- 1 *teaspoon paprika*
- 1 *pound fresh mushrooms, sliced*
- 1 *cup plus 1 tablespoon butter, melted*
- 2 *small onions, thinly sliced*
- 1 *(3 ½-ounce) jar pimientos, thinly sliced*
- 1 *cup fine bread crumbs*
- 2 *tablespoons boiling water*
- 2 *eggs*
- 1 *(2 ¾-ounce) jar stuffed olives, drained and halved*
- ¼ *cup plus 2 tablespoons flour*
- ¾ *cup bacon drippings*
- 1 *teaspoon garlic powder*
- 1 *cup red Burgundy wine*
- 2 *bay leaves*
- 1½ *cups beef broth or 1 (10½ ounce) can consommé*

Sprinkle each steak with ½ teaspoon salt, ¼ teaspoon pepper, and ¼ teaspoon paprika. Sauté the mushrooms in 1 tablespoon butter until tender and spread half the mushrooms and onion slices on each steak. Dot with pimiento strips. Cover each steak with ½ cup bread crumbs. Combine 1 cup butter, boiling water, and eggs together in small saucepan and drizzle mixture over steaks. Arrange olives lengthwise along center of each steak. Roll steaks lengthwise and secure with string.

Dredge steak rolls in ¼ cup flour and brown in hot bacon drippings. Sprinkle with garlic powder and remaining salt, pepper, and paprika. Place steaks in 9 × 13-inch baking dish and add wine and bay leaves. Cover and marinate in refrigerator overnight. Bake, covered, in moderate oven (350° F.) for 2 hours. Remove meat, add broth to drippings, and blend in 2 tablespoons flour, stirring until thickened. Return meat to sauce and heat in oven for 5 minutes. Remove strings and slice.

NEW ENGLAND BOILED DINNER

6 servings

The New England Boiled Dinner was popular in Colonial America, particularly during the winter when little fresh meat was available. The Yankees perfected the art of preserving meat by corning it in brine flavored with peppercorns and other spices. In those days hours of soaking and cooking were needed to achieve tenderness. The modern version doesn't require such a complicated process.

- 4 *to 5 pounds corned brisket of beef*
- 6 *peppercorns*
- 4 *whole cloves*
- 1 *clove garlic*
- 1 *bay leaf*
- 12 *small carrots, peeled*
- 6 *medium potatoes, peeled*
- 6 *small onions, peeled*
- 1 *head cabbage, cut into 6 wedges*
- *Paprika*

Rinse brisket and place in large Dutch oven with close-fitting lid. Gover with cold water. Add peppercorns, cloves, garlic, and bay leaf. Cover and simmer very gently for about 3½ hours, or until tender. Thirty minutes before end of cooking time, add carrots, potatoes, and onions. Add cabbage 8 to 10 minutes before end of cooking time. Remove vegetables and drain. Drain corned beef, arrange on heated platter, and sprinkle generously with paprika. Slice beef across the grain and arrange vegetables around brisket.

BEEF BRISKET WITH ZESTY HORSERADISH SAUCE
8 to 10 servings

½ *cup wine vinegar*
½ *cup white vinegar*
1 *cup water*
¼ *cup sugar*
1 *tablespoon pickling spice*
1 *tablespoon whole cloves*
2 *teaspoons minced garlic*
2 *bay leaves*
5 *pounds boneless beef brisket*
Zesty Horseradish Sauce (see next column)

Combine vinegars, water, sugar, and seasonings in large bowl. Place brisket in marinade, cover, and refrigerate for 8 to 10 hours, turning frequently. Transfer meat and marinade to 5-quart saucepan. Add water just to cover. Simmer for 4 hours, or until the meat is very tender. Serve with Zesty Horseradish Sauce on the side.

ZESTY HORSERADISH SAUCE 1 cup
3 *tablespoons butter, melted*
3 *tablespoons flour*
3 *tablespoons prepared horseradish*
1 *tablespoon Worcestershire sauce*
1 *teaspoon chives*
1 *teaspoon salt*
½ *teaspoon hot dry mustard*
1 *cup milk*

Blend flour, horseradish, and seasonings with butter to make smooth paste. Gradually add milk, stirring until blended. Cook over low heat, stirring constantly, until sauce thickens and begins to boil. Serve with Beef Brisket.

BEEF FONDUE (Fondue Bourguignonne)

6 servings

While the Swiss were enjoying their cheese fondue, their neighbors in Burgundy, France, invented a Beef Fondue, or Fondue Bourguignonne. It is said to have originated during the harvesting of grapes for the famous wines of the region. The busy pickers cooked small chunks of meat in hot oil, fondue-style, right in the vineyard. Today Beef Fondue is accompanied by a variety of sauces.

> 4 *to 6 cups cooking oil*
> 2 *to 3 tablespoons butter*
> 2 *pounds boneless sirloin tip, cut into 1½-inch cubes*
> 1 *pound fresh whole mushrooms, washed*
> *Horseradish Sauce, Hot Mustard Sauce, Chili Sauce, Sherry Butter Sauce, Soy Sauce Marinade, Creamy Tarragon Sauce, Butter Sauce (see next column)*

Heat oil and butter in large saucepan to 375° F. and transfer to metal-lined fondue pot (or use an electric fondue pot). Each person spears the meat and mushrooms with a fondue fork and cooks in oil to taste. Provide sauces and individual plates. Transfer food from fondue fork to individual place fork as fondue forks will be extremely hot.

HORSERADISH SAUCE   1 cup

Combine 1 cup sour cream, 1 small onion, minced, 1 tablespoon prepared horseradish, 1 tablespoon chives, and 1 bouillon cube, crushed. Cook over low heat until thoroughly heated. Serve hot or cold.

HOT MUSTARD SAUCE   1 cup

In saucepan, blend together 3 tablespoons *each* melted butter and flour with 1 tablespoon hot dry mustard. Gradually add 1 cup milk and 1 teaspoon prepared horseradish. Cook over low heat, stirring constantly, until mixture thickens and begins to boil.

CHILI SAUCE   3 cups

> 2 *(15-ounce) cans tomato sauce*
> 1 *apple, peeled and chopped*
> ½ *cup chopped onion*
> ½ *cup chopped green pepper*
> ¼ *cup brown sugar, firmly packed*
> 1 *tablespoon Worcestershire sauce*
> 2 *teaspoons pickling spice, tied in cheesecloth*
> 1 *teaspoon minced garlic*
> ½ *teaspoon oregano*
> ¼ *teaspoon cayenne pepper*

Blend all ingredients together in saucepan. Simmer over low heat for 1 hour. Remove pickling spice before serving.

SHERRY BUTTER SAUCE   1¾ cups

In saucepan, blend 3 tablespoons *each* melted butter and flour. Gradually add 1

(10½-ounce) can consommé, ½ cup sherry, 1 tablespoon Worcestershire sauce, and 2 teaspoons minced garlic. Heat through.

Soy Sauce Marinade

Combine 1 cup water, ½ cup soy sauce, ¼ cup brown sugar, ¼ cup lemon juice, 1 small onion, sliced, 1 teaspoon minced garlic, and 1 bouillon cube, crushed, together in large bowl. Blend 1½ tablespoons cornstarch with small amount of marinade in saucepan. Gradually add remaining marinade and cook over medium low heat until thickened. This may be used as a sauce or as a marinade. Marinate meat for 2 to 3 hours at room temperature or overnight in refrigerator.

TARRAGON.

Creamy Tarragon Sauce ½ cup
½ *cup melted butter*

3 *egg yolks, lightly beaten*

3 *tablespoons dry sherry*

1 *tablespoon tarragon vinegar*

1 *teaspoon Worcestershire sauce*

¼ *teaspoon salt*

Pinch of pepper

Capers or chopped fresh parsley (optional)

Gradually blend butter with egg yolks, then add remaining ingredients. Cook in double boiler over low heat until sauce thickens. Capers or parsley may be added to sauce.

Butter Sauce ½ cup

Combine ¼ pound melted butter, 2 tablespoons Worcestershire sauce, ¼ teaspoon minced garlic, and 1 teaspoon lemon-pepper or freshly ground black pepper in small saucepan. Heat through.

BEEF BURGUNDY
6 servings

2 *pounds sirloin tip or round, cut into 1½ × ½-inch strips*

2 *tablespoons butter, melted*

2 *tablespoons dry sherry*

1 *pound small whole mushrooms*

3 *tablespoons flour*

1½ *cups rich beef broth or 1 (10½-ounce) can consommé*

1 *cup red Burgundy wine*

1 *teaspoon minced garlic*

¼ *teaspoon basil*

¼ *teaspoon crumbled bay leaves*

⅛ *teaspoon ground pepper*

1 *pound small white onions, peeled, or 1 (1-pound) jar small onions, drained*

1 *(8-ounce) package noodles, cooked and buttered*

1 *tablespoon fresh minced parsley*

Sauté beef in butter to brown evenly. Reduce heat, add sherry and mushrooms, and cook for 5 to 7 minutes. Remove beef and mushrooms with a slotted spoon and set aside. Blend flour into meat drippings. Gradually add beef broth, wine, and seasonings. Cook over low heat, stirring constantly, until thickened. Return meat to sauce and add onions (if fresh). Continue cooking over low heat for 1½ hours, or until meat is tender. Add mushrooms and onions (if in jar). Cook for 5 minutes more. Spoon over cooked noodles and sprinkle with parsley.

SWEET MARJORAM

OLD-FASHIONED BEEF PIE WITH HERB CRUST

6 to 8 servings

CRUST

    2 *cups flour*

    ½ *teaspoon* each *thyme and marjoram or 1 teaspoon fines herbes*

    Dash of salt

    ¾ *cup plus 1 tablespoon shortening*

    4 *tablespoons cold water*

FILLING

    1½ *pounds round steak, cut into 1-inch cubes*

    2 *veal kidneys, cut into 1-inch cubes (optional)*

    4 *to 5 tablespoons flour*

    5 *tablespoons butter*

    2 *cups fresh sliced mushrooms*

    1 *medium onion, thinly sliced*

    1¼ *cups beef broth or 1 (10½-ounce) can consommé*

    1 *cup red wine or tomato juice*

    2 *tablespoons Worcestershire sauce*

    1 *teaspoon salt*

    ¼ *teaspoon nutmeg*

    ¼ *teaspoon coarsely ground pepper*

    Milk

Combine flour, herbs, and salt. Cut shortening into mixture until it forms small beads. Add water gradually, tossing lightly with fork.

Form into 2 balls. Roll each on a floured surface into a circle. Line a 10-inch pie plate with half the crust. Reserve second crust for top.

Dredge steak and kidneys in flour. Brown meat on all sides in 3 tablespoons butter. Remove meat and set aside. Add 2 tablespoons butter to meat drippings in pan and sauté mushrooms and onion until soft.

Blend remaining ingredients, except milk, into mushroom-onion mixture. Add meat. Stir in remaining flour and cook until thickened. Spoon mixture into prepared pie plate. Cover with top crust. Brush with milk and slit crust to allow steam to escape. Place strips of foil around outer edge of crust. Bake in hot oven (425° F.) for 45 to 50 minutes, or until crust is browned. Remove foil from crust edges during last 10 minutes of baking.

NOTE: *To prepare kidneys, cover with warm water and 2 tablespoons vinegar and let soak for 1 hour. Drain and rinse in cold water. Devein and core kidneys. Transfer to a saucepan, cover with water, and simmer for 5 minutes. Cut in cubes and follow above recipe.*

If kidneys are not used, substitute an additional ¼ pound round steak.

POT ROASTS

Pot roasts, named for the method of cooking, have been a staple of many ethnic cuisines for several hundred years. The meat is braised in a heavy pot or Dutch oven over low heat for several hours. They are usually made from the economical beef cuts, such as chuck or round, and, properly prepared, have a hearty taste that is hard to beat.

KANSAS CITY POT ROAST WITH POTATO PANCAKES
6 to 8 servings

Yankee pot roast has long been a favorite of New Englanders from Connecticut to Maine. Here is a Midwestern adaptation that combines the classic pot roast with German-style potato pancakes.

    1 (4- to 5-pound) chuck roast
    1 tablespoon shortening
    1 cup sliced onion
    1 cup sliced celery
    1 clove garlic, minced
 1½ teaspoons salt
    6 whole peppercorns
    1 small bay leaf
    1 cup water
    8 medium carrots, thickly sliced
    8 small onions
    1 tablespoon flour
    Potato Pancakes (see next column)
    Applesauce (optional)

Brown meat evenly in hot shortening. Add sliced onion, celery, garlic, 1 teaspoon salt, peppercorns, bay leaf, and ½ cup water. Cover and cook slowly until meat is tender, 2 to 2½ hours. Arrange carrots and onions around meat 30 minutes before end of cooking time and sprinkle with remaining ½ teaspoon salt. When done, remove meat, cover, and keep warm in a moderate oven (350° F.). Remove peppercorns and bay leaf from pan drippings. Blend in flour, add remaining water, and cook until thickened. Serve pot roast with Potato Pancakes and accompanied by gravy and applesauce.

POTATO PANCAKES   12 pancakes
    3 cups well-drained shredded raw potatoes (4 medium potatoes)
  ¼ cup grated onion
    3 tablespoons flour
 1¼ teaspoons salt
  ¼ teaspoon pepper
    2 eggs, beaten slightly
    3 tablespoons butter or bacon drippings

Combine potatoes, onion, flour, salt, pepper, and eggs. Heat a small amount of butter in skillet. Spoon ¼ cup potato mixture into skillet for each pancake and spread carefully to make a 3-inch cake. Cook until browned on both sides, turning once, total cooking time 8 to 10 minutes.

GARLIC.

KENOSHA SPECKBRATEN

6 to 8 servings

Bacon is used as a highlight in this dish of Austrian origin.

    4 *pounds beef chuck roast, 2 inches thick*
    5 *slices bacon, cut into 1½-inch lengths*
    1 *tablespoon shortening*
    1 *cup coarsely chopped onion*
    1 *cup thinly sliced carrots*
    ½ *cup water*
 1¼ *teaspoons salt*
    6 *whole peppercorns*
    1 *bay leaf*
    ¼ *teaspoon leaf thyme*
    1 *cup finely torn soft rye bread cubes*
    ⅓ *cup dry red wine, beef bouillon, or water*
    ⅛ *teaspoon nutmeg*

Using sharp pointed knife, cut slits in both sides of roast about 1 inch deep and insert bacon pieces. Brown meat on both sides in hot shortening in covered skillet or Dutch oven. Add onion, carrots, water, 1 teaspoon salt, peppercorns, bay leaf, and thyme. Cover and cook slowly until meat is tender, 1¾ to 2 hours.

Transfer meat to heated platter and keep warm. Skim fat from drippings and remove peppercorns and bay leaf. Measure drippings and vegetables and add water to make 2 cups liquid. Return to skillet. Add remaining ingredients and ¼ teaspoon salt. Heat, stirring constantly, until bread thickens gravy. If a smooth gravy is desired, whiz in blender.

SAUERBRATEN WITH TANGY GINGERSNAP GRAVY

12 servings

Sauerbraten, long a favorite of Pennsylvania Dutch cooks, is a sweet-sour pot roast tenderized by marinating the meat in vinegar, sugar, and pickling spices.

    4 *to 5 pounds boneless chuck or rump roast*
 3½ *teaspoons salt*
    2 *cups wine vinegar*
    2 *cups water*
 1½ *cups sliced onion*
    ¾ *cup sliced carrots*
    ½ *cup sliced celery*
    6 *to 8 peppercorns*
    6 *whole cloves*
    2 *bay leaves*
    2 *tablespoons shortening*
    ¼ *cup brown sugar, firmly packed*
    ¼ *cup flour*
   10 *gingersnaps, crushed*

Rub meat with 3 teaspoons salt and place in a large bowl. In a saucepan combine vinegar, 1 cup water, vegetables, spices, and herbs and bring to boil. Pour over meat, cover, and refrigerate for 24 to 48 hours, turning often. Remove meat and dry thoroughly.

Brown meat on all sides in hot shortening and sprinkle with brown sugar. Strain marinade. Add vegetables and spices to meat together with 1 cup marinade. Cover and cook very slowly until tender, about 3 hours. Remove meat from pan and keep warm.

Strain cooking liquid and skim off fat. Add marinade as needed to measure 3 cups. Blend together flour, remaining 1 cup water, and ½ teaspoon salt. Add to liquid in pan and cook, stirring constantly, until smooth and thickened. Stir in gingersnaps and heat. Serve gravy over sliced meat.

IRISH POT ROAST

6 to 8 servings

    1 *(4- to 5-pound) chuck roast*
    ¾ *to 1 cup flour*
    ¼ *cup cooking oil or melted shortening*
    1½ *cups beef stock or 1 (10½-ounce) can consommé*
    1 *cup Irish whisky*
    1½ *cups water*
    1 *tablespoon Worcestershire sauce*
    2 *bay leaves, crushed*
    1 *teaspoon salt*
    ½ *teaspoon basil*
    ½ *teaspoon pepper*
    5 *carrots, peeled and quartered*
    4 *potatoes, peeled and quartered*
    3 *onions, peeled and quartered*
    3 *celery stalks, cut in large pieces*
    Parsley for garnish

Dredge roast thoroughly in ½ to ¾ cup flour and brown on all sides in hot oil or shortening. Drain fat or transfer to roasting pan. Combine beef stock or consommé, whisky, 1 cup water, and seasonings together in a bowl and pour over roast. Cover and simmer or pot roast in slow oven (325° F.) for 1 hour. Add vegetables and continue cooking for 1 hour longer. In a small bowl, blend ½ cup cold water and ¼ cup flour to form a paste. Grad-ually add to meat, vegetables, and sauce, stirring lightly until blended. Continue cooking for 5 to 7 minutes, or until thickened. Serve roast and vegetables with gravy. Garnish with fresh parsley.

BRAISED SHORT RIBS

4 servings

Savory fork-tender beef short ribs require long, slow, moist cooking to bring out their excellent flavor. A moderate-priced, nutritious cut of meat, short ribs are delicious when cooked properly.

    3 *pounds short ribs of beef*
    ½ *cup dry red wine*
    2 *tablespoons Worcestershire sauce*
    1 *clove garlic, minced*
    1 *cup sliced onion*
    1 *cup sliced carrots*
    ½ *teaspoon rosemary*
    ¼ *teaspoon marjoram*
    1¼ *teaspoons salt*
    2 *tablespoons shortening*
    1 *cup water*

Place short ribs in plastic bag in shallow pan. Combine next 7 ingredients and 1 teaspoon salt. Pour over meat and close bag securely. Refrigerate for 2 to 3 hours, turning bag carefully several times. Remove short ribs from marinade and brown evenly on all sides in shortening. Add marinade with vegetables, cover, and cook slowly for 2 hours. Transfer short ribs to heated platter and keep warm. Skim off excess fat from pan drippings. Add water and remaining ¼ teaspoon salt and heat through, stirring. Spoon over short ribs.

SPICED SHORT RIBS OF BEEF

4 servings

   3 *tablespoons flour*
   2 *tablespoons brown sugar*
1½ *teaspoons salt*
 ⅛ *teaspoon coarsely ground pepper*
   3 *pounds short ribs of beef*
   2 *tablespoons shortening*
  ½ *cup coarsely chopped onion*
   1 *small bay leaf*
  ¼ *teaspoon whole allspice*
  ½ *cup water*
   8 *medium carrots, peeled*
   8 *small white onions, peeled*
   Horseradish (optional)

Combine flour, sugar, 1 teaspoon salt, and pepper and dredge ribs in mixture. Melt shortening in large skillet or Dutch oven with close-fitting lid and brown ribs evenly on all sides. Sprinkle remaining flour mixture, onion, bay leaf, and allspice over meat. Add water. Cover and cook slowly until meat is tender, about 2 hours. Add vegetables 30 minutes before meat is done and sprinkle with remaining ½ teaspoon salt. Serve plain or with horseradish.

SPICED AND FRUITED BEEF ON COCONUT RICE

6 servings

Sweet and sour meats, popular in South America, the Caribbean, and the Pacific islands, are becoming North American favorites, too. This recipe is sure to become one of your specialties.

   2 *pounds beef chuck or round steak, cut into 1½-inch cubes*
   2 *tablespoons cooking oil*
  ¼ *cup lemon or lime juice*
2¼ *cups water*
   2 *cups sliced onion*
1½ *teaspoons curry powder*
  ¼ *teaspoon ground cloves*
  ¼ *teaspoon cinnamon*
   1 *teaspoon salt*
   3 *cups peeled, cored, and sliced apples*
   3 *tablespoons sugar*
1½ *tablespoons cornstarch*
  ¾ *cup orange juice*
   2 *teaspoons shredded orange peel*
   2 *tablespoons vinegar*
   1 *cup fresh orange sections*
  ¾ *cup drained watermelon pickle*
   6 *servings hot cooked seasoned rice*
  ½ *cup flaked coconut or toasted coconut chips*

In heavy covered skillet, brown beef cubes in oil. Add lemon or lime juice, 1 cup water, onion, curry powder, cloves, cinnamon, and salt. Cover and cook slowly for 40 minutes. Add apple slices and ½ cup water, mixing gently.

Cover and cook over low heat until meat is tender, about 40 minutes.

Mix sugar and cornstarch in saucepan and stir in orange juice, ¾ cup water, and orange peel. Cook slowly, stirring constantly, until thick and clear. Stir in vinegar. Fold in orange sections and watermelon pickle. Fold half the fruit sauce into meat mixture. Mix rice and coconut, turn into serving dish, top with meat mixture, and edge with remaining fruit.

CURRIED BEEF

6 servings

Although not so highly seasoned as the curries of India, those prepared in the United States are savory stews, superbly spiced and simmered slowly.

3 *tablespoons flour*

2 *teaspoons curry powder*

2 *teaspoons salt*

¼ *teaspoon pepper*

2 *pounds boneless beef round or chuck, cut into 1-inch cubes*

2 *tablespoons shortening*

2 *cups sliced onion*

2 *cups peeled, diced apple*

2 *cups sliced celery*

1 *clove garlic, minced*

1½ *cups beef broth or 1 (10½-ounce) can consommé*

½ *cup light raisins*

1 *tablespoon brown sugar*

6 *servings hot cooked seasoned rice*

Condiments: chopped cashew nuts, peanuts or almonds, chutney, coconut, raisins, preserved ginger, chopped pickles

Combine flour, curry powder, salt, and pepper and dredge meat cubes. Brown beef evenly on all sides in hot shortening. Add onion, apple, celery, and garlic and cook until onion is tender. Sprinkle remaining flour mixture over meat, stirring. Add beef broth or consommé, raisins, and sugar. Cover and simmer gently until meat is very tender, 2 to 2½ hours. Serve with rice and one or more curry condiments.

HUNGARIAN GOULASH

6 to 8 servings

A classic of Hungarian cuisine, goulash is a spicy peasant stew seasoned with Hungarian paprika.

3 *to 4 pounds boneless chuck roast, cut into 1½-inch cubes*

2 *tablespoons oil*

2 *large onions, sliced*

1 *green pepper, chopped*

1 *bay leaf, crumbled*

1 *tablespoon sweet Hungarian paprika**

1½ *teaspoons salt*

1 *teaspoon caraway seeds*

½ *teaspoon marjoram*

¼ *to ½ teaspoon pepper*

2 *(1-pound) cans stewed tomatoes*

1 *cup plus 1 to 2 tablespoons water*

1 *tablespoon flour*

1 *cup sour cream (optional)*

Brown meat evenly in oil, drain, and set aside. Sauté onion and green pepper in drippings until soft. Blend in seasonings and meat, tomatoes, and 1 cup water. Simmer, covered, for 1 hour, or until meat is tender. Mix flour with 1 to 2 tablespoons water and blend into goulash. Add sour cream and cook over low heat until thickened.

* Decrease paprika to 1 to 2 teaspoons if using regular paprika.

BEEF STEW PROVENÇAL

6 servings

     1 *cup sliced onion*
     ½ *cup sliced celery*
     2 *cloves garlic, minced*
     3 *tablespoons olive or cooking oil*
     1 *cup dry white or red wine or tomato juice*
  1½ *teaspoons salt*
     ½ *teaspoon rosemary*
     ½ *teaspoon marjoram*
     ¼ *teaspoon leaf thyme*
     3 *pounds boneless lean beef chuck, cut into*
         1½-inch cubes
     6 *slices bacon, diced*
     2 *tablespoons flour*
     1 *cup water*
   18 *small white onions*
   12 *small carrots*
     ⅓ *cup small pitted black olives*

In a heavy skillet sauté onion, celery, and garlic in oil until onion is soft but not brown. Add wine or tomato juice, 1 teaspoon salt, and herbs. Simmer to blend flavors for 10 to 15 minutes. Pour over meat cubes in bowl and mix. Cover and refrigerate about 2 hours, stirring several times.

Drain meat thoroughly and reserve marinade. Pan-fry bacon until crisp in Dutch oven with heatproof handles. Remove bacon pieces. Brown meat cubes evenly on all sides in bacon drippings and sprinkle with flour and remaining ½ teaspoon salt. Add reserved marinade, including vegetables, bacon, and ½ cup water. Simmer, covered, over moderate heat for 5 to 10 minutes. Cook in slow oven (325° F.) for 2¼ hours, or until meat is tender. After 1½ hours add white onions, carrots, and remaining ½ cup water. Cover and continue baking until vegetables are tender. Rinse and drain olives, add to meat mixture, and heat through.

OVEN BEEF STEW WITH DROP BISCUITS

6 servings

  1½ *pounds beef chuck or round, cut into*
         1½-inch cubes
     2 *tablespoons shortening or oil*
     4 *carrots, peeled and sliced*
     1 *pound small onions, peeled*
  1½ *cups fresh green beans or 1 (10-ounce)*
         package frozen
     1 *(12-ounce) can tomato juice*
  1½ *cups beef broth or 1 (10½-ounce) can*
         consommé
     1 *tablespoon Worcestershire sauce*
  1½ *teaspoons salt*
     ¼ *teaspoon pepper*
     ¼ *teaspoon sweet basil*
     2 *bay leaves, crumbled*
     ½ *cup tapioca*
         Baking-powder Biscuits (see index)
         Paprika

In large skillet, brown meat in shortening over low heat. Transfer to 2-quart lightly oiled casserole. Add vegetables, tomato juice, beef broth or consommé, spices, and tapioca. Cover and bake in moderate oven (350° F.) for 2 to 2½ hours, or until tender. Keep stew warm while you make biscuits.

Prepare biscuits according to recipe directions, increasing shortening to ½ cup. Do not roll dough. Drop dough by tablespoonfuls onto hot stew. Sprinkle each biscuit lightly with paprika. Bake in a very hot oven (450° F.) for 10 to 15 minutes, or until biscuits are lightly browned.

NOTE: *Any leftover dough can be baked on a greased cookie sheet for 10 to 15 minutes.*

VIRGINIA SUPPER CASSEROLE

6 servings

  1 *(8-ounce) package noodles*
  2 *tablespoons butter*
  1 *pound ground beef chuck*
  2 *(8-ounce) cans tomato sauce*
  1 *teaspoon salt*
  ⅛ *teaspoon pepper*
  1 *(8-ounce) package cream cheese, at room temperature*
  1 *cup large-curd cottage cheese*
  ½ *cup sour cream*
  ⅓ *cup finely chopped green onion*
  1 *tablespoon chopped green pepper*

Cook noodles according to package directions, drain, and blanch with hot water. Set aside. Melt butter in heavy skillet and cook beef until it loses its bright-red color. Drain off excess fat. Stir in tomato sauce, salt, and pepper and remove from heat. Combine cheeses, sour cream, onion, and green pepper. Spread one half the noodles in a buttered 2-quart (12 × 8 × 2-inch) casserole and cover with one half the cheese–sour cream mixture. Repeat. Spread meat mixture in an even layer over top. Cover casserole tightly with foil and bake in moderate oven (350° F.) for 20 minutes. Uncover and bake an additional 10 minutes.

JAMAICAN-STYLE BEEF STEW

6 servings

  2 *pounds boneless beef chuck*
  3 *tablespoons flour*
  2 *teaspoons salt*
  1 *teaspoon paprika*
  ½ *teaspoon pepper*
  ¼ *cup butter*
  1 *cup water*
  5 *to 6 drops hot pepper sauce*
  1 *pound cabbage, cut into thin wedges*
  2 *cups thick onion slices*
  2 *to 4 leeks, cut into 1½-inch lengths*
  1 *(10-ounce) package frozen whole okra*

Cut beef into 1½-inch cubes. Combine flour, 1 teaspoon salt, paprika, and pepper and dredge meat cubes in mixture. In heavy skillet, brown meat evenly on all sides in butter. Add ½ cup water and hot pepper sauce. Cook, covered, over low heat until meat is almost tender, about 1½ hours. Add cabbage, onion, leeks, remaining ½ cup water, and remaining 1 teaspoon salt. Cover and cook for 20 minutes. Add okra, cover, and cook until vegetables and meat are tender, about 10 minutes.

HAMBURGERS

The hamburger has undergone a considerable evolution since it first appeared in medieval Germany. Said to have originated in the seaport town of Hamburg, it was eaten raw, in much the same way as steak tartare, until some enterprising chef fashioned it into a patty and broiled it. The hamburger was introduced into American cuisine by the German settlers of the Midwest and was first served on a bun during the St. Louis International Exposition of 1904. The billions of hamburgers sold annually attest to their No. 1 rating as America's favorite food.

HAMBURGERS PLAIN AND FANCY

6 to 8 large hamburgers

> 2 *pounds ground beef chuck or round steak*
>
> ⅓ *cup finely chopped onion*
>
> 2 *eggs.*
>
> 2 *teaspoons salt*
>
> ¼ *teaspoon pepper*
>
> *Melted butter or oil*
>
> *Hamburger buns*

Combine first 5 ingredients and shape into 6 or 8 patties. Broil 3 to 4 inches from moderate heat, turning once. Brush with butter or oil. Allow 8 to 9 minutes cooking time per side, depending on doneness desired. Serve on toasted buttered buns or prepare as directed below.

VARIATIONS

Dill Burgers: Blend 1 teaspoon *each* dill weed and prepared horseradish into meat mixture. Cook as directed above. Top each hamburger with a slice of Swiss cheese and a bacon curl and heat until cheese softens. Garnish with a sprig of fresh dill or watercress.

Peanut Butter Burgers: Reduce salt to 1¾ teaspoons. Blend in ⅔ cup finely chopped salted peanuts. Cook as directed above. Top with a dill pickle slice and a dollop of peanut butter. Serve on buns or as an entrée.

Hawaiian Burgers: Combine 3 tablespoons *each* prepared mustard and catsup. Stir in 1½ tablespoons soy sauce. Brush with sauce instead of butter. Top each with a heated pineapple slice. Serve as an entrée.

Neapolitan Burgers: Blend 1 teaspoon oregano and 1 small clove garlic, minced, into meat mixture. Cook as directed above. Top each hot burger with a slice of Provolone cheese and heat to soften cheese. Top with a thin slice of tomato, onion, and red or green pepper.

Mexican Burgers: Blend 1 teaspoon chili powder into meat mixture. Cook as directed above. Mash 1 ripe avocado and stir in ¼ cup *each* finely chopped onion and tomato, 1 tablespoon lemon juice, ¼ teaspoon *each* salt, garlic salt, and chili powder, and 6 drops hot pepper sauce, or to taste. Spoon avocado topping on hot burgers and top each with a tiny hot pepper or black olive and a sprig of parsley.

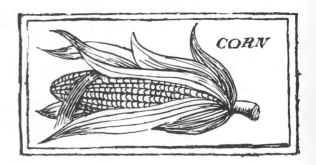

CORN

BEEF LOAF IN CRUST
8 to 10 servings

An adaptation of a well-known European specialty, Beef Wellington, Beef Loaf in Crust is impressive but easy to prepare.

2 *pounds ground beef (chuck or round steak)*

½ *cup fine corn-flake crumbs*

¼ *pound fresh mushrooms, finely chopped*

½ *cup finely chopped onion*

¼ *cup finely chopped celery*

2 *teaspoons salt*

1 *teaspoon fines herbes*

⅓ *cup milk*

3 *eggs*

1 *recipe Pastry for Double-Crust Pie (see index)*

2 *to 3 tablespoons butter, melted*

Blend together first 8 ingredients and 2 eggs. Pack into greased 9 × 5 × 3-inch loaf pan and bake in moderate oven (350° F.) for 50 minutes. Prepare pie crust according to recipe (see index), adding the remaining egg when the shortening is cut in. Wrap dough with plastic film and chill. Remove meat from oven and cool in pan for 40 to 45 minutes. Roll out dough on lightly floured board into 12½ x 19-inch rectangle. Cut 1 inch off the length and reserve.

Roll pastry around rolling pin. Unroll 4 inches of dough in center of greased baking sheet. Center meat loaf lengthwise on edge of crust. Carefully unroll crust and wrap it around meat. Tuck remaining crust under loaf. Fold ends of dough snugly, moistening and pressing edges together firmly. Cut small decorations from reserved pastry, moisten underside, and arrange. Brush crust with melted butter. Bake in hot oven (425° F.) for 15 to 18 minutes. Slice and serve plain or with a favorite sauce or gravy.

SPAGHETTI WITH MEAT SAUCE
6 servings

Marco Polo's chef is credited with the invention of spaghetti in trying to recreate the noodles his master had enjoyed in China. Thomas Jefferson is reputed to have introduced it at a formal dinner in the United States.

2 *pounds ground beef*

¾ *cup chopped onion*

¾ *cup chopped green pepper*

1 *tablespoon shortening*

3 *(6-ounce) cans tomato paste*

2½ *cups hot water*

1⅔ *cups red Burgundy wine*

Shredded or grated Parmesan cheese

1 *tablespoon salt*

2 *teaspoons garlic powder*

2 *teaspoons sugar*

1 *teaspoon oregano*

¾ *teaspoon rosemary*

¾ *teaspoon sweet basil*

3 *bay leaves, crumbled*

1 *(1-pound) package spaghetti*

Sauté first 3 ingredients in hot shortening until vegetables are tender and meat loses its bright-red color. Drain off excess juices. Combine tomato paste, water, wine, 2 tablespoons cheese, and seasonings. Stir into meat mixture. Cover and cook over very low heat for 3 hours. Cook spaghetti as directed on package and turn into heated serving dish. Spoon sauce over spaghetti and sprinkle liberally with Parmesan cheese.

PICADILLO

8 servings

Picadillo originated in Mexico. It is a spicy ground-beef hash that can be used as a filling for enchiladas, stuffed in chili peppers, or as a main course.

  1   *pound lean ground beef*
  1   *cup chopped onion*
  1   *tablespoon flour*
  2   *teaspoons chili powder*
  2   *teaspoons salt*
  ¾   *teaspoon cinnamon*
  ¼   *teaspoon ground cumin seed*
  2   *cups chopped fresh tomato*
  1   *(12-ounce) can whole-kernel corn, drained*
  1   *(4-ounce) can green chilies, drained, seeded, and chopped*
  ⅓   *cup seedless raisins*
  2   *tablespoons vinegar*
  ⅓   *cup sliced pitted ripe olives*
  ⅓   *cup chopped blanched almonds*
  4   *cups shredded lettuce*
  1   *(6-ounce) bag corn chips*
  1   *cup shredded Cheddar or Monterey Jack cheese*

Sauté beef and onion in heavy 10-inch skillet until meat is crumbly. Stir in flour, chili powder, salt, cinnamon, and cumin seed. Add tomato, corn, chilies, raisins, and vinegar, stirring. Simmer, covered, for 30 to 40 minutes, stirring occasionally. Stir in olives and almonds. Serve on shredded lettuce and corn chips and sprinkle with cheese.

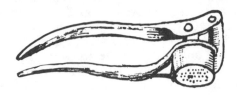

FARMHOUSE STEW

6 servings

  1   *pound ground beef*
  1   *teaspoon butter*
  1   *tablespoon flour*
  2½   *teaspoons salt*
  ⅛   *teaspoon pepper*
  8   *cups finely shredded cabbage (a 1½-pound head)*
  1   *cup chopped onion*
  1   *cup chopped green pepper*
  1   *(8¼-ounce) can tomatoes, undrained*

In 12-inch skillet, sauté beef in butter until crumbly, stirring often. Mix in flour, salt, and pepper. Blend in remaining ingredients and heat thoroughly. Cover and cook over low heat for 30 to 40 minutes, or until cabbage is very tender, stirring occasionally.

RED FLANNEL HASH

4 to 6 servings

Leftovers from a New England boiled dinner, including the segregated red beets, were chopped together and fried in salt pork drippings. The resulting dish was Red Flannel Hash, named for the beet coloring similar to red flannel.

  3   *cups chopped cooked potatoes*
  2   *cups chopped cooked beets*
  1   *to 1½ cups chopped cooked corned beef*
  ⅓   *cup beef bouillon (or liquid left from cooking corned beef)*
  4   *to 6 slices bacon, diced*
  1   *tablespoon butter*
  1   *tablespoon chopped parsley*

Combine first 4 ingredients. Pan-fry bacon in heavy skillet until crisp and set aside. Spread hash evenly over bottom of same skillet and cook over low heat without stirring until hash is browned on bottom. Fold in half and turn out on hot platter. Dot with butter and sprinkle with crisp bacon pieces and parsley.

NOTE: *Leftover beef pot roast and gravy may be substituted for corned beef and beef bouillon.*

VARIATION
QUICK AND EASY RED FLANNEL HASH
6 servings

¼ *pound sliced bacon, cut into 1-inch pieces*

2 *cups thinly sliced onion*

2 *(15½-ounce) cans corned beef hash*

1 *(1-pound) can sliced beets, drained and diced*

6 *round salted crackers, coarsely crushed*

1 *cup sour cream (optional)*

Pan-fry bacon until crisp and drain. Discard all but 2 tablespoons drippings and sauté onion until soft but not brown. Add hash and beets and mix thoroughly. Cook over moderate heat for 15 minutes to brown lightly, turning several times. Stir in cracker crumbs and sprinkle with bacon pieces. Garnish with dollops of sour cream.

GLORIFIED HASH
4 to 5 servings

4 *cups cooked beef, cut into 1-inch cubes*

4 *medium potatoes, peeled, cooked, and diced*

1 *large onion, peeled and chopped*

1 *large green pepper, cored, seeded, and chopped*

¼ *pound fresh mushrooms, sliced*

2 *tablespoons shortening or oil*

1½ *tablespoons salt*

½ *teaspoon coarsely ground pepper*

1½ *cups beef broth or 1 (10½-ounce) can consommé*

3 *tablespoons chili sauce*

Combine beef, potatoes, onion, green pepper, and mushrooms in large skillet and brown over medium heat in shortening. Add remaining ingredients and cook over low heat for 15 minutes, or until heated through.

CHILI CALIENTE
6 servings

Chili recipes differ in various parts of the country, and there is keen competition between the various schools of chili cookery. Here is my entry.

1 *pound ground beef*

1 *(1-pound 14-ounce) can tomatoes*

1 *(8-ounce) can tomato sauce*

2 *(1-pound) cans kidney beans, drained*

1 *cup chili sauce*

⅓ *cup chopped onion*

⅓ *cup chopped green pepper*

2 *tablespoons Worcestershire sauce*

2½ *teaspoons chili powder*

2 *teaspoons salt*

1 *teaspoon sugar*

¼ *to ½ teaspoon ground cumin*

¼ *teaspoon coarsely ground black pepper*

3 *drops of hot pepper sauce*

½ *square (½ ounce) unsweetened chocolate*

Taco shells (optional)

Shredded Cheddar cheese (optional)

Brown meat and drain off excess fat. Blend meat and next 14 ingredients together in a 5-quart saucepan or Dutch oven. Simmer over low heat for 3 to 4 hours, or until spices and sauce are thoroughly blended, stirring occasionally. Serve in bowls or spoon chili into taco shells and top with shredded Cheddar cheese.

GRAND CANYON TACOS

6 servings

In the United States, the corn tortilla is crisply fried and shaped into a half-moon pocket to be stuffed with meat filling, a spicy sauce, and garnished.

 1 *pound ground beef*
 2 *teaspoons butter*
 2 *tablespoons tomato paste*
 1 *teaspoon minced garlic*
 1 *teaspoon chili powder*
 1 *teaspoon salt*
 ½ *teaspoon ground cumin seed*
 6 *taco shells*
 1 *medium tomato, cut into thin wedges*
 6 *mild Italian peppers*
 2 *tablespoons finely chopped onion*
 ⅓ *cup shredded lettuce*
 ⅓ *cup shredded sharp Cheddar cheese*
 1 *(4-ounce) can taco sauce*

In heavy skillet, brown beef in butter, drain excess juices into measuring cup, and add water to measure ½ cup liquid. Return liquid to skillet and add tomato paste, garlic, chili powder, salt, and cumin seed. Cook over low heat until heated through. Spoon an equal amount of meat sauce into taco shells, and layer each taco with 1 or 2 tomato wedges, 1 Italian pepper, 1 teaspoon Cheddar cheese, and 1 to 2 teaspoons taco sauce.

BOWL OF RED

6 servings

In Texas, where it is a specialty, chili is referred to as "bowl of red."

 1 *cup coarsely chopped onion*
 1 *tablespoon oil*
 ¼ *pound beef suet, ground*
 1½ *pounds lean beef (round steak or chuck), coarsely ground*
 1 *clove garlic, minced*
 4 *teaspoons chili powder (or to taste)*
 1½ *teaspoons cumin*
 1 *teaspoon salt (or to taste)*
 2 *to 3 drops hot pepper sauce*
 1½ *teaspoons paprika*
 3 *cups water*
   Choice of tamales, crackers, cheese, and/or relishes

In a Dutch oven, sauté onion in oil until tender but not brown. Add suet and cook over moderate heat. Add beef, garlic, chili powder, cumin, salt, pepper sauce, and paprika, mixing thoroughly. Cook for 10 to 12 minutes, until meat browns, stirring often. Add water and mix well. Simmer, covered, for 1 to 1½ hours, or until meat is tender and flavors are well blended. Serve piping hot with tamales, crackers, cheese, and/or relishes.

CALVES' LIVER WITH ONIONS

6 to 8 servings

 8 *slices bacon*
 2 *large onions, sliced*
 8 *slices (about 2 pounds) calves' liver*
 1 *cup flour*
   Salt and pepper
 ½ *cup water*

Pan-fry bacon until crisp and set aside. Sauté onions in bacon drippings until soft and golden and set aside. Dredge liver in flour, season with salt and pepper, and brown in bacon drippings. Pan-fry until tender. Serve with bacon and onions.

CORNISH PASTIES
8 servings

Introduced to America by Cornishmen, many of whom settled in Wisconsin, these individual meat pies are nourishing and easy to eat on the run.

1½ *pounds round steak, cut into ½-inch cubes*
2 *tablespoons butter*
1½ *tablespoons flour*
1½ *teaspoons salt*
½ *teaspoon seasoned salt*
¼ *teaspoon pepper*
1 *cup water*
1 *cup diced raw potato*
½ *cup finely chopped onion*
½ *cup thinly sliced carrots*
2 *tablespoons chopped parsley*
2 *recipes Pastry for Double-Crust Pie (see index)*

In a heavy skillet, brown meat evenly in butter. Blend in flour, 1 teaspoon salt, seasoned salt, and pepper. Add water and cook, stirring, until mixture thickens. Cover and cook slowly for 45 minutes, or until meat is almost tender. Mix in potato, onion, carrots, parsley, and remaining ½ teaspoon salt. Cover and cook for 5 minutes. Cool.

Divide pie crust into 4 equal portions and roll out on a lightly floured board. Cut out 8 6-inch circles. Divide cooled meat mixture evenly among pastry circles. Moisten pastry edges with water, fold over meat mixture, press edges together, and crimp. Bake in hot oven (400° F.) for 20 to 25 minutes until pastry is browned and done. Serve hot or cold.

BEEF TORTES
2 (8-inch) tortes; 8 to 12 servings

This is a hearty he-man snack, perfect for a post-football-game party.

1 *recipe Roll Dough (see index)*
1 *(1-pound) can tomatoes*
1½ *pounds ground beef*
1 *cup chopped onion*
1 *tablespoon shortening*
⅓ *cup shredded or grated Parmesan cheese*
⅓ *cup chopped parsley*
1½ *teaspoons salt*
1½ *teaspoons basil*
½ *teaspoon oregano*
1½ *cups shredded mozzarella cheese*

Prepare dough according to recipe directions. Turn onto lightly floured board and knead gently. Divide into 3 equal portions. Roll 2 portions of dough into 9-inch rounds. Fit each into greased 8-inch layer cake pans. Roll remaining dough into an 8 × 12-inch rectangle and cut into 1-inch strips.

Meanwhile, prepare meat filling. Drain tomatoes, reserve juice, and chop coarsely. Cook meat and onion in shortening until meat is crumbly. Drain off excess fat. Add reserved tomato juice and simmer, uncovered, until liquid evaporates. Stir in Parmesan cheese, parsley, salt, basil, and oregano. Cool. Cover dough with meat mixture. Top each with equal amounts of chopped tomato and mozzarella cheese. Cover with dough strips lattice-fashion and press down around edges of pans. Let rise in warm place until puffy. Bake in moderate oven (350° F.) for 35 minutes, or until well browned. Remove from pans and invert. Cut each torte into 4 or 6 even wedges and serve hot or cold.

ITALIAN-STYLE VEAL ROAST
8 to 10 servings

1 *(4- to 5-pound) veal arm bone or blade roast*
2 *tablespoons shortening*
2½ *cups beef broth or 2 (10½-ounce) cans consommé*
1 *cup catsup*
1 *medium onion, chopped*
2 *tablespoons Worcestershire sauce*
1 *teaspoon salt*
1 *teaspoon minced garlic*
¼ *teaspoon oregano*
⅛ *teaspoon pepper*
2¼ *cups water (as needed)*
3 *cups thinly sliced zucchini*
1 *green pepper, seeded and cut into ¼-inch rings*
2 *tablespoons flour*

In a large covered skillet or Dutch oven, brown meat on all sides in shortening. Combine broth or consommé, catsup, onion, and seasonings and pour over meat. Cover and cook over low heat for 2½ hours, or until meat is tender. (Add water as needed during cooking.) Add zucchini and pepper rings 20 minutes before end of cooking time. Transfer meat and vegetables to heated serving platter. Mix flour and ¼ cup water until smooth and gradually blend into sauce. Cook over low heat until sauce thickens.

OREGANO

PEACH STREET VEAL CHOPS
6 servings

1 *cup flour*
½ *cup grated Parmesan cheese*
½ *teaspoon salt*
¼ *teaspoon pepper*
¼ *teaspoon paprika*
1 *egg*
¼ *cup milk*
6 *loin veal chops, cut ½ inch thick*
2 *tablespoons shortening or oil*
1 *tablespoon cornstarch*
1½ *cups liquid (peach syrup and water combined)*
½ *cup light brown sugar, firmly packed*
¼ *teaspoon allspice*
⅛ *teaspoon ground cloves*
Pinch of ginger
1 *(1-pound 14-ounce) can sliced peaches, drained*

Combine first 5 ingredients in shallow pan. Beat together egg and milk. Dip chops in egg mixture, drain, and dredge in flour mixture. Brown chops evenly on both sides in hot fat. Remove chops and keep warm. Drain off excess fat. Combine cornstarch and ¼ cup peach liquid in skillet. Gradually add remaining liquid, sugar, and spices. Cook over low heat until thickened, stirring constantly. Return meat to skillet, spooning sauce over. Cover and cook over low heat for 20 to 30 minutes, or until meat is tender. Stir in peach slices and heat through.

VEAL WITH BLUE CHEESE SAUCE

8 servings

¼ *pound fresh mushrooms, sliced (about 1 cup)*

½ *cup butter, melted*

4 *cups Grandma's Bread Stuffing with Herbs (see index)*

3 *tablespoons chopped onion*

8 *veal cutlets*

Blue Cheese Sauce (see below)

¾ *cup fine dry bread crumbs*

Paprika

In a heavy skillet, sauté mushrooms in 2 tablespoons butter until soft. Drain and set aside. Combine stuffing, mushrooms, and onion. Spoon an equal amount of stuffing onto each cutlet, roll up, and fasten with wooden picks or small metal skewers. Brown cutlets evenly in 3 to 4 tablespoons butter and transfer to a shallow 2- or 3-quart baking dish. Spoon Blue Cheese Sauce over cutlets. Combine remaining butter with crumbs. Sprinkle crumbs and paprika over cutlets. Bake in moderate oven (350° F.) for 45 minutes, or until tender.

BLUE CHEESE SAUCE   5 cups

¾ *cup butter*

¾ *cup flour*

4 *cups milk*

2 *teaspoons Worcestershire sauce*

2 *teaspoons salt*

¼ *teaspoon pepper*

2 *to 4 drops hot pepper sauce*

1 *cup sauterne or dry white wine*

⅓ *cup crumbled blue cheese*

Combine butter and flour in a heavy saucepan over low heat. Add milk gradually, stirring constantly. Cook until mixture thickens and begins to boil, stirring constantly. Remove from heat and blend in seasonings, wine, and blue cheese.

VEAL PICCATA JEANETTE

4 servings

Because it is quick, easy, and delicious, this is one of my favorite entrées. I like to serve it with a fresh spinach salad or fresh asparagus garnished with Parmesan cheese and a chilled bottle of white wine.

1¼ *pounds thin boneless veal slices*

½ *cup flour*

⅓ *cup butter, melted*

¼ *teaspoon salt (or to taste)*

⅛ *teaspoon pepper (or to taste)*

2 *large lemons, quartered*

2 *teaspoons brandy*

1 *to 2 tablespoons chopped fresh parsley*

1 *lemon, thinly sliced*

Dredge veal pieces in flour. In large skillet, sauté in butter until golden brown on both sides. Season to taste with salt and pepper. Extract juice from lemons and pour over meat. Reduce heat and simmer for 3 to 5 minutes. Pour brandy over meat just before serving. Sprinkle with parsley and garnish with lemon slices. Serve immediately.

EASY VEAL PROVOLONE

4 to 6 servings

Veal Parmigiana, originally an Italian dish, has become very popular with Americans and is featured in many restaurants. In this simplified adaptation, Provolone cheese may be used in place of mozzarella.

4 to 6 *veal cutlets*

2 *tablespoons butter*

1 *(10¾-ounce) can tomato soup*

½ *cup chili sauce*

1 *tablespoon Worcestershire sauce*

½ *teaspoon salt*

½ *teaspoon minced garlic*

⅛ *teaspoon oregano*

⅛ *teaspoon pepper*

2 *bay leaves*

1 *teaspoon dried chives*

4 to 6 *slices mozzarella or Provolone cheese*

Brown veal cutlets on both sides in butter. Remove from pan and set aside. Lower heat and blend remaining ingredients, except cheese, into meat drippings. Return meat to skillet and spoon sauce over. Simmer, covered, over low heat for 25 minutes, or until tender. Place a slice of cheese on top of each cutlet. Cover and continue cooking until cheese melts, about 3 minutes. Serve cutlets immediately.

VEAL WITH MUSHROOMS

6 servings

2 *cups sliced fresh mushrooms*

⅔ *cup chopped green onion, including tops*

3 *tablespoons melted butter*

6 *veal cutlets*

1½ *cups rich beef broth or 1 (10½-ounce) can consommé*

1 *cup sauterne or dry white wine*

2 *tablespoons chili sauce*

1 *tablespoon Worcestershire sauce*

¼ *teaspoon sweet basil*

¼ *teaspoon chopped bay leaves*

¼ *teaspoon minced garlic*

⅛ *teaspoon pepper*

2 *tablespoons flour*

2 *tablespoons water*

1 *cup frozen peas, thawed and drained*

In large skillet, sauté mushrooms and onion in butter until soft. Remove with a slotted spoon and drain. Brown cutlets on both sides in pan drippings and set aside. Lower heat and add broth or consomme, wine, chili sauce, and seasonings to pan drippings. Make a paste of flour and water and gradually blend paste into sauce. Continue cooking over low heat until sauce thickens, stirring constantly. Add meat, mushrooms, onion, and peas to sauce. Cook, covered, over low heat for 10 to 15 minutes, or until meat is hot and tender.

JAGERSCHNITZEL (Hunter's Schnitzel)

4 servings

Jagerschnitzel is one of many excellent Austrian veal dishes. Schnitzel means "little cut" of meat and, without a prefix, always refers to veal.

1 *pound veal cutlets*
3 *tablespoons butter*
1 *cup thinly sliced carrots*
1 *cup sliced onion*
¼ *pound fresh mushrooms, sliced*
1 *green pepper, seeded and cut in strips*
2 *tablespoons flour*
1 *teaspoon salt*
Dash of pepper
½ *cup water*
½ *cup dry white wine*

Pound cutlets very thin and cut in serving portions. Brown meat in 2 tablespoons butter, turning once. Remove from skillet. Add remaining 1 tablespoon butter and vegetables. Cover and cook, stirring occasionally, over low heat for 10 minutes. Blend in flour, ½ teaspoon salt, and pepper. Add liquid and heat, stirring, until bubbly. Return meat to pan. Sprinkle with remaining ½ teaspoon salt. Cover and simmer for 20 to 25 minutes, or until meat is tender.

SWEETBREADS IN CURRIED FRUIT SAUCE

4 servings

2 *pairs sweetbreads*
4 *quarts cold water*
2 *teaspoons salt*
2 *tablespoons lemon juice*
Curried Fruit Sauce (see below)

Soak sweetbreads for 15 minutes in very cold water. Cover with 2 quarts cold water to which salt and lemon juice have been added. Simmer for 15 minutes. Drain and plunge into ice water to chill before handling. Remove skin and connective tissue. Set aside.

CURRIED FRUIT SAUCE

1 *(1-pound) can pineapple tidbits, drained and juice reserved*
2 *cups pineapple juice (reserved pineapple juice plus additional 1¼ cups)*
3 *tablespoons cornstarch*
1 *teaspoon curry powder*
⅛ *teaspoon nutmeg*
⅛ *teaspoon allspice*
1 *(11-ounce) can mandarin oranges, drained*

In saucepan, blend small amount of pineapple juice with cornstarch to form a paste. Add remaining juice and cook over medium heat until sauce thickens, stirring constantly. Blend in spices and add fruit and sweetbreads. Simmer for 10 minutes and serve immediately.

JEWEL GLAZED HOLIDAY HAM

Prepare this dish for a spectacular holiday presentation. One pound of boneless, rolled, fully-cooked ham will provide three to four servings.

    1 *whole or half boneless, rolled, fully cooked ham*
    ¾ *cup thick orange marmalade*
    2 *tablespoons light corn syrup or honey*
    1 *tablespoon finely shredded orange peel*
    ⅓ *cup chopped mixed candied fruit*
       Pastry Christmas Trees (see below) and large gum drops

Place ham on rack in shallow roasting pan and insert meat thermometer into thickest part, away from fat and bone. Bake, uncovered, in slow oven (325° F.) until meat thermometer registers 140°. Allow about 2 hours for a 6- to 8-pound half ham and 3 hours for a 10- to 12-pound ham.

While ham is baking, prepare glaze. In a saucepan combine marmalade, syrup or honey, and orange peel and bring to a simmer, stirring constantly. Remove from heat at once. Thirty minutes before end of baking time, remove ham from oven and spoon half the glaze over top. Return ham to oven. Add candied fruit to remaining glaze and heat. Transfer ham to heated platter and spoon remaining hot glaze over ham. Garnish platter with pastry trees.

PASTRY CHRISTMAS TREES

Prepare Pastry for Unbaked (9-inch) Pie Shell (see index). Roll half the dough ⅜-inch thick on a lightly floured surface. Wrap remaining pastry in plastic and refrigerate for use at a later time. Cut dough with floured Christmas-tree cutter. Cut off tree trunks. Sprinkle trees lightly with multi-colored candy decorations, pressing into dough.

Bake trees on baking sheet in moderate oven (375° F.) until done, about 8 minutes. Cool on rack. Stand trees upright next to a large gum drop and hold in standing position with a wooden pick pushed through gum drop and into pastry trees. Arrange trees on platter around ham.

ISLANDER PINEAPPLE GLAZED HAM

2 to 3 servings per pound of ham

    1 *whole or half fully cooked or uncooked bone-in ham*
    1 *cup thick pineapple preserves*
    ¼ *cup honey*
    ¼ *cup orange juice*
    ½ *teaspoon grated orange peel*
    ¼ *teaspoon ginger*
    ¼ *teaspoon salt*
    ⅓ *cup fine dry bread crumbs*
    2 *tablespoons sugar*

Place ham, fat side up, on rack in shallow baking pan. Bake, uncovered, in slow oven (325° F.) for time required (see next page).

While ham is baking, prepare glaze. Combine preserves, honey, orange juice and peel, ginger, and salt in saucepan and simmer for 2 minutes. Mix crumbs and sugar. Twenty minutes before end of baking time, remove ham from oven and drain off drippings. Trim off hot rind and score, if desired. Brush fat side with half the glaze and sprinkle with half the crumb mixture. Place ham in lower third of hot oven (400° F.) to brown. Heat for 10 minutes, spoon remaining glaze over ham, and sprinkle with crumbs. Finish browning.

TIME FOR BAKING BONE-IN HAM IN SLOW OVEN (325° F.) (Taken right from refrigerator)

	Weight (Pounds)	Time (Hours)	Internal Temp. (° F.)
Whole Ham, Bone-In			
Fully cooked	12 to 14	3½ to 4	140°
Uncooked	10 to 12	3½ to 4	160°
Uncooked	12 to 15	4 to 4½	160°
Half Ham, Bone-In			
Fully cooked	6 to 8	2	140°
Uncooked	6 to 8	3½ to 4	160°

HAM FLAMBÉ
6 servings

- 6 *slices (¼- to ½-inch thick) boneless fully cooked ham*
- 1 *(1-pound) can sliced peaches*
- ¼ *cup orange juice*
- 3 *tablespoons butter*
- 2 *tablespoons flour*
- ⅓ *cup light brown sugar, firmly packed*
- ⅓ *cup warmed brandy*
- 2 *tablespoons Cointreau or Grand Marnier (optional)*
- 8 *or 10 whole cloves*
- 2 *or 3 cinnamon sticks*
- 1 *tablespoon grated orange peel*

Arrange ham slices in 13 × 9 × 2-inch baking dish and cover with aluminum foil. Bake in moderate oven (350° F.) for 20 to 30 minutes.

While ham is baking, drain peaches and combine peach syrup and orange juice. Melt butter, blend in flour and brown sugar, and stir in orange juice mixture, 3 tablespoons brandy, and Cointreau. Cook over low heat, stirring constantly, until sauce thickens. Fold in peach slices, cloves, cinnamon sticks, and orange peel and heat through. Transfer ham slices to large heated chafing dish and spoon sauce over. Pour remaining brandy over ham and ignite. Remove cloves and cinnamon sticks with a slotted spoon.

BAKED HAM IN CRUST
3 to 4 servings per pound of ham

Baked Ham in Crust is an elegant entrée for a dinner party.

- 1 *(6- to 8-pound) boneless fully cooked ham*
- 2 *recipes dough for Unbaked (9-inch) Pie Shell (see index)*
- ⅓ *cup shortening or butter, melted*
- *Half and half*
- *Rich Mustard Sauce (see index)*

Place ham on rack in shallow baking pan. Bake in slow oven (325° F.) until meat thermometer inserted in center registers 140°, about 2 hours for a 6- to 8-pound ham. Cool and then chill for 30 minutes before covering with the pastry.

Prepare pastry and roll into an 18-inch square. Brush with melted shortening or butter. Fold over in thirds, cover with plastic wrap, and chill for 30 minutes. Repeat rolling, folding, and chilling. Roll out one-third of dough into a rectangle 1½ inches larger than bottom of ham. Transfer to baking sheet and center ham on crust. Trim off excess and reserve. Roll out remaining dough into an oval, ⅜ inch thick, on lightly floured board. Moisten edges of bottom crust. Cover top and sides of ham with crust, pressing it against sides of ham and bottom crust. Be careful not to stretch pastry. Trim off excess crust and reserve. Shape bottom edge of crust into a roll and flute edges with fingers. Roll out reserved pastry scraps ⅜ inch thick and cut into leaf and stem designs. Brush crust with half and half. Arrange leaves and stems on pastry in an attractive pattern and brush with half and half.

Bake in hot oven (400° F.) until crust is done, about 30 minutes. Serve with sauce.

BAKED SMITHFIELD HAM

The distinctive flavor of these fine old-fashioned hams comes from a unique combination of peanut-fed hogs and a method of hanging and smoking that has remained the same for more than three hundred years. To be authentic the hams must be cured in Smithfield, a town on the southern coast of Virginia, and according to government regulations they must be aged six months before being put on the market. They are now available fully cooked and can be sliced thinly and served without additional baking. If you wish, prepare as follows:

Place ham in a deep roasting pan, cover with water, and soak for at least 12 hours. Drain and wash ham. Return to roasting pan, cover with water, and simmer for 4 to 5 hours, or until tender. Cool ham in liquid, remove from pan, and skin.

Score fat and stud with whole cloves. Place ham on rack in shallow roasting pan. Brush fat surface with honey and sprinkle evenly with a mixture of 3 tablespoons each brown sugar and fine dry bread crumbs. Place ham in bottom third of hot oven (425° F.) for 25 to 30 minutes, or until hot and attractively browned. If ham browns before thoroughly heated, cover with a thin sheet of aluminum foil. Slice paper-thin to serve.

CARVING THE HAM

Use a very sharp knife, preferably a long, narrow ham slicer. Place ham on platter, fat side up, and start slicing about 2 inches up on the small end, making first cut straight through to the bone. Slant the knife slightly for each succeeding slice. Slice down to and around the bone. Decrease slant as the slices become larger.

HAM DELIGHTS
8 servings

For a quick treat when unexpected company arrives, Ham Delights make a good choice. Modern boneless fully cooked hams are great time and energy savers.

8   *slices (3 ½ × 3 ½ × ⅛ inch) Swiss cheese*
8   *slices (⅛ to ¼ inch thick) boneless fully cooked ham*
½   *cup crumbled blue cheese*
1   *pound cooked fresh or frozen asparagus spears*
Creamy Sauterne Sauce (see index)
Paprika

Place 1 slice Swiss cheese on each ham slice, top with 1 tablespoon blue cheese and one-eighth of the asparagus. Roll up and secure with wooden picks or metal skewers. Arrange rolls in a greased 13 × 9 × 2-inch baking dish or ovenproof platter and cover with foil. Place in moderate oven (350° F.) for 20 to 25 minutes, or until thoroughly heated. Spoon sauce over top and sprinkle with paprika.

BAKED FRESH HAM WITH SWEET MUSTARD SAUCE
10 to 12 servings

A fresh ham differs from a regular ham in that it is not cured and smoked, but it is just as flavorful.

1   *(8- to 10-pound) fresh ham*
⅓   *cup whole cloves*
1   *(1-pound 14-ounce) can pineapple rings, drained*
Sweet Mustard Sauce (see next column)

Trim excess fat from ham. Score and stud with cloves. Insert meat thermometer so that it does not touch bone or fat. Bake ham on rack in large shallow pan in slow oven (325° F.) for about 30 to 35 minutes per pound. Arrange pineapple rings on top of ham when thermometer registers 150° and secure with wooden picks. Brush ham with half of the sauce. When thermometer registers 160° add the remaining sauce. Continue baking until thermometer registers 170° (boneless) or 185° (bone-in).

SWEET MUSTARD SAUCE

Mix ¾ cup firmly packed brown sugar, 2 tablespoons reserved pineapple syrup, 1 tablespoon white vinegar, and ½ teaspoon dry mustard in small bowl.

GLAZED HAM LOAF

8 servings

Popular since Colonial days, ham loaf is an excellent way to use leftover ham.

1¾ *pounds ground cooked ham*

¾ *pound ground pork*

1½ *cups soft bread crumbs*

⅓ *cup finely chopped onion*

2 *eggs*

1 *(12-ounce) can unsweetened pineapple juice*

1 *teaspoon dry mustard*

¾ *teaspoon ginger*

⅛ *teaspoon pepper*

3 *tablespoons sugar*

1 *tablespoon cornstarch*

¼ *cup apple or currant jelly*

Fruit for garnish (optional)

Blend together meats, crumbs, onion, eggs, ¾ cup pineapple juice, mustard, ½ teaspoon ginger, and pepper. Shape into a loaf in lightly greased baking pan. Bake in moderate oven (350° F.) for 60 to 70 minutes. Combine remaining pineapple juice and ¼ teaspoon ginger, sugar, cornstarch, and jelly and cook, stirring constantly, until thick and clear. Serve over ham loaf.

SWEET HAM PUFFS

8 servings

Everybody will enjoy these Sweet Ham Puffs with their mustardy sweet sauce.

1¼ *pounds ground cooked ham*

1 *pound ground lean pork*

½ *pound ground beef chuck*

1½ *cups crushed graham crackers*

1 *cup milk*

2 *eggs, beaten slightly*

1 *(10¾-ounce) can tomato soup*

⅓ *cup vinegar*

1 *cup light brown sugar, firmly packed*

1 *teaspoon dry mustard*

Combine first 6 ingredients and shape into large balls, using ½ cup of mixture for each. Arrange balls in greased 13 × 9 × 2-inch baking pan. Bake in moderate oven (350° F.) for 20 minutes. While ham balls are baking, combine the remaining ingredients and simmer for 5 minutes. Spoon sauce over ham balls and continue baking for 40 minutes.

HAM ASPARAGUS ROLLS AU GRATIN

4 servings

Serve this tasty, nutritious casserole as a luncheon dish or a late-evening snack.

  3 *tablespoons butter*

  3 *tablespoons flour*

  ¾ *teaspoon salt*

  2 *cups milk*

  1 *cup shredded Swiss cheese*

1⅓ *cups cooked rice*

  8 *thin slices canned ham*

24 *to 32 slender fresh or frozen asparagus spears, cooked and drained*

  ¼ *cup shredded Parmesan cheese*

In a saucepan, melt butter and blend in flour and salt. Add milk and cook, stirring constantly, until thickened. Add Swiss cheese, stirring just until melted. Blend 1 cup sauce into rice. Spoon an equal amount of rice mixture onto each ham slice, top with 3 or 4 asparagus spears, and roll ham around filling. Secure with wooden picks. Arrange rolls in a shallow 2-quart baking dish. Pour remaining sauce over and sprinkle with Parmesan cheese. Bake in moderate oven (350° F.) for 25 to 30 minutes.

DIXIE-STYLE HAM AND YAMS

4 servings

  1 *pound slice (1 inch thick) boneless fully cooked ham*

    Melted butter or oil

    Dixie-style Yams (see index)

Slash fat edges of ham with sharp knife to prevent curling. Place on broiler pan 3 inches from heat. Broil 1-inch thick slice for 5 to 8 minutes per side or bake on rack in shallow pan in slow oven (325° F.) for 25 to 30 minutes. Brush ham with melted butter or oil 2 or 3 times. Serve with Dixie-style Yams.

YORK COUNTY SCHNITZ UND KNEPPE

6 to 8 servings

Probably the most famous of all Pennsylvania Dutch specialties, *Schnitz* (dried apple slices) *und Kneppe* (dumplings) is a savory dish flavored with brown sugar and ham. It is cooked to perfection over low heat until the ham is tender and is topped off with feather-light dumplings.

  1 *(8-ounce) package dried apple rings*

  5 *pounds fully cooked ham hocks*

  3 *tablespoons light brown sugar*

12 *small yeast bread balls or Parsley Dumplings (see index)*

    Chopped parsley

Soak apples in water to cover for 2 to 4 hours. In a large saucepan or Dutch oven cook ham hocks in water to cover very slowly for 2 to 2½ hours, or until meat is tender and falls off the bones. Remove meat from bones, cut into bite-sized pieces, and return to broth. Add apples and water they were soaked in. Sprinkle brown sugar over top. Simmer, covered, for 30 to 40 minutes, or until apples are soft and mushy. About 20 minutes before serving time, drop small balls of yeast dough on top of meat mixture and cover tightly. Do not uncover for 15 minutes or dumplings will collapse. Sprinkle with parsley. Serve at once with cauliflower, green beans, or red cabbage.

Notes: *Fresh sliced apples may be substituted for the dried ones, but the dish will then not be authentic.*

Fully cooked ham butt or pork shoulder picnic may be substituted for shanks.

Baking-powder dumplings may be substituted for yeast bread balls. This does not make true kneppe. *Frozen yeast bread or roll dough can be used. Just thaw dough, let rise as directed on package label, and shape into little balls. Use as directed above.*

PORK TENDERLOIN WITH TOMATO SAUCE

4 to 6 servings

Hogs accompanied Columbus on his second voyage to the New World but were not introduced to mainland America until Hernando De Soto landed in Florida in 1539.

    1 *egg*
    1 *tablespoon milk*
    ½ *cup corn-flake crumbs*
    8 *pork tenderloin patties or 8 thin strips pork tenderloin*
    2 *tablespoons shortening or oil*
    ½ *teaspoon salt*
    ¼ *teaspoon coarsely ground pepper*
    1 *(10¾-ounce) can tomato soup*
    3 *tablespoons chili sauce*
    2 *tablespoons grated sharp Cheddar cheese*
    1 *tablespoon Worcestershire sauce*
    ¼ *teaspoon basil*

Mix egg and milk in small bowl. Measure corn-flake crumbs onto sheet of wax paper. Dip tenderloin patties into egg mixture and then coat with crumbs. Brown meat on both sides in hot shortening or oil. Sprinkle with salt and pepper. Combine soup and remaining ingredients in small bowl. Arrange tenderloin patties in 8 × 8-inch baking dish and spoon sauce over meat. Bake in moderate oven (350° F.) for 50 minutes, or until tender.

PORK ROAST OR CHOPS WITH CHUTNEY SAUCE

4 to 6 servings

Chutney adds a hint of the exotic Orient to American pork.

    1 *(4-pound) pork loin or 6 to 8 chops, ¾ to 1 inch thick*
    1 *teaspoon garlic salt*
    1 *tablespoon cornstarch*
    1½ *teaspoons sugar*
    ¼ *teaspoon curry powder*
    1 *cup orange-pineapple juice*
    ½ *cup finely chopped chutney and syrup or orange marmalade*
    1½ *teaspoons soy sauce*

If a pork roast is used, cut down between bones to within ¼ inch of bottom. Rub meat surface with garlic salt. Assemble chops or arrange loin on rack in roasting pan, fat side up. Run a metal skewer through roast or chops. Cover with aluminum foil and bake in slow oven (325° F.) for 1½ hours.

While meat is baking, prepare sauce. Combine cornstarch, sugar, and curry powder in small saucepan. Stir in orange-pineapple juice, chutney or marmalade, and soy sauce. Cook, stirring constantly, until sauce boils and thickens. Uncover meat and continue baking for about 45 minutes. Baste 2 or 3 times during the last 20 minutes of baking, using ½ cup of sauce. Serve remaining sauce with meat.

GLAZED PORK ROAST
6 to 8 servings

  1 *(4- to 5-pound) boneless pork loin*
  1 *teaspoon salt*
  ¼ *cup red wine vinegar*
  ¼ *cup catsup*
  ¼ *cup orange or pineapple juice*
  ¼ *cup honey*
  1 *tablespoon soy sauce*
  2 *teaspoons cornstarch*
  ½ *teaspoon dry mustard*
  1 *clove garlic, quartered*

Rub roast with salt. Insert meat thermometer into lean part of meat away from bone and fat. Place roast on rack in shallow roasting pan and bake in slow oven (325° F.) for 3 hours, or until meat thermometer registers 170°.

Combine remaining ingredients to form a glaze. Cook, stirring constantly, until thick and clear. Remove garlic. Brush roast with glaze several times during last 30 minutes of roasting. Serve remaining glaze with meat.

BAKED STUFFED PORK CHOPS
6 servings

These are company fare and not difficult to prepare. Have the butcher cut a pocket into the rib side of the pork chops, as it will close more easily over the stuffing while baking.

  1 *cup Grandma's Bread Stuffing with Herbs (see index)*
  ½ *cup grated or shredded Parmesan cheese*
  ¼ *cup chopped onion*
  2 *tablespoons finely chopped parsley*
  2 *tablespoons chopped celery*
  ¼ *cup butter*
  Salt and pepper to taste
  6 *double rib pork chops*

Combine stuffing and cheese in bowl. Sauté onion, parsley, and celery in butter until celery is tender. Add to stuffing-cheese mixture and blend thoroughly. Season with salt and pepper. Fill pocket in pork chops with stuffing, close, and secure with wooden picks or metal skewers. Brown chops on both sides in lightly buttered skillet and arrange in baking dish. Bake, covered, in moderate oven (350° F.) for 35 minutes. Uncover, turn chops, and bake 35 to 40 minutes longer, or until tender.

GRILLED PORK CHOPS WITH SPICY JELLY GLAZE
3 to 6 servings

Cincinnati was once such an important meatpacking center that the city was nicknamed "Porkopolis."

  6 *rib pork chops, fresh or smoked, 1 to 1½ inches thick*
  Cooking oil or melted butter
  Salt to taste
  Spicy Jelly Glaze (see below)

Arrange pork chops on greased grill or in hinged broiler rack. Grill 4 to 6 inches from low to moderate heat. Brown evenly on both sides, basting often with oil or melted butter. Sprinkle with salt. Allow about 15 to 18 minutes per side for 1-inch chops and 20 to 22 minutes per side for 1½-inch chops. Brush with Spicy Jelly Glaze during last 3 to 5 minutes of cooking. Serve any remaining sauce on the side.

SPICY JELLY GLAZE   About ⅔ cup
  ½ *cup apple jelly*
  2 *tablespoons light corn syrup*
  1 *tablespoon lemon juice*
  ½ *teaspoon cinnamon*
  ⅛ *teaspoon cloves*
  ⅛ *teaspoon salt*

Combine ingredients and heat slowly until jelly melts, stirring often.

PUNGENT PORK

4 to 6 servings

Chinese cookery has become immensely popular throughout the United States. Sweet and sour dishes are a specialty of the Honan region of east-central China.

1½ pounds lean pork shoulder, cut into 1-inch cubes
2 tablespoons shortening or oil
¾ teaspoon salt
⅛ teaspoon pepper
1 (1-pound 4-ounce) can pineapple chunks
3 tablespoons cornstarch
1 cup water
½ cup sugar
¼ cup vinegar
2 or 3 tablespoons soy sauce
1 large green pepper, cut into large dice
2 tomatoes, cut in thin wedges
Chow mein noodles

Brown meat evenly in hot shortening or oil, seasoning with salt and pepper. Remove and keep warm. Drain pineapple chunks and add enough water to syrup to measure 1 cup. Blend cornstarch and ¼ cup water thoroughly and stir in remaining ¾ cup water, reserved pineapple syrup, sugar, vinegar, and soy sauce. Cook over medium heat until thickened, stirring constantly. Add meat and coat thoroughly. Simmer, covered, for 25 minutes, or until meat is tender. Fold in pineapple chunks, green pepper, and tomato wedges and heat about 5 minutes. Serve with chow mein noodles.

QUICK AND EASY PORK CHOP BAKE

6 servings

6 pork chops or cutlets (1 inch thick)
3½ tablespoons butter
Salt and pepper to taste
½ cup sliced fresh mushrooms
¼ cup chopped green pepper
¼ cup chopped onion
1½ cups green beans, sliced, or 1 (10-ounce) package frozen, defrosted, and drained
1 (10¾-ounce) can cream of mushroom soup
2 tablespoons milk
½ to 1 teaspoon basil
½ teaspoon Worcestershire sauce
2 or 3 drops hot pepper sauce
1 (3-ounce) can chow mein noodles

Brown pork on both sides in 1½ tablespoons butter. Season with salt and pepper and arrange in shallow baking dish. Sauté mushrooms, green pepper, and onion in remaining 2 tablespoons butter until mushrooms are soft. Spread beans and mushroom mixture over meat. Combine soup, milk, and seasonings and pour over vegetables. Bake in moderate oven (350° F.) for 30 minutes. Sprinkle noodles over top and bake 10 minutes longer.

ALSATIAN-STYLE CHOUCROUTE GARNI

6 generous servings

Old Alsatian recipes for *choucroute garni* (sauerkraut garnished with meat) called for many vegetables and spices, wine, quantities of pork and sausage, and hours of preparation. This simplified version retains the Old World flavor but is geared to modern living.

> ½ *pound thick-sliced bacon, cut into 1-inch pieces*
> 2 *cups coarsely chopped onion*
> 2 *cups peeled, chopped apple*
> 2 *small cloves garlic, minced*
> 2 *quarts sauerkraut, canned or in bulk, well drained*
> ¼ *teaspoon pepper*
> 1½ *cups dry white wine*
> 1½ *pounds spareribs, cut into 4-rib portions*
> ½ *teaspoon salt*
> 1½ *pounds boneless smoked pork shoulder butt*
> 4 *to 6 precooked sausage links (knockwurst, bratwurst, smoked Thuringer, smoked sausage links, or frankfurters)*

Partially cook bacon in large fry pan or Dutch oven, drain off drippings, and reserve. Add onion, apple, and garlic and heat. Mix in sauerkraut and pepper. Pour wine over sauerkraut, cover, and cook slowly for 1 hour. Brown spareribs in bacon drippings and sprinkle with salt. Arrange spareribs and pork shoulder butt on sauerkraut. Cover and cook slowly until meat on spareribs is tender, 1 to 1½ hours. Add sausages during last 15 minutes of cooking. To serve, slice smoked pork butt and arrange meats attractively around sauerkraut on platter.

BARBECUED PORK LOIN

8 to 10 servings

Pork loin is an excellent selection for a barbecue or backyard supper.

> 1 *(4- to 6-pound) rolled, boneless pork loin*
> *Salt*
> ½ *cup finely chopped onion*
> 2 *tablespoons cooking oil*
> 1 *(10-ounce) jar currant jelly*
> ½ *cup catsup*
> ½ *cup water*
> 2 *tablespoons vinegar*
> ½ *teaspoon dry mustard*

Sprinkle meat with salt. Mount on rotisserie spit, securing firmly. Insert meat thermometer into thickest part of roast away from fat pocket. Roast over moderate heat, 350° F. at spit level, until meat thermometer registers 170°, about 2½ to 3 hours.

While meat is roasting, prepare sauce. Sauté onion in oil until tender but not brown. Add remaining ingredients and cook slowly until jelly melts. Simmer to thicken slightly, about 5 minutes. Brush meat with sauce frequently during last 30 minutes of roasting. Serve remaining sauce with meat.

SMOKED SHOULDER AND CABBAGE

8 to 10 servings

For many years smoked shoulder was incorrectly called the butt. Tasty and delicious, this is also a very economical dish.

> 3 *pounds fully cooked smoked shoulder roll (butt)*
> 2 *bay leaves*
> 1 *teaspoon pickling spice*
> 6 *medium potatoes, peeled and halved*
> 1 *large head cabbage, cored and cut into 8 wedges*

Put smoked shoulder in 5-quart saucepan with water to cover. Add bay leaves and pickling spice and simmer for 2 hours, or until tender. Remove smoked shoulder to hot platter and keep warm in slow oven (300° F.). Add potatoes to the stock and cook for 30 minutes. Add cabbage to the stock and cook about 10 minutes more (do not overcook).

VARIATION

Smoked Shoulder with Currant Sauce: Mix 1 (4-ounce) jar currant jelly with 2 or 3 drops lemon juice. Spoon over cooked shoulder. Bake in moderate oven (350° F.) for about 1 hour, basting often.

PORK BALLS IN SOUR CREAM–CAPER SAUCE

6 servings

    2 *cups soft bread crumbs*
    1 *cup milk*
    2 *eggs, beaten*
    ½ *cup finely chopped onion*
    1¾ *teaspoons salt*
    ¼ *teaspoon pepper*
    1 *tablespoon lemon juice*
    1½ *pounds ground pork*
    ½ *pound ground beef*
    2 *tablespoons butter*
    ½ *cup dry white wine*
    1 *bay leaf*
    ¼ *teaspoon leaf thyme*
    ½ *cup sour cream*
    ¼ *cup water*
    1 *tablespoon flour*
    ½ *lemon, sliced*
    1 *tablespoon drained capers*
    6 *servings hot buttered noodles*

Combine bread and milk and let stand until milk is absorbed, about 5 minutes. Combine bread mixture, eggs, onion, 1½ teaspoons salt,

pepper, and lemon juice. Add meats and mix thoroughly (meat mixture will be soft). Shape meat into 24 balls of equal size and brown evenly in butter. Add wine, bay leaf, and thyme. Simmer, covered, for about 30 minutes. Then remove meat balls with a slotted spoon. Combine sour cream, water, flour, and remaining ¼ teaspoon salt and stir into pan drippings. Cook, stirring constantly, until sauce is thickened. Return meat balls to the sauce, add lemon slices and capers, cover, and heat, about 5 minutes. Serve over noodles.

SPARERIBS

At one time spareribs were considered leftovers from the choice cuts of pork and were eaten by the slaves on Southern plantations. The original soul food, spareribs today are universally enjoyed.

OVEN-BARBECUED SPARERIBS

4 to 6 servings

    4 *pounds spareribs, cut into 3-rib portions*
    1½ *teaspoons salt*
    ½ *cup chopped onion*
    2 *tablespoons bacon drippings or oil*
    1 *cup catsup*
    ⅓ *cup water*
    ⅓ *cup brown sugar, firmly packed*
    2 *tablespoons red wine vinegar*
    2 *tablespoons Worcestershire sauce*

Place ribs on rack in a shallow roasting pan and sprinkle with 1 teaspoon salt. Cover with aluminum foil and bake in moderate oven (350° F.) for 1½ hours. While ribs are baking, prepare sauce. In heavy saucepan sauté onion in bacon drippings or oil until tender. Add remaining ½ teaspoon salt and all other ingredients. Simmer to blend flavors for 10 to 15 minutes. Drain off drippings and brush ribs lightly with sauce. Bake, uncovered, for 30 minutes, basting ribs with sauce several times.

MARMALADE-GINGER RIBS

4 to 6 servings

1 *cup lime juice*

1 *cup honey*

3 *to 4 tablespoons soy sauce*

Pinch of ground ginger

5 *pounds spareribs*

1 *cup orange marmalade*

Combine first 4 ingredients to make marinade. Cut ribs into 2- or 3-rib serving portions and pour marinade over ribs. Cover and refrigerate for several hours or overnight, turning ribs frequently. Arrange ribs on rack in one or two shallow baking pans. Bake in slow oven (325° F.) for 45 minutes. Drain excess fat from pan. Stir marmalade into remaining marinade and brush ribs. Bake for 45 minutes longer, basting frequently.

TOURTIÈRE (Canadian Pork Pie)

One 9-inch pie (4 to 6 servings)

Tourtière, a spicy pork pie, is a French-Canadian specialty featured in many restaurants north of the border.

2 *strips bacon, diced*

1½ *pounds ground lean pork*

½ *cup chopped onion*

½ *cup chopped celery*

1 *clove garlic, minced*

2 *tablespoons flour*

1 *cup beef bouillon*

1 *teaspoon salt*

½ *teaspoon chervil (optional)*

¼ *teaspoon mace*

1 *small bay leaf, crushed*

Pork Pie Pastry (see next column)

1 *tablespoon butter, melted*

In large heavy skillet lightly brown bacon and add pork, onion, celery, and garlic. Cook, stirring frequently, until meat is lightly browned. Sprinkle flour over top and stir. Add bouillon, salt, chervil, mace, and bay leaf and cook slowly until mixture thickens. Cover and cook slowly for 30 minutes, then cool for 10 minutes. Roll out half the pie pastry into a circle ⅛ inch thick and 1½ inches larger in diameter than the top of a 9-inch pie pan.

Fit the dough carefully into pan. Roll remaining pastry ½ inch larger than pie pan and prick top to allow escape of steam. Fill crust with pork mixture. Moisten rim, cover with top crust, fold edges under, and flute. Decorate top with pastry leaves. Brush with melted butter. Bake in hot oven (425° F.) for 15 minutes, then reduce oven temperature to moderate (350° F.) and bake for 25 minutes longer.

PORK PIE PASTRY

2 *cups sifted flour*

1 *teaspoon salt*

⅔ *cup shortening*

1 *egg, beaten*

2 *tablespoons water*

Sift flour and salt into mixing bowl and cut in shortening with pastry blender or knives. Add egg and water and mix until dry ingredients are moistened. Roll out as directed.

SAUSAGE

Americans are very fond of all kinds of sausage. The name comes from the Roman word salsus, *meaning salted. Sausages were very popular in ancient Rome and were often included in the elaborate banquets given by the emperors. The less privileged world bought them from roving vendors. Throughout history, certain localities of Europe became famous for their sausage: Frankfurt-am-Main, Germany; Bologna and Genoa, Italy; and Arles, France. Old World sausage makers brought their secrets and talents to the New World, adapting old recipes to the preferences and tastes of modern Americans.*

SAUSAGE ONION PIE

6 servings

2 *cups thinly sliced onion*
3 *tablespoons butter*
2 *tablespoons flour*
1 *teaspoon salt*
⅛ *teaspoon pepper*
1 *cup milk*
⅔ *cup half and half*
2 *teaspoons prepared horseradish*
2 *eggs, beaten*
½ *cup shredded American cheese*
1 *Baked (9-inch) Pie Shell (see index)*
1 *pound (12 to 16) fresh pork sausage links, cooked*

Sauté onion in butter until tender. Stir in flour, salt, and pepper. Add milk, half and half, and horseradish and cook, stirring constantly, until thickened. Stir hot mixture into beaten eggs gradually. Fold in cheese. Pour into baked pie shell and bake in hot oven (400° F.) for 10 minutes. Circle sausages on top of pie. Bake for 10 to 15 minutes longer, cut in wedges, and serve.

BRATWURST AND SAUERKRAUT SANDWICH

8 sandwiches

"Brats" 'n' beer are a great favorite in the state of Wisconsin.

8 *tomato slices, cut in half*
8 *hot-dog buns, toasted and buttered*
1 *(1-pound) can sauerkraut, heated and drained*
8 *thin dill pickle slices*
8 *precooked bratwurst, grilled*
8 *slices brick or Muenster cheese*

For each sandwich, place 2 half tomato slices on bottom half of bun. Top with ¼ cup hot sauerkraut, a pickle slice, and hot bratwurst. Cover with cheese slice and bun top.

SWISS-STYLE SAUSAGE DINNER

4 to 6 servings

4 *cups sliced Bermuda onion*
⅓ *cup butter*
¼ *teaspoon salt*
6 *to 8 fully cooked bratwurst or knockwurst*
Flour
3 *cups hot seasoned mashed potatoes*
1 *cup shredded Swiss cheese*
⅛ *teaspoon nutmeg*
Paprika

In heavy skillet sauté onion in 4 tablespoons butter and salt, stirring often, until tender and honey-colored. Dredge sausage in flour and brown evenly on all sides in remaining butter for 8 to 10 minutes. Combine potatoes, ¾ cup cheese, and nutmeg and blend thoroughly. At one end of heated platter spoon mounds of potato and sprinkle with remaining ¼ cup cheese and paprika. At other end top onions with sausages.

CURRIED FRANKFURTER CASEROLE

6 servings

  1 *pound fully cooked frankfurters*
  1 *(1-pound 4-ounce) can pineapple chunks)*
  ½ *cup sugar*
  3 *tablespoons cornstarch*
  ½ *teaspoon curry powder*
  ¼ *teaspoon salt*
      Dash of pepper
  1 *cup cold water*
  ¼ *cup white vinegar*
  2 *tablespoons soy sauce*
  1 *tablespoon Worcestershire sauce*
  ½ *cup drained mandarin orange sections*
1 ½ *large green peppers, seeded and cut into 1 ½-inch pieces*
  ¼ *cup slivered almonds*
  6 *servings hot cooked seasoned rice*

Cut frankfurters crosswise into 2-inch lengths and reserve. Drain pineapple chunks. Reserve syrup and add enough water to measure 1 cup. In saucepan mix sugar, cornstarch, curry powder, salt, and pepper. Add ½ cup cold water and stir until smooth. Blend in remaining ½ cup water, pineapple syrup, vinegar, soy sauce, and Worcestershire sauce and cook over low heat until thickened. Fold in frankfurters, pineapple chunks, and remaining ingredients except the rice. Pour into shallow 2-quart casserole and bake in moderate oven (350° F.) for 25 minutes, or until hot and bubbly. Serve over rice.

SPIEDINI

8 servings

An Italian favorite, this skewered french-fried sandwich can be prepared in advance and reheated after guests arrive.

  1 *loaf Italian bread*
  ¼ *cup butter*
  1 *clove garlic, finely minced*
  ¼ *teaspoon oregano*
  ¼ *teaspoon rosemary*
 12 *slices cotto salami, summer sausage, cervelat, or bologna*
 24 *cubes (1 × 1 ½ × ¼-inch) mozzarella cheese*
  2 *eggs*
  ⅔ *cup milk*
  ½ *teaspoon salt*
  ⅔ *cup shredded Parmesan cheese*

Trim ends from bread, then cut into 8 1-inch slices. Make three evenly spaced slashes, crosswise, in each bread slice, not quite through. Combine butter, garlic, oregano, and rosemary and spread on cut bread surfaces. Cut sausage slices in half, wrap around a cheese cube, and place in each slash. Thread a long metal skewer through each bread slice. Beat together slightly eggs, milk, and salt. Roll each skewered sandwich in mixture and drain. Sprinkle with cheese and place on baking sheet. Heat in hot oven (400° F.) for 6 to 8 minutes, or until mozzarella cheese melts.

ROSEMARY

SHOULDER LAMB CHOPS WITH CURRANT SAUCE

4 to 6 servings

Shoulder chops are just as tasty as rib or loin chops but are much more economical.

4 *to 6 shoulder lamb chops, cut ¾-inch thick*

Salt and pepper to taste

1 *cup rosé or light red wine*

2 *tablespoons currant jelly*

2 *tablespoons brown sugar*

1 *tablespoon vinegar*

1 *teaspoon whole cloves, tied in a cheese-cloth bag*

2 *teaspoons cornstarch*

Place lamb chops on broiler pan 3 to 4 inches from heat source. Broil 8 minutes per side. Salt and pepper to taste. Combine remaining ingredients in small saucepan and cook over low heat until sauce thickens and starts to boil, stirring constantly. Remove cloves. Spoon sauce over lamb chops before serving.

MEDITERRANEAN LAMB SHANKS

4 servings

4 *lamb shanks (about 12 ounces each)*

2 *teaspoons salt*

¼ *teaspoon pepper*

1 *large onion, thinly sliced*

1 *cup catsup*

1 *cup water*

½ *cup mint jelly, mashed*

2 *tablespoons lemon juice*

1 *teaspoon Worcestershire sauce*

¼ *teaspoon oregano*

In Dutch oven gently simmer lamb shanks in water to cover for 1 hour. Drain off liquid and season with salt and pepper. Combine remaining ingredients and pour over lamb. Cover and cook slowly until tender and sauce thickens, about 60 minutes.

RACK OF LAMB WITH DILL SAUCE

2 to 3 servings

MEAT

2- *to 2½-pound rack of lamb*

½ *to 1 teaspoon salt*

1 *clove garlic, peeled and halved*

DILL SAUCE

2 *tablespoons butter, melted*

2 *tablespoons flour*

1 *cup milk*

3 *tablespoons vinegar*

1 *tablespoon pickling spice*

2 *teaspoons dill weed*

2 *teaspoons dill seed*

¼ *teaspoon basil*

¼ *teaspoon pepper*

1 *tablespoon drained capers*

Cover rib tips with foil to prevent scorching. Rub meat with salt and garlic. Insert meat thermometer. Roast on rack in shallow pan, fat side up, in slow oven (300° F.) for 30 minutes.

To prepare dill sauce, combine butter and flour and add milk gradually. Cook over low heat, stirring constantly, until mixture begins to boil. Remove from heat. Stir in vinegar, spices, and herbs. Simmer for 2 or 3 minutes. Strain. Stir in capers and cook 2 to 3 minutes. Use half the sauce to baste lamb. Roast until thermometer reads 160° for medium rare, 175° for medium, and 180° for well-done lamb. Pass remaining sauce.

ROAST LEG OF LAMB
6 to 8 servings

Roasted lamb was an integral part of the Jewish Passover in Biblical times. Today it is served as a traditional Easter dinner in many Christian homes.

> 1 *(5- to 7-pound) leg of lamb*
> 1 *clove garlic, peeled and halved*
> *Salt and pepper*
> *Lamb Gravy (see below)*
> *Mint Sauce for Lamb (see index)*

If desired, remove the thin paperlike covering of fat, called the "fell," to make carving easier. Rub outside of lamb with garlic, then salt and pepper. Insert meat thermometer into thickest part of leg, away from bone and fat. Roast on rack in shallow baking pan in slow oven (325° F.) 30 to 35 minutes per pound, or until thermometer reaches 180°. Transfer roast to a heated platter and keep warm. Drain and reserve excess fat from pan. Serve with Lamb Gravy or Mint Sauce.

LAMB GRAVY   2 cups

> ¼ *cup reserved pan drippings*
> ¼ *cup flour*
> 1 *teaspoon salt*
> ¼ *teaspoon basil*
> ¼ *teaspoon pepper*
> 2 *cups water*
> 2 *tablespoons Worcestershire sauce*

Measure drippings into saucepan. Blend in flour, salt, basil, and pepper. Add water gradually and cook over moderate heat, stirring constantly, until gravy thickens and begins to bubble. Stir in Worcestershire sauce and simmer 2 to 3 minutes.

MOUSSAKA
8 to 10 servings

> ½ *pound each ground lamb and ground veal, or 1 pound ground beef chuck*
> ¾ *cup cooking or olive oil or a combination (approximate)*
> 2 *cups chopped onion*
> 1 *clove garlic, minced*
> ¼ *cup water*
> ¼ *cup catsup*
> 3 *teaspoons salt*
> ⅛ *teaspoon pepper*
> 2 *eggs, separated*
> 1 *cup fine dry bread crumbs*
> ½ *cup grated Parmesan cheese*
> ⅓ *cup butter*
> ½ *cup flour*
> ¼ *teaspoon nutmeg*
> 4 *cups milk*
> 1 *large eggplant, peeled (optional)*

Brown meat in 2 tablespoons oil and stir in onion, garlic, water, catsup, 1 teaspoon salt, and pepper. Cover and simmer for 10 to 15 minutes. Beat egg whites slightly and mix with bread crumbs. Stir one-half the crumb mixture into meat. Mix remaining crumb mixture with cheese. In saucepan combine butter, flour, remaining 2 teaspoons salt, and nutmeg. Add milk and cook, stirring constantly, until thickened. Add small amount of white sauce to lightly beaten egg yolks. Stir into remaining sauce. Cut eggplant into ½-inch slices and lightly brown in remaining oil. Arrange half the eggplant in buttered 3-quart baking dish. Cover with half the meat mixture, sauce, and crumb mixture. Repeat. Bake in moderate oven (375° F.) for 40 to 45 minutes.

DILL

LAMB STEW WITH DILL

6 servings

2½ *pounds boneless lamb, cut into 1-inch*
    cubes
2 *tablespoons butter*
2 *teaspoons salt*
½ *teaspoon dill weed*
⅛ *teaspoon pepper*
1½ *cups water*
1 *pound carrots, peeled and cut into*
    1½-inch chunks
3 *medium potatoes, quartered*
3 *stalks celery, cut into 2-inch lengths*
2 *cups fresh peas or 1 (10-ounce) package*
    frozen peas, partially defrosted and
    broken apart
¾ *cup milk*
3 *tablespoons flour*
1 *cup sour cream (optional)*
1 *tablespoon chopped parsley*

In a heavy skillet or Dutch oven, brown lamb evenly in butter. Reduce heat and sprinkle salt, dill weed, and pepper over meat and add 1 cup water. Cover and cook for 1¼ hours, or until meat is almost tender. Add remaining ½ cup water, carrots, potatoes, and celery. Cover and cook 20 to 25 minutes, or until carrots are tender. Add peas and heat through. Blend milk and flour until smooth, add to stew, and cook until gravy is thickened, stirring frequently. Fold in sour cream, heat, and sprinkle with parsley.

LAMB CURRY WITH SAFFRON RICE

4 servings

1½ *pounds boneless lamb, cubed*
¼ *cup flour*
3 *tablespoons cooking oil*
1 *cup sliced onion*
1 *clove garlic, minced*
1 *cup peeled, chopped apple*
1 *cup water*
2 *chicken bouillon cubes*
½ *cup tomato sauce*
1 *tablespoon curry powder (or to taste)*
1 *teaspoon light brown sugar*
1 *teaspoon salt*
¼ *teaspoon dry mustard*
¼ *teaspoon ginger*
Saffron Rice (see index)
Condiments: coconut, seedless raisins,
    chopped nuts, chopped pickle, chutney,
    additional curry powder

Dredge lamb in flour. In large skillet, brown evenly in oil. Add onion and garlic. Lower heat, cover, and cook until onion is soft. Add remaining ingredients, except rice and condiments, and mix thoroughly. Simmer, covered, for 1½ to 2 hours, or until meat is tender. Serve with Saffron Rice and condiments.

EGG AND CHEESE DISHES

EGGS BENEDICT

6 servings

> 6 *English muffins, split, toasted, and*
> *buttered*
> 6 *slices grilled Canadian bacon or boned,*
> *rolled, fully cooked ham*
>
> 6 *poached eggs*
> *Hollandaise Sauce (see index)*

Arrange a hot toasted muffin half on each serving plate. Top each with a slice of Canadian bacon or ham and cover with a poached egg. Spoon Hollandaise Sauce over egg. Cut remaining muffin halves in half and put 2 halves on each plate. Serve at once.

VARIATION

Eggs Benedict with Asparagus: Top each meat slice with 3 or 4 hot cooked asparagus spears before topping with egg.

BACON AND EGGS MORNAY

6 servings

> 1 *pound sliced bacon*
> ¼ *cup diced onion*
> ¼ *cup flour*
> 1½ *teaspoons salt*
> ½ *teaspoon paprika*
> 2 *cups milk*
> 2 *tablespoons prepared mustard*
> 1 *cup (¼ pound) shredded American*
> *cheese*
> ⅔ *cup peeled, chopped tomato*
> ¼ *cup diced green pepper*
> 8 *hard-cooked eggs, sliced*
> 6 *patty shells or English muffins*
> *(optional)*

Pan-fry bacon until crisp and reserve 3 tablespoons drippings. Set aside 12 bacon slices for top of casserole. Break remaining slices into 1-inch lengths. Sauté onion in reserved drippings until soft. Blend in flour, salt, and paprika. Add milk and cook, stirring constantly, until thickened. Add mustard, cheese, tomato, and green pepper and cook, stirring. Pour half of the sauce into a shallow 1½-quart baking dish. Add a third of the egg slices and half of the small bacon pieces. Repeat. Bake in moderate oven (350° F.) until heated, about 20 minutes. Top with remaining egg slices and bacon strips and return to oven for 5 minutes. Serve as is or in heated patty shells or on buttered toasted English muffins.

SCALLOPED EGGS AND HAM

6 servings

> ⅓ *cup butter*
> ¼ *cup flour*
> 1 *teaspoon salt*
> ⅛ *teaspoon pepper*
> 2 *cups milk or 1 cup milk and 1 cup half*
> *and half*
> ½ *cup sliced mushrooms*
> 1 *cup diced cooked ham*
> ¼ *cup chopped green pepper (optional)*
> 2 *tablespoons diced pimiento*
> 8 *hard-cooked eggs, sliced*
> ¼ *cup slightly crushed corn flakes*

Melt ¼ cup butter in small heavy saucepan and stir in flour, salt, and pepper. Add milk or milk and half and half and cook, stirring constantly, until smooth and thickened. Blend in mushrooms, ham, green pepper, and pimiento. Layer eggs in a shallow 1½-quart baking dish. Pour sauce over all. Melt remaining butter, add crumbs, and coat evenly. Sprinkle crumbs around edge of baking dish. Bake in moderate oven (350° F.) for 25 minutes, or until hot and bubbly around edges.

EGGS ROBERTO

4 to 6 servings

¼   *cup butter*

4   *green onions (with 2 inches green tops),
      thinly sliced*

8   *eggs, beaten slightly*

¼   *pound shredded Provolone cheese*

3   *tablespoons shredded or grated
      Parmesan cheese*

8   *pitted black olives, sliced*

¾   *teaspoon salt*

⅛   *teaspoon pepper*

Melt butter in heavy fry pan and sauté onions until soft. Combine eggs with remaining ingredients and pour into fry pan. Cook over low heat until cheese melts and eggs are the desired degree of firmness, stirring the mixture frequently.

NOTE: *This dish may be prepared in a chafing dish over direct flame.*

PICKLED EGGS

12 eggs

Pickled eggs, also called "barroom" eggs, may have been one of the first forms of salad served in America. These were very popular in German or Scandinavian households.

3   *cups cider vinegar*

2   *cups water*

1   *medium onion, thinly sliced*

1   *tablespoon peppercorns*

1   *tablespoon whole allspice*

2   *teaspoons finely chopped ginger root
       (optional)*

1½   *teaspoons salt*

1   *teaspoon whole cloves*

3   *bay leaves*

12   *hard-cooked eggs, shelled*

Combine first 9 ingredients in saucepan. Bring to a boil, then lower heat and simmer gently for 8 to 10 minutes. Strain. Pack eggs in hot sterilized jars and pour in hot liquid. Seal jars. Cool, then refrigerate. Use in 4 or 5 days. Serve as salad or appetizer.

HEARTY WESTERN BREAKFAST

4 to 6 servings

Out West breakfast is often a hearty meal of bacon, eggs, and pan-fried potatoes.

¼   *cup butter*

3   *medium potatoes, peeled and diced*

2   *small onions, sliced and separated into
      rings*

1   *teaspoon salt*

⅛   *teaspoon pepper*

8   *eggs, slightly beaten*

3   *tablespoons half and half or milk*

⅓   *cup crisp bacon bits*

1   *tablespoon chopped parsley*

Melt butter in large heavy fry pan. Add potatoes, cover, and cook slowly until a light golden brown on underside. Add onion rings and cook until tender. Season with salt and pepper. Combine eggs and half and half or milk and pour over potato mixture. Cover and cook over low heat until eggs begin to set, stirring carefully during cooking. Sprinkle with bacon bits and parsley before serving. Cut into wedges and serve.

OMELETS

Rumor suggests that the omelet is named for its long flat shape, after the French word amelette. *Omelets make excellent brunch or late supper fare. A good omelet should be light and fluffy in texture and not overcooked, when it gets tough and rubbery. Practically anything can be used as a filling.*

PLAIN OMELET

4 servings

I often have to whip up omelets on the spur of the moment for lingering guests, for which reason I am considered queen of the omelets.

   8 *eggs*
   ¼ *cup milk or half and half*
   1 *teaspoon salt*
   ½ *teaspoon Worcestershire sauce*
   ⅛ *teaspoon pepper*
   2 *tablespoons butter*

Combine first 5 ingredients and beat well. In heavy 10-inch skillet with sloping sides, melt butter. Tilt and rotate pan to coat surface evenly. Pour egg mixture into skillet and cook over low heat until set. Run spatula around edge of pan during cooking. Lift omelet slightly to let uncooked egg flow underneath. Crease omelet in center, fold in half, and roll out onto heated serving platter.

VARIATIONS

Bacon or Ham Omelet: Add ½ to ¾ cup crisp cooked bacon bits or diced cooked ham.

Cheese Omelet: Add ½ to ⅔ cup shredded American, mozzarella, or Provolone cheese.

Fruit Omelet: Omit Worcestershire sauce. Add ½ to ¾ cup drained, canned, crushed pineapple, sliced peaches, apricots, or sweetened sliced fresh strawberries. Fold and sprinkle with confectioners' sugar.

Jelly Omelet: Omit Worcestershire sauce and add ½ cup jelly or preserves.

Mushroom and Onion Omelet: 1½ cups sliced fresh sautéed mushrooms and ½ to ¾ cup chopped green onion or scallions. Either or both may be used plus cheese.

Green Pepper: ½ to ¾ cup chopped and sautéed green pepper.

Tomato: 1 large tomato, peeled, chopped, and sautéed.

Greek: ½ to ¾ cup crumbled feta cheese plus tomato, green pepper, and onion.

PUFFY OMELET

4 servings

   6 *eggs, separated*
   ⅛ *teaspoon cream of tartar*
   ½ *teaspoon salt*
   ⅓ *cup milk*
   Dash of pepper
   1 *tablespoon butter*
   1 *tablespoon cooking oil*
   Strawberry or cherry preserves (optional)
   Confectioners' sugar (optional)

Combine egg whites, cream of tartar, and salt and beat at high speed until stiff peaks form. Beat egg yolks until thick and lemon-colored, adding milk and pepper gradually. Fold egg-yolk mixture into whites with wire whisk or rubber scraper, using an under-and-over motion. Heat heavy 10-inch skillet with sloping sides and heatproof handle.* When a few drops of water sprinkled over surface skitter and disappear quickly the pan is ready. Add butter and oil to pan, tilt, and rotate to spread evenly over surface. Spread egg mixture into skillet in even layer.

Cook without stirring over low heat for 8 to 10 minutes, or until browned on underside. Place in moderate oven (350° F.) for 10 to 12 minutes, or until omelet is firm when pressed gently with finger. Fold in half and turn onto heated serving platter. Serve plain or with strawberry or cherry preserves or sprinkled with confectioners' sugar.

SPANISH DINNER OMELET

4 to 6 servings

  2 *tablespoons butter*
  1 *tablespoon olive or cooking oil*
  ½ *cup coarsely chopped onion*
  1 *medium potato, diced*
  1 *pound fresh asparagus, washed and cut into 1-inch pieces**
  1 *teaspoon salt*
  ½ *pound fully cooked Spanish sausage or smoked pork sausage links, sliced ¼ inch thick*
  6 *eggs*
  ½ *cup milk*
  ½ *teaspoon paprika*
  ¼ *teaspoon pepper*
  2 *to 3 drops hot pepper sauce*

Combine butter and oil in heavy shallow 12-inch fry pan with sloping sides or Spanish omelet pan. Tilt and rotate to coat surface. Add onion, potato, and asparagus and sprinkle with ½ teaspoon salt. Cover pan and cook over low heat for 10 to 12 minutes, or until vegetables are almost tender. Add sausage and heat. Combine eggs, ½ teaspoon salt, and remaining ingredients. Beat slightly and pour over vegetables.

Cover and cook over very low heat for 10 to 12 minutes, or until eggs have set. Lift edges of omelet carefully with a spatula or knife during cooking to let uncooked egg mixture flow under omelet and cook. Cook until egg mixture is set. Do not fold. Cut into wedges and serve.

*1 (10-ounce) package defrosted frozen cut asparagus may be substituted.

SUNDAY-BRUNCH LOX AND EGGS

6 servings

Once a favorite delicacy in Jewish cuisine, lox, or smoked salmon, has become a weekend favorite with everyone.

  ½ *pound fresh mushrooms, sliced*
  ¾ *cup coarsely chopped onion*
  ½ *green pepper, seeded and chopped*
  ⅓ *cup butter*
  ½ *pound lox, finely diced*
  8 *eggs, beaten slightly*
  ¼ *cup light cream or half and half*
  2 *teaspoons chopped parsley*
  ¾ *teaspoon salt*
  ¼ *teaspoon basil*
  ⅛ *teaspoon pepper*
  Dash of hot pepper sauce

In large heavy skillet sauté mushrooms, onion, and green pepper in butter until mushrooms are almost tender, stirring frequently. Add lox and cook slightly. Combine the remaining ingredients and add to skillet. Cook over low heat, stirring constantly, until eggs are of firmness desired.

FAVORITE BRUNCH EGGS

6 servings

> 4 *to 6 slices bacon, diced*
> ¼ *cup butter*
> ¼ *cup flour*
> 1 *teaspoon salt*
> *Dash of pepper*
> 2 *cups milk*
> ⅔ *cup shredded Cheddar cheese*
> 6 *hard-cooked eggs, coarsely chopped*
> *Baking-powder biscuits, corn-bread squares, or English muffins*

Pan-fry bacon in heavy skillet until crisp and drain on paper toweling. Melt butter in heavy saucepan over moderate heat. Stir in flour, salt, and pepper. Add milk and cook until thickened, stirring constantly. Fold in cheese, stirring until melted. Fold in eggs and bacon and heat through. Serve on hot split biscuits, corn-bread squares, or toasted buttered English muffins.

SHIRRED EGGS GRUYÈRE

4 servings

Shirred or baked eggs cooked in a small casserole are one of the oldest known egg dishes.

> 2 *tablespoons butter, melted*
> 4 *slices Gruyère cheese*
> 4 *eggs*
> ¼ *teaspoon salt*
> *Dash of pepper*
> ¾ *cup Tomato Sauce (see index)*
> ¾ *cup shredded Gruyère cheese*

Divide butter equally among 4 individual shirred egg dishes or flat ramekins. Arrange a cheese slice in bottom of each dish. Break eggs, one at a time, into a small dish and then slide onto cheese slice. Sprinkle with salt and pepper. Spoon 3 tablespoons Tomato Sauce

around each egg and sprinkle 3 tablespoons shredded cheese over. Bake in moderate oven (375° F.) for 10 to 15 minutes, or until egg whites are firm.

EGGS FLORENTINE

6 servings

Eggs Florentine is an elegant dish to serve when special guests are coming to Sunday brunch. It consists of poached eggs on a bed of spinach with a cream sauce.

> ⅓ *cup butter*
> ¼ *cup flour*
> 1 *teaspoon salt*
> *Dash of cayenne pepper*
> 2 *cups milk or half and half*
> 2 *(10-ounce) packages frozen chopped spinach, cooked and drained thoroughly*
> 6 *poached eggs*
> ¼ *cup grated Parmesan cheese*
> ¼ *cup heavy cream, whipped*

In a small heavy saucepan melt butter over moderate heat and stir in flour, salt, and cayenne pepper. Add milk or half and half and cook, stirring constantly, until smooth and thickened. Cover and set aside. Divide spinach equally among 6 individual baking dishes or spread over the bottom of a shallow 1½-quart baking dish. Place an egg in each individual baker or 6 eggs in baking dish. Fold cheese and whipped cream into sauce. Pour sauce over eggs. Place in broiler 3 to 4 inches from heat until lightly browned and bubbly.

SHOWBOAT OYSTER SOUFFLÉ

6 servings

2 *(10-ounce) cans frozen oysters*
½ *cup chopped onion*
⅓ *cup butter*
½ *cup flour*
1½ *teaspoons salt*
½ *teaspoon paprika*
Dash of pepper
Dash of nutmeg
1 *cup milk*
4 *eggs, separated*
Creamy Lemon Sauce (see index)

Thaw oysters, drain, and reserve ½ cup liquor. Coarsely chop oysters. Sauté onion in butter until tender but not brown. Stir in flour, salt, paprika, pepper, and nutmeg. Add milk and reserved oyster liquor and cook until thickened, stirring constantly. Remove from heat. Beat egg yolks until thick and lemon-colored. Add egg yolks to hot mixture slowly, stirring constantly. Fold in oysters. Beat egg whites until they hold soft peaks. Carefully fold egg whites into oyster mixture. Pour into an ungreased 2-quart soufflé dish or deep casserole. Bake in slow oven (325° F.) for 60 to 70 minutes, or until soufflé is puffed, brown, and set. Serve with Creamy Lemon Sauce.

SKY-HIGH CHEESE SOUFFLÉ

6 servings

Soufflés are the *pièce de résistance* of egg cookery, but like "time and tide" they wait for no one.

⅓ *cup butter*
⅓ *cup flour*
1 *teaspoon salt*
½ *teaspoon paprika*
Dash of pepper
1½ *cups milk*
2 *cups (½ pound) shredded sharp American cheese*
1 *teaspoon Worcestershire sauce*
6 *eggs, separated*

Melt butter in heavy saucepan and stir in flour, salt, paprika, and pepper. Add milk and cook over low heat, stirring constantly, until sauce is smooth and thickened. Remove from heat. Add cheese gradually, stirring until cheese melts after each addition. Stir in Worcestershire sauce. Beat egg yolks until thick and light-colored. Stir a small amount of hot sauce into egg yolks, then add eggs to sauce slowly in a fine stream, beating constantly. Beat egg whites until they hold soft peaks. Carefully fold egg whites into sauce. Pour into ungreased 2-quart soufflé dish or round casserole. Run tip of knife about 1 inch deep around casserole 1 inch inside of edge. Set soufflé dish in pan of hot water. Bake in moderate oven (350° F.) for 1 hour, or until nicely browned, puffed, and fairly firm to touch or until a silver knife will come out clean when inserted in center of soufflé. Serve at once.

CHEESE FONDUE

The ingenious Swiss discovered that hardened bread could be made not only edible but also delicious when dipped in a combination of melted cheese and wine.

CHEDDAR FONDUE

    2 *pounds grated Cheddar cheese*
    2 *tablespoons cornstarch*
    ¼ *teaspoon dry mustard*
    1 *clove garlic, peeled and halved*
 1½ *cups sherry*
    2 *tablespoons Cherry Heering*
    1 *loaf French bread, cut into large pieces*
    2 *pounds cooked ham, cut into 1-inch cubes*

Blend cheese, cornstarch, and mustard together in bowl. Rub garlic around inside of ceramic or electric fondue pot. Pour in sherry and heat, but do not boil. Gradually add cheese mixture, stirring until completely melted. Cook until mixture begins to bubble, lower heat, and add liqueur. Keep the fondue hot but not boiling. If it becomes too thick, add more liqueur. Dip cubes of French bread and ham into the melted cheese.

NOTE: *Frankfurters, sausages, or salami, cut into 1-inch pieces, may be substituted for the ham.*

SWISS FONDUE

    5 *cups grated Swiss or Gruyère cheese*
    2 *tablespoons cornstarch*
    1 *garlic clove, peeled and halved*
 1½ *cups sauterne or dry white wine*
    3 *tablespoons kirsch*

Follow directions for Cheddar Fondue above.

CHEESE STRATA

6 to 8 servings

On those nights when the kids have friends visiting, this tasty layered casserole is a family favorite.

    2 *tablespoons butter*
   12 *slices firm white bread, crusts removed*
    2 *cups finely diced cooked ham*
    1 *bunch fresh broccoli, cooked, drained, and separated into spears, or 1 (10-ounce) package frozen spears, cooked and drained*
    2 *tablespoons finely chopped onion*
    1 *cup shredded Cheddar cheese*
    6 *eggs, beaten slightly*
 3½ *cups milk*
    1 *(11-ounce) can Cheddar cheese soup*
    ½ *teaspoon salt*
    ½ *teaspoon dry mustard*

Butter bread slices and cut into 1-inch cubes. Arrange half the bread in buttered 13 × 9 × 2-inch pan or shallow 3-quart casserole. Top with even layers of ham, broccoli, onion, and cheese. Top with remaining bread. Combine eggs, milk, soup, salt, and mustard. Pour over top, moistening bread pieces evenly. Bake in moderate oven (350° F.) for 1 hour, or until mixture is set. Let stand 10 to 15 minutes before serving.

MACARONI AND CHEESE WITH CANADIAN BACON

6 servings

Macaroni is said to have been named for an Italian who invented a tubular pasta-making machine.

1 *(7-ounce) package elbow macaroni*
⅓ *cup chopped onion*
2 *tablespoons chopped green pepper*
¼ *cup butter*
3 *tablespoons flour*
½ *teaspoon salt*
¼ *teaspoon paprika*
2 *cups milk*
1 *teaspoon prepared mustard*
2 *cups (½ pound) shredded American cheese*
1 *(7- or 8-ounce) package cooked Canadian bacon, sliced, or New England brand sausage, cut into bite-sized pieces*

Cook macaroni according to package directions, rinse in cold water, and drain thoroughly. In heavy saucepan sauté onion and green pepper in butter until tender but not brown. Blend in flour, salt, and paprika. Stir in milk and mustard. Lower heat and cook until thickened, stirring constantly. Remove from heat and stir in cheese and macaroni. Spread half the macaroni mixture over bottom of 1½-quart casserole and sprinkle with half the meat. Repeat. Cover casserole tightly with aluminum foil. Bake in moderate oven (350° F.) for 25 minutes, remove foil, and continue baking for 10 or 15 minutes longer, or until hot and bubbly.

TOMATO CHEESE PIE

6 servings

A special favorite of mine, Tomato Cheese Pie is very, very rich. It is an elegant dish to serve for a dinner party or buffet.

2 *or 3 tomatoes, sliced (10 slices)*
3 *tablespoons flour*
2 *tablespoons butter*
1 *cup dry, or well-drained, large-curd creamed cottage cheese*
1 *cup sour cream*
3 *eggs, slightly beaten*
¼ *cup thinly sliced green onion*
2 *tablespoons chopped parsley*
1 *teaspoon salt*
1 *teaspoon Worcestershire sauce*
½ *teaspoon basil*
4 *to 6 slices American cheese, cut into thirds*
1 *Unbaked (9-inch) Pie Shell (see index)*
⅓ *cup grated Parmesan cheese*

Dredge tomato slices in 2 tablespoons flour and brown lightly in butter, turning once. Drain and set aside. Combine remaining 1 tablespoon flour, cottage cheese, sour cream, eggs, green onion, parsley, salt, Worcestershire sauce, and basil. Arrange half the cheese slices over bottom of crust. Spoon in half the cottage-cheese mixture and cover with 5 tomato slices. Repeat with remaining cottage cheese and tomatoes. Top with remaining cheese slices and sprinkle with Parmesan cheese. Bake in moderate oven (350° F.) for 30 to 35 minutes, or until set. Cool on wire rack for 15 minutes before serving.

PASTA, NOODLES, AND GRAINS

CANNELLONI

8 to 10 servings

Noodle Squares (see below)

Savory Tomato Sauce (see below)

Beef and Vegetable Filling (see next column)

¼ *cup shredded or grated Parmesan Cheese*

NOODLE SQUARES   About 20 squares

2 *cups sifted flour*

½ *teaspoon salt*

3 *eggs, beaten*

2 *tablespoons water*

2 *tablespoons cooking oil*

Combine ingredients in order listed and blend thoroughly. Dough will be very stiff. Knead on floured board until smooth and shape into ball. Cover and let stand 30 minutes. Divide dough into 2 portions. Roll each as thin as possible and cut into 4-inch squares.

Cook squares in a large amount of boiling salted water with a tablespoonful of oil added for about 10 minutes. Remove with slotted spoon. Place on damp towels and cover with damp towels until ready to use.

NOTE: *Packaged manicotti may be substituted for Noodle Squares. Cook tubes as directed on box and stuff with filling.*

SAVORY TOMATO SAUCE   About 4 cups

1½ *cups chopped onion*

3 *tablespoons cooking or olive oil*

3 *(8-ounce) cans tomato sauce*

1 *cup dry red wine or tomato juice*

1 *teaspoon basil*

½ *teaspoon oregano*

½ *teaspoon leaf thyme*

½ *teaspoon salt*

Sauté onion in oil until tender but not brown. Add remaining ingredients and blend thoroughly. Cover and simmer for about 30 minutes until flavors are blended.

BEEF AND VEGETABLE FILLING   5 cups

1 *cup chopped celery*

1 *cup chopped carrot*

½ *cup chopped onion*

3 *tablespoons cooking or olive oil*

2 *pounds ground beef chuck or round steak*

1 *(8-ounce) can tomato sauce*

2 *teaspoons salt*

⅛ *teaspoon pepper*

½ *cup shredded or grated Parmesan cheese*

¼ *cup chopped parsley*

2 *eggs, beaten*

Sauté celery, carrot, and onion in oil until tender but not brown. Add meat and cook until crumbly. Add tomato sauce, salt, and pepper. Cover and cook slowly to blend flavors, about 30 minutes. Uncover and let any excess moisture evaporate. Cool slightly. Stir in cheese, parsley, and eggs.

PREPARATION

To assemble Cannelloni, spoon 3 tablespoonfuls of filling along one edge of Noodle Squares and roll up. Place, seam side down, one layer deep in two buttered shallow 2-quart casseroles. Divide sauce equally over rolls. Bake, covered, in moderate oven (350° F.) for 30 to 35 minutes, or until hot and bubbly. Serve in casseroles or arrange on heated serving dish. Just before serving, sprinkle with ¼ cup grated or shredded Parmesan cheese.

NOTE: *Beef and Vegetable Filling, Savory Tomato Sauce, and Noodle Squares may be prepared ahead of time. Refrigerate filling and sauce and arrange uncooked Noodle Squares on cookie sheet between sheets of waxed paper. Cover with plastic wrap and refrigerate. Cook just before using. Increase baking time to about 40 minutes.*

LASAGNE IMPERIAL

10 to 12 servings

   1 *(8-ounce) package lasagne noodles*

1½ *pounds ground beef*

 ¾ *cup chopped onion*

 ¾ *cup chopped green pepper*

  1 *(12-ounce) can plus 1 (6-ounce) can tomato paste*

2¼ *cups hot water*

  1 *cup plus 2 tablespoons red Burgundy wine*

1½ *teaspoons minced parsley*

  1 *tablespoon plus 1 teaspoon minced garlic*

  1 *tablespoon salt*

  1 *teaspoon oregano*

 ¾ *teaspoon basil*

 ¾ *teaspoon rosemary*

 ½ *teaspoon coarsely ground black pepper*

  3 *bay leaves, crumbled*

  3 *eggs, slightly beaten*

  1 *quart cottage cheese, drained*

  2 *(6-ounce) packages mozzarella cheese, sliced*

 ⅓ *to ½ cup grated Parmesan cheese*

Cook noodles in 3 quarts boiling salted water until tender, about 15 minutes, and drain. Brown meat, onion, and green pepper over low heat and drain off excess fat. Blend tomato paste, water, wine, and seasonings together in saucepan and bring to boil. Add meat mixture, simmer for 15 minutes, and set aside. Blend eggs with cottage cheese in bowl. Alternately layer half the meat sauce, noodles, and mozzarella cheese (ending with sauce) in a 9 × 13-inch baking dish. Top with cottage cheese–egg mixture. Layer remaining meat sauce, noodles, and mozzarella cheese (again ending with the sauce) and sprinkle top liberally with Parmesan cheese.

Bake in moderate oven (350° F.) for 45 to 50 minutes. Let lasagne stand for 10 to 15 minutes to set before cutting. Lasagne may be baked in advance and reheated, covered with foil, in 350° F. oven for 25 to 30 minutes.

RICE AND PILAF (PILAU)

Rice, which is a mainstay of Southern cooking, was first introduced to South Carolina in the latter 1600s by the captain of a ship sailing from Madagascar. The production of rice has been an important Southern industry ever since. Pilaf originated in the Middle East and consists of rice, onions, raisins, and spices to which meat, poultry, or vegetables are often added.

SAFFRON RICE

6 servings

Rice and saffron are natural companions, but remember that a small amount of the sharp, pungent saffron goes a long way.

 ½ *cup chopped onion*

  1 *small clove garlic, minced (optional)*

  3 *tablespoons butter or olive oil*

  1 *cup long-grain rice*

1½ *cups rich chicken broth or 1 (13¾-ounce) can*

  3 *tablespoons water or dry white wine*

  1 *teaspoon salt*

 ¼ *teaspoon saffron*

    Chopped parsley

Sauté onion and garlic in butter or olive oil until tender but not brown. Add rice. Stir in liquids, salt, and saffron and bring to a boil. Cover and cook over low heat for 15 to 20 minutes, or until liquid is absorbed and rice is tender. Sprinkle with chopped parsley.

SAVANNAH RED RICE
6 to 8 servings

In Georgia, red rice is served daily as an accompaniment to everything from fried chicken to spiced short ribs of beef.

 2 *cups long-grain rice*
 8 *to 10 slices bacon, diced*
 ½ *cup chopped onion*
 1 *(1-pound) can tomatoes or tomato wedges*
 ½ *teaspoon salt*
 ¼ *teaspoon pepper*
 3 *or 4 drops hot pepper sauce*

Cook rice according to package directions and set aside. Pan-fry bacon until crisp, drain, and reserve drippings. Sauté onion in drippings until tender, stirring often. Stir in rice, bacon, and remaining ingredients. Simmer for 10 minutes. Pour into 2-quart casserole. Bake, covered, in moderate oven (350° F.) for 30 minutes, stirring once or twice.

HOPPING JOHN
6 to 8 servings

In the South, Hopping John is traditionally served on New Year's Day to bring luck for the coming year. The name is thought to be derived from the custom of sending children hopping once around the table before the dish was served.

 4 *slices bacon, diced*
 1 *cup chopped onion*
 1 *cup long-grain rice*
 2 *cups water*
 1 *teaspoon salt*
 ¼ *teaspoon hot pepper sauce*
 1 *can (about 15 ounces) pinto or kidney beans or black-eyed peas, drained*

Pan-fry bacon and onion in heavy saucepan until onion is tender but not brown. Stir in rice, water, salt, and hot pepper sauce. Bring to a boil, cover, and cook over low heat for about 15 minutes, or until done. Stir in beans or peas, cover, and heat thoroughly.

CORNMEAL MUSH OR HASTY PUDDING
6 servings

A famous early New England dish, Hasty Pudding made its way to Ohio with pioneers. Below is a recipe written in 1848, followed by the modern method.

"Stir into a half pint of cold water, enough sifted Indian meal to make a thick batter. Have on the fire a pot containing three or four quarts of water; when it boils, pour in the batter, stirring it fast; let it boil a few minutes, then add sifted meal by the handful, till it is quite thick. Keep it boiling slowly, and stir it frequently; the more it is stirred, and the longer it is boiled, the better the pudding. To be wholesome, it must be boiled at least two hours. It should be taken up hot in bowls, and eaten with milk, or upon plates and eaten with butter and sugar, or molasses."

 1 *cup yellow cornmeal*
 1 *cup cold water*
 1½ *cups hot water*
 ½ *teaspoon salt*
 ¼ *cup butter (optional)*

Blend cornmeal and cold water. Combine hot water and salt in heavy saucepan and bring to a boil. Add cornmeal mixture slowly, stirring constantly. Cook, stirring, until thick and fully cooked, about 30 minutes. Stir in butter. Serve with finely shaved maple sugar or sorghum molasses and butter or sugar and cream.

NOTE: *Mixture may be cooked in the top of a double boiler over gently boiling water until fully cooked, 2½ to 3 hours.*

FRIED CORNMEAL MUSH
8 servings (16 slices)

A version of cornmeal mush was served at the first Thanksgiving in 1621.

    3 *cups hot water*
    1 *tablespoon sugar (optional)*
    1 *teaspoon salt*
1⅓ *cups cornmeal*
    1 *cup cold water*
    3 *to 4 tablespoons butter*
      Soft butter and syrup

Combine first 3 ingredients in heavy saucepan and bring to a boil. Mix 1 cup cornmeal and cold water and stir into boiling water a little at a time. Bring to a boil and cook until thickened, stirring often. Cover, turn heat to low, and cook for 5 minutes. Pour into a 9 × 5 × 3-inch loaf pan rinsed with cold water. Cool. Cover top with waxed paper and refrigerate overnight.

Remove mush from pan and cut into slices ½ inch thick. Dip slices in remaining ⅓ cup cornmeal. Fry until golden brown on both sides in butter. Serve hot with soft butter and syrup.

RICE PILAF
8 servings

    ½ *cup butter*
1½ *cups long-grain rice*
    ½ *cup diced celery*
    ¼ *cup chopped onion*
3¾ *cups chicken broth or 2 (13¾-ounce) cans*
    ¾ *cup seedless raisins*
1¼ *teaspoons salt*
    ½ *teaspoon sugar*
    ½ *cup coarsely chopped pecans*
    1 *tablespoon minced parsley*

Melt ¼ cup butter in large skillet, add rice, and brown lightly, stirring frequently. Mix in celery, onion, chicken broth, raisins, salt, and sugar.

Cover and cook over low heat for 15 to 20 minutes, or until rice is tender. Melt remaining butter and brown pecans, stirring constantly. Sprinkle nuts and parsley over rice before serving.

OYSTER PILAF
6 servings

    1 *cup diagonally sliced celery*
    ¼ *cup sliced green onion, with tops*
    ⅓ *cup butter*
    ¼ *pound fresh mushrooms, sliced*
    ½ *pint oysters, drained*
    ⅓ *cup dry white wine*
    3 *cups cooked rice*
    2 *tablespoons chopped parsley*
    1 *teaspoon salt*

Sauté celery and onion in butter until onion is tender. Add mushrooms and cook until tender. Add oysters and cook until edges curl. Add wine and heat until bubbling. Stir in rice, parsley, and salt and heat thoroughly.

WILD RICE MUSHROOM PILAF

10 to 12 servings

Wild rice is not technically a true rice but the seed of a tall aquatic grass that flourishes in the northern United States. It is a costly delicacy, but it makes a magnificent addition to any fowl dinner.

1 *(4-ounce) package wild rice*

1 *cup long-grain rice*

6 *slices bacon, diced*

1 *cup chopped onion*

½ *pound fresh mushrooms, sliced*

1 *cup chopped green pepper*

1 *teaspoon salt*

1 *teaspoon curry powder*

1 *(13¾-ounce) can chicken broth*

Cook both rices as directed on package label. Pan-fry bacon until crisp, drain, and reserve drippings. Sauté onion in bacon drippings until tender but not brown. Add mushrooms and green pepper and cook until mushrooms are tender and most of liquid has evaporated. Sprinkle with salt and curry powder. Combine rices, vegetables, and broth, mixing well. Spoon into buttered round 2-quart casserole. Cover and bake in moderate oven (350° F.) for 25 to 30 minutes. Serve with chicken, duck or turkey or in place of potatoes with any favorite entrée.

CHIPPEWA WILD RICE

4 to 6 servings

Wild rice was a basic food of the Indians living along the shores of the Great Lakes. It was of such importance that for over a hundred years the Sioux and Chippewas battled over rice-growing territories.

2½ *cups hot water*

1 *cup wild rice, washed in cold water*

1½ *teaspoons salt*

4 *slices bacon, diced*

6 *eggs*

¼ *teaspoon pepper*

2 *tablespoons minced chives*

⅓ *cup bacon drippings and butter, combined*

Combine water, rice, and 1 teaspoon salt in heavy saucepan, cover, and bring to a boil. Reduce heat and simmer, uncovered, until tender, about 30 minutes. Pan-fry bacon until crisp, drain, and reserve drippings.

Beat together lightly the eggs, remaining ½ teaspoon salt, and pepper. Pour into skillet in which bacon was cooked and brown eggs slightly. Turn carefully, as you would a pancake, and brown on second side.

When eggs are firm, cut into julienne strips. Lightly toss bacon, egg strips, chives, bacon drippings, plus melted butter, with rice. Serve hot as a main dish.

Combine water, salt, and garlic powder in saucepan and bring to a rapid boil. Add grits in a fine stream and cook, stirring constantly, for 2 to 2½ minutes, or until thick. While hot, stir in butter and cheese spread. Combine eggs and milk and stir into grits.

Pour into buttered 2-quart round casserole. Bake in moderate oven (350° F.) for 40 minutes. Sprinkle shredded Cheddar cheese and paprika over top of casserole 5 minutes before end of baking time.

GRITS

Hominy, or hulled corn, was originally an Indian food but became an important staple in the diet of the early pioneers. Coarse ground hominy or grits is still much appreciated in the South, where a typical breakfast might include eggs, grits, and country ham with red-eye gravy.

EASY CHEESE GRITS

8 servings

  3½ *cups water*
   1 *teaspoon salt*
  ¼ *teaspoon garlic powder*
   1 *cup quick-cooking white hominy grits*
  ¼ *cup butter*
   1 *(5-ounce) jar sharp cheese spread*
   2 *eggs, beaten slightly*
  ½ *cup milk*
  ¼ *cup shredded sharp Cheddar cheese*
Paprika

GRITS PILAF

6 servings

  4½ *cups water*
  ¾ *teaspoon salt*
   2 *chicken bouillon cubes*
   1 *cup regular white hominy grits*
  ½ *cup pecan halves, cut in half*
  ⅓ *cup butter*
   3 *cups diagonally sliced celery*
   1 *cup sliced fresh mushrooms*
  ½ *cup sliced green onion*

Combine water, salt, and bouillon cubes in large heavy saucepan and bring to a boil. Add grits in a fine stream, stirring constantly. Cover and cook slowly for 25 to 30 minutes or until thick, stirring occasionally.

Sauté pecans lightly in 1 tablespoon butter and set aside. Sauté celery, mushrooms, and onion in remaining butter for 5 minutes, or until celery is tender but still crisp. Stir vegetables and pecans into grits and heat through.

VARIATION

Quick Grits Pilaf: Follow above recipe and substitute quick-cooking for regular white hominy grits and reduce water to 3½ cups. Cook, uncovered, 2½ to 5 minutes.

BARLEY CASSEROLE

8 to 10 servings

Barley has been used in a variety of American dishes ever since the Pilgrims first sowed the seeds on the harsh shores of New England.

1 *cup medium barley*

¼ *cup butter*

1 *(13¾-ounce) can chicken broth*

¼ *cup sliced mushrooms*

1 *cup hot water*

¼ *cup sliced green onion*

2 *tablespoons chopped pimiento*

1 *teaspoon salt*

½ *cup sliced almonds*

In a heavy skillet, brown barley lightly in butter. Add chicken broth, mushrooms, water, onion, and pimiento and bring to a simmer. Pour into buttered round 1½-quart casserole. Cover and bake in moderate oven (350° F.) for 1¼ hours, or until barley is tender. Stir and serve.

FRIED OATMEAL SLICES

8 servings (16 slices)

4 *cups water*

2 *teaspoons salt*

4 *cups rolled oats, quick or regular, uncooked*

½ *cup finely chopped onion*

⅓ *cup butter*

4 *eggs, beaten slightly*

2 *cups fine bread or corn-flake crumbs*

Cooking oil for frying

Gravy or syrup and butter

Combine water and salt in a 3- or 4-quart heavy saucepan and bring to a boil. Stir in oats a few at a time. Reduce heat and cook, stirring frequently, until done. Sauté onion in butter until limp and stir into oat mixture. Combine 1 or 2 tablespoons hot mixture with eggs, mix well, and then stir eggs into remaining oats mixture.

Cook over low heat for 2 minutes, stirring constantly. Pour into greased 9 × 5 × 3-inch loaf pan lined with aluminum foil. Cool slightly, cover, and chill overnight. Cut into slices ½ inch thick and coat with crumbs. Pan-fry in heavy skillet until brown on both sides. Serve as a meat accompaniment with a gravy, or with syrup and butter.

CRISPY OATMEAL SLICES

6 servings

3 *cups boiling water*

1 *teaspoon salt*

2 *cups rolled oats, quick or regular, uncooked*

3 *to 4 tablespoons cooking oil*

Butter and syrup

Combine water and salt and bring to a rolling boil. Add oats in a fine stream, stirring constantly. Cook for 1 minute, stirring occasionally. Cover pan, remove from heat, and let stand for 5 minutes.

Pour into buttered loaf pan, cool, and cover. Refrigerate overnight. Slice ½ inch thick. Brown the slices on both sides in oil. Serve with butter and syrup.

PARSLEY DUMPLINGS

8 servings

The dumpling, traditionally associated with Central European cuisine, has been modified for American tastes and is an integral part of many regional specialties.

   2 *cups sifted flour*
   3 *teaspoons baking powder*
   1 *teaspoon salt*
   2 *teaspoons finely chopped parsley*
   3 *tablespoons butter, melted*
   1 *egg, beaten slightly*
   ½ *cup milk (approximate)*

Sift together first 3 ingredients. Stir in parsley, butter, egg, and milk. Batter should be stiff but moist. Add additional milk, if needed, a little at a time. Drop level tablespoonfuls of batter onto simmering mixture. Cover tightly and cook for 20 minutes.

GNOCCHI

8 servings

An Italian pasta with a French flavor, *Gnocchi* are small dumplings poached in boiling water and then garnished with cheese and butter.

   1 *cup sifted flour*
   ½ *teaspoon salt*
   ½ *teaspoon garlic salt*
   ¼ *teaspoon dry mustard*
   1 *cup water*
   ⅔ *cup butter*
   4 *eggs*
   ¼ *cup shredded or grated Parmesan cheese*

Combine first 4 ingredients. In heavy saucepan bring water and ½ cup butter to a boil. Add flour mixture all at once, stirring until mixture forms ball that does not separate. Remove from heat. Add eggs, one at a time, beating well after each addition.

Drop teaspoonfuls of mixture into boiling water. Cook about 5 minutes, keeping water boiling gently. Remove balls with slotted spoon and drain thoroughly. Place in shallow 2-quart baking dish. Melt remaining butter and pour over balls. Sprinkle with cheese. Broil 3 to 4 inches from heat source for 5 minutes.

MILWAUKEE-STYLE SPAETZLE

6 servings

Spaetzle, which means "little sparrow" in German, is a tiny light dumpling that is often served with goulash.

   3¼ *cups sifted flour*
   1 *teaspoon salt*
   ¼ *teaspoon nutmeg*
   ⅛ *teaspoon paprika (optional)*
   4 *eggs, beaten slightly*
   1 *cup milk (approximate)*
   2 *quarts boiling salted water*
   3 *to 4 tablespoons butter*
   Fine dry bread crumbs

Sift together first 4 ingredients into a bowl. Stir in eggs and gradually add milk to make a thick and smooth dough. Force mixture through a colander with large holes into boiling salted water. Boil for 5 minutes. Remove spaetzle with a slotted spoon and blanch with cold water. Drain thoroughly.

In a skillet, melt butter and cook spaetzle until golden brown, stirring often. Spoon into serving dish and sprinkle lightly with crumbs.

150

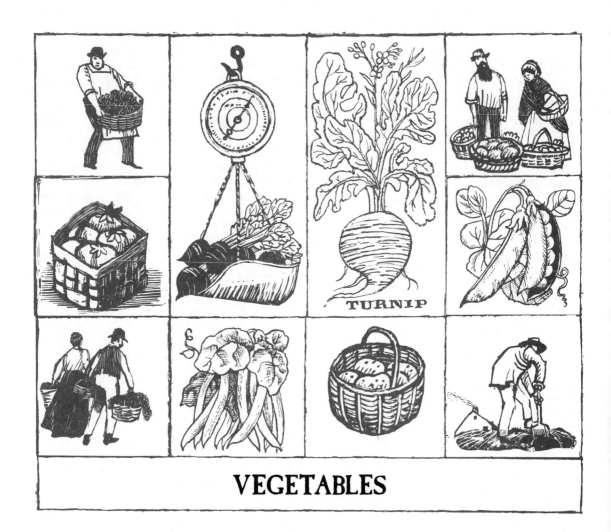

TURNIP

VEGETABLES

ASPARAGUS CASSEROLE IMPERIAL

8 to 10 servings

   4 *pounds fresh asparagus, washed and trimmed, or 4 (10-ounce) packages frozen asparagus spears*

   ½ *cup flour*

   ¾ *cup butter, melted (12 tablespoons)*

   1 *teaspoon Worcestershire sauce*

   ½ *teaspoon salt*

   ¼ *teaspoon pepper*

   4 *to 5 drops hot pepper sauce*

   3 *cups milk*

   1 *to 2 tablespoons sherry*

   1 *(8-ounce) can water chestnuts, drained and sliced*

   1 *tablespoon chopped pimiento*

   1 *cup bread or corn-flake crumbs*

Cook fresh asparagus spears for 5 to 10 minutes or partially cook frozen according to package directions *(do not overcook)*. Drain and set aside. In a medium saucepan blend flour, 6 tablespoons butter, Worcestershire sauce, salt, pepper, and hot pepper sauce, stirring until smooth. Gradually stir in milk and cook until mixture thickens.

Remove from heat and blend in sherry. Layer asparagus, water chestnuts, and sauce alternately in 9 × 12-inch baking dish. ending with the sauce. Sprinkle the top with pimiento. Combine crumbs and remaining 6 tablespoons butter and sprinkle over casserole. Bake in moderate oven (350° F.) for 25 to 30 minutes.

BOSTON BAKED BEANS

6 to 8 servings

Baked beans are a New England specialty. Pilgrims learned to bake a succulent pot of beans by putting them into a hole lined with hot stones. In Puritan colonies no work was done on the Sabbath, so women cooked the Sunday meal of baked beans slowly in brick fireplaces the day before. The beans improved in flavor as they waited.

Though it may seem as if every New England family has its own special recipe, there is almost universal agreement that the beans must be cooked with salt pork and sweetened with molasses and brown sugar.

   1 *pound (2½ cups) dried pea or navy beans*

   1 *teaspoon baking soda*

   ½ *cup light molasses*

   2 *tablespoons dark brown sugar*

   1 *teaspoon salt*

   ½ *teaspoon hot dry mustard*

   ½ *pound lean salt pork*

   1 *onion*

Wash and pick over beans, cover with cold water, and soak overnight in a covered container. In the morning, add baking soda to beans and soaking water and boil until tender and skins crack. Drain beans and turn into 2-quart bean pot or covered casserole. Combine molasses, sugar, salt, and mustard and stir into beans. Cut salt pork almost through rind at ½-inch intervals. Bury onion and salt pork in beans, leaving rind exposed slightly. Add hot water as needed to cover beans.

Cover and bake in slow oven (300° F.) until very tender, 3 to 4 hours. Add additional hot water if they become dry. Remove cover for last 45 minutes of cooking so the pork rind will become crisp and the beans brown.

VARIATIONS

Vermont Baked Beans: Substitute maple syrup for molasses.

Midwestern Baked Beans: Use Great Northern beans. Decrease molasses to ⅓ cup, increase brown sugar to ⅓ cup, firmly packed, salt to 2 teaspoons, and add ½ cup catsup or chili sauce. Omit salt pork and top beans with half slices of thick-sliced bacon 1 hour before end of baking time.

MOTHER'S BAKED BEANS

6 to 8 servings

  1 *pound (2½ cups) dried beans, Great Northern or navy*
  ½ *cup chopped onion*
  1 *cup light brown sugar, firmly packed*
  1 *(8-ounce) can tomato sauce*
  ½ *teaspoon salt*
  ½ *pound salt pork*

Sort and wash beans, put in large bowl, and add cold water to cover. Soak overnight. Drain, put into large saucepan, and cover with cold water. Bring to a boil, reduce heat, and simmer until tender, 1 to 1½ hours. Drain and reserve liquid.

Combine 1 cup reserved liquid and remaining ingredients except salt pork. Pour half the beans into 2-quart bean pot or covered casserole and stir in half the tomato mixture. Cut salt pork almost through rind at ½-inch intervals and place, rind side up, on beans. Cover with remaining beans and sauce.

Bake, covered, in slow oven (300° F.) for 2½ hours. Lift salt pork so rind is just above beans. Add reserved liquid as needed to keep beans juicy. Continue baking until beans are soft, 1 to 1½ hours. Remove cover during last 45 minutes of baking to crisp salt pork.

FRIJOLES REFRITOS
(Refried Beans)

6 servings

Southwesterners eat refried beans as others eat potatoes, either alone or as an accompaniment to other foods.

  1½ *cups dried pink or pinto beans or 1 (15-ounce) can kidney beans, drained*
   6 *cups water*
  ⅓ *cup bacon drippings or lard*
  ⅔ *cup finely chopped onion*
  ¾ *cup tomato sauce*
  1½ *teaspoons salt, or to taste*
  ¼ *teaspoon oregano*
     Hot pepper sauce to taste

Sort and wash beans. Turn into saucepan and cover with water. Bring to a boil and boil 2 minutes. Cover and let stand for 1 hour. Cook over moderate heat until beans are tender. Drain and reserve liquid.

Melt 3 tablespoons drippings or lard in skillet, add beans, and cook 10 to 12 minutes, mashing beans with fork or mallet. Add reserved bean liquid and cook slowly until liquid evaporates, stirring often. Sauté onion until tender in remaining drippings or lard, add tomato sauce, salt, and oregano, and heat. Stir into bean mixture. Add hot pepper sauce as desired.

TENNESSEE-STYLE GREEN BEANS

6 servings

  2 *pounds fresh green or snap beans*
  ¼ *pound salt pork*
  1 *small onion, sliced (optional)*
  1 *cup water*
  1 *teaspoon salt*
     Small piece dried red pepper pod

Wash, string, and break beans into 1- to 1½-inch pieces. Place beans in large heavy covered pot or Dutch oven. Top with salt pork, onion, water, salt, and pepper pod. Cover and bring to a simmer, reduce heat, and cook for 2 to 2½ hours, or until pork is completely tender. Add small amounts of water, as needed, during cooking. Remove pepper pod before serving.

GREEN BEAN CASSEROLE

6 to 8 servings

- 3 *cups julienned green beans or 2 (9-ounce) packages frozen French-cut*
- 2 *tablespoons butter*
- 1 *cup well-drained canned bean sprouts*
- 1 *(8-ounce) can water chestnuts, drained and sliced*
- 2 *tablespoons minced onion*
- 1 *(10½-ounce) can cream of mushroom soup*
- ⅔ *cup milk*
- ¾ *cup shredded sharp Cheddar cheese*
- 1 *(3½-ounce) can French-fried onions*

Cook beans in boiling salted water for 15 minutes or cook frozen green beans as directed on the package. Drain beans and set aside. Melt butter, add bean sprouts, water chestnuts, and onion. Cook, covered, for 3 to 4 minutes, or until onion is soft.

Arrange half the beans in buttered shallow 2½-quart casserole. Top with half the bean-sprout mixture. Combine soup and milk and spoon half over vegetables. Repeat layers of beans, sprouts, and soup. Sprinkle cheese over top and bake, uncovered, in a hot oven (400° F.) for 25 minutes. Remove from oven and cover with onion rings. Return to oven for 5 minutes longer.

MRS. HOWARD'S BAKED CABBAGE

6 servings

I discovered this delectable vegetable dish at a quaint boardinghouse in Rowlesburg, West Virginia.

- 1 *pound cabbage, coarsely shredded (about 7 cups)*
- 1 *teaspoon salt*
- 2 *tablespoons butter*
- 2 *tablespoons flour*

Dash of pepper

- 1¼ *cups milk*
- 1 *teaspoon prepared mustard*
- ½ *cup shredded American cheese (or combination of American and Longhorn cheese)*
- 2 *tablespoons fine corn-flake crumbs*

Cook cabbage in small amount of boiling water for 8 to 10 minutes or just until tender. Drain. Sprinkle with ½ teaspoon salt. Melt butter and stir in flour, remaining ½ teaspoon salt, and pepper. Add milk and mustard and cook until thickened, stirring constantly.

Combine cabbage, sauce, and half the cheese. Spoon into buttered round 1-quart casserole. Sprinkle with remaining cheese mixed with crumbs. Bake in moderate oven (350° F.) for 20 to 25 minutes, or until hot and bubbly.

SWEET AND SOUR RED CABBAGE

6 to 8 servings

Sweet and sour red cabbage has been a favored vegetable dish with German-Americans for many years.

2 *medium tart apples, peeled and sliced*
¼ *cup bacon drippings or butter*
1 *head red cabbage (about 2 pounds), shredded*
¾ *cup water*
½ *cup vinegar*
½ *cup sugar*
1 *tablespoon quick-cooking tapioca*
1 *tablespoon salt*
½ *teaspoon caraway seeds*

Sauté apple slices in bacon drippings or butter until tender. Mix in cabbage. Combine remaining ingredients, stir into cabbage, and heat until bubbling. Cover and cook over low heat for 45 minutes, or until cabbage is of desired tenderness.

MINTED GLAZED CARROTS

6 servings

Carrots originated in the Orient, were introduced into England during the reign of Queen Elizabeth I, and made their way to the colonies in the 1600s.

12 *carrots, peeled*
¼ *cup honey*
¼ *cup butter*
½ *teaspoon salt*
2 *teaspoons finely chopped fresh mint leaves or 1 teaspoon dried*

Cook carrots in boiling salted water until tender (time will depend on the size), then drain. Combine next 3 ingredients in heavy skillet and cook until hot and thoroughly blended, stirring constantly. Add carrots and simmer until glazed, turning as needed. Transfer to serving dish and sprinkle with mint.

CARROT PUDDING

6 servings

Both Indians and colonists used this tasty and easily stored vegetable throughout the winter.

1 *pound carrots, peeled and chopped*
½ *cup chopped onion*
½ *cup water*
2 *tablespoons butter*
¼ *cup chopped celery*
3 *eggs*
1½ *cups milk*
2 *cups soft bread crumbs*
1½ *teaspoons salt*

Combine carrots, onion, water, and butter in saucepan. Bring to a boil, cover, and cook for 15 minutes, or until carrots are tender. Uncover to allow excess moisture to evaporate. Mash carrots with fork. Stir in celery. Combine eggs and milk and beat well. Mix in bread crumbs and salt. Stir in vegetables. Pour into greased round 1½-quart casserole. Bake in moderate oven (350° F.) for 50 to 60 minutes, or until mixture is set.

CAULIFLOWER SCALLOP
6 to 8 servings

Mark Twain once referred to cauliflower as "cabbage with a college education."

1 *large head cauliflower, separated into flowerets*

½ *cup thinly sliced celery*

¼ *cup diced green pepper*

8 *tablespoons butter*

¼ *cup flour*

1½ *teaspoons salt*

¼ *teaspoon pepper*

2½ *cups milk*

2 *cups shelled fresh peas, or 1 (10-ounce) package frozen, defrosted and separated*

1½ *cups shredded sharp Cheddar cheese*

24 *small white onions, peeled and partially cooked, or 1 (16-ounce) jar whole boiled onions, drained*

⅔ *cup slightly crushed corn or whole-wheat flakes*

Cook flowerets until tender in boiling salted water, drain, and set aside. Sauté celery and green pepper in 4 tablespoons butter until tender but not brown, stirring frequently. Stir in flour, salt, and pepper. Add milk and cook until thickened, stirring constantly. Fold in peas and cheese. Combine sauce, onions, and flowerets, mixing carefully. Turn into shallow 2-quart casserole. Melt remaining 4 tablespoons butter, combine with cereal crumbs, and sprinkle over the top. Place in hot oven (400° F.) for 20 to 25 minutes, or until hot and bubbly.

GREAT PLAINS CELERY BAKE
6 servings

4 *cups thinly sliced celery*

8 *tablespoons butter*

⅓ *cup chopped green pepper*

2 *tablespoons flour*

1 *teaspoon salt*

½ *teaspoon paprika*

⅛ *teaspoon pepper*

1½ *cups milk*

1 *cup (¼ pound) shredded American cheese*

½ *cup sliced almonds*

1 *cup coarse cracker crumbs*

Sauté celery in 6 tablespoons butter until tender but not brown. Stir in green pepper, flour, salt, paprika, and pepper. Add milk and cook until thickened, stirring constantly. Stir in cheese and almonds.

Pour into buttered shallow rectangular 1½-quart baking dish. Melt remaining 2 tablespoons butter and evenly coat cracker crumbs. Sprinkle over top of celery mixture. Bake in moderate oven (350° F.) for 20 minutes.

ROASTED CORN ON THE COB
6 servings

12 *ears of corn, in husks*

6 *to 8 quarts water*

Butter

Salt and pepper (to taste)

Soak ears of corn, husks on, in large container of water for several hours. Wrap each ear in small sheet of heavy-duty aluminum foil and seal tightly. Roast on grill over coals for 45 minutes or until done. Turn frequently with tongs so as not to burn corn. Remove foil and husks and serve with butter, salt and pepper.

COUNTRY-STYLE FRESH CORN

6 servings

     6 *large ears of corn*
  1¼ *teaspoons salt*
     2 *tablespoons water*
     ¾ *cup half and half or milk*
     4 *tablespoons butter*
     ⅛ *teaspoon white pepper, or to taste*
     2 *teaspoons minced parsley (optional)*

Cut kernels from ears of corn, using a very sharp knife (this will make about 4 cups). Spread in oblong 1½-quart baking dish. Add salt and water. Cover dish with foil and bake in moderate oven (350° F.) for 30 minutes. Combine half and half and 2 tablespoons butter and cook until butter melts. Pour over corn and sprinkle with pepper. Return to oven for 10 minutes. Just before serving, dot with remaining 2 tablespoons butter and sprinkle with parsley.

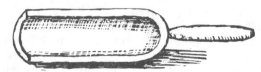

MUSHROOMS IN SOUR CREAM

6 to 8 servings

     1 *pound medium-sized mushrooms, halved*
     ½ *cup sliced green onion with 2 inches of top*
     ¼ *cup butter*
     1 *teaspoon flour*
     ½ *teaspoon salt*
     ½ *teaspoon basil*
     Dash of pepper
     2 *teaspoons lemon juice or 1 tablespoon dry sherry*
     ½ *cup sour cream*
     2 *tablespoons chopped pimiento*

Sauté mushrooms and green onion in butter until mushrooms are tender and most of the liquid has evaporated. Sprinkle with flour, salt, basil, pepper, and lemon juice or sherry and blend thoroughly. Stir in sour cream and pimiento and heat through. Serve at once.

OKRA AND TOMATOES

6 servings

A classic Southern dish, Okra and Tomatoes has gained in popularity throughout the country since frozen okra became readily available in supermarkets.

     1 *cup sliced onion*
     2 *tablespoons butter*
     1 *tablespoon flour*
     1 *pound fresh okra, stemmed, washed, and cut into ½-inch slices, or 1 (10-ounce) package frozen, cut into ½-inch slices*
     1 *(1-pound) can tomato wedges, undrained*
     ½ *teaspoon sugar*
     ½ *teaspoon salt*
     Dash of pepper
     6 *to 8 drops hot pepper sauce*

Sauté onion in butter until tender but not brown. Stir in flour. Add remaining ingredients, cover, and simmer for 8 to 10 minutes, or just until okra is tender.

WILLIAMSBURG CREAMED ONIONS

6 servings

Early American settlers found onions to be a hardy native crop and used them to enhance the flavor of many dishes. Colonial Williamsburg was famed for its good food, and one of the popular recipes was for creamed onions, adapted here for modern use.

- 1½ *pounds small white onions, peeled, or 3 (1-pound) jars, drained*
- 4 *tablespoons butter*
- 3 *tablespoons flour*
- ½ *teaspoon salt*
- ⅛ *teaspoon white pepper*
- ⅛ *teaspoon leaf thyme, basil, or fines herbes*
- 1½ *cups milk or ½ cup milk and 1 cup half and half*
- ¼ *cup finely crushed corn flakes*

   Pimiento diamonds (optional)

Cook fresh onions in boiling salted water for 15 to 20 minutes and drain. Melt 3 tablespoons butter and stir in flour, salt, pepper, and thyme. Add milk and cook over low heat until thickened, stirring constantly. Mix in onions and pour into heated serving dish.

Melt remaining 1 tablespoon butter and brown corn-flake crumbs slightly. Sprinkle crumbs around edge of serving dish. Arrange pimiento diamonds in center of dish. Bake in moderate oven (350° F.) for 20 to 25 minutes.

GLAZED PARSNIPS

6 servings

Parsnips are a much neglected vegetable. Similar to turnips, parsnips sweeten a pot of soup or stew.

- 8 *medium parsnips, peeled*
- ¼ *cup butter*
- ¼ *cup honey*
- 2 *teaspoons minced parsley (optional)*

Slice parsnips lengthwise into thin strips, then crosswise into 1½- to 2-inch lengths. Cook, covered, in boiling salted water for 25 to 30 minutes, or until tender. Drain. Combine butter and honey and heat. Add parsnips and cook over low heat for 4 to 5 minutes, or until parsnips are hot and glazed. Turn into serving dish and sprinkle with parsley.

CONFEDERATE BLACK-EYED PEAS

8 servings

- 1 *(1-pound) package black-eyed peas*
- 6½ *to 7 cups water*
- ½ *cup salt pork, diced*
- 2 *tablespoons bacon drippings*
- 2 *tablespoons chopped green onion*
- 1 *tablespoon Worcestershire sauce*
- ½ *teaspoon salt*
- ¼ *teaspoon pepper*
- 4 *to 5 drops hot pepper sauce or ⅛ teaspoon cayenne pepper*

Wash black-eyed peas, drain thoroughly, and combine with 6 cups water, salt pork, bacon drippings, onion, and seasonings in large kettle. Bring to a boil, then reduce heat and simmer for 2 to 2½ hours, or until tender. Add ½ to 1 cup additional water, as needed, to prevent beans from sticking. Remove salt pork before serving, if desired.

FRESH PEAS WITH MINT

4 servings

- ¼ cup thinly sliced green onion
- 3 tablespoons butter
- 2 cups shelled fresh peas (about 2 pounds in the pod)
- ¼ cup water (approximate)
- 1 to 2 teaspoons chopped fresh mint (or to taste)
- ½ teaspoon sugar
- ¼ teaspoon salt
- ¼ teaspoon rosemary (optional)

Sauté onion in 1 tablespoon butter until tender but not brown. Add peas and remaining ingredients except butter. Cover and simmer until peas are tender but still slightly crisp, 8 to 10 minutes. Add additional water, if needed. Add remaining 2 tablespoons butter and toss until melted.

NOTE: *1 (10-ounce) package defrosted frozen peas may be substituted for fresh, if onion and water are reduced to 3 tablespoons each and butter to 2 tablespoons. Cooking time will be about 5 to 8 minutes, or just until tender.*

SCALLOPED POTATOES

6 servings

- 4 medium potatoes, peeled and thinly sliced (about 4 cups)
- 1 onion, thinly sliced
- 3 tablespoons flour
- 1 teaspoon salt
- ⅛ teaspoon pepper
- 3 tablespoons butter
- 1½ to 2 cups milk

Spread a third of the potatoes and onion in buttered 2-quart casserole. Sprinkle with half the flour, salt, and pepper and dot with 1 tablespoon butter. Cover with half the remaining potatoes and onion. Sprinkle with remaining flour, salt, and pepper and dot with 1 tablespoon butter. Cover with potatoes and onion. Pour milk over potatoes until barely covered and dot with 1 tablespoon remaining butter. Bake, covered, in moderate oven (350° F.) for 1 hour. Uncover and bake for 20 to 30 minutes longer.

MAINE FISHERMAN POTATOES AU GRATIN

6 servings

- 2 tablespoons chopped onion
- 2 tablespoons oil
- 2 tablespoons flour
- 1 teaspoon salt
- Dash of pepper
- 2 cups milk
- 1 cup shredded Cheddar cheese
- 2 teaspoons Worcestershire sauce
- 6 large potatoes, peeled, cooked, and sliced (5 cups)
- 2 (3¾- or 4-ounce) cans Maine sardines, drained
- ¾ cup soft bread cubes
- 2 tablespoons butter, melted
- Paprika

Sauté onion in oil until tender and blend in flour and seasonings. Add milk gradually and cook, stirring constantly, until thickened. Add cheese and Worcestershire sauce, stirring until cheese melts. Arrange half the potatoes in a greased 1½-quart casserole. Cover with sardines and remaining potatoes. Pour sauce over potatoes. Toss bread cubes with butter and scatter over top. Sprinkle with paprika. Bake in a moderate oven (350° F.) for 25 to 30 minutes, or until lightly browned.

RUTABAGAS WITH LEMON BUTTER
4 servings

Rutabagas are often called Swedish turnips. They have been served by my family for many years, especially at holiday time.

2 *pounds rutabagas, peeled and cut into thin slices (about 4 cups)*

1½ *teaspoons salt*

⅓ *cup butter*

2 *teaspoons lemon juice*

¼ *teaspoon dill weed*

Cook rutabagas, covered, in boiling water with 1 teaspoon salt for 20 minutes, or until tender. Drain thoroughly. Melt butter in small saucepan, remove from heat, and stir in remaining ½ teaspoon salt, lemon juice, and dill weed. Pour over rutabagas, mix, and serve.

SPINACH SOUFFLÉ
8 servings

2½ *cups well-drained cooked spinach*

¼ *cup chopped onion*

¼ *cup butter*

¼ *cup flour*

1¼ *teaspoons salt*

⅛ *teaspoon pepper*

1½ *cups milk*

3 *eggs, separated*

2 *tablespoons lemon juice*
Hollandaise Sauce (see index)

Put spinach through a food mill or chop finely in blender. Sauté onion in butter until just tender. Stir in flour, salt, and pepper. Add milk and cook until smooth and thickened, stirring constantly. Stir a small amount of sauce into beaten egg yolks. Stir egg-yolk mixture, spinach, and lemon juice into remaining sauce. Beat egg whites until soft peaks form. Carefully fold whites into spinach mixture.

Pour into ungreased 1½-quart soufflé dish or round casserole. Set in pan of hot water and bake in moderate oven (375° F.) for 35 to 40 minutes. A silver knife inserted in center will come out clean when soufflé is done. Serve at once with Hollandaise Sauce.

BAKED ACORN SQUASH
4 servings

2 *acorn squash (about 3 pounds)*

¼ *cup butter*

¼ *cup light brown sugar, firmly packed*

¼ *cup dry sherry or orange juice*

½ *teaspoon salt*

Wash squash, cut in half lengthwise, and scoop out seeds and string portion. Place, cut side up, in small shallow baking pan. Add 1 tablespoon butter, 1 tablespoon sugar, 1 tablespoon sherry or juice, and ⅛ teaspoon salt in each half. Cover pan tightly with foil. Bake in moderate oven (350° F.) for 1 hour. Remove foil and baste edges of squash with liquid in centers. Bake for 10 to 12 minutes, or until tender and nicely browned.

SUMMER SQUASH SKILLET

6 servings

Called *askoot-asquash*, meaning "green things eaten green," squash is believed to be one of the first foods cultivated by the Indians. The Pilgrims, stumbling over the pronunciation, shortened the name to squash.

2 *crookneck squash (about ¾ pound), unpeeled*

2 *zucchini (about ½ pound), unpeeled*

4 *slices bacon, diced*

⅓ *cup sliced green onion with 2 inches of top*

¾ *teaspoon salt (or to taste)*

¼ *teaspoon curry powder*

2 *tablespoons water (approximate)*

Wash squash, trim off ends, and slice ¼ inch thick. Pan-fry bacon pieces until crisp, remove, and set aside. Add squash and onion to drippings and stir carefully to coat. Sprinkle with salt and curry powder. Add water.

Simmer, covered, for 8 to 10 minutes, or until squash is just tender. Add more water, if needed, to prevent browning. Sprinkle with bacon pieces.

ORANGE-GLAZED SWEET POTATOES

8 servings

6 *sweet potatoes or yams (about 3 pounds)*

1 *cup light corn syrup*

1 *cup sugar*

1 *cup orange juice*

2 *tablespoons grated orange peel*

2 *tablespoons butter*

1 *teaspoon salt*

⅓ *cup toasted slivered or sliced almonds (optional)*

Wash the sweet potatoes but do not peel. Boil in water to cover just until tender, about 15 to 20 minutes. Drain, cool, peel, and slice in half lengthwise. Combine the next 6 ingredients in large heavy skillet, bring to a boil, stirring constantly, and simmer for 5 minutes. Add sweet potatoes and baste with syrup. Cook for 10 to 12 minutes, turning potatoes to glaze evenly. Transfer to serving dish and spoon glaze over potatoes. Sprinkle with toasted almonds just before serving.

NOTE: *Do not overcook potatoes before glazing. They must be tender but not mushy.*

BLUEGRASS SWEET POTATOES

8 servings

2 *(1-pound 1-ounce) cans vacuum-packed sweet potatoes or yams*

⅔ *cup sugar*

⅓ *cup butter*

¼ *cup bourbon whisky or orange juice*

1 *teaspoon salt*

½ *teaspoon vanilla*

1½ *cups miniature marshmallows*

Turn potatoes into heavy saucepan, cover, and cook over moderate heat for 10 to 15 minutes, stirring often. Combine potatoes and next 5 ingredients in large mixer bowl and beat until smooth. Turn into buttered shallow 1½-quart casserole and arrange marshmallows over the top. Bake in moderate oven (350° F.) for 25 to 30 minutes, or until potatoes are hot and marshmallows evenly browned.

BAKED GARLIC TOMATOES

8 servings

¼ *cup butter, melted*

½ *cup fine bread crumbs*

1 *tablespoon shredded or grated Parmesan cheese*

3 *small cloves garlic, minced*

1 *tablespoon Worcestershire sauce*

1 *teaspoon chopped fresh parsley*

½ *teaspoon salt*

⅛ *teaspoon pepper*

4 *medium tomatoes, washed and cut in half crosswise*

Combine first 8 ingredients. Arrange tomatoes on baking pan. Divide crumb mixture equally among tomatoes and pack down firmly. Bake in moderate oven (350° F.) for 15 to 20 minutes, or until tomatoes are tender. Broil 6 inches from heat source for 3 minutes, or until tops are crisp and lightly browned.

DIXIE FRIED TOMATOES

4 to 6 servings

3 *green tomatoes*

½ *cup flour*

½ *cup bacon drippings*

½ *teaspoon salt*

¼ *teaspoon pepper*

¼ *teaspoon sugar*

Wash tomatoes, cut into ⅛-inch slices, and dredge in flour. Heat bacon drippings in large skillet until very hot. Add tomatoes and sprinkle with half the salt, pepper, and sugar. Pan-fry until crisp and golden. Turn, sprinkle remaining salt, pepper, and sugar, and continue pan-frying until slices are crispy-crusted and golden brown.

NOTE: *The traditional method of preparation is to use green tomatoes or those just about to turn. However, ripe tomatoes may be substituted with equal success. This was one of the first dishes my Southern husband asked me, a Yankee, to learn.*

SWEET-POTATO SOUFFLÉ

6 servings

1 *(1 ½-pound) can sweet potatoes, drained*

1 *cup milk*

2 *tablespoons butter*

2 *tablespoons brown sugar*

2 *tablespoons maple syrup*

½ *teaspoon salt*

3 *eggs, separated*

½ *teaspoon nutmeg*

½ *teaspoon cinnamon*

¼ *teaspoon ground cloves*

½ *cup raisins*

½ *cup walnuts*

1 *(11-ounce) can mandarin oranges, drained*

15 *marshmallows (optional)*

Mash sweet potatoes and set aside. In a saucepan, scald milk with butter, sugar, syrup, and salt, blend into potatoes, and beat with electric mixer at medium speed. Beat egg yolks until light and fluffy and blend into potato mixture. Stir in seasonings. Fold in raisins, nuts, and oranges. Beat egg whites until stiff peaks form and fold into mixture. Spoon into 1½-quart casserole. Top with marshmallows. Bake in slow oven (325° F.) for 45 minutes, or until set.

SOUTHERN-STYLE TURNIP GREENS

4 servings

   1 *pound fresh turnip greens*
   ¼ *pound salt pork, or ¼ pound slab bacon, diced*
   2 *to 2½ cups water (approximate)*
   1 *teaspoon chopped onion (optional)*
   ½ *teaspoon salt*
   ¼ *teaspoon pepper*
   Few grains cayenne (optional)

Rinse turnip greens thoroughly three times in cold water and drain thoroughly after each rinsing. Combine salt pork and 2 cups water in saucepan. Bring to a boil, then reduce heat and simmer for 1 hour. Add greens, onion, and seasonings. Cook over medium heat for 30 to 45 minutes, or until tender. Add additional water, as needed, to prevent burning. Bacon or salt pork may be removed before serving.

DIXIE-STYLE YAMS

4 servings

   1 *(17-ounce) can yams*
   1 *cup light brown sugar, firmly packed*
   ⅓ *cup melted butter*
   1 *tablespoon dry sherry (optional)*
   1 *cup broken pecan pieces*

Drain yams and reserve ½ cup liquid. Combine brown sugar, yam liquid, butter, and sherry in large skillet and simmer, stirring, until well blended. Add yams and pecans. Cover and cook over low heat for 30 to 35 minutes, turning yams frequently.

GARDEN-PATCH ZUCCHINI

6 servings

   ½ *cup thinly sliced green onions*
   ¼ *cup butter*
   2 *or 3 zucchini, sliced (2 cups)*
   4 *cups fresh corn kernels (about 6 ears)*
   2 *small tomatoes, peeled and diced*
   1½ *teaspoons salt*
   ⅛ *teaspoon pepper*

Sauté onion in butter until limp but not brown. Stir in zucchini and corn. Cook for 8 to 10 minutes, or until zucchini is tender and corn cooked, stirring occasionally. Stir in tomatoes, salt, and pepper, heat, and serve.

ZUCCHINI FRITTATA

4 to 6 servings

One of the best known of the squash family, zucchini can be prepared in an infinite variety of ways. This zucchini omelet makes a perfect supper dish for a hot summer evening.

   8 *(4-inch) zucchini, peeled and cut into ¼-inch slices*
   2 *tablespoons olive oil*
   3 *tablespoons butter*
   8 *eggs*
   1 *teaspoon salt*
   Dash of pepper
   ¼ *cup shredded or grated Parmesan cheese*

In a heavy skillet with heatproof handle, sauté zucchini in oil and butter until tender. Combine eggs, salt, and pepper, heat slightly, and pour over zucchini. Cook just until eggs are set.

Sprinkle cheese over top and broil 4 inches from heat source until cheese is lightly browned. Let stand a few minutes, cut into wedges, and serve.

NOTE: *To heatproof a handle, cover completely with 2 or 3 layers of aluminum foil.*

SALADS AND SALAD DRESSINGS

SALADS

The first salads were edible herbs or plants flavored with salt, and the word salad *comes from the Latin* sal, *meaning salt. American salads tend to be a combination of a variety of foods, as opposed to the simple greens usually served in France. Salads did not become popular until the latter part of the nineteenth century.*

SUMMER GARDEN BOWL

8 to 10 servings

- ½ *head iceberg lettuce*
- ½ *head curly endive*
- ½ *head Boston or leaf lettuce*
- ½ *head Bibb lettuce or ½ bunch fresh spinach*
- 2 *cups cubed fully cooked ham*
- 6 *slices cooked bacon, crumbled*
- 1 *small onion, sliced in rings*
- ½ *to ¾ cup sliced stuffed green or pitted black olives*
- 1 *tablespoon capers (optional)*
- ⅓ *to ½ cup grated or shredded Parmesan cheese*
- ⅓ *to ½ cup Burgundy Vinaigrette Dressing (see index)*

Wash, drain, and tear greens into bite-sized pieces. Combine all ingredients, except dressing, in salad bowl, reserving 2 or 3 tablespoons cheese. Toss, add dressing, and toss again. Sprinkle with remaining cheese.

ASPARAGUS VINAIGRETTE

4 to 6 servings

Discovered and named by the ancient Greeks, asparagus is a vegetable that is universally liked. Early American colonists found that it thrived in the sandy soils of the Middle Atlantic region.

- 2 *pounds asparagus or 4 (10-ounce) packages frozen*
- ½ *cup salad oil*
- ½ *cup cider vinegar*
- ¼ *cup water*
- 1 *tablespoon sugar*
- 1½ *teaspoons salt*
- 3 *tablespoons sweet pickle relish*
- *Salad greens (optional)*
- *Mayonnaise (optional)*

Clean fresh asparagus and simmer in salted water for 10 to 15 minutes. Cook frozen according to package directions. Cool without draining. Combine oil, vinegar, water, sugar, and salt, stirring until sugar is dissolved. Add pickle relish and mix. Drain asparagus. Arrange a layer of asparagus spears in flat dish. Cover with vinegar-oil mixture. Repeat process until all asparagus is used. Cover and refrigerate for several hours. Serve asparagus in marinade or drain and serve spears on crisp salad greens with mayonnaise.

MOUNT VERNON SALAD

6 to 8 servings

Many early Virginia planters, including George Washington, considered artichokes a delicacy and grew them in greenhouses.

- 1 *(14-ounce) can whole artichoke hearts, drained and chilled*
- 1 *pound fresh asparagus or 2 (10-ounce) packages frozen, cooked, drained, and chilled*
- 4 *cups torn mixed salad greens*
- *Burgundy Vinaigrette Dressing (see index)*

Cut artichoke hearts into halves or quarters and asparagus spears into 1-inch pieces. Combine with salad greens in bowl. Add dressing and toss until greens are well coated.

VEGETABLE MEDLEY MARINADE

8 to 10 servings

2 *large ripe tomatoes*

2 *cucumbers, peeled*

1 *large Spanish onion, peeled*

1 *large zucchini*

2 *medium green peppers*

1 *cup vinaigrette dressing*

Basil

Mixed herbs or Italian seasoning

Pitted ripe olives

Fresh parsley

Thinly slice tomatoes, cucumbers, onion, and zucchini, separating onion into rings. Cut top from peppers, scoop out seeds, and slice. In a large bowl, layer half the vegetables. Pour ¼ cup dressing over mixture and sprinkle with seasonings. Layer remaining vegetables and add ½ cup dressing. Sprinkle with seasonings. Refrigerate for several hours. Just before serving, add more dressing and garnish with ripe olives and parsley.

WILTED LETTUCE

4 servings

Wilted lettuce is possibly a Southern creation that made its way westward with the covered wagons and is now a favorite in the Midwest and Plains States.

3 *large heads leaf lettuce*

4 *slices bacon, diced*

1 *small red or white onion, thinly sliced*

⅓ *cup cider vinegar*

3 *tablespoons sugar*

¼ *teaspoon salt*

Dash of pepper

1 *hard-cooked egg, chopped*

Wash and dry lettuce and tear into large bite-sized pieces. Pan-fry bacon until crisp, remove, and keep warm. Sauté onion in bacon drippings. Add vinegar, sugar, salt, and pepper and cook, stirring, until bubbling. Stir in lettuce and heat just until lettuce is wilted. Sprinkle with chopped egg and bacon pieces. Serve at once.

SUMMER SAVORY.

SCANDINAVIAN GREEN SALAD WITH BACON

4 to 6 servings

This is an adaptation of a well-known Scandinavian salad.

1 *cup heavy cream, chilled thoroughly*

1 *head Boston lettuce*

½ *head leaf lettuce*

6 *slices crisp cooked bacon*

1 *tablespoon sugar*

1 *teaspoon salt*

1 *tablespoon vinegar*

1 *tablespoon minced onion*

Cheese croutons

Paprika

Chill bowl and beaters. Core lettuce, rinse with cold water, drain, and refrigerate. Break bacon into 1-inch pieces and set aside. When ready to serve, beat cream until it forms soft peaks. With the final few strokes, beat in sugar and salt. Gently fold in vinegar and onion. In large bowl, tear lettuce into bite-sized pieces. Spoon in dressing and toss lightly. Serve on individual plates garnished with bacon and croutons and sprinkled with paprika.

ORIENTAL SALAD

8 servings

    4 *cups shelled fresh peas or 2 (10-ounce) packages frozen*
    1 *(16-ounce) can mixed Oriental vegetables*
    1 *cup diced celery*
    1 *(8-ounce) can water chestnuts, drained and sliced*
    1 *(3¼-ounce) package slivered almonds*
    ⅔ *cup vinegar*
    ⅓ *cup oil*
    ⅓ *cup sugar*
    2 *tablespoons soy sauce*
    1 *teaspoon Worcestershire sauce*
    ¼ *teaspoon salt*
    ⅛ *teaspoon pepper*
    3 *drops hot pepper sauce*
    1 *tablespoon chopped pimiento or strips*
    Leaf lettuce or curly endive

Cook fresh peas in boiling salted water until just tender or partially cook frozen peas according to package directions until they are just soft (do not overcook). Drain peas and combine with Oriental vegetables, celery, water chestnuts, and almonds in large bowl. Combine remaining ingredients, except pimiento and greens, in blender or jar and blend or shake thoroughly. Pour over vegetables and garnish with pimiento. Marinate for several hours in refrigerator before serving over greens.

PICNIC COLESLAW

12 servings

Coleslaw was introduced into the American colonies in the early eighteenth century by Dutch settlers, and the Dutch word for salad, *Sla*, soon became Americanized. Coleslaw gained in popularity as winter cabbage was often more readily available.

    2 *pounds cabbage, shredded*
    1 *cup shredded raw carrot*
    Coleslaw Dressing (see below)
    Red or green pepper strips or rings

Combine cabbage and carrot. Add dressing and toss until vegetables are well coated. Garnish with pepper strips or rings.

COLESLAW DRESSING   1½ cups
    ½ *cup sugar*
    1 *tablespoon cornstarch*
    1 *teaspoon dry mustard*
    1 *teaspoon salt*
    1 *egg, beaten*
    ½ *cup water*
    ½ *cup cider vinegar*
    1 *tablespoon butter*

Combine first 4 ingredients in heavy saucepan. Stir in egg, water, and vinegar and cook until thickened, stirring constantly. Stir in butter. Chill, stirring frequently.

QUILTERS' POTATO SALAD

12 servings

A potato salad adds the finishing touch to picnics, barbecues, or backyard cookouts.

Quilters' Salad Dressing

  2 *eggs, beaten slightly*

⅓ *cup vinegar*

⅓ *cup sugar*

  1 *teaspoon prepared mustard*

  1 *teaspoon salt*

¼ *teaspoon pepper*

½ *cup mayonnaise*

½ *to 1 teaspoon chopped chives (optional)*

½ *teaspoon celery seed (optional)*

Salad

2½ *pounds red potatoes, washed*

  1 *cup diced celery*

  1 *cup chopped onion*

Salt and pepper to taste

Paprika (optional)

Parsley sprigs (optional)

To prepare dressing, combine first 6 ingredients in small saucepan and cook over low heat until mixture thickens, stirring constantly. Cool. Blend into mayonnaise, stirring until smooth. Add chopped chives and celery seed.

To prepare salad, cook unpeeled potatoes in salted water to cover for 30 to 40 minutes, or until tender. Drain and set in cold water to cool. Refrigerate until cold. Peel potatoes and cut into 1-inch chunks. Add celery, onion, salad dressing, salt, and pepper, blending thoroughly. Spoon into serving bowl, sprinkle with paprika, and garnish with parsley sprigs.

GARDEN-STYLE HOT POTATO SALAD

6 to 8 servings

Serve this on a cold winter evening.

½ *pound sliced bacon, diced*

  4 *cups sliced cooked potatoes*

  1 *cup thinly sliced celery*

½ *cup sliced green onion*

½ *cup sliced radishes*

  1 *cup water*

⅓ *cup vinegar*

  2 *tablespoons flour*

  2 *tablespoons sugar*

  2 *teaspoons salt (or to taste)*

½ *teaspoon celery seed (optional)*

⅛ *teaspoon pepper*

  4 *cups torn romaine, Boston, or iceberg lettuce*

  1 *pound frankfurters, heated*

  1 *pound smoked sausage links, heated*

Pan-fry bacon until crisp, drain, and set aside. Pour ⅓ cup bacon drippings into large heavy skillet and stir in potatoes, celery, onion, and radishes. Cook over moderate heat. Blend together water, vinegar, flour, sugar, salt, celery seed, and pepper. Pour over potato mixture, reduce heat, and cook until sauce is thickened, stirring occasionally. Fold greens into mixture. Pour into serving dish, sprinkle with bacon, and serve at once with frankfurters and smoked sausage links.

HOT BACON AND SPINACH SALAD

8 servings

    ¾ pound fresh spinach
    1 pound fresh mushrooms, sliced
    1 small red onion, thinly sliced
    8 slices bacon, cut into ¼-inch pieces
    ¾ cup white vinegar
    3 tablespoons sugar
    ¼ teaspoon salt
    ⅛ teaspoon pepper
    1 tablespoon cold water
    1 tablespoon cornstarch
    ⅓ cup seasoned croutons

Wash spinach and remove stems. Tear leaves into small pieces and drain well. Separate onion into rings. Put vegetables into large salad bowl and toss lightly. Refrigerate. Pan-fry bacon until crisp, reduce heat, and add vinegar, sugar, salt, and pepper. Simmer for 5 to 7 minutes. Blend cold water into cornstarch to form a paste and gradually add to dressing, stirring well. Cook until mixture thickens. Pour over vegetables and toss lightly. Garnish with croutons. Serve immediately.

COPENHAGEN SALAD

6 servings

Copenhagen Salad would make an excellent addition to any smorgasbord.

    1 pound fresh spinach
    1 (1-pound) can small beets, drained and
        sliced
    ⅓ cup thinly sliced onion
    ½ teaspoon salt
    ⅛ teaspoon pepper
    3 hard-cooked eggs, cut in wedges or slices
    Sour Cream–Blue Cheese Dressing
        (see next column)

Wash, drain, and tear spinach into bite-sized pieces. Add beets, onion, salt, and pepper and toss. Top with egg wedges or slices. Serve with dressing.

SOUR CREAM–BLUE CHEESE DRESSING
About 2 cups

    1 cup sour cream
    ¾ cup mayonnaise
    ⅓ cup crumbled blue or Roquefort cheese
    2 teaspoons lemon juice

Combine ingredients.

CARLTON HOUSE MUSHROOM SALAD

6 servings

I love mushrooms so much that the chef at the Carlton House Resort Inn in Orlando, Florida, created this salad for me.

    ½ cup olive oil
    ⅓ cup wine vinegar
    1 small clove garlic, sliced
    1 teaspoon chopped chives
    1 teaspoon salt
    Dash of pepper
    1 pound fresh mushrooms, sliced ¼ inch
        thick
    Salad greens
    Tomato wedges
    Sliced hard-cooked eggs
    Chopped green pepper

Combine first 6 ingredients in bowl. Add sliced mushrooms and coat thoroughly. Cover and refrigerate for 3 to 4 hours, stirring occasionally. Remove garlic. Serve on crisp salad greens garnished with tomato wedges, egg slices, and green pepper.

NEW AMSTERDAM SALAD

2½ cups

Many suggest that cucumber-onion pickle was one of the first American salads.

½ *cup vinegar*

⅓ *cup sugar*

¼ *cup water*

2 *tablespoons salad oil*

½ *teaspoon salt*

⅛ *teaspoon pepper*

2 *small cucumbers, washed and thinly sliced*

1 *medium onion, peeled and thinly sliced*

1½ *teaspoons minced parsley*

Combine first 6 ingredients in saucepan and heat, stirring, until sugar dissolves. Cool slightly. Arrange vegetables in refrigerator dish and pour vinegar mixture over vegetables. Blend carefully. Refrigerate, covered, for 4 to 6 hours or overnight before serving.

GELATIN SALADS

Jellied or gelatin salads are a distinctly twentieth-century American innovation. A Pennsylvania housewife who won a national prize for a jellied salad in the early 1900s is rumored to have set off the demand. Old-fashioned Perfection Salad is one of the oldest recipes and is still popular.

PERFECTION SALAD

8 to 10 servings

2 *envelopes unflavored gelatin*

½ *cup cold water*

2 *cups hot water*

½ *cup sugar*

1 *teaspoon salt*

⅓ *cup cider vinegar*

¼ *cup lemon juice*

1¼ *cups finely shredded cabbage*

¾ *cup finely diced celery*

⅓ *cup finely chopped green pepper*

¼ *cup diced pimiento*

¼ *cup shredded carrot*

Salad greens

Pimiento for garnish

Mayonnaise

Soften gelatin in cold water for 5 minutes. Combine hot water, sugar, and salt in saucepan and bring to a simmer. Remove from heat and add softened gelatin, stirring until dissolved. Add vinegar and lemon juice. Cool until mixture starts to thicken and fold in diced, chopped, and shredded vegetables. Pour into 8 to 10 oiled individual molds or into oiled 9 × 9 × 2-inch pan. Chill until firm. Unmold on crisp salad greens, garnish with pimiento, and serve with mayonnaise.

BAYOU TOMATO SALAD

4 servings

Tomatoes were not widely eaten in the United States until after the Civil War, as many people feared they might be poisonous. In 1890, growers petitioned the Supreme Court to change the tomato classification from fruit to vegetable to help increase sales. Fresh tomatoes are not often used in gelatin salads. The flavor of this one is tangy and delicious.

- 1 *(3-ounce) package lemon gelatin*
- 1 *teaspoon salt*
- 1 *cup boiling water*
- ½ *cup cold water*
- 1 *tablespoon vinegar*
- *Dash of pepper*
- 2 *tablespoons minced green pepper*
- 3 *tablespoons minced green onion*
- 1 *cup drained diced fresh tomato*
- *Salad greens*
- *Mayonnaise*

Combine first 3 ingredients, stirring until gelatin is dissolved. Stir in cold water, vinegar, and pepper. Chill until mixture starts to set. Fold in green pepper, onion, and tomato. Pour into an oiled 4-cup mold. Chill until firm. Unmold on salad greens and serve with mayonnaise.

AVOCADO RING WITH FRUITS

6 to 8 servings

- 1 *(3-ounce) package lime or lemon gelatin*
- 1 *cup boiling water*
- 2 *tablespoons lemon juice*
- ¼ *teaspoon salt*
- 1 *cup mashed ripe avocado*
- ¾ *cup Tangy Cooked Salad Dressing (see index)*
- ½ *cup heavy cream, whipped*
- 2½ *to 3 cups well-drained assorted fresh or canned fruits*
- *Mint sprigs*
- *California Fruit Dressing (see index)*

Dissolve gelatin in boiling water and stir in lemon juice and salt. Chill until mixture begins to thicken. Fold in avocado, salad dressing, and whipped cream. Pour into an oiled 4-cup ring mold and chill until firm. Unmold on serving plate and fill center with fruits. Garnish with mint sprigs. Serve with dressing.

CUCUMBER MOUSSE

8 servings

- 1 *(3-ounce) package lime gelatin*
- 1 *cup boiling water*
- 1 *tablespoon lime juice*
- 2 *cups seeded and finely diced cucumber*
- 2 *cups sour cream*
- ½ *cup Tangy Cooked Salad Dressing (see index)*
- 2 *teaspoons prepared horseradish*
- 1 *teaspoon Worcestershire sauce*
- 1 *teaspoon salt*
- ½ *teaspoon white pepper*
- ¼ *teaspoon hot pepper sauce*
- *Salad greens*
- *Tomato slices or cherry tomatoes (optional)*

Dissolve gelatin in boiling water and chill. Sprinkle lime juice over cucumbers, let stand 5 minutes, and drain thoroughly. Combine with remaining ingredients except salad greens and tomatoes. Fold mixture into gelatin when it starts to set. Pour into an oiled 4½-cup ring mold or 8 oiled individual molds. Chill until firm. Serve on crisp salad greens. Garnish with tomato slices or cherry tomatoes.

ASPIC SPECTACULAR

8 to 10 servings

   1 *(3-ounce) package lemon gelatin*
1¼ *cups tomato juice*
   2 *tablespoons chili sauce*
   2 *tablespoons lemon juice*
   1 *tablespoon vinegar*
   1 *tablespoon Worcestershire sauce*
   1 *tablespoon horseradish*
   2 *to 3 drops hot pepper sauce*
   1 *cup chopped celery*
   ⅓ *cup chopped green pepper*
   ⅓ *cup grated onion*
   Dash of salt and pepper

In saucepan, dissolve gelatin in hot tomato juice. Blend in remaining ingredients and pour into lightly oiled 2½-quart mold. Refrigerate until firm. Add Cream Gelatin Layer.

CREAM GELATIN LAYER
   1 *(3-ounce) package lemon gelatin*
   1 *(3-ounce) package cream cheese, softened*
   1 *cup boiling water*
   ½ *cup cold water*
   2 *tablespoons lemon juice*
   2 *teaspoons Worcestershire sauce*
   3 *to 4 drops hot pepper sauce*
1½ *cups sour cream*
   2 *cups diced fully cooked ham*
   1 *cup shredded Cheddar cheese*
   ½ *cup sliced stuffed green olives*
   ½ *cup chopped walnuts*

Cream gelatin with cream cheese at low speed of electric mixer until light and fluffy. Dissolve gelatin–cream-cheese mixture in hot water (use low-speed electric mixer if necessary). Blend in cold water, lemon juice, Worcestershire sauce, and hot pepper sauce. Refrigerate until mixture just begins to thicken. Blend in remaining ingredients, mixing well. Pour on top of first layer and refrigerate for several hours until firm.

NOTE: *If only preparing aspic, double recipe and pour into lightly oiled 2-quart mold.*

CRANBERRY-ORANGE MOLD

8 to 10 servings

CRANBERRY LAYER

  1 (3-ounce) package cherry gelatin
1¼ cups boiling water
  1 (10-ounce) package frozen cranberry
    with orange
  2 teaspoons grated orange peel

ORANGE LAYER

  1 (3-ounce) package orange gelatin
  1 cup boiling water
1½ cups miniature marshmallows
  1 (13½-ounce) can crushed pineapple,
    undrained
  1 (3-ounce) package cream cheese, at
    room temperature
½ cup mayonnaise
⅛ teaspoon salt
½ cup heavy cream, whipped
  Salad greens
  Tangy Fruit Dressing (see index)

Dissolve cherry gelatin in boiling water. Add cranberry mixture and stir until defrosted. Fold in orange peel. Chill until mixture starts to thicken. Pour into an oiled 6½-cup ring mold. Chill until firm. In saucepan dissolve orange gelatin in boiling water. Add marshmallows and cook over low heat, stirring, until marshmallows melt. Stir in pineapple. Chill until mixture starts to thicken. Beat cream cheese until smooth, adding mayonnaise and salt. Fold into gelatin mixture with whipped cream. Pour over cranberry layer. Chill until firm. Unmold on crisp salad greens. Serve with Tangy Fruit Dressing.

LUNCHEON SALADS

Seafood and meats are popular additions to a salad that can be served as a light entrée. Salads can be both nutritious and low in calories, a great boon to diet-conscious Americans.

SCALLOP SALAD BOWL

6 servings

1½ pounds Alaska or other scallops
1½ cups water
  3 tablespoons lemon juice
1½ teaspoons salt
  3 peppercorns
  3 slices onion
½ cup tarragon vinegar
⅓ cup salad oil
⅓ cup sugar
  1 clove garlic, sliced
1½ cups diagonally sliced celery
  6 servings salad greens
¾ cup sliced radishes
  3 hard-cooked eggs, sliced
  1 pint cherry tomatoes, halved, or 2
    tomatoes cut in wedges
¼ pound Cheddar cheese, cut into thin
    strips
  French or oil-and-vinegar dressing
    (optional)

Rinse scallops in cold water and drain. Combine in saucepan water, lemon juice, ½ teaspoon salt, peppercorns, and onion. Bring to a boil and simmer for 5 minutes. Add scallops, cover, and simmer gently for 5 to 10 minutes, or until scallops are tender. Remove scallops with a slotted spoon and drain. Combine vinegar, oil, sugar, remaining 1 teaspoon salt, and garlic, stirring until sugar is dissolved. Pour over scallops. Cover and chill for several hours. Mix in celery, drain, and reserve marinade. Arrange greens in large salad bowl. Pile scallops and celery in center of bowl and arrange radishes, sliced eggs, tomatoes, and cheese around the edge. Serve with reserved marinade or dressing.

MARINATED SHRIMP

4 to 6 servings

 ½ *cup chopped green onions and tops*
 ½ *cup olive or salad oil*
 ⅓ *cup tarragon vinegar*
 ⅓ *cup horseradish mustard*
 2½ *tablespoons paprika*
 2 *tablespoons catsup*
 1 *teaspoon salt*
 ¾ *teaspoon cayenne pepper*
 2 *cloves garlic, minced*
 1 *pound shrimp, cooked, peeled, and deveined*
 Lettuce

Combine first 9 ingredients in jar and shake well. Marinate shrimp in sauce in refrigerator for several hours. Serve on lettuce.

CRUNCHY CHICKEN SALAD

2½ cups

Chicken salad is reputed to have been served to George Washington and his fellow delegates of the Virginia House of Burgesses.

 2 *cups diced cooked chicken*
 ½ *cup finely chopped celery*
 ½ *cup chopped water chestnuts or cashew nuts*
 ¼ *cup thinly sliced quartered radishes*
 2 *tablespoons sliced green onion with 2 inches of top*
 2 *tablespoons chopped pimiento*
 ⅔ *cup Tangy Cooked Salad Dressing (see index)*

 1 *teaspoon seasoned salt*
 1 *teaspoon lemon juice*
 ½ *teaspoon dill weed*

Combine first 6 ingredients in bowl. Blend together salad dressing, salt, lemon juice, and dill weed and mix together with chicken and vegetables. Cover and chill for at least 1 hour.

PAINTED DESERT TACO SALAD

6 to 8 servings

Tacos, kidney beans, and avocados are typical Southwestern foods that go well together in a salad.

 1 *pound lean ground beef*
 1 *tablespoon flour*
 1 *teaspoon salt*
 ½ *teaspoon chili powder*
 ⅛ *teaspoon pepper*
 2 *(4-ounce) cans taco sauce*
 1 *(8¼-ounce) can kidney beans, drained*
 6 *cups shredded lettuce*
 1½ *cups chopped tomato*
 ½ *cup sliced green onion with 2 inches of top*
 1 *(6-ounce) bag corn chips*
 1 *cup shredded Cheddar or Monterey Jack cheese*
 Cable-Car Avocado Dressing (see index)

Sauté beef in heavy skillet until crumbly. Stir in flour, salt, chili powder, and pepper. Mix in taco sauce and kidney beans. Cover and simmer for 20 to 25 minutes, stirring occasionally. Combine lettuce, tomato, and green onion in bowl. Add hot meat mixture and toss quickly. Serve edged with corn chips and topped with cheese and Avocado Dressing.

CALIFORNIA CURRIED RICE SALAD

6 servings (5½ cups)

California Curried Rice Salad is an excellent hot-weather entrée.

 1 *cup long-grain rice*
1½ *cups chicken broth or 1 (13¾-ounce) can*
 ¼ *cup water*
1¼ *teaspoons salt*
 2 *(6-ounce) jars marinated artichoke hearts*
 10 *pimiento-stuffed olives, halved crosswise*
 ½ *cup chopped green pepper*
 2 *tablespoons sliced green onion*
 ¼ *teaspoon curry powder*
 ⅓ *cup mayonnaise*
  Salad greens
 6 *cooked ham slices or 2 cups cooked ham cubes*

Combine first 4 ingredients in heavy saucepan and bring to a boil. Cover and cook over low heat for 15 minutes, or until liquid is absorbed. Chill thoroughly. Drain artichoke hearts and reserve ⅓ cup of the marinade. Combine chilled rice, artichoke hearts, olives, green pepper, onion, curry powder, mayonnaise, and the reserved marinade, mixing lightly. Cover and chill for at least 1 hour. Serve on crisp salad greens circled with ham slices or cubes.

LA JOLLA WATERMELON BOWL

10 to 12 servings

A perfect party salad or dessert, La Jolla Watermelon Bowl first gained popularity in California, where fresh fruits are available year round.

 6- *to 7-inch slice watermelon, cut from one end*
 1 *small cantaloupe, peeled and cut into bite-sized pieces*
 1 *small honeydew melon, peeled and cut into bite-sized pieces*
 2 *cups fresh or canned pineapple chunks*
 1 *cup fresh strawberry halves or Bing cherries*
 2 *bananas, cut into ½-inch slices*
 6 *to 8 clusters sugar-frosted green grapes*

Cut a thin slice from end of watermelon so it will stand upright. Scoop out watermelon, leaving a 1-inch layer at the bottom. Remove seeds from scooped-out meat and cut into bite-sized pieces. Cut large scallops around top edge of watermelon rind. Chill shell and fruits. Combine all fruits except grapes. Arrange watermelon bowl on shallow serving dish. Spoon fruits into watermelon bowl. Arrange sugar-frosted grapes around bowl.

SALAD DRESSINGS

TANGY COOKED SALAD DRESSING

1 cup

A bottled cooked commercial dressing is a time-saver, but if you would like a homemade flavor, here is my recipe.

 2 *tablespoons flour*
 3 *tablespoons sugar*
 1 *teaspoon salt*
 1 *teaspoon hot dry mustard*
  Pinch of cayenne (or to taste)
 2 *egg yolks, slightly beaten*
 ¾ *cup milk*
 ⅓ *cup white vinegar*
 1 *teaspoon butter*

Combine flour, sugar, salt, mustard, and cayenne in top of double boiler over hot water. Add egg yolks and milk and cook, stirring, until thickened. Add vinegar and butter and blend thoroughly. Cool. Seal and refrigerate. If dressing should separate, stir with a wire whisk or wooden spoon.

NOTE: *Increase egg yolks to 3 and vinegar to ½ cup for a tangier dressing.*

VARIATIONS

Curry Dressing: Add ½ to 1 teaspoon curry powder to dry ingredients.

Herbed Dressing: Add ½ to 1 teaspoon fines herbes to dry ingredients.

Honey Dressing: Blend 1 to 2 tablespoons honey into cooked dressing.

MAYONNAISE
About 2½ cups

- 2 *eggs*
- ½ *teaspoon salt*
- 1 *tablespoon sugar*
- 1¼ *teaspoons dry mustard*
- ½ *teaspoon paprika*
- ¼ to ½ *teaspoon celery salt*
- ⅛ *teaspoon white pepper*
- ⅓ *cup cider vinegar*
- 2 *cups salad oil*

Combine first 8 ingredients and ¼ cup oil in blender container. Cover and blend at medium speed for 1 minute. Add remaining oil in a fine stream until thick and smooth.

THOUSAND ISLAND DRESSING
1¾ cups

- ½ *cup chili sauce*
- 1 *pimiento, finely chopped*
- 1 *tablespoon grated onion*
- 2 *tablespoons finely chopped green pepper*
- 1 *cup mayonnaise*

Blend all the ingredients together and chill.

CHIFFONADE DRESSING
About 1 cup

- ½ *cup olive oil*
- 3 *tablespoons cider vinegar*
- 1 *hard-cooked egg, grated*
- 1 *teaspoon finely chopped chives or scallions*
- 1 *tablespoon chopped green pepper*
- 1 *teaspoon salt*
- ½ *teaspoon freshly ground pepper*
- 1 *teaspoon paprika*

Combine all the ingredients in a glass jar and shake thoroughly. Chiffonade is an excellent dressing for mixed greens.

RUSSIAN DRESSING
About 2 cups

- 1¼ *cups mayonnaise*
- ½ *cup chili sauce*
- 1 *hard-cooked egg, finely chopped*
- 1 *tablespoon lemon juice or vinegar*
- 1 *teaspoon finely chopped chives or grated onion*
- ½ *teaspoon Worcestershire sauce*
- ½ *teaspoon prepared horseradish*
- *Dash of cayenne pepper*

Combine ingredients in order listed, mix, and chill thoroughly. Delicious served with shrimp, crab, or tossed green salads.

LEMON CREAM DRESSING
About 1¼ cups

- 1 *cup sour cream*
- 2 *tablespoons lemon juice*
- 1 *tablespoon chopped parsley*
- 2 *teaspoons prepared horseradish*
- ¼ *teaspoon salt*

Blend all ingredients together and chill.

CALIFORNIA FRUIT DRESSING

3½ cups

    3 eggs
    1 cup sugar
    ¼ teaspoon salt
    ½ cup pineapple juice
    ¼ cup lemon juice
    1 cup heavy cream, whipped

Beat eggs, sugar, and salt together in heavy saucepan. Stir in fruit juices. Cook, stirring constantly, until thickened. Chill thoroughly. Store in covered container. Fold in whipped cream just before serving. Good with any fruit salad.

TARRAGON.

GREEN GODDESS SALAD DRESSING

About 3 cups

    3 cups mayonnaise flavored with 2
       tablespoons tarragon vinegar
    1 green onion, finely sliced
    ½ cup chopped parsley
    2 tablespoons diced fresh tarragon or 2
       teaspoons dried
    ¼ cup finely cut chives
   10 anchovy fillets, finely diced

Combine all the ingredients and let stand for at least 1 hour for flavors to blend. An excellent accompaniment for all fish and seafood salads.

COOKED SOUR CREAM DRESSING

1¾ cups

    ¼ to ⅓ cup sugar
         2 tablespoons flour
         1 teaspoon dry mustard
         ⅛ teaspoon salt
         ½ cup vinegar
         2 eggs, beaten
         1 cup sour cream

Combine first 4 ingredients in a heavy saucepan. Stir in vinegar. Cook, stirring constantly, until mixture comes to a boil and thickens slightly. Remove from heat. Gradually add a small amount of the hot mixture to eggs, beating constantly, then stir into hot mixture. Cool, stirring frequently. Fold in sour cream. Excellent for potato, vegetable, or meat salads.

ESTHER'S SPECIAL DRESSING

About 1¾ cups

    ½ cup salad oil
    ½ cup catsup
    ½ cup honey
    ⅓ cup cider vinegar
    3 tablespoons sugar
    1 tablespoon Worcestershire sauce
    1 teaspoon celery salt
    ½ teaspoon paprika
    ½ teaspoon onion powder
    ¼ teaspoon dry mustard
    1 or 2 drops hot pepper sauce (optional)

Combine ingredients in order listed in blender container, cover, and whiz until well mixed. Refrigerate in a tightly covered jar. Let stand at room temperature for 10 to 15 minutes before using. Shake well.

BURGUNDY VINAIGRETTE DRESSING

1¼ cups

½ *cup salad oil*

½ *cup white vinegar*

2 *tablespoons red Burgundy wine*

½ *teaspoon sugar*

¼ *teaspoon Worcestershire sauce*

¼ *teaspoon salt*

¼ *teaspoon coarsely ground pepper*

¼ *teaspoon salad herbs*

¼ *teaspoon minced garlic*

2 *or 3 drops hot pepper sauce*

Combine ingredients in jar with close-fitting cover and shake well. Refrigerate. Shake well before using.

BLUE CHEESE-FRENCH DRESSING

2¾ cups dressing

1 *(10¾-ounce) can tomato soup*

¾ *cup malt or cider vinegar*

½ *cup salad oil*

3 *tablespoons sugar*

1 *tablespoon Worcestershire sauce*

1 *teaspoon salt*

⅛ *teaspoon white pepper*

½ *clove garlic*

⅓ *cup (2 ounces) blue cheese, crumbled*

Combine ingredients in quart jar. Cover, shake, and refrigerate. Remove garlic when ready to serve.

CABLE-CAR AVOCADO DRESSING

About 2¾ cups

¾ *cup mashed ripe avocado*

2 *tablespoons lemon juice*

1 *teaspoon grated lemon peel*

1 *teaspoon grated orange peel (optional)*

Pinch of salt

⅓ *cup sifted confectioners' sugar*

1 *cup cream, whipped*

Combine first 5 ingredients. Fold sugar into whipped cream. Carefully fold whipped cream into avocado mixture. Serve with fruit salads.

TANGY FRUIT DRESSING

1⅓ cups

½ *cup mayonnaise*

1 *tablespoon orange juice*

¼ *teaspoon celery seed*

⅛ *teaspoon grated orange peel*

½ *cup heavy cream*

1 *tablespoon sugar*

Dash of paprika

Combine first 4 ingredients. Combine cream and sugar and whip until soft peaks form. Fold into salad-dressing mixture. Spoon into serving dish and sprinkle with paprika. Excellent with any fruit salad.

QUICK POPPY-SEED DRESSING

About 1½ cups

½ *cup cream*

½ *cup Tangy Cooked Salad Dressing (see index)*

2 *tablespoons honey*

1 *tablespoon poppy seeds*

Chill beaters and bowl. Whip cream until it forms soft peaks. Fold in dressing, honey, and poppy seeds. Serve with fresh fruit or fruited gelatin salads.

SAUCES AND GRAVIES

BASIC CREAM SAUCE
(Béchamel)

1 cup

2 *tablespoons butter*

2 *tablespoons flour*

½ *teaspoon salt*

Dash of pepper

Dash of paprika (optional)

1 *cup milk or ½ cup milk and ½ cup half and half*

Melt butter in heavy saucepan and stir in flour and seasonings. Add milk or milk and half and half, stirring until smooth and thickened.

VARIATIONS

Thin Cream Sauce: Reduce butter and flour to 1 tablespoon each.

Thick Cream Sauce: Increase butter and flour to ¼ cup each.

Cheese Sauce: Fold 1 cup (¼ pound) shredded American, Cheddar, or Swiss cheese into hot sauce and stir until cheese melts. Yield: about 1¼ cups.

Horseradish Sauce: Stir in 2 to 3 tablespoons prepared horseradish and a drop of hot pepper sauce.

Mustard Sauce: Stir 1½ to 2 tablespoons prepared mustard into sauce. Fold in ½ cup sour or whipped cream (optional). Yield: 1½ cups sauce if sour or whipped cream is used.

HOLLANDAISE SAUCE

1¾ cups

1 *cup butter*

3 *egg yolks*

2 *tablespoons hot water*

1 *tablespoon white vinegar*

1½ *teaspoons lemon juice*

Pinch of salt

Pinch of white pepper

3 *or 4 drops Worcestershire sauce*

3 *or 4 drops Tabasco sauce*

Melt butter and keep warm. Combine remaining ingredients in top of double boiler, heating until well mixed. Cook over hot water, beating constantly, until thick. Remove from heat. Add melted butter slowly, a tablespoon at a time, beating constantly until thoroughly blended. May be kept hot in top of double boiler over simmering water.

NOTE: *If sauce should separate, add a tablespoon or two of boiling water and beat with a rotary beater.*

BÉARNAISE SAUCE

About 2½ cups

¼ *cup tarragon or cider vinegar*

2 *teaspoons finely chopped shallots or onion*

1 *teaspoon minced parsley*

¼ *cup dry white wine or water*

3 *egg yolks*

½ *cup butter, melted*

1 *cup Tangy Cooked Salad Dressing (see index)*

Salt and pepper to taste

Combine first 3 ingredients in saucepan and simmer gently until liquid is reduced by half. Add white wine or water. Beat egg yolks until very thick and lemon-colored, using an electric or hand beater. Beat in butter. Place egg mixture in top of double boiler over hot, not boiling, water. Do not let bottom of insert touch water. Cook, stirring constantly, until mixture thickens. Remove from heat and blend in wine mixture. Fold in salad dressing. Add salt and pepper to taste. Serve with broiled meats or fish.

CREAMY SAUTERNE SAUCE
1 cup

In preparing this sauce, use the dry white domestic table wine known as sauterne rather than the sweeter French variety.

½ *cup butter*
6 *egg yolks, lightly beaten*
3 *tablespoons dry sauterne*
1 *tablespoon white vinegar*
¼ *teaspoon salt*
Dash of pepper

Melt butter and cool slightly. Add to egg yolks gradually, stirring constantly. Pour into top of double boiler and stir in remaining ingredients. Cook over gently boiling water until sauce thickens, stirring constantly.

SPANISH SAUCE
1⅓ cups

¼ *cup chopped onion*
2 *tablespoons chopped green pepper*
1 *tablespoon butter*
2 *teaspoons flour*
¼ *teaspoon salt*
¼ *teaspoon sugar*
Dash of cayenne pepper
1 *(8¼-ounce) can tomatoes, chopped fine*
¼ *cup catsup*
¼ *cup sliced stuffed or pitted ripe olives*

Sauté onion and green pepper in butter until onion is tender but not brown. Add flour, salt, sugar, and cayenne, stirring until smooth. Stir in tomatoes and catsup and cook until sauce thickens, stirring constantly. Fold in olives and heat through.

QUICK BORDELAISE SAUCE
About 1⅔ cups

Excellent with meat loaf or meat balls.

½ *cup sliced fresh mushrooms*
1 *tablespoon chopped onion*
2 *teaspoons minced parsley*
1 *tablespoon butter*
1 *(10½-ounce) can beef gravy*
½ *cup dry red wine*
1 *or 2 drops hot pepper sauce (optional)*

Sauté mushrooms, onion, and parsley in butter for about 4 minutes, or until mushrooms are tender, stirring often. Stir in gravy, wine, and hot pepper sauce and simmer to heat through.

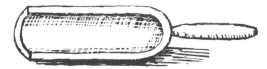

TOMATO SAUCE
About 3 cups

½ *cup chili sauce*
¼ *cup brown sugar, firmly packed*
1½ *teaspoons prepared mustard*
1 *(1-pound) can tomatoes*
1 *(6-ounce) can tomato paste*
½ *teaspoon Worcestershire sauce*
¼ *teaspoon garlic powder*
¼ *teaspoon onion powder*
¼ *teaspoon sweet basil*
¼ *teaspoon oregano*
1 *bay leaf*
Drop of hot pepper sauce
¼ *cup dry sherry (optional)*
1 *(4-ounce) can mushrooms, drained*

Combine all ingredients in saucepan and simmer to blend flavors. Serve hot or cold.

EGG SAUCE
About 2 cups

  ¼ *cup butter*
  2 *tablespoons flour*
  ½ *teaspoon salt*
  ¼ *teaspoon dry mustard*
     Dash of pepper
1½ *cups milk*
  3 *hard-cooked eggs, chopped*

Melt butter and stir in flour, salt, mustard, and pepper. Add milk and cook, stirring constantly, until thickened. Fold in chopped eggs and heat through. This sauce is an excellent accompaniment to boiled or baked fish.

TARTAR SAUCE FOR FISH
About 1 cup

  ⅔ *cup mayonnaise or Tangy Cooked Salad Dressing (see index)*
  ¼ *cup well-drained sweet pickle relish*
  1 *tablespoon minced green onion*
  1 *tablespoon finely chopped pimiento*
  ¼ *teaspoon grated lemon peel (optional)*

Blend all the ingredients together and chill. Traditionally served with fish.

RÉMOULADE SAUCE
1½ cups

  1 *cup mayonnaise or Tangy Cooked Salad Dressing (see index)*
  ½ *cup finely chopped green onion*
  1 *tablespoon drained sweet pickle relish*
  1 *tablespoon tarragon or cider vinegar*
  2 *teaspoons prepared mustard*
  1 *teaspoon chopped parsley (optional)*
  ½ *teaspoon leaf thyme*
     Salt and pepper to taste

Combine all the ingredients and blend thoroughly. Serve hot or cold. Ideal with lobster or fish.

SEAFOOD SAUCE
About 1½ cups

  ½ *cup catsup*
  ½ *cup chili sauce*
  3 *tablespoons lemon juice*
  1 *tablespoon prepared horseradish*
  1 *tablespoon mayonnaise or Tangy Cooked Salad Dressing (see index)*
  1 *teaspoon Worcestershire sauce*
  ½ *teaspoon grated onion*
  ¼ *teaspoon salt*
  3 *drops hot pepper sauce*
     Dash of pepper

Blend together all the ingredients and chill.

CREAMY LEMON SAUCE
About 1¾ cups

    2 *tablespoons butter*
    2 *tablespoons flour*
  ½ *teaspoon salt*
  ¼ *teaspoon paprika*
1¼ *cups milk*
  ½ *cup Tangy Cooked Salad Dressing (see index)*
    1 *tablespoon lemon juice*

Melt butter and stir in flour, salt, and paprika. Add milk and cook until thickened and smooth, stirring constantly. Blend in mayonnaise or dressing and lemon juice and heat through.

DILL SAUCE
About 1 cup

  ⅔ *cup mayonnaise or Tangy Cooked Salad Dressing (see index)*
  ⅓ *cup sour cream*
  ½ *teaspoon sugar*
  ½ *teaspoon dill weed*
  ¼ *teaspoon salt*
      Dash of white pepper

Blend together all the ingredients and chill. Serve on or with hot or cold fish or seafood.

SHERRY MUSHROOM GRAVY
2 cups

  ½ *pound fresh mushrooms, sliced*
    2 *tablespoons sliced green onion with 2 inches of top*
    2 *tablespoons butter*
    1 *tablespoon cider vinegar*
    1 *tablespoon flour*
  ½ *teaspoon salt*
  ¼ *teaspoon tarragon leaves*
    1 *cup half and half*
  ½ *cup milk*
    3 *tablespoons dry sherry*

Sauté mushrooms and onion in butter until mushrooms are tender and most of liquid has evaporated. Add vinegar and heat. Stir in flour, salt, and tarragon leaves. Add half and half and milk and cook until thickened, stirring constantly. Stir in sherry and heat through. Serve with chicken or fish.

TANGY SOUR CREAM GRAVY
About 1¼ cups

    1 *cup sour cream*
    2 *tablespoons prepared mustard*
    1 *tablespoon minced onion*
    2 *teaspoons Worcestershire sauce*
    2 *drops red pepper sauce*
      Salt to taste
      Pepper to taste

Combine ingredients and blend thoroughly. Good with beef or duck.

TANGY BARBECUE SAUCE FOR DUCKLING

1¼ cups

  ¾ *cup catsup*
  ¾ *cup water*
  ¼ *cup red wine or cider vinegar*
  ½ *cup chopped onion*
  2 *tablespoons brown sugar*
  ½ *teaspoon chili powder*
  ½ *teaspoon oregano*
  ¼ *teaspoon salt*

Combine all the ingredients in heavy saucepan and bring to a boil. Simmer for 20 to 30 minutes to blend flavors. Brush over duckling quarters during last 30 minutes of cooking time.

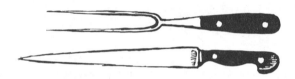

BARBECUE SAUCE FOR STEAK

About 1¼ cups

  ½ *cup finely chopped onion*
  ¼ *cup finely chopped celery*
  1 *tablespoon cooking oil*
  1 *(8-ounce) can tomato sauce*
  ¼ *cup water*
  1 *teaspoon Worcestershire sauce*
  ½ *teaspoon sugar*
  ¼ *teaspoon dry mustard*
  ¼ *teaspoon basil*
  ¼ *teaspoon oregano*

Sauté onion and celery in oil until tender. Stir in remaining ingredients. Simmer over low heat for 8 to 10 minutes, stirring occasionally. Serve with steak.

CHEESE-HERB BUTTER

About 1½ cups

  ½ *cup butter*
  2 *cups finely shredded Cheddar cheese*
  ½ *cup sliced green onion*
  ½ *teaspoon dill weed*
  ½ *teaspoon dry mustard*

Cream butter until soft and smooth. Add cheese and blend thoroughly. Stir in onion, dill weed, and mustard. Spread on hot steaks.

HERB-ONION BUTTER

About ¾ cup

  ½ *cup butter*
  ½ *small clove garlic, minced*
  3 *tablespoons sliced green onion*
  ½ *teaspoon dry mustard*
  ½ *teaspoon fines herbes*

Cream butter. Add remaining ingredients and blend thoroughly.

CAPER SAUCE

About 1½ cups

  2 *tablespoons butter*
  2 *tablespoons flour*
  ½ *teaspoon salt*
  Dash of pepper
  1 *cup milk*
  ½ *cup half and half*
  2 *or 3 tablespoons drained capers*

Melt butter and blend in flour, salt, and pepper. Add milk and half and half. Cook until thickened and smooth, stirring constantly. Fold in capers.

CREAMY TARRAGON SAUCE FOR LAMB

½ cup

- ¼ *cup melted butter*
- 3 *egg yolks, beaten lightly*
- 3 *tablespoons dry sherry*
- 1 *tablespoon tarragon vinegar*
- 1 *teaspoon Worcestershire sauce*
- ¼ *teaspoon salt*
- *Pinch of pepper*
- 2 *teaspoons drained capers (optional)*
- ½ *teaspoon chopped fresh parsley (optional)*

Add butter to egg yolks slowly, stirring constantly. Stir in remaining ingredients except capers and parsley. Cook in top of double boiler over gently boiling water until sauce thickens, stirring often. Capers or chopped parsley may be added.

MINT SAUCE FOR LAMB

1½ cups

- 2 *tablespoons cornstarch*
- 1 *cup water*
- ¾ *cup mint jelly, mashed*
- 2 *teaspoons lime juice*
- 1 *teaspoon lemon juice*
- ¼ *teaspoon Worcestershire sauce*
- ¼ *teaspoon salt*
- ¼ *teaspoon basil*
- ⅛ *teaspoon salad herbs*

Blend cornstarch and ¼ cup water in heavy saucepan, then stir in remaining ¾ cup water. Cook over low heat until thick and clear, stirring constantly. Remove from heat and stir in remaining ingredients. Continue cooking over low heat until jelly melts.

SOUR CREAM MUSTARD SAUCE

About 1⅓ cups

Sour Cream Mustard Sauce is an excellent accompaniment to ham, beef, or corned beef.

- 1 *cup sour cream*
- ⅓ *cup Tangy Cooked Salad Dressing (see index)*
- 2 *teaspoons prepared mustard*
- ½ *to 1 teaspoon prepared horseradish*

Combine ingredients and heat slowly in small heavy saucepan, stirring constantly. May also be served cold.

RICH MUSTARD SAUCE

1⅔ cups

This is an excellent sauce to serve with ham.

- 2 *tablespoons butter*
- 2 *tablespoons flour*
- ¾ *teaspoon salt*
- 1½ *cups milk*
- 2 *egg yolks, beaten*
- 2 *tablespoons prepared mustard*

Melt butter and stir in flour and salt. Add milk and cook, stirring constantly, until thickened. Add a small amount of hot sauce to egg yolks, beating constantly. Return to hot sauce, add mustard, and cook slowly for about 2 minutes, stirring constantly.

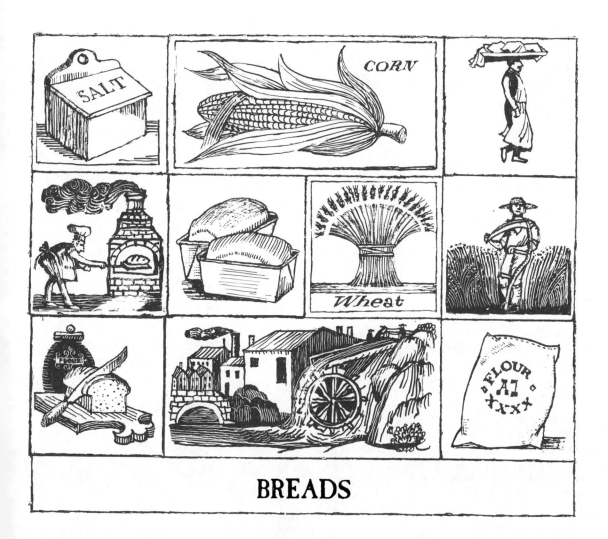

BREADS

OLD-FASHIONED WHITE BREAD

2 loaves

What can one say about home-baked bread? It's just good, good, good!

Defined as a food made from flour or meal by moistening, kneading, and baking, bread is truly the "staff of life."

    1¾ *cups milk, scalded*
    ¼   *cup shortening*
    3   *tablespoons sugar*
    1   *tablespoon salt*
    2   *packages active dry yeast*
    1   *cup warm water (105° to 115° F.)*
    6½ *to 7 cups sifted flour (approximate)*
        Melted butter

Combine first 4 ingredients and cool to lukewarm. Soften yeast in warm water and add to mixture. Stir in 3 cups flour, beating thoroughly. Add remaining flour, ½ cup at a time, to make a stiff dough.

Turn onto lightly floured board and knead until smooth and elastic. Place in greased bowl and turn once to coat surfaces. Cover and let rise in a warm place (85° F.) until doubled in bulk, about 1½ to 2 hours. Punch down, turn onto lightly floured board, and shape into two loaves. Place in greased 9 × 5 × 3-inch loaf pans. Let rise again, covered, until doubled in bulk, about 1 hour.

Bake on lower rack of hot oven (400° F.) for 35 to 40 minutes, or until well browned. Remove loaves from pans and cool on racks. Brush tops lightly with melted butter.

VARIATIONS

Cinnamon-Raisin Bread: Increase sugar to ¼ cup and stir in ¾ cup seedless raisins when the 3 cups flour are stirred into liquids. Roll each portion of dough into a 15 × 9-inch rectangle. Brush surface with water and sprinkle each with a mixture of ¼ cup sugar and 1 teaspoon cinnamon. Roll up tightly, starting at the narrow end of rectangle, tuck ends under, and place loaves in well-greased 9 × 5 × 3-inch loaf pans, seam side down.

Old-Fashioned Whole-Wheat Bread: Substitute 2 tablespoons *each* honey and molasses or brown sugar for granulated sugar and 3 cups whole-wheat flour for 3 of the cups of white flour.

HEARTY MIXED-GRAINS BREAD

2 loaves

This bread combines delicious eating with vitamins and minerals that are good for you.

    1   *cup milk, scalded*
    ¾   *cup boiling water*
    1   *cup yellow cornmeal*
    ⅓   *cup butter or shortening*
    ¼   *cup light molasses*
    ¼   *cup brown sugar, firmly packed*
    1   *tablespoon salt*
    2   *packages active dry yeast*
    ½   *cup warm water (105° to 115° F.)*
    2   *cups whole-wheat flour*
    1   *cup rye or buckwheat flour*
    ¾   *cup seedless raisins*
    2   *to 2½ cups sifted flour*

Combine milk and boiling water and stir in cornmeal gradually. Add butter or shortening, molasses, sugar, and salt. Cool to lukewarm. Soften yeast in warm water. Add yeast, whole-wheat and rye or buckwheat flours, and raisins to cornmeal mixture. Add enough sifted flour to make a moderately stiff dough.

Knead on lightly floured board until smooth and elastic. Place in greased bowl and turn once to grease top. Cover and let rise in a warm place (85° F.) until doubled in bulk, about 1½ to 2 hours. Punch down, turn onto lightly floured board, and shape into two loaves. Place in greased 8½ × 4½ × 2⅝-inch loaf pans. Let rise again, covered, until doubled in bulk, about 1 hour.

Bake in moderate oven (375° F.) for 40 minutes, or until done. Remove from pans and cool on wire rack.

GERMAN RYE BREAD

2 loaves

German Rye Bread is equally delicious with cold meats and hearty cheeses or spread with butter.

2 *cups milk, scalded*
2 *tablespoons butter or shortening*
⅓ *cup molasses*
2 *tablespoons caraway seeds*
1 *tablespoon salt*
2 *packages active dry yeast*
½ *cup warm water (105° to 115° F.)*
2½ *cups rye flour*
3½ *to 4 cups sifted flour*

Combine first 5 ingredients and cool to lukewarm. Soften yeast in warm water and add to liquids. Stir in rye flour, beating until smooth. Cover and let rise in a warm place until bubbly. Gradually add enough sifted flour to make a moderately stiff dough.

Turn onto lightly floured board and knead until smooth and elastic. Place in greased bowl, turning to coat the surface. Cover and let rise in a warm place (85° F.) until doubled in bulk. Punch down the dough and return to greased bowl to let rise again until doubled in bulk, about 1 to 1½ hours. Turn onto floured board and divide in two. To shape loaves, roll each into an 18 × 9-inch rectangle. Roll up dough, starting at the narrow end, and fold ends under. Place seam side down in greased 9 × 5 × 3-inch loaf pans. Cover and let rise in a warm place until doubled in bulk, about 1 hour. Bake in moderate oven (375° F.) for 30 to 35 minutes, or until done. Remove from pans and cool on wire rack.

VARIATION

Onion Rye Bread: Increase caraway seeds to 3 tablespoons and stir 1 cup finely chopped onion into batter after first rising before adding flour needed to make a stiff dough. Shape into round loaves, brush tops with cream, and sprinkle with coarse salt. Cover, let rise, and proceed as directed above.

PUMPERNICKEL

2 loaves

Though the word *pumpernickel* actually derives from two German words, *pumpern* and *nickel*, that described its supposed indigestibility, many anecdotes explain the bread's name in other fashions. One suggests that a Swiss baker named Pumper Nickel developed the bread during a shortage of wheat flour. Another reports that Napoleon scoffed at the bread's flavor and texture, declaring, "*Bon pour Nickel.*" (Nickel was Napoleon's horse.)

3 *packages active dry yeast*
1½ *cups warm water (105° to 115° F.)*
1¼ *cups warm milk (105° to 115° F.)*
½ *cup light molasses*
3 *tablespoons butter*
2 *tablespoons sugar*
1 *to 2 tablespoons caraway seeds*
1 *tablespoon salt*
3 *cups rye flour*
1½ *cups whole-wheat flour*
3 *to 3½ cups sifted flour*
Cornmeal

Soften yeast in warm water. Combine milk, molasses, butter, sugar, caraway seeds, and salt. Stir in softened yeast and rye and whole-wheat flours, beating well. Add enough sifted flour to make a moderately stiff dough.

Turn onto lightly floured board and knead until smooth and elastic. Place in greased bowl, turning once to grease top. Cover and let rise in a warm place (85° F.) until doubled in bulk, about 1½ to 2 hours. Punch down and turn onto lightly floured board. Shape into 2 loaves, 14 inches long, or rounds. Place each loaf on a greased baking sheet sprinkled lightly with cornmeal. Cover and let rise again until doubled in bulk, about 1 to 1½ hours. Make several slashes in top of loaves with very sharp knife or razor blade. Bake in moderate oven (375° F.) for 30 to 35 minutes, or until done. Remove from pans and cool on wire rack.

OAT BREAD

2 loaves

Here is an old-fashioned bread chock full of whole-grain nutrition and tasty eating. It is delicious served right from the oven with butter or jam.

   1 *cup milk, scalded*

 ⅓ *cup butter or shortening*

 ¼ *cup brown sugar, firmly packed*

 ¼ *cup light molasses*

   2 *teaspoons salt*

   1 *package active dry yeast*

 ½ *cup warm water (105° to 115° F.)*

   1 *egg, beaten*

   2 *cups uncooked rolled oats, quick or old-fashioned*

4½ *cups sifted flour (approximate)*

Combine first 5 ingredients and cool to lukewarm. Dissolve yeast in warm water and add to milk mixture. Stir in egg, 1½ cups oats, and enough flour to make a soft dough.

Turn onto lightly floured board and knead until smooth and elastic, about 10 minutes. Place in greased bowl and turn to grease top. Cover and let rise in a warm place (85° F.) until doubled in bulk, about 1½ to 2 hours. Punch dough down and turn out on lightly floured board. Divide in half and roll out each half into an 18 × 8-inch rectangle. Roll up, beginning at short side, and turn ends under loaf. Brush with water and roll in reserved ½ cup oats. Place loaves, seam side down, in well-greased 8½ × 4½ × 2⅝-inch loaf pans. Cover and let rise again until doubled in bulk, about 1 hour.

Bake in moderate oven (350° F.) for 40 to 45 minutes, or until done. Let cool in pans for 5 minutes, then turn onto wire rack.

NOTE: *If 8½ × 4½ × 2⅝-inch pans are not available, 9 × 5 × 3-inch ones may be substituted.*

SALLY LUNN

2 loaves

Delicious served warm with butter and jam, this bread, originally made as a bun, is also superb when sliced and toasted. One theory about the name comes from the appearance. The golden tops and white bottoms were thought to resemble the sun and moon—*soleil* and *lune* in French. Both the name and presentation underwent a significant transformation by the time the bread was brought to America.

   1 *package active dry yeast*

 ¼ *cup warm water (105° to 115° F.)*

1¾ *cups milk, scalded*

   2 *tablespoons sugar*

 ¼ *cup butter*

   1 *teaspoon salt*

   2 *eggs, well beaten*

   5 *cups sifted flour (approximate)*

Dissolve yeast in warm water. Combine milk, sugar, butter, and salt in mixing bowl and let cool. Stir in yeast, eggs, and 3 cups flour. Add enough additional flour to make a soft dough. Place in greased bowl and turn once to coat all surfaces. Cover and let rise in a warm place (85° F.) until doubled in bulk, about 1½ hours.

Punch down and turn out onto a lightly floured board. Knead until smooth and elastic. Divide dough in half and form into two loaves. Turn into greased 9 × 5 × 3-inch loaf pans. Cover and let rise until doubled in bulk, about 1 hour. Bake in a hot oven (400° F.) for 15 minutes, then reduce oven temperature to 350° F. and bake for 15 to 18 minutes longer, or until done. Remove from pans and cool on wire rack.

BOHEMIAN HOUSKA

2 loaves

Houska, flavored with lemon peel, mace or nutmeg, raisins and nuts, and braided, is synonymous with Christmas to those of Bohemian ancestry.

¼ *cup warm water (105° to 115° F.)*
1 *package active dry yeast*
⅓ *cup sugar*
4½ *to 5 cups sifted flour*
1 *cup milk, scalded*
¾ *cup butter or shortening*
1½ *teaspoons salt*
2 *eggs*
½ *teaspoon mace or nutmeg*
¾ *cup currants or seedless raisins*
½ *cup finely chopped blanched almonds*
2 *teaspoons grated lemon peel*
Melted butter
Confectioners' Sugar Icing
    (see index—optional)

Combine warm water, yeast, 1 tablespoon sugar, and 2 tablespoons flour, beating thoroughly. Cover and let rise in warm place until bubbly. Combine milk, butter or shortening, salt, and remaining sugar and cool to lukewarm. Add yeast mixture and eggs, beating well. Mix in 2 cups flour, mace or nutmeg, currants or raisins, almonds, and lemon peel. Add remaining flour as needed to make a moderately stiff dough. Cover and let rise in a warm place (85° F.) until doubled in bulk, 1½ to 2 hours.

Turn onto lightly floured board and divide dough into two portions. Divide each half into three pieces, roll each into a rope about 15 inches long, and braid. Place in greased 8½ × 4½ × 2⅝-inch loaf pans. Cover and let rise in warm place until doubled in bulk, about 1 to 1½ hours. Brush tops lightly with melted butter and bake in moderate oven (350° F.) for 30 to 35 minutes. Remove from pans and cool on wire rack. If desired, drizzle Confectioners' Sugar Icing over top of loaves while still warm.

BULGHUR WHEAT BREAD

2 loaves

Bulghur, or cracked wheat, is both nutritious and delicious. The grainy texture it gives to bread resembles that of old-fashioned bread of a century or two ago. In the Middle East bulghur is often served with chicken or lamb. The wheat is available in most gourmet shops and in some supermarkets.

⅓ *cup bulghur wheat, cooked according to*
    package directions
½ *cup boiling water*
¼ *cup butter*
½ *cup milk*
¼ *cup sugar*
2 *teaspoons salt*
1 *package active dry yeast*
¼ *cup warm water (105° to 115° F.)*
1 *egg*
4 *to 4½ cups sifted flour*

Combine bulghur, boiling water, and butter, stirring until butter melts. Add milk, sugar, and salt and cool to lukewarm. Soften yeast in warm water and add with egg to bulghur mixture. Stir in enough flour to make a moderately stiff dough.

Turn onto lightly floured board and knead until smooth and elastic. Place in greased bowl and turn once to grease top. Cover and let rise in a warm place (85° F.) until doubled in bulk, about 1½ to 2 hours. Turn onto lightly floured board and shape into 2 loaves. Place loaves in greased 8½ × 4½ × 2⅝-inch loaf pans. Cover and let rise until doubled in bulk, about 1 hour.

Bake in moderate oven (350° F.) for 40 minutes, or until done. Remove from pans and cool on wire rack.

ANADAMA BREAD

1 large loaf

An amusing tale has been handed down from one generation to the next concerning the famed Anadama bread. As the story goes, a disgruntled husband, irate over his lazy wife's slovenly cooking, took a pot of cornmeal mush from her, added some ingredients, and with a flare of temper exclaimed, "Damn it, Anna, bake some bread!"

  1½ *cups cold water*
   ⅓ *cup plus 2 teaspoons yellow or white cornmeal*
   1 *teaspoon salt*
   ⅓ *cup light molasses*
  1½ *tablespoons shortening*
   1 *package active dry yeast*
   ¼ *cup warm water (105° to 115° F.)*
   4 *to 4½ cups sifted flour*
   2 *teaspoons butter, melted*

Combine cold water, ⅓ cup cornmeal, and salt in 1-quart saucepan and bring to a boil, stirring constantly. Remove from heat and stir in molasses and shortening. Cool to lukewarm (100° to 105° F.). Soak yeast in warm water until dissolved, and stir into cooled cornmeal mixture. Add enough flour to make a soft dough.

Turn onto a lightly floured board and knead until smooth and elastic, about 10 minutes. Place in greased bowl and turn once to coat all surfaces. Cover and let rise in a warm place (85° F.) until doubled in bulk, about 1 to 1½ hours. Punch dough down, turn onto lightly floured board, and roll out into 18 × 9-inch rectangle. Starting at narrow end, roll up dough. Press ends of roll down with side of hand and fold ends under. Place in a well-greased 9 × 5 × 3-inch loaf pan. Let rise again until doubled in bulk, about 1 hour.

Brush top gently with melted butter and sprinkle evenly with remaining 2 teaspoons cornmeal. Bake in moderate oven (375° F.) for 45 minutes, or until done. Remove from pan and let cool on wire rack.

YANKEE-STYLE BROWN BREAD

2 loaves

Coarse texture and old-fashioned goodness are found in this yeast bread, which is similar to European black bread. Cornmeal provides texture, and molasses and raisins add extra flavor.

   1 *cup milk, scalded*
   ¼ *cup shortening*
   ¼ *cup light molasses*
   1 *tablespoon salt*
   1 *package active dry yeast*
   1 *cup warm water (105° to 115° F.)*
   2 *cups whole-wheat flour*
  1½ *cups yellow cornmeal*
  1½ *cups rye flour*
   1 *cup seedless raisins*

Blend first 4 ingredients and cool to lukewarm. Soften yeast in warm water and add liquids. Stir in 1½ cups whole-wheat flour, cornmeal, and rye flour, beating well. Stir in raisins. Cover and let rise in a warm place (85° F.) until doubled in bulk, 1½ to 2 hours. Turn onto floured board, using remaining ½ cup whole-wheat flour as needed, and knead until smooth and elastic. Place in greased bowl and turn once to grease top. Cover and let rise in a warm place until doubled in bulk, about 1 to 1½ hours.

Punch down, turn onto lightly floured board, and shape into 2 round loaves. Place on opposite corners of large greased baking sheet. Cover and let rise until doubled in bulk, about 1 to 1½ hours. Bake in moderate oven (375° F.) for 30 to 35 minutes, or until done.

ALASKAN SOURDOUGH STARTER AND BREAD

Sourdough hotcakes, the main breakfast dish of Alaskan prospectors, differ from other breads or hotcakes because the batter is leavened with a yeast starter and soda. The starter must be set 36 hours before it is to be used. Replenished regularly with flour and water, the starter will last weeks, even years. Some Alaskans are still using a starter traced back to an original starter brought into the state with the gold rush. To them the sourdough pot is a prized possession.

ALASKAN SOURDOUGH STARTER

1 *package active dry yeast*

2 *cups warm water (105° to 115° F.)*

2 *cups sifted flour*

1 *tablespoon sugar*

Soften yeast in warm water in large glass or ceramic bowl. Stir in flour and sugar, beating until smooth. Let stand in a warm place (85° F.) about 36 hours , stirring occasionally. Stir well just before using. Pour out the amount of starter needed. Replenish remaining starter by adding 1 cup *each* flour and warm water, beating well. Let stand in warm place until bubbly. Place in covered jar and refrigerate for future use.

ALASKAN SOURDOUGH BREAD   2 loaves

1 *cup Alaskan Sourdough Starter (see above)*

2 *cups plus 1 tablespoon warm water (105° to 115° F.)*

2 *tablespoons sugar*

1 *tablespoon salt*

6½ *to 7 cups sifted flour*

2 *tablespoons shortening, melted and cooled*

½ *teaspoon baking soda*

Cornmeal

Combine starter, 2 cups warm water, sugar, salt, and 2 cups flour, beating well. Cover loosely and let stand in a warm place (85° F.) for 18 to 24 hours. Stir sponge down. Add shortening, soda dissolved in 1 tablespoon warm water, and flour to make a stiff dough.

Turn onto lightly floured board and knead until smooth and elastic. Place in greased bowl and turn once to grease top. Cover and let rise in warm place (85° F.) until doubled in bulk, 1½ to 2 hours. Punch down and turn onto lightly floured board. Shape into 2 loaves, 14 inches long, or rounds. Place each loaf on a greased baking sheet sprinkled with cornmeal and make 3 slashes on top of each, using a razor blade or very sharp knife. Cover and let rise again in warm place until doubled in bulk, about 1 hour. Bake in moderate oven (375° F.) for 45 to 50 minutes, or until done.

TILLAMOOK CHEESE BREAD
1 loaf

Tillamook cheese is similar to Cheddar. Bright yellow in color, and pungent in flavor, it is produced in Tillamook, Oregon. This bread is quick and easy to make.

½ *cup hot water*

2 *tablespoons sugar*

2 *tablespoons shortening*

1 *teaspoon salt*

1 *cup shredded Tillamook, Monterey Jack, or Cheddar cheese*

1 *package active dry yeast*

¼ *cup warm water (105° to 115° F.)*

1 *egg*

2⅓ *to 2⅔ cups sifted flour*

Combine hot water, sugar, shortening, salt, and cheese. Cool to lukewarm. Soften yeast in warm water and add to cheese mixture. Stir in egg and enough flour to make a stiff dough. Cover and let rise in a warm place (85° F.) until doubled in bulk, about 1½ hours.

Turn onto a lightly floured board and knead until smooth and elastic. Shape into a loaf. Place in greased 8½ × 4½ × 2⅝-inch loaf pan. Let rise again until doubled in bulk, about 1 hour.

Bake in moderate oven (375° F.) for 30 to 35 minutes, or until done. Cool bread in pan for 5 minutes, then transfer to wire rack to finish cooling.

SWEDISH LIMPA

2 loaves

Limpa originated in Scandinavia and it is very popular in Minnesota and North Dakota, where the Scandinavian settlers of the mid-1800s established farms. Being of Swedish descent, I consider this one of my favorite breads.

1½   *cups warm water (105° to 115° F.)*

⅓   *cup brown sugar, firmly packed*

¼   *cup light molasses*

¼   *cup shortening*

1½   *tablespoons grated orange peel*

1   *tablespoon caraway seeds (optional)*

1   *tablespoon salt*

1   *teaspoon anise seeds*

2   *packages active dry yeast*

2½   *cups rye flour*

3   *cups sifted flour (approximate)*

Melted butter or milk-sugar glaze

Combine 1 cup warm water, brown sugar, molasses, and shortening. Heat until sugar dissolves and shortening melts, stirring constantly. Add orange peel, caraway seeds, salt, and anise seeds. Cool to lukewarm. Dissolve yeast in remaining ½ cup warm water and add to liquids. Stir in rye flour and enough sifted flour to make a soft dough.

Turn onto lightly floured board and knead until smooth and elastic. Put into a greased bowl and turn once to grease top. Cover and let rise in a warm place (85° F.) until doubled in bulk, about 1 to 2 hours. Punch down and turn onto lightly floured board. Cut in half, knead each half 6 to 8 times, and shape into 2 round loaves. Place in 2 greased pans or in opposite corners of large greased baking sheet. Let rise again until doubled in bulk, about 1 hour.

Bake in moderate oven (375° F.) for 35 to 40 minutes, or until done. Remove from oven and immediately brush tops and sides with melted butter or milk-sugar glaze (½ teaspoon sugar dissolved in 1 tablespoon milk).

CHRISTMAS STOLLEN

1 large stollen

Although baking was done primarily at home in the Midwest of the late 1800s, the German bakery was an important institution. Many delicious baked goods came from these little shops situated in the German sections of Chicago, Cincinnati, St. Louis, and Milwaukee. One of these items was Stollen, a traditional German Christmas bread that became a frequent Sunday treat.

1   *package active dry yeast*

¼   *cup warm water (105° to 115° F.)*

½   *cup milk, scalded*

¼   *cup sugar*

¼   *cup butter*

½   *teaspoon salt*

1   *egg*

1   *teaspoon grated lemon peel*

1   *teaspoon vanilla*

½   *teaspoon mace or nutmeg*

¼   *cup each chopped candied red cherries, citron, currants or seedless raisins, and blanched almonds*

2½ *to 2¾ cups sifted flour*

Melted butter

Confectioners' sugar or Confectioners' Sugar Icing (see index)

Candied fruit and nuts for decoration (optional)

Soften yeast in warm water. Combine milk, sugar, butter, and salt and cool to lukewarm. Add egg, lemon peel, vanilla, mace or nutmeg, and softened yeast, beating until smooth. Add fruits, almonds, and enough flour to make a moderately stiff dough.

Knead on lightly floured board until smooth and elastic. Place in greased bowl, turning once to grease top. Cover and let rise in a warm place (85° F.) until doubled in bulk, about 1 to 2 hours. Punch down and turn onto lightly floured board. Shape into a 14 × 9-inch oval and brush with melted butter. Fold in half lengthwise and place on well-greased baking sheet. Let rise again, covered, until doubled in bulk, about 45 minutes to 1 hour.

Bake in moderate oven (375° F.) for 30 to 35 minutes, or until done. Brush with melted butter. Cool slightly and sprinkle generously with confectioners' sugar or frost with Confectioners' Sugar Icing and decorate with candied fruit and nuts.

NARSKE JULEKAGE (Norwegian Christmas Cake)

2 loaves or cakes

Julekage is one of the many rich and fragrant baked goods introduced by the Scandinavians. Ground cardamom seeds give this fruit bread its unusual flavor.

- 1 *package active dry yeast*
- ¼ *cup warm water (105° to 115° F.)*
- 1 *cup milk, scalded*
- ½ *cup sugar*
- ½ *cup butter*
- 1 *teaspoon salt*
- 1 *teaspoon cardamom*
- 2 *eggs*
- 1 *cup currants or seedless raisins*
- ½ *cup chopped mixed candied fruits*
- ½ *cup chopped blanched almonds*
- ¼ *cup chopped candied orange peel*
- 5 *to 5 ½ cups sifted flour*
- *Melted butter*
- *Confectioners' Sugar Icing (see index)*

Soften yeast in warm water. Combine milk, sugar, butter, salt, and cardamom and cool to lukewarm. Add eggs and softened yeast, beating until smooth. Add currants or raisins, candied fruits, almonds, and orange peel. Add enough flour to make a moderately stiff dough.

Turn onto lightly floured board and knead until smooth and elastic. Place in greased bowl, turning once to grease top. Cover and let rise in a warm place (85° F.) until doubled in bulk, about 1 to 1½ hours. Punch down, turn onto lightly floured board, and divide in half. Shape into 2 loaves and place in greased 9 × 5 × 3-inch loaf pans or shape into 2 rounds and place in greased 9-inch layer pans. Cover and let rise again until doubled in bulk, about 1 hour. Bake loaves in moderate oven (350° F.) for 45 minutes, or until done. Bake round cakes in moderate oven (375° F.) for 30 minutes, or until done. Let cool in pans for 10 minutes, then turn onto wire rack. Brush with melted butter. Cool slightly and frost with Confectioners' Sugar Icing, if desired.

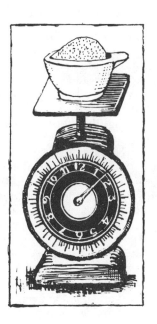

MORAVIAN SUGAR CAKE

2 coffeecakes

Prepared during the Easter season by people of Moravian ancestry living in Salem, North Carolina, and environs, the dough for this coffeecake is rich and buttery. The mashed potatoes make the cake very moist.

CAKE DOUGH

1 *package active dry yeast*

¼ *cup warm water (105° to 115° F.)*

1 *cup milk, scalded*

½ *cup sugar*

½ *cup butter or shortening*

1 *cup hot unseasoned mashed potatoes*

1½ *teaspoons salt*

2 *eggs*

4½ *to 5 cups flour*

TOPPING

1½ *cups light brown sugar, firmly packed*

1 *teaspoon cinnamon*

½ *cup butter, melted*

To prepare cake dough, soften yeast in warm water. Combine milk, sugar, butter or shortening, potatoes, and salt and cool to lukewarm. Add eggs and softened yeast, beating until smooth. Add enough flour to make a moderately stiff dough.

Knead on lightly floured board until smooth and elastic. Place in greased bowl and turn once to grease top. Cover and let rise in a warm place (85° F.) until doubled in bulk, about 1½ hours. Punch down, turn onto lightly floured board, and divide in half. Roll out each half into a 13 × 9-inch rectangle and place in greased 13 × 9 × 2-inch pans. Cover and let rise again until doubled in bulk, about 45 minutes. With finger, punch holes in raised dough.

To prepare topping, combine brown sugar and cinnamon and sprinkle evenly over cake tops. Brush with melted butter. Bake in moderate oven (375° F.) for 25 minutes, or until done.

CARDAMOM BRAIDS

2 coffee braids

1½ *cups milk, scalded*

¾ *cup sugar*

1 *package active dry yeast*

5 *to 5 ¼ cups sifted flour*

½ *cup butter, softened*

3 *egg yolks*

1½ *to 2 teaspoons cardamom*

½ *teaspoon salt*

Additional milk and sugar for top

Cool milk to lukewarm (100° to 105° F.). Add 1 tablespoon sugar and yeast, stirring until dissolved. Add 2½ cups flour, beating until smooth. Cover and let rise in a warm place (85° F.) until doubled in bulk, about 1½ to 2 hours. Beat in butter, remaining sugar, egg yolks, cardamom, and salt. Add flour as needed to make a moderately stiff dough.

Turn onto lightly floured board and knead until smooth and elastic. Place in greased bowl and turn once to grease top. Cover and let rise again until doubled in bulk, about 1 to 1½ hours. Punch down and turn onto lightly floured board. Divide dough in half and then divide each half into 3 equal pieces. Roll out each piece into rope about 16 inches long. Pinch 3 ends together, braid, and pinch opposite ends together. Repeat process. Place each braid on a greased baking sheet and let rise until double in bulk, about 1 to 1½ hours.

Brush tops with milk and sprinkle lightly with sugar. Bake in moderate oven (375° F.) for 25 to 30 minutes, or until done.

ROLL DOUGH

About 3 dozen rolls

Various kinds of rolls have been developed over the years, and some have historic significance. The *kipfels,* or crescent rolls, of Vienna symbolize the Viennese foiling of a Turkish invasion. These were later brought by

Marie Antoinette to France, where, made of a richer dough, they became known as *croissants*.

2 *packages active dry yeast*
½ *cup warm water (105° to 115° F.)*
1½ *cups milk, scalded*
½ *cup butter or shortening*
¼ *cup sugar*
2 *teaspoons salt*
2 *eggs, beaten*
6 *cups sifted flour (approximate)*
Melted butter

Soften yeast in warm water. Combine milk, butter or shortening, sugar, and salt. Cool to lukewarm and stir in yeast, eggs, and 2 cups flour, beating until smooth. Add flour as needed to make a moderately stiff dough.

Turn onto lightly floured board and knead until smooth and elastic. Place in greased bowl, turning once to grease top. Cover and let rise in a warm place (85° F.) until doubled in bulk, about 1 to 1½ hours. Punch down, turn onto lightly floured board, and shape as desired (see variations). Arrange rolls on lightly greased baking sheet, cover, and let rise until doubled in bulk, about 45 minutes.

Brush tops lightly with melted butter. Bake in hot oven (400° F.) for 15 to 20 minutes.

VARIATIONS

Parker House Rolls: Roll out dough ¼ inch thick. Cut into 2½- or 3-inch circles with floured cutter. Mark a crease across circle to one side of center. Brush surface with melted butter. Fold larger side over smaller one and press edges together. Bake as directed above.

Cloverleaf Rolls: Pinch off dough as needed to make 1-inch balls. Shape each piece with fingertips, tucking edges under until top of ball is smooth. Place 3 balls, smooth side up, in well-greased 2½-inch muffin cups.

Crescent Rolls: Roll out dough ¼ inch thick into an 8- or 9-inch circle. Brush surface lightly with melted butter. Cut circle into 6 or 8 wedges. Roll up each wedge starting at outside and rolling toward point.

BRIOCHE
3 dozen rolls

The round "bun with a little hat" is traditionally French and was brought to the New World by the early settlers of New Orleans. Originating in the district of Brie, it was once made with the cheese of the area, hence the name Brioche.

½ *cup milk, scalded*
1 *cup butter*
⅔ *cup sugar*
1½ *teaspoons salt*
2 *packages active dry yeast*
½ *cup warm water (105° to 115° F.)*
6 *to 6½ cups sifted flour*
4 *eggs, beaten*

EGG WASH

1 *egg*
1 *tablespoon water*

Combine milk, butter, sugar, and salt, stir until sugar is dissolved, and cool to lukewarm. Soften yeast in warm water. Add yeast and 2 cups flour to liquids, beating well. Cover and let rise in a warm place (85° F.) until bubbly. Stir in eggs. Add flour as needed to make a soft dough.

Turn dough onto lightly floured board and knead until smooth and elastic. Place in greased bowl and turn once to grease top. Cover and let rise again until doubled in bulk about 1½ to 2 hours. Punch down and turn onto lightly floured board. Cut into 36 pieces of equal size. To shape brioche, cut one-fourth of dough from each piece and shape both into balls. Place the large ball in well-greased 2½-inch muffin cup. Press a deep indentation in center with thumb and press small ball into indentation. Continue process until all dough is used. Cover and let rise in warm place until doubled in bulk, about 45 minutes. Prepare egg wash. Beat egg and water together and carefully brush over tops of rolls. Bake in moderate oven (350° F.) for 15 minutes, or until done.

DAKOTA ROLLS

18 rolls

ROLLS

    1 *package active dry yeast*
    ¼ *cup warm water (105° to 115° F.)*
    1 *cup milk, scalded*
    3 *tablespoons butter or shortening*
    3 *tablespoons sugar*
    1 *teaspoon salt*
    1 *egg*
  3⅓ *to 3½ cups sifted flour*

FILLING

    2 *tablespoons butter, melted*
    ½ *cup light brown sugar, firmly packed*

TOPPING

    ½ *cup light brown sugar, firmly packed*
    ¼ *cup light corn syrup*
    2 *tablespoons butter*

To prepare roll dough, soften yeast in warm water. Combine milk, butter or shortening, sugar, and salt and cool to lukewarm. Add egg and softened yeast. Beat in enough flour to make a soft dough. Beat vigorously. Cover and let rise in warm place (85° F.) until doubled in bulk, about 1 to 1½ hours.

Turn out on lightly floured board and roll into 18 × 10-inch rectangle. Brush dough with melted butter and sprinkle with brown sugar. Roll up jelly-roll fashion, starting with long side. Cut in 1-inch slices.

To prepare topping, combine brown sugar, corn syrup, and butter in a 13 × 9 × 2-inch pan. Heat slowly until butter melts, mixing thoroughly. Set aside to cool. Place rolls flat on brown-sugar mixture. Cover and let rise again until doubled in bulk, about 45 minutes to 1 hour.

Bake in moderate oven (375° F.) for 25 minutes, or until done. Let stand in pan about 2 minutes, then turn out onto baking sheet. Serve warm.

PHILADELPHIA STICKY BUNS

24 buns

Sticky buns are a specialty of the City of Brotherly Love. Derived from the cinnamon rolls (*schnecken*) of the people of Germantown, these gooey yeast rolls have been favorites with Philadelphians since the late 1600s.

DOUGH

    1 *cup milk, scalded*
    ½ *cup butter*
    ⅓ *cup sugar*
  1½ *teaspoons salt*
    1 *package active dry yeast*
    ¼ *cup warm water (105° to 115° F.)*
    3 *eggs*
  5¼ *to 5¾ cups sifted flour*

FILLING

    ½ *cup butter, softened*
    1 *cup light brown sugar, firmly packed*
    2 *teaspoons cinnamon*
    ⅔ *cup seedless raisins or currants*
    ⅔ *cup chopped pecans*
    1 *cup dark corn syrup*

Combine first 4 ingredients and stir until butter melts and sugar dissolves. Cool to lukewarm. Soften yeast in warm water and add to liquids. Stir in eggs and enough flour to make a soft moderately stiff dough.

Turn onto lightly floured board and knead until smooth and elastic. Place in greased bowl, turning once to coat thoroughly. Cover and let rise in a warm place (85° F.) until doubled in bulk, about 1½ to 2 hours. Turn dough onto lightly floured board, and divide in half. Roll out each half ¼ inch thick into an 18 × 10-inch rectangle.

Spread each rectangle with ¼ cup softened butter. Combine sugar and cinnamon and sprinkle half over each rectangle. Scatter half the raisins or currants and nuts over each piece of dough. Butter two 9 × 9 × 2-inch pans thoroughly and drizzle ½ cup syrup over surface of each. Roll each portion of dough jelly-roll fashion, starting on long side. Cut each roll into 12 slices and place flat on pans. Cover and let rise until doubled in bulk, about 45 minutes to 1 hour.

Bake in moderate oven (350° F.) for 30 minutes, or until done. Turn out of pans onto baking sheet immediately.

KOLACH

24 to 30 kolaches

Kolach, or *koláč*, is a Czechoslovakian contribution to American cookery. Similar to Danish pastry, these round yeast buns are light and delicate and contain a fruit filling of prunes, apricots, or preserves.

   1 *cup milk, scalded*

   ⅔ *cup butter or shortening*

   ½ *cup sugar*

   2 *teaspoons salt*

   2 *packages active dry yeast*

   ½ *cup warm water (105° to 115° F.)*

   3 *eggs, beaten*

   1 *teaspoon grated lemon peel*

   ½ *teaspoon nutmeg*

   6 *cups sifted flour (approximate)*

   Fruit filling (see below)

   Melted butter

   Confectioners' sugar

Combine first 4 ingredients and cool to lukewarm. Soften yeast in warm water. Add yeast, eggs, lemon peel, and nutmeg to liquid, mixing well. Stir in enough flour to make a soft dough.

Turn onto lightly floured board and knead until smooth and elastic. Place in greased bowl and turn once to grease top. Cover and let rise in a warm place (85° F.) until doubled in bulk, about 1 to 2 hours. Punch dough down and turn onto lightly floured board. Divide into 24 or 30 pieces, shape each into a ball, and flatten to make 3½- or 4-inch circle. Place 2 inches apart on greased baking sheet. Cover and let rise again until doubled in bulk, about 45 minutes, or until done.

Make a deep depression in center of each bun, using thumb or the back of a melon-ball cutter. Spoon desired filling into hole. Brush dough lightly with melted butter. Bake in moderate oven (350° F.) for 18 to 20 minutes, or until done. Remove from pan and cool on wire racks. Dust with confectioners' sugar when slightly warm.

Prune Nut Filling

   1 *cup finely chopped pitted prunes*

   ½ *cup water*

   ¼ *cup sugar*

   ½ *teaspoon grated lemon peel*

   ¼ *teaspoon cinnamon*

   ¼ *cup chopped walnuts*

Combine first 3 ingredients in saucepan, bring to a boil, and cover. Reduce heat and simmer for 10 minutes. Remove cover and cook until thickened, stirring constantly. Stir in lemon peel, cinnamon, and nuts. Yield: 1¼ cups, enough for 24 to 30 rolls.

Apricot Filling

Follow recipe for Prune Nut Filling and substitute 1 cup chopped dried apricots for the prunes, increase lemon peel to 1 teaspoon, and omit nuts.

Jam and Preserve Fillings

For fillings, use any thick jam, marmalade, or preserves.

HOT-CROSS BUNS
20 or 26 buns

"Hot-Cross Buns!
Hot-Cross Buns!
One a penny, two a penny,
Hot-Cross Buns!
Hot-Cross Buns!
If you have no daughters,
Give them to your sons."
—1916 Mother Goose

Served traditionally on Good Friday, Hot-Cross Buns were first baked by pre-Christian inhabitants of England to honor the goddess of spring. Bakers added the cross when Christianity was introduced.

DOUGH

    2 *packages active dry yeast*
    ½ *cup warm water (105° to 115° F.)*
    1 *cup milk, scalded*
    ⅔ *cup softened butter or shortening*
    ⅔ *cup sugar*
    2 *teaspoons salt*
    3 *eggs, beaten*
    1 *teaspoon cinnamon*
    ½ *teaspoon nutmeg*
    2 *teaspoons grated lemon peel*
    1 *cup seedless raisins or currants*
    ½ *cup chopped mixed candied fruits or citron*
 5½ *to 6 cups sifted flour*
    1 *egg yolk*
    2 *tablespoons cold water*

FROSTING

    1 *tablespoon milk*
    2 *teaspoons softened butter*
    ½ *teaspoon vanilla*
    1 *cup sifted confectioners' sugar (approximate)*

Soften yeast in warm water. Combine milk, butter or shortening, sugar, and salt, stirring until sugar is dissolved. Cool to lukewarm and add yeast, eggs, spices, lemon peel, fruit, and 2 cups of flour, mixing thoroughly. Add flour as needed to make a soft dough.

Turn onto lightly floured board and knead until dough is smooth and elastic. Place in greased bowl and turn once to grease top. Cover and let rise in a warm place (85° F.) until doubled in bulk, about 1½ to 2 hours. Punch dough down, turn onto floured board, and divide into 20 to 26 pieces of equal size. Shape each piece into a bun. Place buns, 2 inches apart, on lightly greased baking sheet. Use scissors to snip small cross on top of each bun. Cover and let rise in warm place until doubled in bulk, about 45 minutes.

While buns are rising, prepare egg wash. Combine egg yolk and cold water, beating slightly. Brush egg wash over tops of buns just before baking. Bake in moderate oven (375° F.) 18 to 20 minutes for large buns, 15 minutes for smaller ones, or until done. Remove buns from baking sheet and cool. While buns are still warm, frost a small cross on top of each bun.

To prepare frosting, blend together milk, butter, vanilla, and ½ cup confectioners' sugar. Stir in additional sugar to achieve spreading consistency.

LOVE-FEAST BUNS
8 large or 16 medium-sized buns

The love feast, or agape, is a religious custom dating back to early Christian days. No love feast is complete without the symbolic breaking of bread among the congregation. The Moravians, who settled in the New World in Pennsylvania and South Carolina, celebrated this rite using traditional flat yeast buns now known as Love-Feast Buns. In early times the buns were prepared in the Brothers' House in Old Salem, but in 1774 a community bakery was established because some people felt it improper for young women to go to the single Brothers' House.

2 *packages active dry yeast*

1 *cup warm water (105° to 115° F.)*

1 *cup sugar*

¼ *cup butter*

¼ *cup shortening*

1 *egg*

½ *cup warm mashed potatoes*

1½ *teaspoons salt*

4¼ *to 4¾ cups sifted flour*

Cream or melted butter

Soften yeast in warm water. Cream sugar, butter, and shortening. Beat in egg, potatoes, and salt. Add softened yeast to sugar mixture. Add enough flour to make a soft dough.

Turn onto lightly floured board and knead until smooth and elastic. Place in greased bowl, turning once to grease top. Cover and let rise in a warm place (85° F.) until doubled in bulk, about 1½ to 2 hours. Turn onto lightly floured board. Cut into 8 or 16 equal portions and shape into balls. Place 3 inches apart on a greased baking sheet. Cover and let rise again until double in bulk, about 45 minutes to 1 hour. Bake in moderate oven (375° F.) 20 to 25 minutes for large buns, 15 minutes for medium-sized, or until done. Remove from oven and brush tops lightly with cream or melted butter.

PLANTATION CORN BREAD

12 to 16 servings

Corn was an important part of the diet of the Indians and Colonial Americans. Pounded into meal, it was used to make a variety of breads, porridges, cakes, and other foods. Corn bread was one such food. Numerous varieties of corn bread have been developed over the years with such whimsical names as hoecake, ashcake, and Johnny cake. Hoecakes were so christened because they were actually baked on a hoe over an open fire. Similarly, ashcakes, wrapped in palm or cabbage leaves, were baked in hot ashes. The name "Johnny cake" is an alteration of "Shawnee cake" and is derived from a kind of bread made by the Shawnee Indians.

Yankee and Southern corn breads differ because of the type of cornmeal used in each locale. Yellow corn was mostly grown in New England, while white was predominant in the South. In general, Southern corn bread is richer because plantation cooks used more buttermilk and shortening in their recipes.

2 *cups white cornmeal*

½ *cup sifted flour*

2 *teaspoons baking powder*

1 *teaspoon salt*

½ *teaspoon baking soda*

1 *cup buttermilk*

1 *cup milk*

¼ *cup shortening, melted and cooled*

2 *eggs, beaten*

Preheat oven to 450° F. Five minutes before mixing, place a well-greased 9 × 9 × 2-inch pan on bottom shelf of oven. Sift together first 5 ingredients in bowl. Add milk, shortening, and eggs and stir just until dry ingredients are moistened.

Pour batter into prepared pan. Bake *at once* in top half of very hot oven (450° F.) for 25 to 30 minutes, or until done. Serve hot.

VARIATION

Yankee-Style Corn Bread: Substitute 2 cups yellow cornmeal for the white, and increase milk to 2 cups, omitting buttermilk and soda. Sift in ¼ cup sugar with dry ingredients. Increase shortening to ⅓ cup.

BACON OR CRACKLIN' BREAD
8 to 10 servings

Cracklings are the crisp pieces of pork rind remaining after lard has been rendered. They were used extensively in Southern dishes of a century ago. Today cracklings can be purchased in the gourmet sections of food shops and are often used as hors d'oeuvres.

> 6 *slices bacon, diced, or ⅓ cup crisp cracklings*
> 1½ *cups yellow or white cornmeal*
> ¼ *cup sifted flour*
> 1 *teaspoon baking soda*
> 1 *teaspoon salt*
> 2 *cups buttermilk*
> 1 *egg, beaten*

Pan-fry bacon until crisp, drain on paper towels, and crumble finely. Combine cornmeal, flour, soda, and salt. Add buttermilk, egg, and crumbled bacon or cracklings, mixing just until dry ingredients are moistened.

Pour into hot greased 10-inch skillet with heatproof or removable handle. Bake in hot oven (400° F.) for 30 minutes, or until done. Cut in wedges and serve hot.

KANSAS APPLESAUCE CORN BREAD
12 to 16 squares

> 1 *cup sifted flour*
> 1 *cup yellow cornmeal*
> 3 *tablespoons sugar*
> 4 *teaspoons baking powder*
> 1½ *teaspoons salt*
> 1 *egg, beaten*
> 1½ *cups milk*
> ½ *cup applesauce*
> ¼ *cup butter or shortening, melted*

Place a greased 8 × 8 × 2-inch pan in a hot oven (425° F.) to heat while mixing batter. Sift together first 5 ingredients. Combine remaining ingredients and blend into dry ingredients, stirring just until dry ingredients are moistened.

Pour batter into prepared pan and bake for 25 minutes, or until done. Cut into squares and serve hot or warm.

MEXICAN CORN BREAD
8 servings

Jalapeño peppers add an unusual taste to the traditional Colonial corn bread. A favorite in the Southwest, Mexican Corn Bread combines elements of Spanish and Indian cooking. The original recipe came via Mexico and Texas.

> 1 *cup yellow or white cornmeal*
> ¾ *teaspoon salt*
> ½ *teaspoon baking soda*
> 1 *(8¾-ounce) can cream-style corn*
> 1 *cup milk*
> ¼ *cup bacon drippings*
> 2 *eggs, beaten*
> ½ *cup finely chopped onion*
> 1 *or 2* jalapeño *peppers, chopped*
> 1 *cup (¼ pound) shredded sharp Cheddar cheese*

Combine first 3 ingredients. Mix together next 6 ingredients in mixing bowl. Add the dry ingredients and stir just until they are moistened.

Pour half the batter into a hot well-greased 10-inch skillet with heatproof or removable handle. Sprinkle cheese over batter. Top with remaining batter. Bake in hot oven (400° F.) for 45 minutes, or until done. Cut into wedges and serve hot.

HUSH PUPPIES

Hush Puppies and catfish are inseparable throughout the South. A delightful tale has evolved surrounding the name. As dogs caught the odor of frying fish and began to whine, the fisherman tossed them bits of newly fried cornmeal with the soothing words, "Hush, puppy!"

SOUTH CAROLINA HUSH PUPPIES

20 hush puppies

  ¾ *cup white cornmeal*
  ¼ *cup sifted flour*
  1 *teaspoon sugar*
  1 *teaspoon baking powder*
  ¾ *teaspoon salt*
  ½ *teaspoon baking soda*
  ½ *cup buttermilk*
  1 *egg, beaten*
  ¼ *cup finely chopped onion*
  Fat for deep frying

Sift together first 6 ingredients in bowl. Add next 3 ingredients and stir until blended.

Drop by teaspoonfuls into deep hot fat (350° F.). Fry 2 to 3 minutes, turning as needed to brown evenly. Drain on paper towels.

NOTE: *Self-rising cornmeal may be substituted and baking powder and soda omitted.*

QUICK AND EASY BAKED HUSH PUPPIES

16 large or 36 small hush puppies

These are very tasty, and they freeze and reheat well.

  1 *cup yellow or white cornmeal*
  1 *cup sifted flour*
  2 *teaspoons baking powder*
  1 *teaspoon sugar*
  1 *teaspoon salt*

  ⅛ *teaspoon cayenne pepper*
  2 *eggs, beaten*
  ¾ *cup milk*
  ½ *cup finely chopped onion*
  ¼ *cup melted fat or cooking oil*

Sift together first 6 ingredients in bowl. Add remaining ingredients and stir just until blended.

Spoon batter into well-greased muffin pans, filling about two-thirds full (use 1¾ × 1-inch or 2½ × 1¼-inch pans). Bake in hot oven (425° F.) 10 minutes for tiny muffins or 15 minutes for large ones, or until done.

NAVAJO FRY BREAD

18 to 20 rounds

Navajo Fry Bread was a favorite accompaniment to mutton stew among the pueblo dwellers of the Southwest. The Spanish originally introduced both wheat and sheep into the region.

  2 *cups sifted flour*
  2 *teaspoons baking powder*
  ½ *teaspoon salt*
  1 *tablespoon shortening*
  1 *cup water (approximate)*
  Cooking oil for frying

Sift together flour, baking powder, and salt and cut in shortening with two knives or pastry blender until mixture resembles coarse meal. Add enough water to make a soft dough. Knead on lightly floured board until smooth and elastic. Pinch off enough dough to make 1½-inch balls. Roll or slap back and forth from hand to hand until each ball is a flat 4-inch round.

Fry in skillet in ¼-inch-deep hot fat at 400°F. until lightly brown on both sides, turning once. Bread becomes puffy as it fries. Drain on paper towels. Serve hot, plain, or with jam, honey, or favorite tortilla topping.

NOTE: *These are much like tortillas. Kids would have fun making them.*

SPOON BREAD

Spoon Bread, traditional food of the South, traces its ancestry to a cornmeal and water porridge called sappawn *by the Indians. Folklore has it that a forgetful housewife left an earthen crock of porridge too long on the fire. It was no longer a porridge but a concoction that was crisp around the edges but creamy inside. Spooned from the pot, it was eaten hot with lots of butter. Later eggs and milk were added for a richer flavor. In Virginia, a slightly different version was made called Batter Bread. Today Spoon Bread is prepared in many variations and has become a favorite for brunch or dinner as an accompaniment to ham or turkey in many areas of the United States.*

TEXAS SPOON BREAD

6 servings

The dash of cayenne pepper gives this spoon bread a Texas accent.

    1 *cup white or yellow cornmeal*
    2 *teaspoons sugar (optional)*
    1 *teaspoon salt*
    3 *cups milk*
    2 *tablespoons butter*
    ¼ *teaspoon paprika (optional)*
    Dash of cayenne pepper (optional)
    3 *eggs, separated*
    2 *teaspoons baking powder*

Combine cornmeal, sugar, and salt in heavy saucepan. Stir in 2 cups milk. Cook over low heat, stirring constantly, until mixture is very thick. Remove from heat and stir in butter, paprika, and cayenne. Beat in remaining 1 cup milk, then well-beaten egg yolks and baking powder. Beat egg whites until they hold soft peaks and carefully fold into cornmeal mixture.

Pour into greased 2-quart casserole or soufflé dish. Bake in moderate oven (350° F.) for 50 minutes, or until puffed and brown. Serve *at once* with soft butter and jam.

VARIATIONS

Cheese Spoon Bread: Omit paprika and cayenne and add 1 cup of shredded Cheddar or American cheese to batter with egg yolks. If desired, ½ teaspoon of fines herbes may be added with the cheese.

Virginia Spoon Bread: Use white cornmeal, increase sugar to ¼ cup, and omit paprika and cayenne.

COLONIAL BROWN BREAD

3 loaves

Brown bread, hot and steaming, served with baked beans is traditionally identified with New England. Although cornmeal was an important staple in early Yankee cookery, wheat and rye flours were used as they became available. Authentic brown bread must contain three kinds of flour and meal. Molasses, another essential ingredient, was brought from the West Indies by the New England traders.

    1 *cup rye flour*
    1 *cup yellow cornmeal*
    1 *cup whole-wheat flour*
    1 *teaspoon baking powder*
    1 *teaspoon salt*
    ½ *teaspoon baking soda*
    1½ *cups buttermilk*
    ¾ *cup light molasses*
    2 *tablespoons butter, melted*
    1 *cup seedless raisins*

Select 3 empty 1-pound cans and grease insides throughly. Cut rounds of aluminum foil or waxed paper the size of the can bottom, grease, and place in bottom of each can. Combine first 6 ingredients. Mix together buttermilk, molasses, and butter. Blend dry ingredients into liquids and stir in raisins. Fill cans about two-thirds full and cover tightly. Place on rack in large covered kettle and add boiling water to reach halfway up sides of cans. Cover tightly and simmer for 2 hours.

Transfer cans to baking pan. Bake in slow oven (300° F.) for 30 minutes. Cool in cans for 10 minutes, remove from cans, discarding foil or waxed paper, and finish cooling on rack.

NOTE: *This stores and freezes well.*

IRISH SODA BREAD

1 8-inch loaf; 8 servings

First brought to New England in the 1800s by the Irish settlers, Irish Soda Bread has become a popular St. Patrick's Day delight. It is a cross between a biscuit and a coffeecake.

  2 *cups sifted flour*

  ⅓ *cup sugar*

  1 *teaspoon salt*

  ¾ *teaspoon baking soda*

  ½ *cup seedless raisins*

  1 *teaspoon caraway seeds (optional)*

  ¾ *cup buttermilk*

  ¼ *cup butter or shortening, melted*

  1 *egg, beaten*

Sift together first 4 ingredients into bowl and stir in raisins and caraway seeds. Add remaining ingredients and stir just until dry ingredients are moistened.

Spread evenly in greased 8-inch layer cake pan. Bake in moderate oven (350° F.) for 30 to 35 minutes, or until done.

NOTE: *If a smooth top is desired, reduce buttermilk to ⅔ cup and turn dough onto lightly floured board and knead lightly. Shape into an 8-inch round and place in a greased 8-inch layer cake pan. Mark into 8 even wedges, using a table knife and cutting into dough about ½ inch.*

WEST COAST DATE-WALNUT BREAD

1 large loaf

Modern methods of packaging and trsnsportation have enabled date-walnut bread to become a popular item throughout the United States. Dates and walnuts were probably brought to America by Spanish missionaries.

  1 *cup coarsely chopped pitted dates*

  1 *cup sugar*

  ½ *cup shortening*

  1 *cup boiling water*

  2 *cups sifted flour*

  2½ *teaspoons baking powder*

  ½ *teaspoon salt*

  2 *eggs, beaten*

  2 *teaspoons lemon juice*

  1 *teaspoon grated lemon peel*

  1 *cup coarsely chopped walnuts*

Combine dates and sugar in bowl. Add shortening to boiling water and simmer just until shortening melts. Pour over dates and sugar, stirring until sugar dissolves, then cool. While mixture is cooling, sift together flour, baking powder, and salt. Add eggs, lemon juice and peel to date mixture. Add dry ingredients, stirring just until blended. Fold in nuts.

Pour into greased and floured 9 × 5 × 3-inch loaf pan. Bake in slow oven (325° F.) for 1 hour, or until done. Cool in pan on wire rack for 5 minutes, then transfer to rack to finish cooling. When cold, wrap in aluminum foil and store in refrigerator.

NOTE: *This bread freezes well. For easier handling, allow bread to cool completely, slice, put foil between each slice, and freeze. Good plain, it is also delicious spread with cream cheese, butter, marmalade, or jelly.*

MINNESOTA APPLESAUCE BREAD

1 loaf

Some of the country's best apples come from Minnesota. I've walked the orchards of La Crescent, Minnesota, located on the Mississippi River, to pick and eat out of hand the delicious apples. The beauty and fragrance of the blossoms in spring are magnificent.

2½ *cups sifted flour*
¾ *cup sugar*
3 *teaspoons baking powder*
1½ *teaspoons salt*
½ *teaspoon cinnamon*
½ *teaspoon nutmeg*
½ *cup chopped walnuts*
2 *eggs, well beaten*
1 *(15-ounce) jar applesauce*
¼ *cup shortening, melted*

Sift together first 6 ingredients and stir in walnuts. Add eggs, applesauce, and shortening, mixing just until dry ingredients are moistened.

Pour into greased 9 × 5 × 3-inch loaf pan. Smooth top with knife. Bake in moderate oven (350° F.) for 60 to 70 minutes, or until done. Cool in pan for 10 minutes and turn onto wire rack. Cool thoroughly before slicing.

OREGON FRESH APPLE BREAD

1 loaf

This recipe comes from the Hood River region of Oregon.

2 *cups sifted flour*
2 *teaspoons baking powder*
1 *teaspoon salt*
½ *teaspoon cinnamon*
¼ *teaspoon nutmeg*
½ *cup butter or shortening*
1¼ *cups sugar*
2 *eggs*
1½ *cups peeled, finely grated apple*
½ *cup chopped walnuts or pecans*

Sift together first 5 ingredients and set aside. Cream butter or shortening and sugar until light and fluffy. Beat in eggs, one at a time, beating well after each addition. Stir in dry ingredients and apple, half at a time. Fold in nuts.

Pour into well-greased and floured 9 × 5 × 3-inch loaf pan. Bake in moderate oven (350° F.) for 1 hour, or until done. Cool in pan for 10 minutes and turn onto wire rack. Cool completely before slicing.

GLAZED LEMON BREAD

1 loaf

2½ *cups sifted flour*
3 *teaspoons baking powder*
1 *teaspoon salt*
⅓ *cup butter or shortening*
1¼ *cups sugar*
2 *tablespoons grated lemon peel*
2 *eggs*
1 *cup milk*
½ *cup finely chopped walnuts*
⅓ *cup lemon juice*

Sift together first 3 ingredients and set aside. Cream butter or shortening, 1 cup sugar, and 1 tablespoon lemon peel. Add eggs, one at a time, beating well after each addition. Add dry ingredients and milk alternately, half at a time, stirring just until batter is smooth. Fold in nuts.

Pour into greased 9 × 5 × 3-inch loaf pan and smooth top with knife. Bake in slow oven (325° F.) for 60 to 70 minutes, or until done. Just before end of baking time, combine lemon juice and remaining ¼ cup sugar and 1 tablespoon lemon peel in saucepan. Heat slowly until sugar dissolves, stirring constantly. Glaze bread with lemon syrup immediately upon removing from oven. Cool in pan on rack for 30 minutes. Remove from pan and cool for 2 to 4 hours before slicing.

DOWN EAST CRANBERRY NUT BREAD

1 loaf

"Craneberries" were one of the first native American fruits shipped to the Old World. Wild cranberries were cooked with honey or maple sugar by the Indians, and sailors ate them at sea to prevent scurvy.

    2¼ *cups sifted flour*
    1 *cup sugar*
    2 *teaspoons baking powder*
    1½ *teaspoons salt*
    ½ *teaspoon baking soda*
    3 *tablespoons grated orange peel*
    ½ *cup orange juice*
    ⅓ *cup warm water*
    ⅓ *cup butter or shortening, melted*
    1 *egg, beaten*
    1½ *cups halved cranberries*
    ½ *cup chopped pecans or walnuts*

Sift together first 5 ingredients and stir in orange peel. Combine liquids, butter or shortening, and egg. Add to dry ingredients and

stir only enough to moisten dry ingredients. Fold cranberries and nuts into batter with fewest possible strokes.

Pour into well-greased 9 × 5 × 3-inch loaf pan. Bake in moderate oven (350° F.) for 1 hour, or until done. Cool in pan for 10 minutes, then transfer to wire rack. Allow to age for 1 day before serving.

PUMPKIN BREAD

1 loaf

Like pumpkin pie, Pumpkin Bread is an American invention. Spicy as gingerbread, it is delicious eaten with plenty of butter or spread with cream cheese.

    2 *cups sifted flour*
    2 *teaspoons baking powder*
    1 *teaspoon salt*
    1 *teaspoon cinnamon*
    ½ *teaspoon cloves*
    ½ *teaspoon nutmeg*
    ¼ *teaspoon ginger*
    ¼ *teaspoon baking soda*
    ½ *cup shortening*
    1 *cup light brown sugar, firmly packed*
    2 *eggs*
    1 *cup canned pumpkin*
    ½ *cup milk*
    ½ *cup chopped pecans*
    ¼ *cup halved seedless raisins*

Sift together first 8 ingredients. Cream shortening and sugar well and beat in eggs. Stir in pumpkin. Add dry ingredients and milk alternately to the creamed mixture, beginning and ending with dry ingredients. Fold in pecans and raisins.

Pour into greased 9 × 5 × 3-inch loaf pan and bake in moderate oven (350° F.) for 50 to 60 minutes, or until done. Cool for 10 minutes in pan, then transfer to wire rack.

BANANA NUT BREAD

1 loaf

Banana Nut Bread is one of many tasty recipes developed in recent decades to help popularize bananas.

- 2 *cups flour*
- 3 *teaspoons baking powder*
- 1 *teaspoon salt*
- ¼ *teaspoon nutmeg (optional)*
- ½ *cup butter*
- ¾ *cup sugar*
- 2 *eggs*
- 1 *cup mashed banana (about 3 medium bananas)*
- ½ *cup chopped pecans or walnuts*

Sift together first 4 ingredients. Beat butter and sugar until creamy. Add eggs, one at a time, beating well after each addition. Add dry ingredients and banana alternately to creamed mixture, stirring gently just until dry ingredients are moistened. Fold in nuts.

Pour into greased 9 × 5 × 3-inch loaf pan. Bake in moderate oven (350° F.) for 50 to 60 minutes. A metal cake tester inserted into center of loaf will come out clean when done. Cool in pan on rack for 5 minutes, then transfer loaf to rack.

SQUAW BREAD

18 pieces

This is an adaptation of a recipe from the Indians of Oklahoma.

- 2 *cups sifted flour*
- 3 *teaspoons baking powder*
- ½ *teaspoon salt*
- ½ *teaspoon sugar*
- 1 *cup milk*
- ½ *tablespoon shortening, melted and cooled*
- *Fat for deep frying*

Sift together flour, baking powder, salt, and sugar into bowl. Add milk and shortening to make soft dough. Turn onto lightly floured board and roll or pat to ½-inch thickness. Cut into 1 × 3-inch strips. Make a lengthwise slit in center of each strip.

Fry in deep hot fat (375° F.) about 2 minutes total time, turning once. Drain on paper towels. Serve with syrup, honey, or preserves.

BROWN COUNTY SOUR CREAM COFFEECAKE

1 (10-inch) cake

Brown County is one of Indiana's most picturesque regions. It is a mecca for landscape artists, but the county is also famous for its wholesome food and many excellent cooks. This coffeecake is rich enough to be served as a dessert.

NUT FILLING

- ½ *cup sugar*
- ¼ *cup flour*
- 2 *teaspoons cinnamon*
- ¼ *teaspoon salt*
- ¼ *cup butter*
- ¾ *cup chopped pecans*

BATTER

- 2¾ *cups sifted flour*
- 3 *teaspoons baking powder*
- ½ *teaspoon baking soda*
- ½ *teaspoon salt*
- 1 *cup plus 1⅓ tablespoons softened butter*
- 1½ *cups sugar*
- 1½ *teaspoons vanilla*
- 3 *eggs*
- 1 *cup sour cream*

To prepare filling, mix together sugar, flour, cinnamon, and salt. Cut butter into sugar mixture, stir in pecans, and set aside.

To prepare batter, sift together first 4 ingredients. Cream 1 cup butter, sugar, and vanilla until light and fluffy. Add eggs, one at a time, beating well after each addition. Add dry ingredients and sour cream alternately, half at a time, and stir just until dry ingredients are moistened.

Spread one-third of the batter evenly into a buttered and floured 10-inch tube (angel-food) pan. Sprinkle one-third of the nut filling evenly over batter and press it down with back of spoon. Repeat twice. Bake in moderate oven (350° F.) for 1 hour, or until done. Melt remaining 1⅓ tablespoons butter and brush on top of coffeecake while hot. Cool in pan for 15 minutes, then lift out center of pan and finish cooling on wire rack. When cold, remove coffeecake from tube.

HAWAIIAN COCONUT COFFEECAKE

16 squares

  1½ *cups sifted flour*
  ⅔ *cup sugar*
  2½ *teaspoons baking powder*
  ½ *teaspoon salt*
  1 *(8-ounce) can crushed pineapple, drained*
  1 *egg, beaten*
  ½ *cup butter, melted*
  ¾ *cup flaked coconut*
  ½ *cup light brown sugar, firmly packed*

Sift together first 4 ingredients. Add pineapple, egg, and ⅓ cup butter, stirring only enough to moisten ingredients.

Spread in an even layer in greased 8 × 8 × 2-inch pan. Blend coconut, brown sugar, and remaining butter and sprinkle evenly over batter. Bake in moderate oven (350° F.) for 25 minutes, or until done. Cut into squares and serve warm.

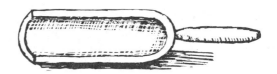

SOPAIPILLAS (Hot Puffed Bread)

About 3 dozen

Of Mexican and Indian origin, *Sopaipillas* are presented as the very first course in New Mexican restaurants that feature traditional Spanish or Mexican food. When the small pieces of dough are cooked in hot oil they puff out and form bread with a crispy crust and hollow center. They are served hot, coated with honey, or rolled in cinnamon sugar.

  3 *cups sifted flour*
  2½ *teaspoons baking powder*
  1 *teaspoon salt*
  3 *tablespoons butter or shortening*
  3 *eggs*
  ¼ *cup sugar*
  ⅓ *cup water (approximate)*
  Cooking oil for frying
  Cinnamon Sugar (see below) or honey

Sift together flour, baking powder, and salt into bowl. Cut in butter or shortening with pastry blender until mixture resembles coarse meal. Beat eggs and sugar well and add to dry ingredients with enough water to make soft dough. Knead on floured board until smooth and elastic. Cover with towel and let stand for 30 minutes. Roll out to ⅛-inch thickness and cut into 2½- or 3-inch squares.

Fry in deep hot fat (385° to 400° F.) for 2½ to 3 minutes total cooking time, turning often, or until browned. Drain on paper towels. Serve hot with honey or roll in Cinnamon Sugar.

Cinnamon Sugar: Combine ½ cup sugar and 1 teaspoon cinnamon. If more is desired, maintain this ratio of sugar and cinnamon.

BLUEBERRY BUCKLE
9 to 12 servings

The early settlers arriving in New England found a profusion of wild berries. Combining the culinary heritage of their homeland with the foods available in the New World, these hard-working settlers created many tasty and oftentimes whimsically named concoctions. One such creation, a coffeecake or quick bread, was called Blueberry Buckle.

BATTER

> 2 *cups sifted flour*
> 2 *teaspoons baking powder*
> ¾ *teaspoon salt*
> ¼ *cup softened butter*
> ¾ *cup sugar*
> 1 *egg*
> 2 *teaspoons lemon juice*
> 1 *teaspoon grated lemon peel*
> ½ *cup milk*
> 1 *to 2 cups blueberries, fresh or frozen*

TOPPING

> ⅓ *cup sugar*
> ⅓ *cup sifted flour*
> ¼ *teaspoon salt*
> ¼ *teaspoon cinnamon*
> 3 *tablespoons butter*

Sift together first 3 batter ingredients. Cream butter, sugar, egg, lemon juice, and lemon peel until light. Add dry ingredients and milk alternately, half at a time, stirring until dry ingredients are moistened. Fold in blueberries. Turn into a greased 9 × 9 × 2-inch baking pan.

To prepare topping, combine sugar, flour, salt, and cinnamon. Cut butter into fine pieces and cut into dry ingredients, using knives or pastry blender. Sprinkle evenly over batter. Bake in moderate oven (375° F.) for 45 minutes. Serve warm or cooled.

NOTE: *Drain canned berries or defrost frozen ones.*

SOUR CREAM CRUMB CAKE
(Streusel Kuchen)
1 coffeecake

This is one of my Grandma Keller's specialties.

> 3 *cups sifted flour*
> 1½ *cups light brown sugar, firmly packed*
> 1 *teaspoon salt*
> 1½ *teaspoons cinnamon*
> ¼ *teaspoon nutmeg*
> 1 *cup butter*
> ⅓ *cup chopped pecans or walnuts (optional)*
> 1 *teaspoon baking soda*
> 1 *cup sour cream*
> 2 *eggs, beaten*

Sift together first 5 ingredients. Cut butter into dry ingredients with pastry blender or two knives until mixture is crumbly. Remove 2 cups of the crumb mixture, mix in nuts, and reserve for topping. Stir soda into remaining crumb mixture. Add sour cream and eggs and stir only enough to moisten dry ingredients. Spoon into greased 9 × 9 × 2-inch pan. Sprinkle crumb mixture over top and press down lightly. Bake in moderate oven (350° F.) for 50 to 60 minutes. Serve as dessert or coffeecake.

MUFFIN GEMS
10 to 12 muffins

European bakers have been concocting muffins for several centuries. Nursery rhymes and songs have been composed about this delightful small round bread that can be leavened with baking powder, yeast, or baking soda. However, the quick bread typical to the United States is made without yeast.

2 *cups sifted flour*

¼ *cup sugar*

3 *teaspoons baking powder*

½ *teaspoon salt*

1 *egg, beaten*

1 *cup milk*

¼ *cup butter or shortening, melted and cooled*

Sift first 4 ingredients together into bowl. Combine remaining ingredients. Add all at once to dry ingredients and stir only enough to moisten dry ingredients (*do not overmix*).

Fill greased muffin pans (2¾ inches in diameter) two-thirds full. Bake in hot oven (400° F.) for 20 to 25 minutes, or until lightly browned.

VARIATIONS

Spicy Apple Muffins: Add 1 teaspoon pumpkin pie spice mix to dry ingredients, increase eggs to 2, reduce milk to ½ cup, and fold 1 cup chopped raw apple into batter.

Fruity Muffins: Fold ½ to ⅔ cup currants, seedless raisins, chopped pitted dates, or chopped dried apricots into batter.

Cranberry Nut Muffins: Fold 2 teaspoons grated orange peel, ½ cup halved fresh washed cranberries, and ⅓ cup chopped pecans into batter.

Nutty Muffins: Substitute ½ cup light brown sugar for the granulated and fold ½ to ¾ cup chopped pecans or walnuts into batter.

OLD-FASHIONED BLUEBERRY MUFFINS
12 muffins

2 *cups sifted flour*

⅓ *cup sugar*

4 *teaspoons baking powder*

½ *teaspoon salt*

1 *cup milk*

1 *egg, beaten*

¼ *cup butter or shortening, melted*

1 *cup fresh blueberries*

Sift together first 4 ingredients into bowl. Add milk, egg, and butter or shortening. Stir just until dry ingredients are moistened (batter will be lumpy). Fold in blueberries. Spoon into 12 well-greased muffin pans (2¾ inches in diameter), filling pans two-thirds full. Bake in hot oven (400° F.) for 20 to 25 minutes, or until done.

NOTE: *1 cup thawed, frozen, or drained canned blueberries may be substituted.*

BAKING POWDER BISCUITS

15 to 20 biscuits, depending on thickness

These feathery, light biscuits, now popular throughout the United States, originated in plantation kitchens of the South. Delicate and crusty, they were a must at most meals. In the days before commercial baking powder, homemakers made their own by combining cream of tartar with baking soda.

Beaten biscuits, another Southern favorite, differ from Baking Powder Biscuits. They are made light by beating air into the dough with 100 strokes or "more for company." These biscuits are thin and crisp and are traditionally served with thin slices of country-cured ham in many areas of the South.

A third typically Southern biscuit is the Buttermilk. Buttermilk was used more frequently for cooking in the South than in other sections of the country. Perhaps the reason for this is that plantation households were larger and more butter was churned, thus producing more buttermilk for use in cooking.

   2 *cups sifted flour*
   1 *tablespoon baking powder*
   1 *teaspoon salt*
   ½ *teaspoon sugar (optional)*
   ⅓ *cup shortening*
   ¾ *cup milk*

Sift dry ingredients together into bowl and cut in shortening with two knives or pastry blender until mixture resembles coarse meal. Add milk and stir with fork just until dry ingredients are moistened. Turn onto lightly floured board and knead lightly 6 to 10 times. Roll or pat dough ½ to ¾ inch thick. Cut with lightly floured biscuit cutter.

Place biscuits on ungreased baking sheet and bake in very hot oven (450° F.) about 10 minutes for biscuits ½ inch thick, 15 minutes for biscuits ¾ inch thick, or until done.

NOTE: *For a richer, crustier biscuit, increase shortening to ½ cup.*

VARIATION

Buttermilk Biscuits: Follow the recipe for Baking Powder Biscuits and substitute buttermilk for sweet milk. Decrease baking powder to 2 teaspoons and sift ½ teaspoon baking soda with dry ingredients.

MARYLAND BEATEN BISCUITS

3½ dozen biscuits

   3 *cups flour*
   ½ *teaspoon salt*
   ½ *teaspoon baking powder*
   ¼ *teaspoon baking soda*
   3 *tablespoons shortening*
   ¾ *cup cold milk*

Sift together first 4 ingredients. Cut in shortening very finely, using a pastry blender. Stir in milk to make a stiff dough. Turn onto floured board and knead thoroughly. Beat dough on board with mallet or end of rolling pin until dough blisters and cracks, 25 to 30 minutes or about 100 whacks, folding edges of dough in toward the center and turning after every 3 or 4 whacks. Roll dough ¼ to ⅜ inch thick and cut into biscuits with very small round cutter. Prick top of biscuits with 4-tined fork 2 or 3 times.

Arrange on lightly greased baking sheet and bake in moderate oven (375° F.) for 30 minutes, or until light beige in color. Serve hot or cold.

SCOTCH SCONES
12 scones

When I think of scones I remember the lovely Gleneagles Hotel near Perth, Scotland, a crisp cold afternoon, and tea served in the Scottish tradition—piping hot and accompanied by delicious rich scones slathered with butter and jam. Brought to the United States by Scottish and English settlers, scones are said to have been a favorite of the people of Scone, the site of Scottish coronations.

 2 *cups flour*
 ¼ *cup plus 2 teaspoons sugar*
 3 *teaspoons baking powder*
 1 *teaspoon salt*
 ⅓ *cup shortening*
 2 *eggs*
 ⅓ *to* ½ *cup milk or half and half*

Sift together flour, ¼ cup sugar, baking powder, and salt. Cut in shortening, using a pastry blender, until mixture resembles fine crumbs. Beat 1 whole egg and 1 yolk, reserving 1 egg white for top. Add beaten egg mixture and milk or half and half as needed to make a soft dough, stirring just until dry ingredients are moistened (mixture will be lumpy—do not overmix).

Turn onto lightly floured surface and knead gently 5 or 6 times. Roll dough into a circle ½ inch thick. Beat remaining egg white slightly and brush on dough. Sprinkle with remaining 2 teaspoons sugar. Cut into 12 wedge-shaped pieces, using a floured knife.

Transfer to baking sheet and reassemble wedges into a circle. Bake in hot oven (400° F.) for 15 minutes, or until browned.

VARIATIONS

Alaskan Scones: Stir ½ cup currants into dry ingredients and use just 1 egg. Do not top dough with egg white or sugar. Cut circle of dough into 8 wedges. Place wedges on lightly greased griddle over low heat (325° F.) and cook for 8 to 10 minutes on each side. Delicious with soft butter and jam. Yield: 8 scones.

Old-Fashioned Cream Scones: Substitute cream for milk and use butter instead of shortening. Cut circle into sixths. Arrange wedges 1 inch apart on baking sheet. Brush tops with slightly beaten egg white and sprinkle with sugar. Yield: 6 scones.

MILE-HIGH POPOVERS
8 popovers

Popovers are a uniquely American invention. In Colonial Williamsburg they were called Breakfast Puffs. Light and airy, the popovers can be poured into baking cups, frozen, and "popped" into the oven with a few minutes' additional baking time.

 1 *cup sifted flour*
 ½ *teaspoon salt*
 1 *cup milk*
 2 *eggs*
 2 *tablespoons butter, melted*

Combine flour and salt. Beat together milk, eggs, and butter. Add dry ingredients and beat at medium speed for about 1 minute, or until thoroughly blended. Fill 8 well-greased popover pans or custard cups about one-third full.

Arrange custard cups on baking sheet. Bake in hot oven (400° F.) for 35 to 40 minutes, or until well browned and crisp. Serve at once.

VARIATIONS

Herb Popovers: Add ½ teaspoon mixed herbs or fines herbes to flour.

Oatmeal Popovers: Add ½ cup uncooked quick oats with flour, increase eggs to 3 and milk to 1½ cups. Yield: 12 popovers.

ALL-AMERICAN PANCAKES

1 dozen 4-inch pancakes

Griddle cakes, or pancakes, are the oldest form of bread. Originally made of pounded grain mixed with water and spread on a hot rock to dry, they are now known in many versions. From appetizers to dessert, they are a welcome part of any meal. In England, pancakes are traditionally served on Shrove Tuesday, the day before Lent. Great sport is made of the preparation, for the person preparing the pancakes must flip them in front of family and friends. Flipping pancakes has become such a popular sport that it is an annual competition at the Mrs. America pageant. I proudly remember the time when I was Mrs. Iowa and I managed to toss a pancake that reached the rafters of the San Diego Coliseum.

    1⅓ cups sifted flour
     3 tablespoons sugar
    2½ teaspoons baking powder
     1 teaspoon salt
     2 eggs, beaten slightly
    1¾ cups milk
     ½ teaspoon vanilla
     ¼ cup melted shortening or cooking oil

Sift first 4 ingredients together into bowl. Combine eggs, milk, and vanilla and add to dry ingredients, beating just until dry ingredients are moistened. Stir in shortening or oil.

For each pancake, pour ¼ cup batter onto a hot, lightly greased griddle or electric griddle set at 375° F. Turn pancakes when puffed, full of bubbles, and the edges are cooked.

VARIATIONS

Buttermilk Pancakes: Reduce baking powder to 1½ teaspoons, add 1 teaspoon baking soda, and substitute 2 cups buttermilk for the 1¾ cups milk.

Blueberry or Huckleberry Pancakes: Omit vanilla and fold 1 cup washed fresh blueberries or huckleberries and ½ teaspoon grated lemon peel into batter before baking.

Crispy Pancakes: Increase eggs to 3 and shortening to ⅓ cup.

Dollar-Size Pancakes: Pour tablespoonfuls of any batter desired onto hot, lightly greased griddle and bake.

Iowa Corn Cakes: Substitute 1 cup sifted flour and ¾ cup yellow cornmeal for the 1⅓ cups flour. Omit vanilla and fold 1 cup well-drained whole-kernel corn into batter. Yield: about 16 4-inch cakes.

Quick-Made Buckwheat Pancakes: Substitute ¾ cup *each* sifted flour and buckwheat flour for the 1⅓ cups sifted flour. Substitute 1⅔ cups milk and 2 tablespoons molasses for the 1¾ cups milk and omit vanilla.

Sour Cream Pancakes: Substitute 1 cup *each* sour cream and milk or half and half for the 1¾ cups milk. Add a dash of mace or nutmeg to batter (optional).

WAFFLES

3 (9-inch) waffles

Kitchens of Southern plantations were well known for their waffles during Colonial and antebellum eras. A typical Southern waffle was made with baking soda and buttermilk. The following recipe is an adaptation of one belonging to a Miss Beecher and dates from 1858.

     2 cups sifted flour
     2 tablespoons sugar
     3 teaspoons baking powder
     ¾ teaspoon salt
    1½ cups milk
     3 eggs, separated
     ½ cup butter or shortening, melted and cooled

Sift together first 4 ingredients into bowl. Combine milk and egg yolks and beat in butter or shortening. Add liquid to dry ingredients, stirring only enough to moisten dry ingredients. Beat egg whites until soft peaks form and fold into batter. Bake in preheated waffle iron until steaming stops, about 5 minutes.

VARIATIONS

Southern Waffles: Substitute 2 teaspoons baking powder and 1 teaspoon baking soda for the 1 tablespoon baking powder and use 2 cups buttermilk instead of 1½ cups milk.

Bacon or Ham Waffles: Sprinkle 1½ to 2 tablespoons finely chopped cooked bacon or ham over batter before closing iron. Serve with soft butter and honey or maple syrup.

Blueberry Waffles: Fold ½ to ¾ cup fresh blueberries into batter just before baking. Serve with soft butter and confectioners' sugar or favorite syrup.

FRENCH QUARTER CRÊPES

18 crêpes

We owe the delicate thin pancake known as the crêpe to the French settlers of New Orleans. Crêpes may be served as an hors d'oeuvre, light entrée, or dessert.

1½ *cups sifted flour*
3 *tablespoons sugar*
½ *teaspoon salt*
4 *eggs*
1¼ *cups milk (approximate)*
¾ *cup half and half*
2 *tablespoons brandy (optional)*
Melted butter

Sift together first 3 ingredients. Beat eggs until very light. Stir in milk, half and half, and dry ingredients. Add brandy and beat until smooth.

To make crêpes, preheat and lightly grease a 5- or 6-inch crêpe or omelet pan or skillet. Pour in 2 to 3 tablespoons of batter all at once. Tilt pan quickly and rotate to distribute batter evenly over surface. Cook the crêpe quickly on both sides. Remove crêpe from pan and brush lightly with melted butter. Repeat until all batter is used. Stack cakes and cover with towel to keep warm.

NOTE: *Crêpes are time-consuming to make. The above recipe can be made in advance, with foil or plastic wrap then placed between each crêpe. The crêpes may be frozen. To reheat, drop thawed crêpes, one at a time, into a lightly buttered pan. Cook over moderate heat until warm, turning once.*

TENNESSEE LACY-EDGED BATTER CAKES

Sixty 3-inch pancakes

An adaptation of two recipes dating from the late 1800s, this recipe makes very tasty batter cakes. The following is an excerpt from one of the original recipes: "The batter should not be so thin that it will run, or so thick it will have to be spread with a spoon. Sometimes fresh buttermilk may be too sour; that will have to be corrected by adding a little more soda. Test the batter by dropping a little on griddle to see if there is enough soda or not. The bottled meal of cities is not as good as sifted country meal."

2 *cups yellow cornmeal*
½ *teaspoon baking soda*
½ *teaspoon salt*
2½ *cups buttermilk*
2 *eggs*
2 *tablespoons melted shortening*

Combine first 3 ingredients in bowl. Combine remaining ingredients, beating slightly. Stir liquids into dry ingredients and mix thoroughly.

Pour 1 tablespoonful of batter onto hot greased griddle. Fry until browned on both sides.

NOTE: *These are small, thin cakes. Count on 4 to 6 per serving. Serve hot with butter, applesauce, syrup, honey, sorghum, or preserves.*

FRENCH TOAST

Popular throughout America today, French Toast can be traced back as far as the fourteenth century. Appearing in many cuisines, it is whimsically known in England as the "poor knights of Windsor," in France as "pain perdue," in Sweden as "Rich Knights," and in Austria as "arme Ritter."

FAMOUS DINING-CAR FRENCH TOAST

4 servings

During the heyday of transcontinental train travel, Dining-Car French Toast was a favorite breakfast and the specialty of many railroad dining-car chefs.

6 *slices slightly dry bread (2 or 3 days old), cut ¾ inch thick*

4 *eggs*

1 *cup cream or half and half*

¼ *teaspoon salt*

Dash of nutmeg

Cooking oil for frying

Confectioners' sugar

Jelly, maple syrup, or marmalade

Trim crusts from bread and cut each slice in half diagonally. Beat slightly the eggs, cream or half and half, salt, and nutmeg. Soak bread slices, a few at a time, in egg mixture and drain.

Fry in ¼ inch of hot oil (325° F.) until golden on both sides. Drain on paper toweling. Place on baking sheet and heat in hot oven (400° F.) for 3 to 5 minutes, or until puffed. Sprinkle with confectioners' sugar and serve with jelly, maple syrup, or marmalade.

BAGELS

18 medium or 24 small bagels

The name *Bagel* was most probably derived from the German word *Bougel*, meaning ring, or from the Yiddish word *biegen*, meaning to twist. In any case, the chewy, doughnut-shaped roll has been a traditional favorite with Jewish people and has since become a popular staple in most urban delicatessens.

1 *cup milk, scalded*

¼ *cup butter*

2 *tablespoons sugar*

1½ *teaspoons salt*

1 *package active dry yeast*

¼ *cup warm water (105° to 115° F.)*

1 *egg, separated*

3½ *to 3¾ cups sifted flour*

1 *teaspoon water*

Coarse salt or poppy seeds (optional)

Combine first 4 ingredients and cool to lukewarm. Soften yeast in warm water and add with egg white to liquids. Add flour as needed to make a stiff dough.

Knead on lightly floured board until smooth and elastic. Place in greased bowl and turn once to grease top. Cover and let rise in a warm place (85° F.) until doubled in bulk, about 1 to 1½ hours. Turn onto lightly floured board. Divide into 18 or 24 pieces and roll out each into a strip 6 to 7 inches long. Press ends together to make circle and shape with fingers until it resembles a doughnut. Let stand for 10 minutes, or until they begin to rise.

Drop 3 or 4 bagels at a time into a large pan of hot water held just below the boiling point. Cook on first side until puffy, turn, and cook on second side. Total cooking time is 5 to 7 minutes. Remove bagels from water with slotted spoon, drain, and place on greased baking sheet. Beat egg yolk and water and brush tops of bagels. Leave plain or sprinkle with coarse salt or poppy seeds. Bake in hot oven (400° F.) for 20 to 25 minutes, or until done.

Variation

Light Rye Bagels: Substitute 1½ cups rye flour for 1½ cups sifted flour and add 1½ teaspoons caraway seeds.

Note: *This preparation is more involved than the one for rolls, but it's certainly worth the effort. Don't get scared—the recipe* does *work and it's not as hard as it seems.*

FRENCH QUARTER DOUGHNUTS

5 dozen doughnuts

Romantic visions of cobblestoned old New Orleans and the Vieux Carré, or French Market, come to mind when tasting hot crisp puffs of dough known as French Quarter Doughnuts. Horse-drawn carriages still pull up to the Café du Monde in order that the passengers may taste the famous doughnuts and enjoy a steaming cup of coffee fortified with chicory.

　½ *cup boiling water*
　¼ *cup sugar*
　¼ *cup shortening*
　1 *teaspoon salt*
　½ *cup milk or half and half*
　1 *egg, beaten*
　1½ *teaspoons active dry yeast (½ package)*
　¼ *cup warm water (105° to 115° F.)*
　3¼ *cups sifted flour (approximate)*
　Cooking oil for frying
　Confectioners' sugar

Combine boiling water, sugar, shortening, and salt, stirring until shortening is melted. Blend in milk or half and half and egg and cool to lukewarm. Soften yeast in warm water. Add softened yeast and 2 cups flour to egg mixture, beating hard. Add remaining 1¼ cups flour or as needed to make a medium soft dough. Place in greased bowl, turn to grease top, and cover. Refrigerate until ready to use. One-third or one-half of the dough may be covered and refrigerated overnight to be fried the following day. Roll about half the dough at a time to ⅛-inch thickness on a lightly floured board. With a sharp knife or fluted pastry wheel cut in 2½- or 3-inch squares.

Fry dough at once—do not let rise—in deep hot fat (360° to 370° F.) about 2 minutes total cooking time, turning once. Drain on paper towels. Dust generously with confectioners' sugar while hot and serve at once.

BRIGHAM'S BUTTERMILK DOUGHNUTS

18 doughnuts

Emily Young, wife of Brigham Young, was an excellent cook. The following recipe is an adaptation of her buttermilk doughnuts.

　2½ *cups sifted flour*
　1 *teaspoon baking soda*
　¾ *teaspoon salt*
　¾ *teaspoon grated nutmeg*
　½ *teaspoon baking powder*
　1 *cup buttermilk*
　½ *cup sugar*
　1 *egg, beaten*
　1 *teaspoon vanilla (optional)*
　2 *tablespoons butter or shortening, melted*
　Oil for frying
　Confectioners' sugar (optional)

Sift together first 5 ingredients. Blend buttermilk, sugar, egg, and vanilla. Beat liquid mixture into dry ingredients, then stir in butter or shortening. Chill dough thoroughly for about 30 minutes. Roll out on lightly floured board to ⅜- or ½-inch thickness. Cut with floured 2½-inch doughnut cutter.

Fry in about 3 inches of hot fat (375° F.) until golden brown on both sides, turning once, about 2 minutes total cooking time. Drain on paper towels and dust with confectioners' sugar while warm. Fry doughnut holes in same manner.

BISMARCKS (Jelly-Filled Doughnuts)

About 1½ dozen doughnuts

Traditionally served in Germany on *Fastnacht* or Shrove Tuesday, jelly doughnuts are called Bismarcks in Berlin after the illustrious Prussian statesman. My childhood memories include the weekly Saturday-morning visit to a Chicago bakery for Bismarcks and other pastries. However, my most vivid experience with these marvelous doughnuts occurred in Yugoslavia halfway through a hazardous and hair-raising mountain drive in a car that wouldn't shift out of fourth gear. Shaken with fright, I still managed to down, in almost one gulp, the most divine-tasting jelly doughnut I've ever eaten.

> 1 *package active dry yeast*
>
> ¼ *cup warm water (105° to 115° F.)*
>
> ⅓ *cup milk, scalded*
>
> ¼ *cup butter or shortening, melted*
>
> ⅓ *cup sugar*
>
> 1 *teaspoon salt*
>
> 3 *eggs, beaten slightly*
>
> 1½ *teaspoons vanilla*
>
> ¼ *teaspoon nutmeg or mace*
>
> 3½ *cups sifted flour (approximate)*
>
> ⅔ *cup thick preserves (apricot, strawberry, or raspberry)*
>
> *Oil for frying*
>
> *Glaze (see next column) or confectioners' sugar (optional)*

Dissolve yeast in warm water. Combine milk, butter or shortening, sugar, and salt. Cool to lukewarm and stir in yeast, eggs, vanilla, and nutmeg or mace. Beat in 1 cup flour. Add enough flour to make an easy-to-handle dough. Place in large greased bowl and turn to grease top. Cover and let rise in a warm place (85° F.) until doubled in bulk, about 1 to 1½ hours.

Turn onto floured board and roll out to ¼-inch thickness. Cut into rounds with a 3-inch floured cookie cutter. Center 1 teaspoonful of preserves on half the rounds. Moisten edges and cover with remaining dough rounds. Press outside edges together firmly and recut with a slightly smaller cutter (2¾ inch). Place on floured baking sheet and cover. Let rise until doubled in bulk, about 1 hour.

Fry in deep hot fat (350° F.) until browned, about 4 minutes, turning once. Drain on paper towels. Glaze while hot or sprinkle cooled doughnuts with confectioners' sugar.

GLAZE

> ¼ *cup butter*
>
> 1 *teaspoon vanilla*
>
> ¼ *teaspoon salt*
>
> 2 *cups sifted confectioners' sugar*
>
> 3 *to 4 tablespoons hot water*

Melt butter and add vanilla and salt. Stir in sugar and water, a little at a time, until the proper consistency to spread over doughnuts.

POTATO DOUGHNUTS

About 2 dozen doughnuts

Mashed potatoes add both flavor and moistness to this tasty doughnut. The trick to making good doughnuts is to have a soft dough. Chilling the dough and breaking off small amounts at a time to roll and fry helps prevent the dough from drying out.

3 *cups sifted flour*

4½ *teaspoons baking powder*

1 *teaspoon salt*

1 *teaspoon nutmeg*

½ *teaspoon cinnamon*

2 *eggs*

¾ *cup sugar*

⅔ *cup cooled seasoned mashed potatoes*

3 *tablespoons shortening, melted and cooled*

1 *teaspoon vanilla*

½ *teaspoon grated lemon peel (optional)*

⅔ *cup milk*

Cooking oil for frying

Granulated or confectioners' sugar (optional)

Sift together first 5 ingredients. Beat eggs until light, add sugar gradually, and beat until very light and fluffy, about 2 minutes. Add mashed potatoes and beat until smooth. Stir in shortening, vanilla, and lemon peel. Add dry ingredients alternately with milk, stirring just until well blended. Cover bowl and chill for at least 2 hours. Roll out half the dough at a time to ½-inch thickness on lightly floured board. Cut with floured doughnut cutter.

Fry doughnuts in 3 to 4 inches of hot fat (365° F.) until brown on both sides, turning once. Drain on paper towels. Fry doughnut holes in same manner. Dust with granulated or confectioners' sugar when slightly warm.

SWEET FRITTERS

About 2¼ cups batter

Fritters are the English version of the French *beignet*. Perhaps the name comes from the French word *friture*, meaning something fried. All fritters are made with a batter, but the variety is infinite. A perfect fritter should be light, golden brown, and crisp outside, and full of rich goodness inside. What follows is my basic recipe for fruit fritters.

BATTER

1½ *cups sifted flour*

3 *tablespoons sugar*

2 *teaspoons baking powder*

½ *teaspoon salt*

3 *eggs*

¾ *cup milk*

2 *tablespoons cooking oil*

1 *teaspoon vanilla*

½ *teaspoon grated lemon peel (optional)*

Sift together first 4 ingredients. Combine remaining ingredients and beat well. Add dry ingredients and beat just until free of lumps.

Use batter in one of the following ways:

Fruit Fritters: Wash and dry fruits such as strawberries and cherries. Peel fresh fruits such as peaches, bananas, and pineapple. Drain canned fruits well and dry on paper towels. Dust each piece of fruit with flour, shaking off excess. Dip floured fruit into sweet fritter batter and drain off excess. Fry in 2 to 3 inches of hot oil (375° F.) until golden brown on both sides, turning once. Drain on paper towels.

Apple Fritters: Peel and core 4 small eating apples and cut into rings ¼ inch thick. Proceed as directed for Fruit Fritters. Serve at once with maple syrup or sprinkled with confectioners' or cinnamon sugar. Yield: about 16 fritters.

Peach or Apricot Fritters: Drain 1 (1-pound 13-ounce) can of peach or apricot halves. Cut peach halves into thirds or halves, leaving apricot halves whole. Proceed as directed for Fruit Fritters. Serve with confectioners' sugar or favorite butterscotch or chocolate sauce. Yield: 4 to 6 servings.

Strawberry Fritters: Wash, stem, and dry 1½ pints strawberries. Proceed as directed for Fruit Fritters. Serve with confectioners' sugar or favorite chocolate or rum sauce.

AEBLESKIVERS (Danish Pancake Balls)

2 dozen balls

Neither a doughnut nor a pancake, an *aebleskiver* is a small ball made of batter and filled with fruit or jam. *Aebleskiver* translates as apple slices because the Danish tradition was to serve them split with applesauce. Today, they can be filled with apple slices, apple butter, cherries, and other fruits or jams.

    1 *cup sifted flour*
    4 *teaspoons sugar*
    1 *teaspoon baking powder*
    ½ *teaspoon salt*
    ¼ *teaspoon cardamom*
    ¼ *teaspoon nutmeg*
    2 *eggs, separated*
    ¾ *cup milk*
    2 *tablespoons butter, melted*
    Cooking oil
    ½ *cup apple butter, thick jam, or preserves*
    Confectioners' sugar

Sift together first 6 ingredients into bowl. Beat egg yolks slightly. Add yolks, milk, and butter to dry ingredients, beating just until smooth. Beat egg whites until they hold soft peaks and fold into batter.

Brush wells of a heated *aebleskiver* pan with oil. Fill two-thirds full with batter. Spoon a teaspoonful of apple butter, jam, or preserves into center of each *aebleskiver*. Cover filling with a small amount of batter if not covered when it sinks down. Cook over moderate heat until browned on both sides. Sprinkle with confectioners' sugar and serve hot.

EAST COAST CORN FRITTERS

24 fritters

This recipe was adapted from one written in 1848.

    1½ *cups sifted flour*
    1 *tablespoon sugar*
    2 *teaspoons baking powder*
    ½ *teaspoon salt*
    Dash of cayenne pepper (optional)
    ¼ *cup milk*
    2 *eggs, beaten*
    1 *(8¾-ounce) can cream-style corn*
    1 *tablespoon butter, melted*
    Cooking oil for frying
    Confectioners' sugar, applesauce, honey, or syrup

Sift together first 5 ingredients into bowl. Combine milk, eggs, corn, and butter and add to dry ingredients, stirring just until ingredients are mixed.

Drop slightly rounded tablespoonfuls of batter into deep hot oil (375° F.). Cook until brown on both sides, 4 to 5 minutes, turning once. Drain on paper towels. Serve hot with confectioners' sugar, applesauce, honey, or syrup.

OLYKOEKS DOUGHNUTS

About 6 dozen doughnuts

The Dutch settlers of New Amsterdam had a great liking for *olykoeks* (oil cakes). These irregularly shaped yeast cakes were originally made with raisins or chopped apple placed in the center. Although not as sweet and light as later doughnuts, they were a favorite at gossip time when the Dutch fathers would gather to exchange news, munch *olykoeks*, and sip caudle, a hot spicy drink made of ale or wine. Later, when the Dutch opened bakeries, *olykoeks* became known as doughnuts.

1 *package active dry yeast*

¼ *cup warm water (105° to 115° F.)*

4 *cups sifted flour*

¼ *cup sugar*

2 *teaspoons salt*

½ *teaspoon nutmeg*

1½ *cups warm milk (105° to 115° F.)*

¼ *cup shortening, melted*

1 *cup seedless raisins or currants, halved or quartered*

2 *eggs, beaten*

Cooking oil for frying

Confectioners' or cinnamon sugar or Rum Syrup (see below)

Soften yeast in warm water. Sift together flour, sugar, salt, and nutmeg. Combine milk and shortening. Stir in softened yeast, raisins or currants, eggs, and flour mixture, mixing thoroughly. Cover and let rise in a warm place (85° F.) until doubled in bulk, about 2 hours.

Drop level tablespoonfuls of dough into deep hot fat (360° to 365° F.). Fry until done and lightly browned, turning if doughnuts do not turn themselves, 3 to 4 minutes total cooking time. Drain on paper towels and dust with confectioners' or cinnamon sugar or Rum Syrup.

Rum Syrup

Olykoeks soaked in rum and accompanied by peach preserves were served as a dessert by the Dutch. *Olykoeks* may be soaked in the following syrup, which is similar to a baba-au-rhum syrup and adds an interesting flavor to the doughnuts.

1½ *cups sugar*

¾ *cup water*

1½ *to 2 teaspoons grated orange peel*

⅓ *cup rum*

Combine sugar, water, and orange peel, bring to a boil, and simmer until syrup thickens, 5 to 7 minutes. Remove from heat,

cool slightly, and stir in rum. Drizzle over doughnuts and let stand until syrup is absorbed.

FUNNEL CAKES
About 12 cakes

A deft forefinger and an agilely handled funnel are the most important requirements for making this Pennsylvania Dutch specialty. Once the staple fare at the midmorning meal served to early-rising and hard-working farmers, these batter cakes are now fun for a special breakfast or brunch. The kids will love making them, using their artistic imaginations to create interesting designs.

Cooking oil for frying

2 *cups sifted flour*

¼ *cup sugar*

2 *teaspoons baking powder*

½ *teaspoon salt*

2 *eggs, beaten*

1 *cup milk (approximate)*

Confectioners' sugar

Maple syrup (optional)

Pour oil into a 3- or 4-quart saucepan to a depth of 2 inches. Sift together flour, sugar, baking powder, and salt in mixing bowl. Add eggs and milk, beating until smooth. Let batter stand while oil heats to 370° to 375° F.

Select a funnel with ½-inch tip opening. Hold funnel with finger over opening. For each cake, fill funnel with ¼ cup batter. Keep the spout closed and remove finger as needed to let batter flow smoothly into the hot fat, moving funnel in a spiral fashion. Start at center and continue spiraling until a cake 5 or 6 inches in diameter is made. Fry until a golden brown on both sides, turning once (total cooking time about 1 minute). Drain thoroughly on paper towels. Fry just one cake at a time. Sprinkle cakes lightly with confectioners' sugar and serve with maple syrup.

DESSERTS

OLD-FASHIONED VANILLA ICE CREAM

About 3 quarts

2 *cups sugar*

3 *tablespoons cornstarch*

¼ *teaspoon salt*

3 *cups half and half or milk*

4 *eggs, slightly beaten*

4 *cups chilled heavy cream*

2 *tablespoons vanilla*

Custard should be prepared ahead of time and chilled in refrigerator for at least 4 hours or overnight before freezing. Combine first 3 ingredients in top of double boiler and stir in half and half or milk. Cook over gently simmering water, stirring constantly, until mixture thickens and cornstarch is cooked. Add a small amount of hot mixture to eggs in fine stream, stirring constantly. Stir in remaining hot mixture and continue cooking for 5 to 6 minutes, stirring constantly. Remove from heat and cool slightly. Stir in cream and vanilla. Refrigerate until freezing time. Freeze in a hand-crank or electric freezer, following instructions given for either.

VARIATIONS

Butter Pecan Ice Cream: Substitute 1 cup light brown sugar, firmly packed, for 1 cup of the granulated sugar. Lightly toast 1 cup chopped pecans in 2 tablespoons butter, drain on paper toweling, and cool. When ice cream starts to thicken, remove cover and add nuts. Cover container and finish freezing process.

Chocolate Ice Cream: Increase sugar to 2½ cups. Melt 4 squares (ounces) unsweetened chocolate and stir into hot custard mixture before adding eggs.

Peppermint-Stick Ice Cream: Reduce sugar to 1½ cups and add ½ cup finely crushed peppermint-stick candy to custard mixture before cooking. Reduce vanilla to 2 teaspoons and add ½ teaspoon peppermint extract. When ice cream starts to thicken, remove cover and add 1 cup coarsely chopped peppermint-stick candy. Cover container and finish freezing process.

Rum Ice Cream: Reduce vanilla to 1 tablespoon and stir ½ to 1 cup light or dark rum into custard mixture just before freezing.

Strawberry Ice Cream: Increase sugar to 2¼ cups. Reduce vanilla to 2 teaspoons. While custard is chilling, crush 2 cups fresh strawberries and add to custard mix just before freezing.

BRANDY ICE

6 to 8 servings

A dessert fit for a king, Brandy Ice is easy to make and will star at any dinner party. Especially popular in my home city of Chicago, it takes on extra elegance when served in chilled tulip wineglasses.

3 *pints hand-packed vanilla ice cream*

1 *cup brandy*

Grated nutmeg

Chill mixing bowl and spoons in freezer. Put ice cream in chilled bowl and break up into small chunks. Set bowl in refrigerator for a few minutes to soften ice cream slightly. Mix brandy into ice cream *very quickly* with beater and return it to freezer to harden. Chill tulip wineglasses in freezer. Spoon Brandy Ice into cold glasses and place in freezer until serving time. Just before serving, sprinkle top lightly with a bit of nutmeg.

ORANGE

DESSERT SOUFFLÉS

Soufflé means to poof or puff in French. You may have to wait for a soufflé, and it is worth the waiting, but a soufflé will wait for no one.

ORANGE SOUFFLÉ

6 servings

¼ *cup butter*

½ *cup flour*

¼ *teaspoon salt*

1 *cup milk*

½ *cup sugar*

3 *eggs, separated*

¼ *cup orange juice*

1 *tablespoon lemon juice*

2 *tablespoons orange-flavored liqueur or additional orange juice*

1 *tablespoon grated orange peel*

Orange Sauce for Soufflés (see below)

Butter a 1½-quart soufflé dish or casserole. Melt ¼ cup butter, stir in flour and salt, and blend thoroughly. Stir in milk, ¼ cup sugar and cook over moderate heat, stirring constantly, until very thick and smooth. Beat egg yolks and add a small amount of hot mixture in a fine stream, stirring constantly. Beat into remaining hot mixture. Stir in fruit juices, orange liqueur, and orange peel. Beat egg whites until white and foamy. Add remaining ¼ cup sugar, 1 tablespoonful at a time, and continue beating until egg whites are stiff and glossy, not dry. Carefully fold egg whites into orange mixture.

Pour into prepared soufflé dish and place in pan of hot water. Bake in slow oven (325° F.) for 1 hour, or until puffed, firm, and lightly browned. Serve at once with Orange Sauce.

ORANGE SAUCE FOR SOUFFLÉS   1½ cups

½ *cup sugar*

4 *teaspoons cornstarch*

¼ *teaspoon salt*

1¼ *cups orange juice*

¼ *cup water*

4 *teaspoons grated orange peel*

3 *tablespoons orange-flavored liqueur (optional)*

Combine first 3 ingredients in heavy saucepan. Stir in orange juice, water, orange peel, and liqueur. Cook over moderate heat, stirring constantly, until clear and thick.

LEMON SOUFFLÉ WITH FRAMBOISE SAUCE

6 servings

Butter a 2-quart soufflé dish or casserole. Follow recipe for Orange Soufflé (see above) and increase egg yolks to 4 and egg whites to 6. Substitute ¼ cup lemon juice for orange and lemon juice, omit orange-flavored liqueur, and substitute grated lemon peel for orange peel. Set soufflé dish in pan of hot water and bake in slow oven (325° F.) for 1 hour, or until puffed, firm, and lightly browned. Sprinkle with confectioners' sugar. Serve hot with Framboise Sauce.

FRAMBOISE SAUCE   ¾ cup

1 *egg plus 1 egg yolk*

5 *tablespoons sugar*

⅛ *teaspoon salt*

¼ *cup framboise or raspberry brandy*

Combine ingredients in top of double boiler and beat. Place over gently boiling water and cook, beating constantly, until mixture puffs and holds soft peaks, about 8 minutes.

CHOCOLATE SOUFFLÉ
8 servings

   1 *cup sugar*
2½ *squares (ounces) unsweetened chocolate*
   ¼ *cup hot water*
   ⅓ *cup butter*
   ⅓ *cup flour*
   ¼ *teaspoon salt*
1½ *cups milk*
   1 *tablespoon brandy (optional)*
   6 *eggs, separated*
1½ *teaspoons vanilla*
   ⅛ *teaspoon cream of tartar*
   Whipped cream (optional)
   Double Chocolate Sauce (see index)
      (optional)

Lightly butter a 2-quart soufflé dish or deep casserole with straight sides. Sprinkle 2 tablespoons sugar evenly over buttered surfaces: Melt chocolate in top of double boiler over hot water, stir in ¼ cup sugar and hot water, stirring until smooth, and set aside. Melt butter in heavy saucepan, stir in flour and salt, and add milk, stirring constantly. Cook over low heat until thick and smooth, stirring constantly. Remove from heat and stir in chocolate mixture and brandy. Cool for 15 minutes, stirring often. Beat egg yolks, 6 tablespoons sugar, and vanilla until thick and lemon-colored. Stir into cooled chocolate mixture. Beat egg whites and cream of tartar until they hold soft peaks. Add remaining ¼ cup sugar, 1 tablespoonful at a time, and beat until stiff and glossy. Fold egg whites into chocolate mixture.

Pour into prepared soufflé dish. Make a deep cut all around soufflé 1 inch from outside edge. Place dish in pan of hot water and bake in moderate oven (350° F.) for 1¼ hours, or until puffed, firm, and done. Serve at once with whipped cream or sauce.

GRAND MARNIER SOUFFLÉ
6 servings

   3 *tablespoons butter*
   ⅓ *cup flour*
   ¼ *teaspoon salt*
   1 *cup half and half or milk*
   ½ *cup sugar*
   6 *eggs, separated*
   ⅓ *cup Grand Marnier*
1½ *teaspoons grated orange peel*
   Confectioners' sugar
   Sweetened red raspberries or sliced
      strawberries

Lightly butter a 2-quart soufflé dish or casserole. Melt butter in heavy saucepan and blend in flour and salt. Stir in half and half or milk and ¼ cup sugar. Cook over low heat, stirring constantly, until thick and smooth. Remove from heat. Beat egg yolks and stir in ½ cup of hot mixture gradually, beating constantly. Blend into remaining hot mixture. Stir in Grand Marnier and orange peel. Beat egg whites until white and foamy. Add remaining ¼ cup sugar, 1 tablespoonful at a time, and continue beating until stiff and glossy but not dry. Carefully fold egg whites into egg-yolk mixture.

Pour into prepared dish. Sprinkle confectioners' sugar lightly over top. Bake in pan of hot water in moderate oven (350° F.) for 45 minutes, or until puffed and lightly browned. Serve at once with red raspberries or strawberries spooned over each serving.

BAKED PRUNE OR APRICOT FRUIT WHIP

6 servings

Related to soufflés, fruit whips are light and airy. They can be served hot or cold and require little skill to prepare.

> 1 *cup drained cooked pitted prunes or dried apricots*
> 2 *tablespoons prune or apricot juice*
> 2 *tablespoons lemon or orange juice*
> 2 *egg whites, at room temperature*
> ¼ *teaspoon salt*
> ⅓ *cup sugar*
> *Sweetened whipped cream (optional)*

Combine first 3 ingredients in blender at low speed until fruit is smooth, stopping to scrape down sides as necessary. Transfer fruit to mixing bowl. Beat egg whites and salt until white and foamy. Add sugar, 1 tablespoonful at a time, and beat until stiff and glossy. Fold egg whites into fruit mixture.

Spoon into six 5-ounce custard or soufflé cups, filling cups two-thirds full. Place cups in shallow baking pan and fill pan with hot water to within ¾ inch of cup tops. Bake in slow oven (325° F.) for 40 minutes, or until center is firm. Serve warm or cooled, plain or with whipped cream.

NOTE: *If no blender is available, fruit may be put through a food mill or whipped with an electric beater or mashed and sieved.*

OLD-FASHIONED STRAWBERRY SHORTCAKE

8 to 10 servings

In pre-Civil War days, the slaves on Southern plantations were given shortnin' bread in place of cake.

DOUGH

> 4 *cups sifted flour*
> 4 *teaspoons baking powder*
> ⅔ *cup sugar*
> ½ *teaspoon salt*
> ½ *cup butter*
> ½ *cup shortening*
> 1½ *cups milk*
> 2 *eggs, beaten*

FILLING AND TOPPING

> *Softened butter*
> 6 *to 8 cups washed, drained, sliced sweetened fresh or defrosted frozen strawberries*
> *Sweetened whipped cream*

Sift together first 4 ingredients. Cut in butter and shortening with two knives or pastry blender until mixture resembles fine crumbs. Add milk and eggs all at once and stir only enough to moisten dry ingredients.

Spread evenly into 2 greased 9-inch round pans. Bake in hot oven (425° F.) for 20 minutes until lightly browned. (Shortcake is done when cake tester inserted in center comes out clean.) Let stand for 5 minutes, then remove from pans. Cool to lukewarm.

Turn one shortcake layer bottom side up on large round dessert platter. Spread with softened butter and half the berries. Cover with remaining layer. Spread with butter and spoon remaining berries over top. To serve, cut into wedges and serve topped with a generous amount of sweetened whipped cream.

VARIATIONS

Easy-to-Serve Strawberry Shortcake for a Crowd:

Prepare strawberries and whipped cream as directed above and refrigerate. Prepare shortcake dough and spread in an even layer in greased 13 × 9 × 2-inch baking pan. Mark off 12 equal servings with sharp knife. Sprinkle top lightly with sugar. Bake in hot oven (425° F.) for 30 minutes or until done and lightly browned. Cool in pan 5 minutes.

When lukewarm, cut into 12 serving portions. To serve, split each serving in half. Spread with butter and spoon strawberries over shortcake. Cover with top half, more berries, and whipped cream. Yield: 12 servings.

Jersey State Blueberry Shortcake: Prepare ½ recipe Old-Fashioned Strawberry Shortcake dough, spooning dough into 6 equal round portions ¾ inch thick, 3 inches apart, on greased baking sheet. Bake in hot oven (425° F.) for 20 minutes or until done and lightly browned.

While shortcake is baking, fold 4 cups washed and dried blueberries into 2 cups sweetened whipped cream. Refrigerate. Split each biscuit in half while hot. Spoon half the blueberry-whipped-cream mixture over shortcakes, cover with top halves, and top with remaining blueberry mixture. Yield: 6 servings.

JAN'S SHORTCUT SHORTCAKE

6 to 8 servings

The following is a very short shortcake, a godsend for the cook whose time is limited by a crowded schedule.

  2⅓ *cups prepared biscuit mix*
  6 *tablespoons sugar*
  6 *tablespoons melted butter*
  ½ *cup light cream or half and half*

Mix all ingredients with a fork to form a soft dough. Drop by spoonfuls onto an ungreased cookie sheet to form shortcakes, slightly smoothing tops. Bake in hot oven (425° F.) for 10 minutes, or until golden brown. Top each with sweetened blueberries, strawberries, or peaches, and sweetened whipped cream.

MERINGUES

Made of stiffly beaten egg whites that are baked in a slow oven until a light ivory color, meringues are rumored to have been invented by a Swiss pastry cook working in the small German town of Meyringen. Meringues made their way into American cookery as an elegant dessert. They are usually filled with ice cream or a fruit or dessert sauce.

INDIVIDUAL MERINGUES

12 meringues

Meringues are sensitive to weather conditions, so don't bake them on humid days.

  6 *egg whites, at room temperature*
  1 *teaspoon vanilla*
  ½ *teaspoon cream of tartar*
  ½ *teaspoon salt*
  1½ *cups sugar*

Cover 2 baking sheets with heavy brown paper. Draw six 3½- to 4-inch circles about 2 inches apart on each sheet of brown paper. Beat together first 4 ingredients until white and foamy. Add sugar, 1 tablespoonful at a time, and continue beating until sugar is completely dissolved and egg whites are glossy and hold very stiff peaks. Spoon mixture into circles or put through a pastry bag with a large fluted tip. Hollow out the center of each mound with the back of a teaspoon. Bake in very slow oven (275° F.) for 50 to 60 minutes, or until dry and a very light ivory color. Turn off heat and let meringues cool in oven. Remove from paper. Serve filled with ice cream and top with sweetened fresh fruit.

VARIATION

Chocolate Meringues: Increase sugar to 1¾ cups and sift ¼ cup cocoa in with the last ¼ cup sugar. Delicious filled with ice cream and served with chocolate, raspberry, or strawberry sauce.

SCHAUM TORTE (Meringue Shells)

12 servings

Considered the queen of tortes by many, *Schaum Torte* is a German contribution to the American cuisine.

MERINGUE LAYERS

> 8 *egg whites, at room temperature*
>
> 2 *teaspoons vanilla*
>
> 1 *teaspoon vinegar*
>
> ½ *teaspoon cream of tartar*
>
> ½ *teaspoon salt*
>
> 2 *cups sugar*

FILLING

> 3 *cups fresh strawberries or 2 cups red raspberries*
>
> ⅓ *cup sugar*
>
> 4 *cups sweetened whipped cream*
>
> 2 *to 4 tablespoons toasted slivered almonds*

Cover 3 baking sheets with heavy brown paper. Draw a 9-inch circle in center of each and butter lightly. Prepare meringue layers. Beat together first 5 ingredients until egg whites are white and foamy. Add sugar, 1 tablespoonful at a time, and continue beating until sugar is entirely dissolved and egg whites stand in very stiff, glossy, firm peaks.

Spoon mixture onto the 3 circles, spreading over entire circle and building up the edges slightly. Bake in very slow oven (250° F.) for 45 minutes, or until dry and a light ivory color. Turn off heat. Remove meringues from paper and return to oven to cool.

Prepare filling. Reserve a few perfect berries for garnish and slice remaining berries. Combine berries and sugar and fold into whipped cream. Place one meringue layer on serving plate and spoon one-third of the whipped cream-fruit mixture over meringue. Top with second meringue and half the remaining fruit mixture. Repeat again. Sprinkle top with slivered almonds and garnish with reserved berries. Serve at once.

ICY MERINGUES WITH FLAMING RASPBERRY SAUCE

6 servings

Served on blue plates, this makes a dramatic red, white, and blue dessert.

> 6 *Individual Meringues (see index)*
>
> 2 *pints vanilla or French vanilla ice cream*
>
> 1 *pint fresh red raspberries or 1 (10- or 12-ounce) package frozen*
>
> 2 *tablespoons framboise (optional)*
>
> 2 *tablespoons sugar*
>
> 1½ *tablespoons cornstarch*
>
> 3 *tablespoons cold water*
>
> ¼ *cup light rum, warmed*

Ahead of serving time, fill meringues with a scoop of ice cream, arrange on individual serving dishes or on a tray, and store in freezer. At serving time, mix raspberries, framboise, and sugar in small chafing dish or metal fondue pan and place over moderate heat (or direct flame).

While raspberries are heating, mix cornstarch and water until smooth and stir into fruit. Cook, stirring constantly, until mixture thickens. Just before serving, stir in 1 tablespoon rum. Spoon remaining rum over sauce and ignite at edge of pan. When flame dies, spoon sauce over ice cream-filled meringues. Serve immediately.

HUGUENOT TORTE
6 servings

Thousands of French Huguenots fled France during the political and religious quarrels of the sixteenth and seventeenth centuries. Many settled in America, particularly New York, Massachusetts, Virginia, and the Carolinas. Their style of cooking was wholesome and simple, as the following recipe suggests.

⅓ *cup sifted flour*
1½ *teaspoons baking powder*
2 *eggs*
1½ *cups sugar*
2 *teaspoons vanilla*
⅛ *teaspoon salt*
1 *cup chopped nuts*
1 *cup peeled, finely chopped raw apple*
Sweetened whipped cream
Bits of maraschino cherries or chopped nuts for garnish

Sift together flour and baking powder. Combine eggs, sugar, vanilla, and salt, beating until thick and lemon-colored. Fold in dry ingredients, then nuts and apples.

Pour into buttered 2-quart round covered casserole and bake in slow oven (325° F.) for 45 minutes. Uncover and continue baking 15 minutes longer.

To serve, spoon torte, warm or cold, into serving dish and top with sweetened whipped cream and bits of maraschino cherry or chopped nuts.

DATE-NUT TORTE
9 to 12 servings

Date-Nut Torte is a California creation. Dates were first brought to California by the Spanish missionaries and were thought to be a symbol of life, fertility, and riches.

1½ *cups confectioners' sugar*
⅓ *cup flour*
¾ *teaspoon baking powder*
¼ *teaspoon salt*
3 *eggs, beaten*
1½ *teaspoons vanilla*
1½ *cups chopped pitted dates*
1 *cup chopped pecans or walnuts*
Sweetened whipped cream or vanilla ice cream

Sift together first 4 ingredients. Combine eggs and vanilla, beating slightly. Add dry ingredients, dates, and nuts and stir until well mixed.

Grease a 9 × 9 × 2-inch baking pan and line with greased waxed paper. Pour batter in and bake in moderate oven (350° F.) for 25 to 30 minutes, or until a wooden pick inserted in center comes out clean.

Cool in pan for 10 minutes. Turn out of pan, peel off paper, and turn right side up on wire rack to cool. Cut in serving pieces. Serve warm or cold topped with whipped cream or ice cream.

DUTCH APPLE CAKE

8 to 10 servings

Teatime was a favorite hour of the day in New Amsterdam homes. Among the delicious assortment of cakes and pastries that might be presented to honored guests, Dutch Apple Cake was a favorite with old and young alike.

APPLE LAYER

  ½ *cup sugar*

  1 *tablespoon lemon juice*

  1 *teaspoon cinnamon*

  4 *cups peeled, sliced tart apples*

CAKE BATTER

  2 *cups sifted flour*

  ⅓ *cup sugar*

  2 *teaspoons baking powder*

  ½ *teaspoon salt*

  ⅓ *cup butter*

  1 *cup milk*

  1 *egg, beaten*

  Additional sugar (optional)

  Sauce (see next column)

Blend together sugar, lemon juice, and cinnamon and coat apple slices well. Arrange evenly over bottom of 9-inch square pan.

Sift together flour, sugar, baking powder, and salt. Cut in butter with two knives or pastry blender until mixture resembles fine crumbs. Stir in milk and egg, mixing until smooth. Spoon over apple slices in even layer. Sprinkle top with small amount of sugar, if desired. Bake in moderate oven (350° F.) for 35 to 40 minutes, or until done. Serve warm with sauce.

SAUCE   About 1⅓ cups

  ½ *cup dark brown sugar, firmly packed*

  3 *tablespoons flour*

  ¼ *teaspoon salt*

  1 *cup boiling water*

  1 *tablespoon butter*

  1 *teaspoon lemon juice*

  ½ *teaspoon vanilla*

Combine first 3 ingredients in heavy saucepan and stir in boiling water. Cook over moderate heat until thickened, stirring constantly. Remove from heat, add butter, lemon juice, and vanilla and stir until butter is melted.

CHOCOLATE MINT TORTE

12 servings

A modern dessert for the busy homemaker, Chocolate Mint Torte is loaded with calories and tastes delicious. Even the novice cook will find it easy to prepare and impressive to serve.

  ¾ *cup butter*

  1 *cup fine vanilla wafer crumbs*

  3 *cups sifted confectioners' sugar*

  2 *teaspoons vanilla*

  1 *teaspoon peppermint extract*

  2 *eggs*

  4 *squares (ounces) unsweetened chocolate, melted and cooled*

  1 *cup heavy cream*

  3 *cups miniature marshmallows*

  Maraschino cherry pieces, crushed peppermint-stick candy, chocolate curls or sprinkles

Line a 9 × 9 × 2-inch baking pan with aluminum foil. Melt 2 tablespoons butter and mix with crumbs. Press crumbs evenly over bottom of prepared pan. Cream remaining butter, add 2⅔ cups sugar gradually, and beat until light and fluffy. Beat in vanilla and ½

teaspoon peppermint extract. Add eggs, one at a time, beating about 2 minutes after each addition. Fold in chocolate and continue stirring until evenly blended. Spoon in an even layer over crumbs. Chill while preparing topping. Combine remaining ⅓ cup sugar and ½ teaspoon peppermint extract with cream and whip until cream holds soft peaks. Fold in marshmallows. Spread evenly over chocolate mixture. Freeze. Cut into squares with sharp knife. Garnish with maraschino cherry pieces, crushed peppermint-stick candy, chocolate curls or sprinkles.

CHOCOLATE FONDUE EXTRAORDINAIRE

2½ cups sauce

Fun for family and friends, bite-sized pieces of cake, marshmallows, or fruits are twisted in the hot chocolate mixture with long two-pronged fondue forks. Much of the fun stems from the attempt to get the dipped chocolate morsel from pot to mouth without dripping.

1 *(3-ounce) package cream cheese, at room temperature*
½ *cup half and half*
2 *(8-ounce) packages milk chocolate, broken in small squares*
½ *cup Cherry Heering, orange, coffee, or chocolate liqueur*

Beat cream cheese until smooth. Add half and half slowly, beating constantly. Pour cheese mixture into electric fondue pot, set at low temperature. Add chocolate pieces, a few at a time, stirring constantly until sauce is thick and smooth. Stir in liqueur. Serve bite-sized pieces of pound cake, chunks of angel food or sponge cake, big marshmallows, chunks of cantaloupe or honeydew melon, Bing cherries, banana chunks, canned or fresh pineapple or strawberries for dipping.

NOTE: *If an electric fondue pot is not available, use a regular fondue pot set over a low flame or the top of a double boiler over hot water. If cheese mixture becomes lumpy, beat lightly with an egg beater.*

VARIATIONS

Chocolate Mint Fondue: Substitute 3 or 4 tablespoons crème de menthe for the Cherry Heering. For a mintier fondue, substitute 1 (8-ounce) package mint-flavored chocolate pieces for 1 package milk chocolate or add ½ to 1 teaspoon mint flavoring.

Nutty Chocolate Fondue: Omit Cherry Heering and stir in 1 teaspoon vanilla and 3 tablespoons Cointreau or Grand Marnier. Fold in ¼ cup very finely chopped pecans or toasted almonds. If a less exotic fondue is desired, omit Cointreau, increase vanilla to 2 teaspoons, and fold in ¼ cup very finely chopped salted peanuts.

NOTE: *Both variation mixtures are great for big marshmallows, pound-cake cubes, doughnut or banana chunks, or large maraschino cherries.*

CHESUNCOOK VILLAGE BLUEBERRY DUMPLING

6 servings

Located in Piscataquis County, Maine, Chesuncook Village was known first as an Indian settlement and later as a logging site. The blueberry dumpling of Chesuncook Village has remained popular, although the population of the village is now numbered at zero.

CRUST

    2 *cups sifted flour*

    2 *tablespoons sugar*

2½ *teaspoons baking powder*

  ½ *teaspoon salt*

  ½ *cup shortening*

  ½ *cup milk*

FILLING

  ¾ *cup sugar*

  ½ *cup melted butter*

  ½ *teaspoon cinnamon*

   2 *cups blueberries, fresh or frozen*

    Cream, sweetened whipped cream, or vanilla ice cream

To prepare crust, sift together first 4 ingredients. Cut in shortening with pastry blender until mixture resembles coarse meal. Stir in milk. Turn onto lightly floured board, knead 6 to 8 times, and roll into a 12-inch square. Trim edges of square with fluted pastry wheel or sharp knife. Place crust diagonally in greased 8 × 8 × 2-inch pan and press to fit into pan, leaving corners hanging over center of each pan side.

To prepare filling, blend together sugar, butter, and cinnamon. Stir in blueberries. Spoon in even layer over crust and bring corners of dough up over blueberry mixture to meet in center.

Bake in hot oven (400° F.) for 30 to 35 minutes, or until blueberries are hot and crust is done and browned. Serve warm with desired accompaniments.

ROANOKE APPLE DUMPLINGS

6 dumplings (6 servings)

Here is my reconstruction of the dessert my husband remembers as his childhood favorite.

CRUST

    2 *cups sifted flour*

    2 *teaspoons baking powder*

  ½ *teaspoon salt*

  ⅓ *cup shortening*

  ⅓ *cup butter*

  ½ *cup milk*

FILLING

   6 *medium-sized tart baking apples (about 2 pounds), peeled and cored*

  ⅓ *cup granulated sugar*

  ½ *cup light brown sugar, firmly packed*

   1 *teaspoon cinnamon*

   4 *tablespoons lemon juice*

   3 *tablespoons butter*

    Milk or cream

    Additional granulated sugar

    Cream, sweetened whipped cream, or vanilla ice cream

To prepare crust, sift together flour, baking powder, and salt. Cut in shortening and butter with pastry blender until mixture resembles fine crumbs. Stir in milk. Knead 10 to 12 strokes on lightly floured board. Roll dough into a 14 × 21-inch rectangle. Cut into six 7-inch squares, using a fluted pastry cutter or sharp knife.

To prepare filling, center an apple on each crust square. Combine granulated and brown sugars and cinnamon. Pour 2 teaspoons lemon juice over each apple. Sprinkle an equal amount of sugar mixture into cavity and over top of each apple. Dot each apple with 1½ teaspoons butter. Moisten edges of pastry. Bring four corners of pastry together over center of apple and seal edges completely. Arrange in a shallow baking dish, brush with milk or cream, and sprinkle with a small amount of granulated sugar.

Bake in moderate oven (375° F.) for 50 to 60 minutes, or until pastry is lightly browned and apples tender. Serve warm or cold with cream, whipped cream, or ice cream.

WISCONSIN APPLE SLICES

24 slices

A favorite of mine for many years, this recipe comes from Wisconsin. Apple slices make good lunchbox fillers or after-school treats. Marvelous as a dessert, they are also especially good at breakfast.

CRUST

    2 *cups sifted flour*
    1 *teaspoon salt*
    ⅔ *cup shortening*
    1 *egg, beaten*
    ⅔ *cup milk*

FILLING

    1 *tablespoon lemon juice*
    6 *cups peeled, sliced cooking apples (about 1¾ pounds)*
    1 *cup sugar*
    2 *tablespoons flour*
    2 *tablespoons butter*

LEMON GLAZE

    1 *cup sifted confectioners' sugar*
    1 *tablespoon softened butter*
    1 *tablespoon lemon juice*
    1 *to 2 teaspoons milk (approximate)*

To prepare crust, sift together flour and salt. Cut in shortening with pastry blender until mixture resembles fine crumbs. Add egg and milk, stir to moisten dry ingredients, and press together. Roll out half the crust into a 13 × 9-inch rectangle and press into bottom of 13 × 9 × 2-inch baking pan. Roll out remaining crust into 13 × 9-inch rectangle.

To prepare filling, sprinkle lemon juice over apples. Combine sugar and flour and sprinkle over apples, mixing to coat slices thoroughly. Arrange apples in even layer over bottom crust. Dot with butter and top with second crust.

Bake in moderate oven (375° F.) for 35 to 40 minutes, or until crust is brown and apples are tender. Cool for about 15 minutes.

To prepare lemon glaze, beat sugar, butter, and lemon juice together. Stir in milk as needed, beating until smooth. Spread glaze over top. Cool and cut into slices, 3 inches long and 1½ inches wide.

BAKED PEACH PLEASERS

4 servings

    1 *(1-pound) can cling peach halves*
    2 *tablespoons light brown sugar*
    ¼ *teaspoon cinnamon*
    ⅛ *teaspoon nutmeg*
    Pinch of ginger
    ½ *cup chopped or slivered almonds*

Drain peach halves and reserve ¼ cup syrup. Combine syrup, sugar, cinnamon, nutmeg, ginger. Arrange peach halves, cavity side up, in 9-inch and pie plate and spoon an equal amount of mixture into each peach half. Sprinkle with almonds. Bake in moderate oven (350° F.) for 25 minutes, basting frequently with sauce.

FRESH PEACH COBBLER

4 to 6 servings

A fruit cobbler resembles a deep-dish fruit pie. Speculation suggests that the name comes from the phrase "to cobble up"—to put together hurriedly.

½ recipe Pastry for Double-Crust Pie (see index)

4 cups peeled, sliced fresh peaches

1 tablespoon lemon juice

1 cup sugar

3 tablespoons flour

¼ teaspoon salt

⅛ teaspoon cinnamon (optional)

2 tablespoons butter

Cream or melted butter

Sweetened whipped cream or vanilla ice cream (optional)

Roll pastry to fit top of a 1½-quart baking dish. Cut several slashes in crust for steam vents. Mix peach slices and lemon juice. Combine sugar, flour, salt, and cinnamon, sprinkle over peaches, and mix carefully. Turn into greased baking dish. Dot with butter and cover with pastry. Brush crust lightly with cream or melted butter.

Bake in hot oven (425° F.) for 25 minutes, or until crust is lightly browned and peaches tender. Serve warm or slightly cooled, plain or with whipped cream or ice cream.

VARIATION

Quick Peach Cobbler: Substitute 1 (1-pound 12-ounce) can sliced peaches, well drained, for fresh ones. Reduce flour to 2 tablespoons, sugar to 3 tablespoons, and butter to 1 tablespoon. Serve as suggested for Fresh Peach Cobbler above.

IOWA RHUBARB COBBLER

4 to 6 servings

1¼ cups sugar

2 tablespoons cornstarch

⅓ cup water

4 cups sliced fresh rhubarb

2 tablespoons butter

2 tablespoons lemon or orange juice

1 teaspoon grated lemon or orange peel

1 cup sifted flour

2 teaspoons baking powder

½ teaspoon salt

¼ cup shortening

1 egg, beaten

½ cup milk

Cream or ice cream (optional)

Combine 1 cup sugar, cornstarch, water, and rhubarb in large saucepan and bring to a boil, stirring carefully. Cook for 1 minute and stir in butter.

Pour into 8 × 8 × 2-inch buttered baking pan. Pour in fruit juice and sprinkle peel over rhubarb. Combine remaining ¼ cup sugar, flour, baking powder, and salt. Cut shortening into dry ingredients with pastry blender. Stir in egg and milk (*do not overmix*). Spoon onto fruit.

Bake in hot oven (400° F.) for 20 minutes. Serve warm, plain or with cream or ice cream.

NEW ENGLAND BLUEBERRY SLUMP
6 servings

The origin of the word *slump* is lost to history; one can only guess. Perhaps an early New England cook created a cobbler that "slumped" or fell in the middle.

BLUEBERRY MIXTURE
  3 *cups blueberries, fresh or frozen*
  ½ *cup sugar*
  2 *tablespoons lemon juice*
  ¼ *teaspoon grated lemon peel*
  ¼ *teaspoon cinnamon*
  ⅛ *teaspoon nutmeg*

CRUST
  1 *cup sifted flour*
  3 *tablespoons sugar*
  1½ *teaspoons baking powder*
  ¼ *teaspoon salt*
  ¼ *cup shortening*
  ½ *cup milk*
  1 *tablespoon butter, melted*
  Half and half, cream, or vanilla ice cream, as desired

Combine blueberry mixture ingredients in 1½-quart casserole. Cover and bake in hot oven (400° F.) for 15 minutes. Uncover and stir well.

While berries are heating, prepare crust. Sift together flour, 2 tablespoons sugar, baking powder, and salt. Cut in shortening with pastry blender until mixture resembles fine crumbs. Add milk and stir only enough to moisten dry ingredients. Drop by small spoonfuls onto blueberry mixture, covering fruit completely. Drizzle butter over top and sprinkle with remaining 1 tablespoon sugar.

Return to hot oven and bake for 25 to 30 minutes, or until topping is cooked and browned. Serve warm with half and half, cream, or vanilla ice cream.

APPLE PANDOWDY
One 12 × 8-inch pie

Apple Pandowdy's picturesque name comes from the last step of the recipe in which the top crust or "coffin" is chopped up and "dowdied" or pushed into the pie.

  ½ *cup butter*
  Pastry for Double-Crust Pie (9-inch) (see index)
  ⅔ *cup sugar*
  ½ *teaspoon cinnamon*
  ¼ *teaspoon nutmeg*
  ⅛ *teaspoon ground cloves*
  ¼ *teaspoon salt*
  8 *cups peeled, cored, thinly sliced apples*
  ⅓ *cup light molasses*
  ¼ *cup water*
  Melted butter and thick cream

Melt and cool ¼ cup butter. Prepare crust, roll into a 16 × 12-inch rectangle on a lightly floured board, and brush with melted butter. Fold pastry in half. Roll out again, brush with butter, and fold again. Repeat rolling, brushing, and folding twice more, using up the ¼ cup of melted butter. Wrap dough in plastic film and chill for 30 to 40 minutes.

Combine sugar, spices, and salt, add to apples, and toss lightly to coat slices. Arrange in 12 × 8 × 2-inch baking dish. Melt remaining ¼ cup butter, combine with molasses and water, and pour over apples. Roll pastry into a 14 × 10-inch rectangle and place over apples. Roll edges of crust under at rim of dish and flute. Bake in hot oven (400° F.) for 10 minutes. Reduce heat to slow (325° F.) and bake for 40 to 45 minutes longer, or until apples are tender and crust is browned.

"Dowdy" by cutting through crust and apples with sharp knife or by spooning the crust into the apples. Serve warm with melted butter and thick cream.

SWEDISH FRUIT SOUP

8 to 10 servings

In Swedish households, this traditional recipe may precede or follow the main course and is often included in a smorgasbord. At Christmas, I like to serve it at a buffet in a large glass bowl or as a special dessert topped with whipped cream. Hearty and refreshing, it also makes a good hot-weather luncheon entrée.

> ¾ *cup dried apricots*
> ¾ *cup pitted prunes*
> ⅓ *cup seedless raisins*
> 6 *cups water*
> 2 *cups peeled, cored, sliced apples*
> ½ *cup sugar (approximate)*
> ¼ *cup quick-cooking tapioca*
> 1 *(3-inch) stick cinnamon*
> 4 *whole cloves*
> 4 *thin lemon slices*
> ⅛ *teaspoon salt*
> 1 *cup fruit syrup, raspberry or grape juice*
> ¼ *cup blanched slivered almonds (optional)*

Place dried fruits and water in large saucepan. Cover and simmer for 30 minutes. Add apples, sugar, tapioca, cinnamon, cloves, lemon slices, and salt. Cover and simmer until fruit is tender, about 30 minutes. Add fruit syrup. Taste and add more sugar, if desired. Chill thoroughly. Just before serving, sprinkle with almonds.

NEW ORLEANS FLAMING BANANAS

4 servings

Flaming bananas is a specialty dessert in New Orleans, where colorful banana boats from Central and South America have unloaded their valuable cargoes for over a century.

> ¼ *cup light brown sugar, firmly packed*
> 2 *tablespoons butter*
> 2 *tablespoons water*
> 2 *teaspoons lemon juice*
> 2 *medium-sized ripe bananas, peeled and cut in half lengthwise and then crosswise*
> 3 *tablespoons warmed cognac*
> *Whipped cream or vanilla ice cream*
> *Flaked coconut (optional)*

Melt sugar and butter in chafing dish over direct heat or in electric fry pan set at moderate, stirring constantly. Stir in water and lemon juice and continue stirring until sugar is melted.

Add banana quarters and cook until hot and tender, turning once. Add warmed cognac, ignite, and shake pan until flame dies. Serve bananas immediately topped with whipped cream or ice cream and sprinkled with coconut.

FLAMING FRUIT DESSERT

8 servings

> 1 *(1-pound 4-ounce) can whole blue plums*
> 1 *(1-pound) can peach halves*
> ½ *cup sugar*
> 12 *whole cloves*
> 2 *sticks cinnamon*
> ¼ *cup warmed brandy*
> *Sweetened whipped cream (optional)*

Drain plums and peaches and reserve syrup. Remove pits from half the plums and whiz in blender or put through a sieve. Combine mashed plums, fruit syrups, sugar, and spices in a saucepan, bring to a boil, and cook until sugar is dissolved. Pour juice over remaining fruit and refrigerate for 2 to 3 hours.

To serve, heat in chafing dish. Just before serving, remove cinnamon sticks and pour warmed brandy over fruit and ignite. Serve when flame dies. Top with whipped cream.

NESSELRODE CUSTARD
(Fruited Rum Custard)
6 to 8 servings

A creation of a French chef named Mouy, Nesselrode Custard was named for the chef's Russian master, Count Karl Robert Nesselrode, an eminent nineteenth-century diplomat. This elegant dessert is a rich concoction of candied fruits, maraschino cherries, and whipped cream.

- ⅔ cup sugar
- 1 envelope unflavored gelatin
- ¼ teaspoon salt
- 3 eggs, separated
- 1 cup half and half
- 2 tablespoons rum
- 1 teaspoon vanilla
- ⅓ cup finely chopped mixed candied fruit
- ¼ cup quartered maraschino cherries
- ½ cup heavy cream, whipped
- Additional whipped cream (optional)
- Chocolate curls or chopped chestnuts or pecans (optional)

Combine ⅓ cup sugar, gelatin, and salt in a heavy saucepan. Beat egg yolks slightly and add to saucepan with half and half. Cook over low heat, stirring constantly, until gelatin dissolves and mixture coats the spoon. Stir in rum and vanilla. Chill until mixture starts to set, stirring occasionally. Beat egg whites until foamy. Add remaining ⅓ cup sugar, 1 tablespoonful at a time, and continue beating until stiff and glossy but not dry. Beat gelatin mixture thoroughly and carefully fold in egg whites, fruits, and whipped cream. Spoon into a large glass or ceramic serving bowl and chill until firm. Serve plain or top with a circle of whipped cream and garnish with chocolate curls or chopped nuts.

VARIATION
Nesselrode Pie: Prepare custard as directed above and spoon into a Baked (9-inch) Pie Shell (see index). Chill until firm and garnish as desired.

SWEDISH RICE MOLD
10 to 12 servings

- *Vanilla Pudding (see below)*
- 1 envelope unflavored gelatin
- ¼ cup cold water
- ⅔ cup long-grain rice
- 2 to 4 tablespoons sugar (or to taste)
- ¼ teaspoon salt
- 2 teaspoons vanilla
- 1 cup heavy cream, whipped
- *Melba Sauce (see index)*

Prepare Vanilla Pudding. Soften gelatin in cold water then add to pudding, stirring until dissolved. Cook rice according to package directions. Stir hot rice, sugar, and salt into pudding. Cool then chill thoroughly, stirring occasionally. Fold in vanilla and whipped cream. Spoon mixture into an oiled 6-cup ring mold. Chill until firm. Unmold and serve with Melba Sauce.

VANILLA PUDDING   4 to 6 servings
- ⅓ cup sugar
- 2 eggs, slightly beaten
- 3 tablespoons cornstarch
- ¼ teaspoon salt
- 2½ cups milk
- 1½ teaspoons vanilla
- ¼ teaspoon almond extract

Combine sugar, eggs, cornstarch, and salt. Gradually blend in milk. Cook over medium heat, stirring constantly, until mixture thickens. Cook 2 or 3 minutes more. Add vanilla and almond extract. Cover with plastic film and chill.

STRAWBERRIES WITH GRAND MARNIER

6 to 8 servings

A White House favorite under many administrations, Strawberries with Grand Marnier is not only delicious but easy to prepare.

  1 *egg white*
  ⅛ *teaspoon cream of tartar*
  Pinch of salt
  ⅓ *cup sugar*
  1 *teaspoon vanilla*
  ½ *cup cream*
  4 *cups fully ripe strawberries, washed, hulled, and left whole*
  ⅓ *cup strawberry preserves*
  ¼ *cup Grand Marnier*
  2 *tablespoons kirsch*
  Mint sprigs (optional)
  Sweetened whipped cream (optional)

Combine first 3 ingredients in small bowl and beat until egg white is frothy. Add sugar gradually, 1 tablespoonful at a time, and continue beating until egg white forms stiff peaks. Fold in vanilla. Whip cream until it holds soft peaks and fold into egg whites. Spread mixture into shallow serving bowl. Stand strawberries, pointed end up, in egg-cream mixture. Thin preserves with Grand Marnier and kirsch and spoon over berries. Garnish with mint sprigs. Serve with sweetened whipped cream and favorite pound cake, tea cakes, or rich cookies.

ZABAGLIONE CREAM

6 servings

  ½ *cup sugar*
  1 *teaspoon unflavored gelatin*
  ½ *cup dry sherry*
  6 *eggs, separated, plus 3 egg whites*
  1 *tablespoon brandy*
  1 *teaspoon vanilla*
  1 *cup cream*
  ⅛ *teaspoon cream of tartar*
  Dash of salt
  Fresh strawberries or chocolate curls for garnish

Combine ⅓ cup sugar and gelatin in top of double boiler and stir in sherry. Beat egg yolks until very light, fluffy, and lemon-colored. Add to double boiler and cook over gently boiling water until thickened, stirring constantly. Remove from heat and cool. Stir in brandy and vanilla.

Whip cream and fold into egg mixture. Combine 9 egg whites, cream of tartar, and salt, beating until whites are foamy. Add remaining sugar and continue beating until whites are stiff. Fold into custard. Spoon into tall dessert dishes. Chill thoroughly (at least 1 hour). Garnish with strawberry halves or chocolate curls.

POTS DE CRÈME À LA VANILLE

6 servings

  6 *egg yolks*
  ⅔ *cup sugar*
  ⅛ *teaspoon salt*
  3 *cups half and half or cream, scalded*
  1 *tablespoon vanilla*
  Sweetened whipped cream (optional)
  Chocolate curls (optional)

Combine first 3 ingredients and beat slowly just until mixed. Add half and half or cream very slowly, beating constantly. Stir in vanilla. Strain into 6 ungreased 5-ounce crème pots, soufflé dishes, or custard cups. Place dishes in pan of hot water and bake in slow oven (300° F.) for 35 minutes, or until a knife inserted to one side of center comes out clean. Chill 4 hours or overnight. Serve topped with whipped cream or chocolate curls.

VARIATIONS

Pots de Crème à l'Orange: Substitute 1 tablespoon grated orange peel and 2 tablespoons Grand Marnier for vanilla and do not strain.

Pots de Crème au Chocolat: Add ½ pound grated sweet chocolate to scalded half and half or cream and stir until chocolate has melted, stirring constantly.

Pots de Crème à la Carlton: Stir ⅓ cup sugar and salt into scalded half and half or cream. Increase egg yolks to 8 (optional). Beat yolks and remaining ⅓ cup sugar until light and lemon-colored. Add the hot mixture to egg yolks in a very fine stream, stirring constantly with a wire whisk. Pour into top of double boiler over hot water and cook, stirring, until custard thickens and coats the spoon. Transfer to a bowl and set in a pan of cold water to stop the cooking. Stir in flavoring. Pour into individual crème pots, soufflé dishes, or custard cups. Chill thoroughly for at least 6 hours or overnight.

INDIAN PUDDING

6 servings

One of the true American puddings, Indian Pudding was a favorite Saturday dessert in Colonial New England. Baked in a slow oven with the usual pot of baked beans, it was richer than ordinary Indian cornmeal mush. Flavored with molasses, cinnamon, ginger, and possibly raisins, it can be eaten plain or with cream or whipped cream.

- ¼ *cup sugar*
- 1 *teaspoon cinnamon*
- ½ *teaspoon ginger or nutmeg*
- 1 *teaspoon salt*
- ½ *cup light molasses*
- 3 *eggs, beaten*
- ⅓ *cup yellow cornmeal*
- ½ *cup cold milk*
- 3 *cups scalded milk*
- 1 *tablespoon butter*
- ½ *cup seedless raisins (optional)*
- *Cream or sweetened whipped cream*

Combine first 4 ingredients. Stir in molasses and eggs and set aside. Combine cornmeal and cold milk in heavy saucepan. Stir in scalded milk and cook over low heat for 10 minutes, stirring constantly. Add butter. Remove from heat and add molasses mixture in a fine stream, beating constantly. Fold in raisins.

Pour into a greased 8 × 8 × 2-inch baking dish. Place baking pan in a shallow pan filled with 1 inch hot water. Bake in slow oven (325° F.) for 50 minutes, or until silver knife inserted in center comes out clean. Serve hot or cold with cream or whipped cream.

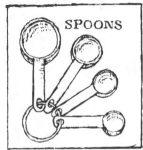

FARM-COUNTRY BREAD PUDDING

6 to 8 servings

In the tradition of early New England grunts and slumps, bread pudding was a favorite dessert during long cold winters. Sometimes made with apples, it can be made with other fruits and is an excellent budget stretcher.

> 4 *cups day-old white or French bread cubes, crusts removed*
> ½ *cup seedless raisins*
> 3 *tablespoons melted butter*
> 4 *eggs*
> 1 *teaspoon cinnamon*
> ½ *teaspoon nutmeg*
> ½ *teaspoon salt*
> ⅔ *cup sugar*
> 3 *cups milk, scalded*
> 1½ *teaspoons vanilla*
> *Spiced Milk (see next column) or sweetened whipped cream*

Arrange bread cubes and raisins in buttered 1½-quart baking dish or casserole and drizzle with butter. Combine eggs, cinnamon, nutmeg, and salt, beating slightly. Dissolve sugar in milk and add to eggs in a fine stream, stirring constantly. Stir in vanilla.

Pour over bread cubes and bake in moderate oven (350° F.) for 55 to 60 minutes, or until a silver knife inserted in center comes out clean. Serve slightly warm or chilled, plain, or with Spiced Milk or whipped cream.

SPICED MILK

> ½ *teaspoon cinnamon*
> ½ *teaspoon nutmeg*
> ¼ *teaspoon sugar*
> *Pinch of salt*
> 2 *cups chilled milk or half and half*

Combine first 4 ingredients. Add milk or half and half and stir until sugar dissolves. Serve cold with bread pudding.

QUEEN'S PUDDING

6 to 8 servings

A favorite with the Victorians, Queen's Pudding is still popular today. Possibly named for Queen Victoria, it consists of three layers—a bread custard spread with fruit preserves or marmalade and topped with a meringue. The pudding is baked until the meringue turns a golden brown.

> 4 *cups day-old bread cubes, crusts removed*
> 4 *eggs*
> ¾ *cup sugar*
> ½ *teaspoon salt*
> ½ *teaspoon nutmeg (optional)*
> 2 *teaspoons vanilla*
> 2 *tablespoons butter*
> 3 *cups scalded milk*
> ½ *cup red raspberry preserves, currant jelly, or orange marmalade*
> ⅛ *teaspoon cream of tartar*
> 1 *tablespoon water*

Arrange bread cubes in buttered 1½-quart casserole. Combine 2 whole eggs and 2 egg yolks, beating slightly. Stir in ½ cup sugar, salt, nutmeg, and vanilla. Add butter to scalded milk, let it melt, and add to egg mixture slowly, stirring constantly. Pour over bread cubes.

Place casserole in shallow pan filled with 1

inch hot water and bake in moderate oven (350° F.) for 1 hour, or until silver knife inserted in center of pudding comes out clean. Remove from oven and spread with preserves, jelly, or marmalade.

Beat remaining 2 egg whites and cream of tartar until frothy. Add water gradually and continue beating. Add remaining ¼ cup sugar gradually, 1 tablespoonful at a time, and continue beating until meringue is glossy and holds soft peaks. Spread over pudding. Return to oven for about 10 minutes, or until meringue is browned. Serve hot or cold.

OZARK PUDDING

6 to 8 servings

> ½ *cup sifted flour*
> 2½ *teaspoons baking powder*
> ¼ *teaspoon salt*
> 2 *eggs*
> 1½ *teaspoons vanilla*
> 1 *cup light brown sugar, firmly packed*
> 1¼ *cups peeled, finely chopped apples*
> 1¼ *cups chopped walnuts*
> *Sweetened whipped cream*
> *Chopped walnuts or maraschino cherries (optional)*

Sift together first 3 ingredients. Beat eggs until frothy. Add vanilla and sugar, ¼ cup at a time, beating very well after each addition. Fold in dry ingredients, apples, and nuts.

Pour into well-buttered 10-inch pie plate or 9 × 9 × 2-inch pan. Bake in moderate oven (350° F.) for 30 minutes. Serve warm or cold, cut in wedges or squares. Top each serving with a dollop of whipped cream. Garnish with nuts or cherry pieces.

RICE CUSTARD WITH CARAMEL TOPPING

6 to 8 servings

> 3 *eggs, beaten slightly*
> 1 *teaspoon salt*
> ½ *teaspoon nutmeg*
> ⅔ *cup sugar*
> 3 *cups milk, scalded*
> 1 *tablespoon butter*
> 1 *cup well-drained cooked rice*
> 2 *teaspoons vanilla*
> ¼ *cup toasted slivered almonds*
> ⅓ *cup brown sugar, firmly packed*
> *Whipped cream (optional)*

Combine first 3 ingredients. Dissolve sugar in milk, add butter, and stir until melted. Add milk to eggs in fine stream, stirring constantly. Stir in rice and vanilla. Pour into buttered shallow 1½-quart baking dish.

Bake in pan of hot water in moderate oven (350° F.) for 35 minutes, or until silver knife inserted to one side of center comes out clean. (Stir twice during baking.) Remove baking dish from hot water and sprinkle nuts and brown sugar evenly over top.

Place in broiler 3 to 4 inches from heat source to melt sugar. Watch constantly, as sugar burns quickly. Remove from broiler the instant the sugar melts. Serve warm or chilled, plain or with whipped cream.

VARIATION

Old-Fashioned Rice Pudding: Soak ¾ cup seedless raisins in hot water for 10 minutes. Drain thoroughly and stir into rice mixture with ½ teaspoon cinnamon. Reduce nutmeg to ¼ teaspoon. Omit almond-brown sugar topping.

J. ROBERT'S MACAROON PUDDING

10 to 12 servings

Long a favorite with my Southern husband, this is an adaptation of a pudding he remembers from his childhood but couldn't find in written form. He insists the pudding did not include maraschino cherries and pecans but their addition enhances the overall flavor.

    2 *envelopes unflavored gelatin*

 3½ *cups milk*

  ¾ *cup sugar*

  ¼ *teaspoon salt*

    4 *eggs, separated*

  ⅓ *cup rum*

    2 *teaspoons vanilla*

  ¼ *teaspoon almond extract*

  ½ *cup chopped pecans*

  ½ *cup quartered red maraschino cherries*

  ½ *pound almond macaroons, crumbled (about 2½ cups)*

  ½ *cup heavy cream, whipped*

Soften gelatin in ½ cup milk. Combine remaining 3 cups milk, ½ cup sugar, salt, and egg yolks in heavy saucepan, beating thoroughly. Cook, stirring constantly, until mixture reaches the boiling point (if mixture curdles, lower heat and beat with egg beater). Remove from heat. Add softened gelatin and stir until melted.

Chill until mixture begins to set. Blend in rum, vanilla, and almond extract. Stir in pecans and cherries. Beat egg whites until white and foamy. Beat in remaining ¼ cup sugar, 1 tablespoonful at a time, and continue beating until stiff and glossy. Fold into gelatin mixture. Chill until mixture mounds well.

Reserve ½ cup macaroon crumbs for decorating top. Sprinkle half the remaining crumbs into a chilled 2-quart serving bowl. Spoon half the gelatin mixture over crumbs. Repeat. Chill for several hours or until mixture sets. Serve topped with whipped cream and sprinkle with reserved crumbs.

RICHARDS FAMILY SUET PUDDING

10 servings

Suet pudding has been served, especially at holiday time, since early Colonial times. This recipe is a very old one that has been handed down from generation to generation by the Richards family of Iowa.

 1½ *cups flour*

    1 *teaspoon baking powder*

  ½ *teaspoon cinnamon*

    1 *cup sugar*

    1 *egg, slightly beaten*

    2 *tablespoons blackstrap molasses*

    1 *cup finely ground suet, lightly packed*

    1 *teaspoon baking soda*

    1 *cup buttermilk*

    1 *teaspoon vanilla*

    1 *cup raisins*

Suet Pudding Sauce (see next column)

Sift together first 3 ingredients and set aside. Combine sugar, egg, and molasses in large bowl and beat until thoroughly mixed. Mix in suet. Add baking soda to buttermilk and add to molasses mixture, blending well. Add dry ingredients to mixture, stirring or beating lightly until well mixed. Blend in vanilla and ½ cup raisins.

Pour into a greased 2½-quart casserole or 9-inch round cake pan. Sprinkle remaining ½

cup raisins over top. Cover tightly with aluminum foil. Fill a steamer with water to a depth of 1 inch. Set casserole on rack in steamer and cover. Cook over medium heat for 3 hours. Serve with sauce.

NOTE: *An improvised steamer may be made from any large kettle or roaster.*

If desired, dry pudding, covered, in 300° F. oven for 10 minutes. Pudding is of a moist, soft consistency when removed from steamer and becomes more cakelike in texture if dried in the oven.

SUET PUDDING SAUCE

    1 *tablespoon butter*
    1 *cup confectioners' sugar*
    1 *egg, slightly beaten*
    1 *teaspoon vanilla*
    3 *cups heavy cream*

Cream butter and sugar together until light and fluffy. Blend in egg and vanilla. Chill large bowl and beaters and beat cream until soft peaks form. Fold sugar mixture into whipped cream until well blended.

BAKED CUSTARD

6 servings

    3 or 4 *eggs, beaten slightly*
    ½ *cup sugar*
    ¼ *teaspoon salt*
    2 *cups milk or half and half, scalded and cooled slightly*
    1½ *teaspoons vanilla*

Stir first 3 ingredients together. Add milk or half and half to eggs in a fine stream, stirring constantly. Stir in vanilla. Pour into 6 lightly buttered 5- or 6-ounce custard cups or a 1-quart casserole. Place cups or casserole in a shallow pan filled with 1 inch of hot water. Bake in slow oven (325° F.) 40 minutes for cups, 60 minutes for casserole, or until knife inserted to one side of center comes out clean. Chill. To unmold cups, run a knife around top edge and gently down sides to let in air. Custard should fall out on to serving dish. Serve plain or with sweetened whipped cream, red raspberries, strawberries, or sliced peaches.

VARIATIONS

Coconut-Topped Custard: Ten minutes before end of baking time sprinkle lightly toasted flaked or shredded coconut over the top of custard.

Rum Custard: Use 4 eggs and stir ¼ cup light rum or 1½ teaspoons rum extract into custard mixture. Chill baked custard and serve plain or with raspberry or strawberry sauce.

BOILED CUSTARD

3½ cups

Brought to the American colonies by early English settlers, boiled or soft custard served in a variety of ways has long been a favorite, easy-to-digest dessert.

    ¾ *cup sugar*
    1 *tablespoon cornstarch*
    ¼ *teaspoon salt*
    2 *cups half and half*
    4 *eggs, beaten*
    2 *teaspoons vanilla*

Combine first 3 ingredients in heavy saucepan. Blend in half and half and cook, stirring constantly, until hot. Pour about one-third of the hot mixture over eggs, stirring constantly. Stir into hot mixture. Cook, stirring constantly, about 2 minutes, or until mixture coats spoon and thickens slightly. Stir in vanilla. Chill thoroughly.

PLUM PUDDING
10 to 12 servings

Plum Pudding had its beginnings as "plum soup," a concoction of mutton stock, currants, prunes, raisins, and sherry. Eventually bread was added as a thickening, and "plum soup" became plum porridge. Gradually it grew sweeter and appeared at the end of the meal minus the meat. During the Puritan reign in England, Plum Pudding was outlawed as "sinfully rich."

  1 *cup sifted flour*
  1 *teaspoon each salt, baking soda, nutmeg, and cinnamon*
  ¼ *teaspoon each ground cloves, allspice, and ginger*
  1 *cup halved seedless raisins*
  1 *cup halved golden raisins*
  1 *cup currants*
  1 *cup chopped mixed candied fruits*
  ¼ *cup chopped candied cherries*
  ¼ *cup chopped candied orange peel*
  ½ *cup chopped walnuts or pecans*
  2 *teaspoons grated orange peel*
  1 *teaspoon grated lemon peel*
1½ *cups soft bread crumbs*
  3 *eggs*
  1 *cup light brown sugar, firmly packed*
  2 *cups (½ pound) finely ground beef suet*
  ⅓ *cup orange juice or brandy*
  ¼ *cup apple or currant jelly*
     Hard Sauce or Brandy Sauce (see index)

Grease a 2-quart or two 1-quart pudding molds and set aside. Sift together flour, salt, baking soda, and spices. Combine fruits, nuts, orange and lemon peel, and bread crumbs and mix thoroughly. Beat eggs and sugar until light. Stir in suet, liquid, and jelly. Stir in fruit and dry ingredients, blending thoroughly.

Pack in prepared molds, filling three-fourths full. Cover molds tightly and place on rack in deep kettle. Fill kettle with hot water to within 1 inch of top of mold. Cover kettle and bring water to a boil. Reduce heat to simmer and steam pudding until done, 4 to 5 hours for a 2-quart mold, 3 hours for two 1-quart molds. Replenish hot water as it evaporates.

Loosen pudding on one side of mold and gently turn out onto heated serving plate. Serve hot with Hard or Brandy Sauce. Garnish with sprigs of holly.

VOLUNTEER STATE ORANGE CREAM CUSTARD
About 2 cups

An old, old recipe from Tennessee, Orange Cream Custard has a delicate tangy flavor. Excellent as a dessert, it may also be used as a topping for cake.

  1 *cup drained fresh orange sections, white membrane removed*
  ½ *cup sugar*
  2 *tablespoons flour*
  ⅛ *teaspoon salt*
  1 *cup half and half or light cream*
  3 *egg yolks, beaten*
  1 *teaspoon grated orange peel*
  ¼ *cup orange juice (optional)*

Cut orange sections in half crosswise and reserve. Combine sugar, flour, and salt in top of double boiler. Stir in half and half or cream, egg yolks, grated orange peel, and orange pieces. Cook over gently boiling water, stirring often, until the consistency of mayonnaise.

If a thinner sauce is desired, stir in half and half or orange juice a little at a time until desired consistency is reached. Serve as a dessert topped with sweetened whipped cream or on sponge- or pound-cake slices.

TRIFLE
10 to 12 servings

Introduced into America by the British, Trifle was a favorite dessert in Colonial Virginia. Some recipes called for cake slices, ladyfingers, or macaroons to be soaked with rum or sherry and layered with jam and custard in an elegant crystal bowl.

    2 *dozen ladyfingers*
    1 *(12-ounce) jar raspberry or strawberry preserves or currant jelly*
    ¼ *pound (1¼ cups) almond macaroons, crumbled*
    ¾ *cup cream or sweet sherry*
    ¼ *cup brandy*
    Boiled Custard, chilled (see index)
    ¾ *cup chopped candied fruits or fresh fruit in season*
    2 *egg whites*
    ½ *teaspoon vanilla*
    2 *tablespoons sugar*
    ½ *cup cream, whipped*

Split ladyfingers and spread bottom halves with preserves or jelly, using ½ cup. Put ladyfingers back together. Stand 12 ladyfingers upright around edge of 2-quart glass or china serving bowl and make a layer of ladyfingers over the bottom. Sprinkle one-third of the macaroon crumbs over ladyfingers. Combine sherry and brandy and sprinkle one-third of the mixture over crumbs. Spoon one-third of remaining preserves over top and cover with one-third of the chilled custard. Sprinkle with one-third of the fruit. Repeat twice to make 3 layers.

Chill for several hours. Just before serving, beat egg whites and vanilla until white and foamy. Add sugar, 1 tablespoonful at a time, and continue beating until stiff and glossy. Fold in whipped cream and spoon over Trifle. Serve immediately.

TIPSY PARSON OR SQUIRE CAKE
12 servings

Similar to a trifle and named for its alcoholic content, Tipsy Parson is a favorite dessert to serve on New Year's in many areas of the South. In old days it was the traditional dessert to serve when important visitors came to call.

    Light and Fluffy Sponge Cake (see index)
    ½ *cup slivered blanched almonds*
    1 *cup cream or sweet sherry (old cookbooks say 2 cups)*
    Boiled Custard, chilled (see index)
    Sweetened whipped cream
    Maraschino cherries or blanched almonds (optional)

Place tube cake, upside down, on large serving plate or in large glass bowl. Stud top and sides with almonds. Drizzle sherry very slowly over entire top. Spoon custard into hole and over top of cake. Chill for several hours or overnight. Serve topped with whipped cream. A few maraschino cherry quarters or almonds sprinkled over cream adds to the beauty.

CHRISTMAS AMBROSIA

8 servings

A Southern favorite, Ambrosia alludes to the fabled "food of the gods." According to Greek and Roman mythology, ambrosia confers immortality, and mortals who ate of it gained in strength and beauty

    8 *large seedless oranges, peeled and white membrane removed*

1½ *cups flaked or shredded coconut*

1½ *cups fresh, canned, or defrosted frozen pineapple chunks*

    ½ *cup orange juice*

    ¼ *cup superfine or confectioners' sugar*

    Sherry or Grand Marnier (optional)

    Maraschino cherries or strawberry halves

    Mint sprigs (optional)

    Orange Cream (see below—optional)

Several hours before serving, cut oranges in segments, chunks, or slices. Spread one-fourth of the orange pieces over bottom of a large glass or china serving bowl. Sprinkle one-third of the coconut over top. Spread one-third of the pineapple pieces over coconut. Repeat process, finishing with orange pieces.

Combine orange juice and sugar, stirring until sugar dissolves, and pour over fruit. Add a small amount of sherry or Grand Marnier. Cover and chill until serving time. Garnish with maraschino cherries or strawberry halves and mint sprigs. Serve with Orange Cream.

NOTE: *If desired, three small seedless grapefruit, trimmed of white membrane and cut in segments or chunks, may be substituted for 4 of the oranges.*

ORANGE CREAM

Whip 1 cup well-chilled heavy cream and fold in ¼ cup superfine or confectioners' sugar and 1 to 1½ tablespoons grated orange peel. Spoon into serving bowl. Garnish with a few pieces of shredded orange peel.

BANBURY TARTS

2 dozen tarts

Although these resemble tarts, they were known in England as cakes. The tarts were a specialty of Banbury in Oxfordshire, where they were hawked by street vendors who carried them in round wicker baskets.

    ½ *cup chopped seedless raisins*

    ½ *cup chopped pitted dates*

    ½ *cup chopped mixed candied fruits*

    ½ *cup chopped red candied cherries*

    1 *cup sugar*

    2 *tablespoons flour*

    2 *eggs, beaten*

    ⅓ *cup lemon juice*

    1 *tablespoon grated orange peel*

    1 *teaspoon grated lemon peel*

    2 *recipes Pastry for Double-Crust Pie (see index)*

    Water

    Melted butter

    Additional sugar

Combine first 8 ingredients in a small, heavy saucepan, mixing thoroughly. Cook over low heat, stirring constantly, until thickened. Stir in grated peels and chill.

Roll out pastry, half at a time, on a lightly floured board to ⅛-inch thickness. Cut into 4-inch squares. Place a slightly rounded tablespoonful of filling in one corner of each square. Brush edges of pastry with water, fold in half diagonally, and press edges together, sealing with tines of a dinner fork. Prick steam vents in top 3 or 4 times with tines of fork. Brush top of each tart with melted butter and sprinkle lightly with sugar.

Place on ungreased baking sheet and bake in hot oven (400° F.) for about 15 minutes, or until pastry is lightly browned. Cool on wire racks. Serve warm or cold.

CREAM PUFFS (Choux)
12 to 15 cream puffs

Cream puffs are called *choux* in France, their country of origin. They were named for their resemblance, when baked, to miniature cabbages. A round, airy cake, they may be filled with cream or ice cream or served as an appetizer with a meat, egg, or shellfish filling.

1 *cup water*

½ *cup butter or shortening*

1 *cup sifted flour*

¼ *teaspoon salt*

4 *eggs*

French Cream Custard Filling (see below) or sweetened whipped cream or ice cream

Confectioners' sugar or Glossy Chocolate Frosting (see index)

Combine water and butter or shortening in small, heavy saucepan and bring to a full rolling boil. Reduce heat to medium. Add flour and salt, all at once, stirring vigorously until mixture leaves the sides of the pan and forms a stiff ball. Remove from heat. Add eggs, one at a time, beating until mixture is smooth and shiny after each addition.

Drop rounded tablespoonfuls of dough, 2½ inches apart, onto ungreased baking sheet. Bake in hot oven (425° F.) for 35 minutes, or until puffed, browned, and dry. Prick puffs with point of sharp knife to allow steam to escape. Cool away from drafts. Cut off tops and remove any soft dough. Fill with French Cream Custard Filling or whipped cream or ice cream. Replace tops and sprinkle with confectioners' sugar or frost with Glossy Chocolate Frosting.

FRENCH CREAM CUSTARD FILLING
About 4 cups

1 *cup sugar*

¼ *cup cornstarch*

2 *tablespoons flour*

½ *teaspoon salt*

3 *cups milk*

3 *egg yolks, beaten slightly*

2 *teaspoons vanilla*

½ *cup heavy cream, whipped*

Combine first 4 ingredients in heavy saucepan. Stir in milk. Cook, stirring constantly, until sauce is thickened and smooth. Add about ¼ cup of hot mixture to egg yolks, stirring constantly, and stir into hot mixture. Cook, stirring constantly, for 2 minutes. Cool, then chill. Fold in vanilla and whipped cream.

VARIATIONS

Large Cream Puffs: Drop mixture onto ungreased baking sheet using about 3 tablespoons for each puff. Bake in hot oven (400° F.) for 45 minutes, or until puffed, browned, and dry. Proceed as directed above. Yield: 8 to 10 large cream puffs.

Miniature or Appetizer-Sized Puffs: Drop dough by rounded teaspoonfuls onto ungreased baking sheet 1½ inches apart. Bake in hot oven (400° F.) for 15 to 20 minutes, or until puffed, browned, and dry. Cool as directed for Cream Puffs. Cut in half and fill with favorite appetizer or salad mixture or favorite sweet filling. Yield: 3½ to 4 dozen tiny cream puffs.

Chocolate Éclairs: Spoon cream-puff dough into 12 long oval-shaped portions 1 inch wide, 2 inches apart on ungreased baking sheet. Bake in hot oven (425° F.) for 30 to 35 minutes, or until puffed, browned, and dry. Proceed as directed for Cream Puffs. To fill, cut in half lengthwise. Fill bottom half with French Cream Custard Filling or ice cream. Cover and top with Hot Fudge Sauce (see index) or frost with Glossy Chocolate Frosting (see index). Yield: 12 éclairs.

LEMON

HOT LEMON SAUCE

About 1½ cups

  ½ *cup sugar*

  2 *tablespoons cornstarch*

  ¼ *teaspoon salt*

  1 *cup water*

  3 *tablespoons lemon juice*

1½ *tablespoons butter*

1½ *teaspoons grated lemon peel*

Combine sugar, cornstarch, and salt in saucepan. Stir in water. Cook over low heat until mixture thickens and becomes clear, stirring constantly. Stir in lemon juice, butter, and lemon peel. Serve hot or warm over puddings and cakes.

VARIATION

Hot Rum Sauce: Reduce lemon juice to 1 tablespoon, omit peel, and stir in 3 tablespoons rum with butter. Serve on hot gingerbread.

RASPBERRY SAUCE WITH FRAMBOISE

6 servings

  1 *pint red raspberries*

  ½ *cup sugar*

  2 *teaspoons lemon juice*

  2 *tablespoons framboise (or to taste)*

Fresh mint leaves (optional)

Combine first 3 ingredients in blender and blend until the sugar is dissolved and purée is thick. Add framboise and chill. Serve over fresh or poached peaches, ice cream, or ice-cream-filled meringues. If desired, garnish with fresh mint leaves.

MELBA SAUCE

About 1½ cups

  1 *pint red raspberries or 1 (10-ounce) package frozen, defrosted*

  ½ *cup currant jelly*

  2 *tablespoons cold water*

  1 *tablespoon cornstarch*

Blend ingredients in blender until raspberries are very finely chopped. Pour into saucepan and cook, stirring constantly, until clear and slightly thickened. Cool. Serve over fresh or cooked peach or pear halves, fruit-topped pound-cake slices, angel food à la mode, atop pineapple, lemon, or orange ice or sherbet, or vanilla ice cream.

CHERRY SAUCE

1½ to 2 cups

  1 *(1-pound) can pitted red tart cherries in syrup*

  2 *tablespoons sugar*

  1 *tablespoon lemon juice*

  3 *whole allspice*

  3 *whole cloves*

Drain cherries and reserve syrup. Add water to cherry syrup to measure 1 cup liquid. Combine sugar and cornstarch in saucepan. Add liquid, lemon juice, and spices. Cook, stirring constantly, until thickened. Use ¼ cup sauce for glazing duckling. Add cherries to remaining sauce and heat. Serve sauce over duckling.

CHERRY KIRSCH CUSTARD SAUCE

2 cups

2 *eggs*

1 *cup sifted confectioners' sugar*

1 *cup half and half, scalded*

3 *tablespoons chopped maraschino cherries*

1 *tablespoon kirsch*

1 *teaspoon vanilla*

Beat eggs well. Add sugar gradually and continue beating until very light and fluffy. Gradually add half and half. Pour into top of double boiler and cook over gently boiling water, stirring constantly, until mixture thickens slightly and coats the spoon. Stir in cherries, kirsch, and vanilla. Serve warm or chilled on sliced pound or sponge cake.

NOTE: *Sauce may be cooked in heavy saucepan over very low heat.*

LINGONBERRY SAUCE

About 1½ cups

2 *cups canned lingonberries, drained*

¼ *cup water*

½ *cup sugar*

Wash berries and turn into small, heavy saucepan. Add water. Place over low heat and bring to a boil. Add sugar slowly in a fine stream and stir until dissolved. Reduce heat and simmer for 6 to 8 minutes. Chill.

CRANBERRY-ORANGE SAUCE

1¼ cups

⅓ *cup sugar*

2 *teaspoons cornstarch*

½ *cup orange juice*

½ *cup water*

1 *cup raw cranberries*

2 *teaspoons grated orange peel*

Combine sugar and cornstarch in 2-quart saucepan. Add orange juice and water and cook, stirring constantly, until mixture comes to a boil. Add cranberries and cook for 5 minutes, or until skins pop, stirring occasionally. Fold in orange peel.

SOUSED CRANBERRY SAUCE

About 2¼ cups

2 *tablespoons cornstarch*

½ *cup water*

1 *(1-pound) can whole cranberry sauce*

¼ *cup orange liqueur (Cointreau or Grand Marnier) or orange juice*

1½ *tablespoons grated orange peel*

Combine cornstarch and water in heavy saucepan. Stir in cranberry sauce. Heat until mixture is clear and thick, stirring constantly. Stir in liqueur or orange juice and orange peel. Serve hot or cold with poultry or meats or spooned hot over cake, crêpes, pancakes, or waffles.

DOUBLE CHOCOLATE SAUCE
2 cups

    1 *(6-ounce) package semisweet chocolate bits*

    2 *squares (ounces) unsweetened chocolate, quartered*

    1 *cup sifted confectioners' sugar*

    ⅔ *cup half and half or undiluted evaporated milk*

    ½ *cup light corn syrup*

    2 *tablespoons butter*

    ½ *teaspoon salt*

    1 *tablespoon vanilla*

Place chocolate bits and quarters in blender container. Combine next 5 ingredients in saucepan and heat until bubbles appear around edge of pan. Pour over chocolate. Add vanilla. Blend until satin smooth. Serve warm on ice cream or cake. Sauce may be refrigerated in an airtight container and reheated in top of double boiler over gently boiling water just before serving.

Note: *If blender is not available, sauce may be made in heavy saucepan over low heat, stirring constantly until thick and smooth.*

HOT FUDGE SAUCE
1¼ cups

    ½ *cup half and half*

    1 *(6-ounce) package semisweet chocolate bits*

    1 *cup miniature marshmallows*

    ¼ *teaspoon salt*

    1 *teaspoon vanilla*

Heat half and half in heavy saucepan over low heat until bubbles form around edge of pan. Stir in chocolate bits, marshmallows, and salt. Heat, stirring constantly, until both chocolate and marshmallows melt. Remove from heat and stir in vanilla. Serve over ice cream, cake, or brownies.

Variations

Chocolate Mint Sauce: Substitute 1 (6-ounce) package mint-flavored chocolate bits for semisweet.

Chocolate Rum Sauce: Omit vanilla. Stir 2 to 3 tablespoons rum into sauce.

Chocolate Orange Sauce: Omit vanilla. Stir 2 to 3 tablespoons Cointreau and ½ teaspoon grated orange peel into sauce.

HOT BUTTERED RUM SAUCE
About 2½ cups

    1 *cup sugar*

    1 *tablespoon cornstarch*

    ¼ *teaspoon salt*

    ¾ *cup boiling water*

    ½ *cup lemon juice*

  1½ *teaspoons grated lemon peel*

    ⅓ *cup butter*

    ⅛ *to ¼ teaspoon grated nutmeg*

    ½ *cup light rum*

Combine first 3 ingredients in heavy saucepan. Stir in boiling water. Cook, stirring constantly, until mixture starts to thicken. Add remaining ingredients and cook, stirring constantly. Serve hot over hot mince pie or plum pudding.

Sugar Cane

HARD SAUCE FOR DESSERTS
2½ cups

  ½ *cup butter*
1½ *cups sifted confectioners' sugar*
  1 *tablespoon light cream*
  1 *teaspoon vanilla*
  ½ *teaspoon lemon extract*
  1 *to 1½ teaspoons shredded orange or*
     lemon peel

Cream butter until light and fluffy. Add sugar gradually and continue creaming. Add cream, vanilla, lemon extract, and peel, blending thoroughly. Chill. Serve with heated plum pudding or other desserts.

VARIATION
Brandy or Rum Hard Sauce: Omit last 4 ingredients and add 2 to 3 tablespoons brandy or rum.

BRANDY OR COGNAC SAUCE
About 2⅓ cups

  ½ *cup butter*
  2 *cups sifted confectioners' sugar*
  2 *egg yolks*
  ½ *cup heavy cream*
  3 *tablespoons brandy or cognac*

Cream butter until light and fluffy. Add sugar gradually, beating constantly. Add egg yolks and beat until thick and lemon-colored. Add cream slowly, beating constantly. Turn into top of double boiler. Place over gently simmering water for 5 to 6 minutes, stirring constantly. Stir in brandy or cognac and serve warm.

BRANDIED PEACH SAUCE
2 cups

  ¾ *cup sugar*
  2 *tablespoons cornstarch*
  1 *(12-ounce) package frozen sliced*
     peaches, defrosted
  1 *tablespoon butter*
  2 *tablespoons apricot brandy*

Combine sugar and cornstarch in saucepan. Add peaches, stirring until cornstarch is lump-free. Cook over low heat, stirring constantly, until clear and thickened. Stir in butter and then the brandy. Serve over pancakes, waffles, cake squares, or ice cream.

CAKES, FROSTINGS, AND FILLINGS

LADY BALTIMORE CAKE

Two-layer 9-inch cake

Popular in Charleston and throughout the South for many decades, Lady Baltimore Cake was a reputed favorite of President Lincoln. It was immortalized when Owen Wister described it and used its name for the title of his book *Lady Baltimore*, published in 1906. The cake takes its name from its frosting—a fluffy white concoction rich in fruit and nuts. Originally the fruits were soaked overnight in brandy or sherry and used as a filling between layers and to cover sides and top of cake.

2½ *cups sifted cake flour*

2½ *teaspoons baking powder*

½ *teaspoon salt*

⅔ *cup shortening*

1½ *cups sugar*

1 *teaspoon vanilla*

½ *teaspoon almond extract*

1¼ *cups milk*

4 *egg whites (about ½ cup)*

Lady Baltimore Frosting (see next column)

Sift together first 3 ingredients. Cream shortening, 1¼ cups sugar, vanilla, and almond extract until light and fluffy. Add dry ingredients alternately with milk, beginning and ending with dry ingredients, stirring just until smooth after each addition. Beat egg whites until foamy. Add remaining ¼ cup sugar, 1 tablespoonful at a time, beating constantly until soft peaks form. Fold egg white into batter.

Pour into 2 greased 9-inch round layer pans. Bake in moderate oven (375° F.) for 20 to 25 minutes, or until cake tester inserted in center comes out clean. Let stand in pans for 5 to 10 minutes. Remove and cool on wire racks. Frost.

LADY BALTIMORE FROSTING

½ *cup diced seedless raisins*

½ *cup chopped red maraschino cherries*

½ *cup chopped pecans or walnuts*

¼ *cup chopped figs or dates*

½ *teaspoon grated orange or lemon peel*

3 *tablespoons brandy or orange liqueur (Cointreau or Grand Marnier)*

Old-Fashioned 7-Minute Frosting (see index)

Combine fruits, nuts, peel, and brandy or liqueur. Cover tightly and let stand overnight so that the fruits absorb the liquid. Prepare frosting and fold in fruit mixture. Spread between layers and on top and sides of Lady Baltimore Cake.

LORD BALTIMORE CAKE

Two-layer 9-inch cake

If there is a Lady Baltimore Cake, it stands to reason that there be a Lord Baltimore Cake! It is thought that it is named for George Calvert, Lord Baltimore, the English statesman who founded the colony of Maryland. The cake uses the egg yolks not needed in a Lady Baltimore Cake.

Prepare Gold Cake (see index) and cool. Fill and frost top and sides of cake with Lord Baltimore Cake Frosting (see index).

THREE-LAYER WHITE CAKE
One 9-inch cake

White layer cake is similar to the White Mountain Cake or Colorado Cake in which the batter was sometimes baked in graduated pans. When the layers were assembled and frosted with a fluffy white icing, the cake resembled a snow-peaked mountain.

3¼ *cups sifted cake flour*

3½ *teaspoons baking powder*

½ *teaspoon salt*

1 *cup butter*

2 *cups sugar*

1 *cup milk*

2 *teaspoons vanilla*

8 *egg whites*

Sift together first 3 ingredients. Cream butter, add 1½ cups sugar gradually, and continue beating until mixture is light and fluffy. Add dry ingredients alternately with milk and vanilla, starting and ending with dry ingredients. Stir until mixture is smooth. Beat egg whites until white and foamy, add remaining ½ cup sugar gradually, and continue beating until mixture is glossy and holds soft peaks. Fold egg whites into batter.

Pour into 3 greased 9-inch round layer pans. Bake in moderate oven (350° F.) for 25 to 30 minutes, or until cake tester inserted in center comes out clean. Cool in pans for 10 minutes, then transfer to wire racks. Spread Cream Filling for Cakes (see index) between layers and frost as desired with White Satin Frosting, Butter Cream Frosting, or Smooth Chocolate Frosting (see index).

VARIATION

Southern Rum Cake: Prepare Three-Layer White Cake. While layers are cooling, prepare Creamy Rum Frosting (see index). Spread between layers and frost top and sides of cake. Chill thoroughly.

LANE CAKE
Two-layer 9-inch cake

Made extensively in the South, Lane Cake has a rich egg-yolk filling of coconut, raisins, and nuts. It is thought that this famous dessert takes its name from Emma Rylander Lane because it appeared in a cookbook she edited in 1880.

Prepare a Lady Baltimore Cake (see index). While cake layers are cooling, prepare Lane Cake Filling (see below). Spread filling between layers and frost top and sides of cake. Refrigerate until used.

LANE CAKE FILLING

8 *egg yolks, beaten*

1 *cup sugar*

⅛ *teaspoon salt*

½ *cup butter*

1 *(3½-ounce) can flaked coconut*

¾ *cup chopped pecans*

½ *cup seedless raisins, chopped*

½ *cup finely chopped red candied cherries*

¼ *cup brandy*

1½ *teaspoons vanilla*

Beat egg yolks, sugar, and salt in top of double boiler. Beat in butter. Cook over hot water, stirring constantly, until hot and thickened. Remove from heat. Stir in remaining ingredients and cool. Spread between well-cooled cake layers and on top and sides of cake.

GRANDMOTHER'S 1-2-3-4 CAKE
Two- or three-layer 9-inch cake

Probably one of the most popular American cakes of all times, the recipe is contained in the title: 1 cup butter, 2 cups sugar, 3 cups flour, and 4 eggs. Before the days of standardized measurements, the same measurer could be used for the ingredients, thereby ensuring success.

3 *cups sifted cake flour*

4 *teaspoons baking powder*

1 *teaspoon salt*

1 *cup butter*

2 *cups sugar*

4 *eggs, separated*

1 *cup milk*

2 *teaspoons vanilla*

Sift together first 3 ingredients. Cream butter, add 1½ cups sugar gradually, and cream until very light and fluffy. Add egg yolks, one at a time, beating well after each addition. Combine milk and vanilla. Add dry ingredients and liquids alternately, beginning and ending with dry ingredients. Beat until smooth. Beat egg whites until white and foamy. Add remaining ½ cup sugar, 1 tablespoonful at a time, and continue beating until stiff and glossy. Fold egg whites into cake batter. Pour into 2 or 3 greased 9-inch round layer pans.

Bake in moderate oven (350° F.) for 25 to 35 minutes, depending on thickness of cake, or until cake tester inserted in center comes out clean. Cool cakes in pans for 5 minutes, then transfer to wire racks to finish cooling. Fill and frost as desired.

VARIATIONS

Apricot Layer Cake: Make a two-layer Grandmother's 1-2-3-4 Cake. Spread Apricot Filling (see index) between layers and chill for 20 minutes. Frost top and sides with Old-Fashioned 7-Minute Frosting (see index). Sprinkle top of cake with a few chopped pecans (optional).

Coconut Layer Cake: Fold 1 cup shredded fresh or canned coconut into Grandmother's 1-2-3-4 Cake batter before pouring into two 9-inch round layer pans and baking. Spread Cream Filling for Cakes (see index) between cooled cake layers. Frost top and sides of cake with Old-Fashioned 7-Minute Frosting (see index). Sprinkle shredded fresh or canned coconut over top and sides of cake.

Lemon Coconut Cake: Spread Lemon Filling (see index) between cake layers and frost top and sides of three-layer cake with Old-Fashioned 7-Minute Frosting (see index). Sprinkle top and sides of cake with flaked or shredded coconut.

Old-Fashioned Chocolate Layer Cake: Spread Smooth Chocolate Frosting (see index) between layers and on top and sides of three-layer cake.

LOUISIANA LEMON RICE CAKE
16 to 25 squares

This Lemon Rice Cake has a grainy consistency and somewhat resembles a cheesecake as it ages. Adapted from a mid-nineteenth-century recipe, it is a marvelous dessert for those on wheat-free diets. Rice flour is available throughout the country in many large groceries or specialty shops.

1 *cup butter*

¼ *teaspoon salt*

2 *cups sugar*

6 *eggs, separated*

3 *or 4 tablespoons grated lemon peel*

2¼ *cups rice flour (not sifted)*

3 *tablespoons fresh lemon juice*

Confectioners' sugar or sweetened whipped cream (optional)

Cream butter and salt until very light and fluffy. Gradually beat in 1 cup sugar. Beat egg yolks and add, with lemon peel, to creamed mixture. Stir in rice flour and lemon juice. Beat egg whites until foamy. Add remaining 1 cup, 2 tablespoons at a time, beating until egg whites hold soft peaks. Carefully fold egg whites into creamed mixture.

Pour or spoon batter into well-greased and floured 9 × 9 × 2-inch pan. Bake in moderate oven (350° F.) for 55 minutes. Cool for 10 minutes before removing from pan. Cut in squares. Sprinkle top with confectioners' sugar before slicing or top each square with a dollop of whipped cream.

DOLLY VARDEN CAKE
Four-layer 9-inch cake

Adapted from a recipe popular in Georgia in the late nineteenth century, this two-color cake is named for a character in Charles Dickens' *Barnaby Rudge*. Not much is heard of that particular Dickens book today, but Dolly Varden Cake maintains its popularity.

⅓ cup finely chopped nuts
⅓ cup chopped maraschino cherries
¼ cup currants
¼ cup halved seedless raisins
1 teaspoon cardamom
1 teaspoon cinnamon
½ teaspoon nutmeg
3 cups sifted cake flour
3 teaspoons baking powder
½ teaspoon salt
¾ cup shortening
2 cups sugar
2 teaspoons vanilla
1¼ cups milk
4 egg whites
White Satin Frosting (see index)
6 or 8 well-drained maraschino cherries, quartered (optional)

Combine first 7 ingredients and set aside. Sift together flour, baking powder, and salt. Cream shortening, 1½ cups sugar, and vanilla until light and fluffy. Add dry ingredients alternately with milk, starting and ending with dry ingredients. Stir until mixture is smooth. Beat egg whites until white and foamy. Add remaining ½ cup sugar, 1 tablespoonful at a time, and continue beating until mixture is glossy and holds soft peaks. Fold egg whites into batter.

Divide batter in half. Stir fruit-spice mixture into half the batter and pour each half into a greased 9-inch round layer pan. Bake in moderate oven (350° F.) for 35 to 40 minutes, or until cake tester inserted in center comes out clean. Cool in pans for 10 minutes, then transfer to wire racks to finish cooling. When cake is cool, split each layer in half, using a sharp knife. Fill and assemble alternating white and spice layers with White Satin Frosting and frost top and sides of cake. Scatter bits of cherry over top.

SPICED CARROT CAKE
One 10-inch tube cake

Carrot cake with cream cheese frosting is one of my favorites. A moist cake with a hint of spice, it provides some Vitamin A along with all those calories.

2½ cups sifted flour
1 teaspoon baking powder
1 teaspoon baking soda
1 teaspoon salt
1 teaspoon cinnamon
½ teaspoon nutmeg
1 cup butter
1½ cups sugar
4 eggs
1½ cups finely shredded raw carrot
1 cup buttermilk
½ cup chopped pecans
Creamy Cheese Frosting (see index) or confectioners' sugar

Sift together first 6 ingredients. Cream butter, gradually add sugar, and cream well. Add eggs, one at a time, beating well after each addition. Stir in carrot. Add dry ingredients alternately with buttermilk, beginning and ending with dry ingredients. Fold in pecans.

Pour into greased and floured 10-inch tube pan. Bake in moderate oven (350° F.) for 1 hour, or until cake tester inserted in center comes out clean. Cool in pan 15 minutes, then transfer to wire rack to finish cooling. Sift confectioners' sugar over top or frost with Creamy Cheese Frosting.

SPICE CAKE
Three-layer 9-inch cake

Sugar and spice, everything nice, that's what Spice Cake is made of.

  3 *cups sifted flour*
  3 *teaspoons baking powder*
  1 *teaspoon cinnamon*
  ½ *teaspoon salt*
  ½ *teaspoon ground cloves*
  ½ *teaspoon nutmeg*
  ¼ *teaspoon ginger*
  ¼ *teaspoon allspice*
  ⅔ *cup butter*
1½ *cups sugar*
  1 *egg plus 3 egg yolks*
1¼ *cups milk*
  2 *tablespoons light molasses*
  1 *teaspoon vanilla*
  Ivory Satin Frosting (see index)

Sift together first 8 ingredients. Cream butter, adding sugar gradually, and continue beating until light and creamy. Add egg and egg yolks, one at a time, beating well after each addition. Combine milk, molasses, and vanilla. Add dry ingredients and liquid alternately, a small amount at a time, starting and ending with dry ingredients. Stir until mixture is smooth.

Pour into 3 greased 9-inch round layer pans. Bake in moderate oven (350° F.) for 25 minutes or until cake tester inserted in center comes out clean. Cool in pans for 5 minutes, remove from pans, and cool on wire racks. Fill and frost with Ivory Satin Frosting.

BLACKBERRY JAM CAKE
Two-layer 9-inch cake

Kentucky is famous for its blackberries, which grow in abundance in mountain clearings and along the roadsides, and for its blackberry dishes. Jam cake is traditionally served at Christmas. It is similar to a fruit cake but not as rich. The jam enriches the batter. Many like the cake with a caramel icing.

  2 *cups sifted flour*
  1 *teaspoon baking soda*
  1 *teaspoon cinnamon*
  ½ *teaspoon ground cloves*
  ½ *teaspoon salt*
  ¾ *cup shortening*
  ¾ *cup sugar*
  3 *eggs*
  1 *(10-ounce) jar seedless blackberry jam*
  ½ *cup buttermilk*
  1 *cup halved seedless raisins*
  Old-Fashioned 7-Minute Frosting or Caramel Frosting (see index)

Sift together first 5 ingredients. Cream shortening and sugar well. Add eggs, one at a time, beating well after each addition. Beat in jam. Add dry ingredients alternately with buttermilk, beginning and ending with dry ingredients, stirring until dry ingredients are moistened. Stir in raisins.

Pour into 2 greased 9-inch round layer pans. Bake in moderate oven (350° F.) for 40 to 45 minutes, or until cake tester inserted in center comes out clean. Cool in pans on wire racks for 10 minutes. Remove from pans and finish cooling on wire racks. Fill and frost cake layers as desired.

DEY MANSION ORANGE CAKE
One 10-inch tube cake

Headquarters for General George Washington from July to November 1780, Dey Mansion is located in Wayne, New Jersey. Built in 1740 by the Deys, a family of Dutch ancestry, the house is situated on some 600 acres purchased in 1717 for $500. Filled with eighteenth-century antiques, the mansion is now maintained as a museum by the New Jersey Park Commission.

CAKE

- 2½ cups sifted flour
- 1 teaspoon baking powder
- 1 teaspoon baking soda
- 1 teaspoon mace
- 1 teaspoon salt
- ¾ cup butter
- 1½ cups sugar
- 3 eggs
- 1 cup buttermilk
- 1 navel orange, finely chopped
- 1 cup seedless raisins
- ½ cup chopped walnuts

SYRUP

- 1 cup sugar
- ⅓ cup orange juice

To prepare cake, sift together first 5 ingredients. Cream butter, add sugar gradually, and cream thoroughly. Add eggs, one at a time, beating well after each addition. Add dry ingredients alternately with buttermilk, beginning and ending with dry ingredients. Stir until dry ingredients are moistened. Stir in orange, raisins, and walnuts.

Pour into greased and floured 10-inch tube or bundt pan. Bake in slow oven (325° F.) for 60 to 70 minutes, or until cake tester inserted in center comes out clean. Just before cake is done, prepare syrup. Combine sugar and orange juice in saucepan. Heat slowly, stirring constantly, until sugar is dissolved. Spoon over hot cake. Cool on wire rack for about 30 minutes to absorb syrup. Remove from pan. Finish cooling on wire rack.

TOMATO SOUP SPICE CAKE
One 13 × 9-inch cake

History doesn't tell us who developed this unusual cake. Originally made with canned tomatoes, it was a popular cake to serve during the winter. When condensed soup came into being, the recipe was changed, and one of the leading soup companies has had it in its files since the early 1920s. Surprisingly, the soup does not give the cake a tomato flavor but does give it moistness. The spices provide a zesty flavor.

- 2½ cups sifted flour
- 1 teaspoon baking soda
- 1 teaspoon cinnamon
- ½ teaspoon ground cloves
- ½ teaspoon nutmeg
- ½ teaspoon salt
- ¾ cup shortening
- 1½ cups light brown sugar, firmly packed
- 2 eggs
- 1 (10¾-ounce) can tomato soup
- ½ cup chopped walnuts or pecans
- ½ cup seedless raisins
- Lemon Cream Frosting or Creamy Cheese Frosting (see index)

Sift together first 6 ingredients. Cream shortening and brown sugar well. Add eggs, one at a time, beating well after each addition.

Add dry ingredients and soup alternately, beginning and ending with dry ingredients. Stir until smooth. Fold in nuts and raisins.

Pour into greased and floured 13 × 9 × 2-inch baking pan. Bake in moderate oven (350° F.) for about 35 minutes, or until cake tester inserted in center comes out clean. Let stand in pan 10 minutes. Then transfer to wire rack to cool. Frost top and sides with Lemon Cream Frosting or Creamy Cheese Frosting.

NASHVILLE BUN CAKE
One 13 × 9 × 2-inch cake

A favorite recipe of one of my friends, Nashville Bun Cake should be served slightly warm.

CAKE BATTER

2½ cups sifted flour
2 teaspoons baking powder
1 teaspoon baking soda
1 teaspoon salt
1 teaspoon nutmeg
½ teaspoon ground cloves
¾ cup butter
1½ cups light brown sugar, firmly packed
1 teaspoon vanilla
2 eggs plus 2 egg yolks
1 cup buttermilk

TOPPING

2 egg whites
1 cup light brown sugar, firmly packed
⅓ cup finely chopped pecans or walnuts

To prepare cake batter, sift together first 6 ingredients. Cream butter until smooth, gradually adding sugar. Add vanilla. Add eggs and yolks, one at a time, beating well after each addition. Add dry ingredients alternately with buttermilk, beginning and ending with dry ingredients. Stir until dry ingredients are moistened. Spread evenly in greased and floured 13 × 9 × 2-inch baking pan.

To prepare topping, beat egg whites until white and foamy. Gradually add sugar, a tablespoon at a time, and beat until stiff and glossy. Spread over cake batter. Sprinkle with nuts. Bake in moderate oven (350° F.) for 40 to 45 minutes, or until cake tester inserted in center comes out clean. Cover top of cake loosely with a sheet of aluminum foil if top gets too brown. Cool in pan.

TENNESSEE GINGER PUDDING
One 10-inch tube cake

In reality a cake, this is an adaptation of a recipe written in 1897.

4 cups sifted flour
1 tablespoon ginger
1½ teaspoons baking soda
1 teaspoon cinnamon
1 teaspoon salt
1 cup butter
1 cup sugar
2 eggs
1 cup light molasses
1 cup buttermilk
1 cup currants
Lemon Cream Frosting (see index)

Sift together first 5 ingredients. Cream butter thoroughly, add sugar, a small amount at a time, and continue creaming until light and fluffy. Beat in eggs, one at a time. Beat in molasses. Add dry ingredients alternately with buttermilk, one-third of each at a time, beating well after each addition. Fold in currants.

Pour into greased and floured 10-inch tube pan. Bake in moderate oven (350° F.) for 60 minutes, or until a cake tester inserted in center comes out clean. Cool right side up on wire rack for 10 minutes. Remove cake from pan and finish cooling on rack. Frost with Lemon Cream Frosting.

SERGEANT BLUFF APPLESAUCE CAKE

One 13 × 9-inch cake

Named for a charming town in Iowa, this cake is a family recipe that is over a century old. Eggs weren't always available, but soda was and applesauce could be depended on to keep the cake moist.

> 2 *cups sifted flour*
> 1½ *teaspoons cinnamon*
> 1 *teaspoon baking powder*
> 1 *teaspoon cocoa*
> ½ *teaspoon baking soda*
> ½ *teaspoon salt*
> ½ *teaspoon ground cloves*
> ½ *cup butter*
> 1 *cup sugar*
> 2 *teaspoons lemon extract*
> 2 *eggs*
> 1½ *cups unsweetened applesauce*
> 1 *cup seedless raisins*
> 1 *cup chopped pecans or walnuts*
> *Sergeant Bluff Fudge Frosting (see below)*

Sift together first 7 ingredients. Cream butter and sugar until smooth and add lemon extract. Beat in eggs, one at a time, beating well after each addition. Add dry ingredients alternately with applesauce, mixing well after each addition. Fold in raisins and nuts.

Pour into greased and floured 13 × 9 × 2-inch pan. Bake in moderate oven (350° F.)

for 30 to 35 minutes. Let stand in pan for 5 to 10 minutes, then transfer to wire rack to finish cooling. Frost when cool.

Sergeant Bluff Fudge Frosting

> 1½ *cups sugar*
> ⅓ *cup milk*
> ⅓ *cup butter*
> ½ *cup semisweet chocolate bits*
> 1 *teaspoon vanilla*

Combine sugar, milk, and butter in saucepan over low heat, stirring constantly, until butter is melted. Bring to a hard boil over high heat, stirring constantly, and boil for 30 seconds. Remove from heat and add chocolate bits and vanilla, stirring until chocolate melts. Cool quickly by setting pan in a bowl of cold water. Stir constantly but gently until mixture becomes the proper consistency for spreading. Spread at once over top of cooled cake.

Variation

Farm-Style Applesauce Cake: Omit cocoa and add ⅓ cup chopped pecans or walnuts. Bake in a 13 × 9 × 2-inch cake pan or two 9-inch layer cake pans. Bake as directed above. Fill and frost with Caramel Frosting or Ivory Satin Frosting (see index). Sprinkle an additional ⅓ cup chopped nuts over top (optional).

ELECTION-DAY CAKE

One 10-inch tube cake

A century ago elections were gala occasions in New England. No matter what the results, people gathered to celebrate victory or defeat. A favorite food on such occasions was Election-Day Cake, said to have originated in Hartford, Connecticut. Mary Todd Lincoln served it often, as did many hostesses of her era.

1 *cup currants or halved seedless raisins*

½ *cup brandy*

2 *packages active dry yeast*

1 *cup warm milk (105° to 115° F.)*

½ *cup plus 1 tablespoon granulated sugar*

4 *cups sifted flour*

1 *teaspoon salt*

1 *teaspoon mace*

1 *teaspoon cinnamon*

¾ *cup butter*

½ *cup light brown sugar, firmly packed*

2 *eggs*

1 *tablespoon lemon juice*

1½ *teaspoons vanilla*

1 *teaspoon grated lemon peel*

½ *cup chopped mixed candied fruits*

Election Cake Glaze (see below)

Combine currants or raisins and brandy, cover tightly, and let stand overnight. Soften yeast in warm milk. Stir in 1 tablespoon sugar and 1 cup flour. Cover and let rise in a warm place (85° F.) for 1 hour, or until bubbly. Sift together remaining 3 cups flour, salt, and spices. Cream butter, brown sugar, and ½ cup granulated sugar. Beat in eggs, one at a time. Beat in lemon juice, vanilla, and lemon peel. Stir in mixed fruits, currants or raisins with brandy and yeast mixture. Stir in dry ingredients, mixing well. Turn into greased 10-inch tube pan. Cover and let rise in warm place until doubled in bulk, 1½ to 2 hours. Bake in moderate oven (375° F.) for 50 minutes. Cool in pan for 15 minutes, then turn out and finish cooling on wire rack. Spoon glaze over top and allow to run down sides.

ELECTION CAKE GLAZE

1¼ *cups sifted confectioners' sugar*

¼ *cup warm orange juice*

2 *teaspoons grated orange peel*

1 *teaspoon grated lemon peel*

Combine ingredients and beat thoroughly. Invert cake onto serving plate and spread glaze over top, allowing it to drizzle down the sides of the cake.

MOUNT VERNON GINGERBREAD

One 13 × 9 × 1½-inch gingerbread

Gingerbread was one of Martha Washington's favorite desserts. The following is a modern adaptation of an old recipe. No topping is needed, but a hot lemon or rum sauce, or even sweetened whipped cream, can be added.

2¾ *cups sifted flour*

2½ *teaspoons ginger*

1 *teaspoon salt*

1 *teaspoon baking soda*

½ *teaspoon cinnamon*

½ *teaspoon nutmeg*

½ *teaspoon ground cloves*

1 *cup light molasses*

½ *cup light brown sugar, firmly packed*

½ *cup butter or shortening*

¾ *cup buttermilk or sour milk*

¼ *cup orange juice or brandy*

2 *eggs, beaten*

Hot Rum Sauce or Hot Lemon Sauce (see index) or sweetened whipped cream (optional)

Sift together first 7 ingredients. Combine molasses, sugar, and butter or shortening in saucepan and bring to a simmer, stirring 2 or 3 times. Cool to lukewarm. Stir cooled molasses mixture and buttermilk or sour milk into dry ingredients. Add orange juice or brandy and eggs, stirring until smooth.

Pour into well-greased 13 × 9 × 2-inch pan and bake in moderate oven (350° F.) for 30 to 35 minutes. Serve warm or cold with sauce or whipped cream.

MAE'S TIDEWATER CAKE

One 10-inch tube cake

    3 *cups cake flour*
    1 *teaspoon cinnamon*
    1 *teaspoon baking soda*
    1 *teaspoon salt*
    2 *cups sugar*
    3 *eggs, slightly beaten*
 1½ *cups cooking oil*
    1 *(8-ounce) can crushed pineapple,
       undrained*
    1 *(7-ounce) can coconut*
    2 *medium ripe bananas, diced*
    1 *cup finely chopped pecans*
 1½ *teaspoons vanilla*

Sift dry ingredients together in large bowl. Blend in remaining ingredients, stirring until well mixed. Do not beat. Pour into a greased and floured 10-inch tube pan. Bake in slow oven (325° F.) for 1 hour and 20 minutes. Remove from oven and cool for 10 minutes.

NOTE: *Wrapped in foil and sealed tightly, the cake will last for several weeks in refrigerator.*

BLACK FOREST CHERRY TORTE

Three-layer 8-inch cake

CHOCOLATE CURLS

    ½ *pound semisweet chocolate squares*

CAKE

    ¾ *cup sifted cake flour*
    ½ *cup unsweetened cocoa*
    ¼ *teaspoon salt*
    6 *eggs*
    1 *teaspoon vanilla*
    1 *cup sugar*
    ¼ *cup butter, melted and cooled slightly*

SYRUP

    ¾ *cup water*
    ½ *cup sugar*
    ¼ *cup kirsch*

FILLING

    1 *(17-ounce) can pitted dark sweet
       cherries*
    2 *tablespoons sugar*
    2 *tablespoons cornstarch*

TOPPING

    2 *cups heavy cream*
    ½ *cup sifted confectioners' sugar*
    2 *tablespoons kirsch*
    Fresh sweet or maraschino cherries

Prepare chocolate curls with a vegetable peeler. Using steady strokes, slice across edge of chocolate squares. Arrange chocolate curls on tray and refrigerate until used.

To prepare cake, sift together flour, cocoa, and salt. Beat eggs and vanilla until foamy. Add sugar gradually and continue beating until mixture is thick and fluffy, about 10 minutes. Carefully fold in one-fourth of the flour mixture at a time. Quickly fold in butter. Pour into 3 greased and floured 8-inch round layer pans. Bake in moderate oven (350° F.) for 18 to 20 minutes, or until done. Let cool in pans for 5 minutes, then remove from pans and cool on wire racks.

To prepare syrup, combine water and sugar in saucepan over low heat, stirring until sugar dissolves. Bring to boil and boil for 5 minutes. Cool to lukewarm. Stir in kirsch. Prick cake layers with wooden pick. Spoon syrup over surface and let stand for 15 minutes.

To prepare filling, drain cherries and reserve syrup. Combine sugar, cornstarch, and cherry syrup in heavy saucepan. Cook, stirring constantly, until sauce is thick. Add in cherries and cool.

To prepare topping, combine cream, confectioners' sugar, and kirsch. Chill thoroughly. Whip until cream mixture holds soft peaks.

To assemble torte, place a cake layer on serving plate. Spread with a thin layer of whipped cream. Spoon half the cherry filling over cream. Top with second cake layer and repeat process. Top with third cake layer. Spread top and sides with remaining whipped cream. Press chocolate curls over top and sides of cake and chill. Before serving, garnish with cherries.

DEVIL'S-FOOD CAKE
Two-layer 9-inch cake

Perhaps only the devil himself could pinpoint the beginnings of Devil's-Food Cake. There are many theories about its origin but few facts. Martha Washington is said to have served it to her guests. Some speculate that with the invention of angel-food cake there had to be a Devil's-Food Cake. Others declare there was no mention of Devil's-Food Cake until the turn of the twentieth century. Still other sources suggest that it is an improved Spanish creation. Mrs. William Vaughn Moody, a Chicago hostess of the late 1880s

known for her chocolate cakes, wins the most votes as the originator of this "devilishly good" cake.

> 4 *squares (ounces) unsweetened chocolate*
> 1¾ *cups sugar*
> 1 *cup water*
> 2¼ *cups sifted flour*
> 1½ *teaspoons baking powder*
> 1 *teaspoon baking soda*
> ½ *teaspoon salt*
> ¼ *teaspoon cinnamon*
> 1 *cup butter*
> 2 *teaspoons vanilla*
> 3 *eggs*
> ¼ *teaspoon red food coloring (optional)*
> ⅔ *cup buttermilk*
>
> *Smooth Chocolate Frosting,*
> *Old-Fashioned 7-Minute Frosting, or*
> *Mint Frosting (see index)*

Combine chocolate, 1 cup sugar, and water in heavy saucepan over low heat, stirring constantly, until slightly thickened. Cool to room temperature, stirring occasionally. Sift together flour, baking powder, baking soda, salt, and cinnamon. Cream butter, add remaining ¾ cup sugar gradually, and cream until smooth. Beat in vanilla and eggs, one at a time, beating well after each addition. Beat in chocolate mixture. Stir red food coloring into buttermilk. Add dry ingredients alternately with buttermilk, beginning and ending with dry ingredients, stirring until batter is smooth.

Pour into 2 greased and floured 9-inch round layer pans. Bake in moderate oven (350° F.) for 30 to 35 minutes, or until cake tester inserted in center comes out clean. Cool in pans 10 minutes. Turn out on wire racks and finish cooling. Fill and frost top and sides of cake as desired.

Pecan

ATLANTA CRUNCH CAKE
One 10-inch tube cake

Originating in the pecan country of Georgia, this cake with crunchy goodness is easy to prepare and wins a blue ribbon for flavor.

CRUNCH MIXTURE

½ cup sifted confectioners' sugar
⅓ cup granulated sugar
⅓ cup fine vanilla wafer crumbs
⅓ cup finely chopped pecans
⅓ cup chopped flaked coconut
3 tablespoons melted butter

CAKE BATTER

2½ cups sifted flour
1½ teaspoons baking powder
1 teaspoon salt
¼ teaspoon mace
1 cup shortening
1½ cups granulated sugar
1 tablespoon vanilla
4 eggs, separated
1 cup milk
1 teaspoon cream of tartar

To prepare crunch mixture, blend together first 5 ingredients. Add butter and mix well. Press mixture evenly over bottom and 2½ inches up sides of greased 10-inch tube pan. Set aside.

Prepare cake batter by sifting together first 4 ingredients. Cream shortening, 1 cup sugar, and vanilla thoroughly. Add egg yolks, one at a time, beating well after each addition. Add dry ingredients alternately with milk, beginning and ending with dry ingredients. Stir until mixture is smooth. Beat egg whites and cream of tartar until white and foamy. Add remaining ½ cup sugar, a tablespoonful at a time, and continue beating until stiff and glossy. Fold egg whites into cake batter.

Pour into prepared pan and bake in moderate oven (350° F.) for 1 hour, or until cake tester inserted in center comes out clean. Cool in pan for 15 minutes. Turn out of pan and finish cooling, bottom side up, on wire rack.

FEATHERY POUND CAKE
Two loaf cakes

Of English origin, pound cake has been popular since the days of the founding fathers. As with Grandmother's 1-2-3-4 Cake, the original recipe was based on its name: 1 pound butter, 1 pound flour, and 1 pound sugar.

3½ cups sifted cake flour
1 teaspoon salt
¼ teaspoon mace
1½ cups margarine (3 sticks)
1 pound confectioners' sugar (4½ cups)
6 eggs
⅓ cup milk
2 teaspoons vanilla

Sift together first 3 ingredients. Cream butter and add sugar gradually, beating well. Add eggs, one at a time, and continue beating until very creamy. Combine milk and vanilla. Add dry ingredients alternately with milk mixture, beginning and ending with dry ingredients, stirring until well blended after each addition.

Spoon into 2 greased and floured 9 × 5 × 3-inch loaf pans. Bake in slow oven (325° F.) for about 70 minutes, or until browned and cake tester inserted in center comes out clean. Cool in pan for 10 minutes, then turn out on wire rack to finish cooling.

NOTE: *Do not use whipped margarine. Butter may be substituted, but the cake will not be as high.*

SOUR CREAM POUND CAKE
One 10-inch tube cake

>   3 *cups sifted cake flour*
> ¼ *teaspoon baking soda*
> ¼ *teaspoon baking powder*
> ¼ *teaspoon salt*
> ½ *cup butter*
> ½ *cup shortening*
>   3 *cups sugar*
>   6 *eggs, separated*
>   1 *cup sour cream*

Sift together first 4 ingredients. Cream butter and shortening until smooth. Add sugar gradually, beating well. Add egg yolks, one at a time, and continue beating until very creamy. Add dry ingredients to creamed mixture alternately with sour cream, beginning and ending with dry ingredients, stirring until well blended after each addition. Beat egg whites until they hold stiff peaks, and carefully fold into batter, one-third at a time.

Spoon batter into greased and floured 10-inch tube pan and bake in slow oven (325° F.) for about 1½ hours (the top will be brown and crusty). Cool in pan for 10 minutes, then remove from pan and finish cooling. Let stand overnight to enhance flavor.

Note: *1 cup butter may be used and shortening omitted.*

CHOCOLATE FANTASY CAKE
One 10-inch cake

Similar to a pound cake, Chocolate Fantasy Cake is an excellent dessert to serve at buffets, parties, or other large gatherings.

>   3 *cups sifted flour*
>   2 *teaspoons baking powder*
> ½ *teaspoon salt*
>   1 *cup butter or shortening*
>   2 *cups sugar*
>   2 *teaspoons vanilla*
>   3 *eggs*
>   1 *cup milk*
> ¾ *cup chocolate syrup*
> ¼ *teaspoon baking soda*
>
> *Confectioners' sugar, Butter Cream Frosting, Mocha Frosting, or Chocolate Frosting (see index)*

Sift together first 3 ingredients. Cream butter or shortening well. Add sugar gradually and continue creaming until light and fluffy. Beat in vanilla. Add eggs, one at a time, beating well after each addition. Add dry ingredients alternately with milk, beginning and ending with dry ingredients, stirring until smooth after each addition.

Pour two-thirds of the batter into a greased and floured bundt or 10-inch tube pan. Combine chocolate syrup and baking soda and stir into remaining batter. Spoon chocolate over yellow batter. *Do not mix.* Bake in moderate oven (350° F.) for 70 to 75 minutes, or until cake tester inserted in center comes out clean. Cool in pan for 15 minutes. Turn out, top side up, onto wire rack to finish cooling. Sprinkle with confectioners' sugar or frost.

LIGHT AND FLUFFY SPONGE CAKE

One 10-inch tube cake or four 9-inch sponge cake layers

  1½ *cups sifted cake flour*

  1½ *cups sugar*

   1 *teaspoon salt*

   8 *eggs, separated*

  ¼ *cup cold water*

   2 *teaspoons vanilla*

   2 *teaspoons lemon juice*

  ¾ *teaspoon cream of tartar*

Sift flour, ¾ cup sugar, and salt into bowl. Beat together egg yolks, water, vanilla, and lemon juice. Add to dry ingredients and beat at medium speed with electric mixer until mixture is smooth. Beat egg whites and cream of tartar until white and foamy. Add remaining ¾ cup sugar gradually, a small amount at a time, beating at high speed until mixture is stiff and glossy. Carefully fold egg-yolk mixture into egg whites.

Pour batter into an ungreased 10-inch tube pan or 4 ungreased 9-inch round layer pans. Gently cut through batter with knife to break up any air pockets. Bake in moderate oven (350° F.) for 55 to 60 minutes for cake in tube pan or 15 minutes for sponge layers, or until cake tester inserted in center comes out clean. Place tube pan or layers upside down on wire rack until cake is cool. Remove from pan.

GENERAL LEE CAKE
Four-layer 9-inch cake

Reputed to have been the favorite cake of the South's most beloved general, one is not surprised that it was subsequently named for him. There are many versions of the recipe, but its basic makeup is a four-layer sponge cake put together with lemon filling and frosted with a lemon-orange icing, although some recipes call for a white icing.

Prepare Light and Fluffy Sponge Cake (see index) batter and pour into four ungreased 9-inch round layer pans. Bake as directed for layers in cake recipe. Cool layers thoroughly and remove from pans.

While cake layers finish cooling, prepare Lemon Curd Filling (see index) and spread filling between layers. Frost top and sides of cake with Lemon Orange Frosting (see index). Chill thoroughly.

CARLTON LIME CAKE
Four-layer 10-inch tube cake

If there's another version of this cake, we haven't found it. We like limes, so we created it. We hope you like it, too.

Prepare Light and Fluffy Sponge Cake (see index) baked in 10-inch tube pan. Turn cold cake upside down and slice into 4 equal layers.

Prepare Key Lime Cake Filling (see index) and spread between layers. Chill while preparing frosting. Spread top and sides of cake with Old-Fashioned 7-Minute Frosting (see index) or sweetened whipped cream. Chill until ready to serve. Sprinkle 1 to 2 teaspoons grated lime peel over top (optional).

ANGEL-FOOD CAKE
One 10-inch tube cake

St. Louis, Missouri, claims the honor of inventing Angel-Food Cake. Although the creator's name is lost to history, in the 1880s the cake was featured at the Hotel Beers. The hotel went so far as to advertise the cake's distinguished qualities in its catalogue. The cake passed all taste tests and has become an all-American favorite.

   1   *cup sifted cake flour*

1½   *cups sugar*

 12   *egg whites (1½ cups), at room temperature*

1¼   *teaspoons cream of tartar*

   2   *teaspoons vanilla*

   ¼   *teaspoon almond extract (optional)*

   ¼   *teaspoon salt*

      Confectioners' sugar or frosting

Combine flour and ½ cup sugar and sift 4 times. Combine egg whites, cream of tartar, vanilla, almond extract, and salt in large beater bowl. Beat until egg whites form soft peaks. Sprinkle remaining 1 cup sugar over egg whites, 2 tablespoonfuls at a time, beating well after each addition. Continue beating until egg whites are stiff and glossy. Sift about ¼ cup of flour-sugar mixture over egg whites and fold in gently but thoroughly (about 15 times), using a wire whisk or oil-free rubber spatula. Repeat until all flour-sugar mixture is used. Turn into ungreased 10-inch tube pan. Gently run knife through batter to eliminate large air pockets. Bake in center of moderate oven (375° F.) for 30 to 35 minutes, or until cake tester inserted in center comes out clean or until cake springs back when touched lightly with finger. Turn pan upside down on wire rack. Let cake "hang" until cold. Remove cake from pan and sift confectioners' sugar over top or frost as desired.

VARIATION

Chocolate Angel Food: Substitute ½ cup unsweetened cocoa for ½ cup flour before sifting. Omit almond extract and fold 2 drops red food coloring (optional) into egg-white-sugar mixture before dry ingredients are added. Sift confectioners' sugar over top of baked cake or spread top and sides with Glossy Chocolate Frosting (see index).

GOLD CAKE
Two-layer 9-inch cake

Gold Cake can be made at the same time as an angel-food cake to use the egg yolks not needed in the angel food.

2¾   *cups sifted cake flour*

   4   *teaspoons baking powder*

   ½   *teaspoon salt*

   ¾   *cup butter*

1¼   *cups sugar*

   2   *teaspoons vanilla*

   8   *egg yolks*

   ¾   *cup milk*

Sift together first 3 ingredients. Cream butter, sugar, and vanilla until light and fluffy. Add egg yolks, 2 at a time, creaming very well after each addition. Add dry ingredients alternately with milk, beginning and ending with dry ingredients. Stir just until batter is smooth after each addition.

Pour into 2 greased 9-inch round layer pans. Bake in moderate oven (350° F.) for 25 minutes, or until cake tester inserted in center comes out clean. Let stand in pans for 5 minutes, then transfer to wire rack to finish cooling.

PECAN BOURBON CAKE

One 10-inch tube cake

Kentucky is famous for its whisky and its bourbon cakes.

½ *pound seedless raisins, cut in half*

2 *teaspoons nutmeg*

⅔ *cup bourbon whisky*

3 *cups sifted flour*

1½ *teaspoons baking powder*

1 *teaspoon salt*

½ *cup butter*

½ *cup shortening*

1½ *cups sugar*

1 *teaspoon vanilla*

6 *eggs*

2 *cups chopped pecans*

Additional bourbon (optional)

Confectioners' sugar

Combine first 3 ingredients in bowl and let stand 30 minutes. Sift together flour, baking powder, and salt. Cream butter and shortening, add sugar gradually, and cream until light and fluffy. Add vanilla. Beat in eggs, one at a time, beating well after each addition. Add dry ingredients alternately with raisin-bourbon mixture, beginning and ending with dry ingredients. Stir until all dry ingredients are moistened.

Pour into greased and floured 10-inch tube pan. Bake in slow oven (325° F.) for 1 hour and 15 minutes, or until cake tester inserted in center comes out clean. Cool in pan for 15 minutes. Turn cake out of pan and finish cooling on wire rack. If desired, drizzle 2 to 3 tablespoons bourbon over cake. Wrap in foil and store for 2 to 3 days before serving. Just before serving, sift confectioners' sugar over top. Cut in thin slices.

Sugar Cane

BURNT SUGAR CAKE

One 9-inch layer cake

Another American invention, popularized after the introduction of baking powder, Burnt Sugar Cake is named for the caramelized or "burnt" sugar used in the recipe.

2½ *cups sifted cake flour*

3 *teaspoons baking powder*

¾ *teaspoon salt*

¾ *cup shortening*

¾ *cup sugar*

1 *teaspoon vanilla*

3 *eggs, separated*

⅔ *cup milk*

½ *cup Burnt Sugar Syrup (see next column)*

Burnt Sugar Frosting (see next column)

Sift together first 3 ingredients. Cream shortening, ½ cup sugar, and vanilla until light and fluffy. Add egg yolks, one at a time, beating well after each addition. Combine milk and Burnt Sugar Syrup. Add dry ingredients alternately with liquids, a small amount at a time, beginning and ending with dry ingredients. Stir just until smooth after each addition. Beat egg whites until white and foamy. Add remaining ¼ cup sugar, 1 tablespoon at a time, beating constantly until mixture holds soft peaks. Fold egg whites into cake batter.

Pour into 2 greased 9-inch round layer pans. Bake in moderate oven (350° F.) for 25 to 30 minutes, or until a cake tester inserted in center comes out clean. Cool in pans for 5 minutes, remove from pan and transfer to wire rack to finish cooling. Fill and frost with Burnt Sugar Frosting.

BURNT SUGAR SYRUP   ¾ cup

Pour ¾ cup sugar into a heavy skillet over medium heat. Stir until sugar is melted, becomes dark brown, and begins to smoke. Remove from heat at once. Add ¾ cup boiling water gradually, stirring constantly. Return to heat and stir until sugar is dissolved and mixture begins to bubble. Remove from heat. Cool. Use ½ cup syrup for preparing cake and ¼ cup for Burnt Sugar Frosting.

BURNT SUGAR FROSTING

    1 *cup sugar*
    ¼ *cup Burnt Sugar Syrup (see above)*
    2 *tablespoons water*
    2 *tablespoons light corn syrup*
    ⅛ *teaspoon salt*
    2 *egg whites*
    1 *teaspoon vanilla*

Combine first 6 ingredients in top of double boiler over boiling water. Beat rapidly with electric mixer for 7 to 8 minutes, or until mixture forms stiff peaks. Remove from heat and beat in vanilla. Spread between layers and on top and sides of cake.

ORANGE CHIFFON CAKE
One 10-inch tube cake

A newcomer on the baking scene, chiffon cake was the rage of the 1950s. Introduced by a prominent food company in May 1948, it was promoted as "the first really new cake in a hundred years." Very different from butter cakes in texture, chiffon cakes are made with liquid cooking oil instead of butter. The use of the word *chiffon* comes from the light, airy texture of a cake that is good to the last crumb.

    2¼ *cups cake flour*
    1½ *cups sugar*
     3 *teaspoons baking powder*
     1 *teaspoon salt*
     ½ *cup cooking oil*
     ½ *cup water*
     ¼ *cup orange juice*
     2 *tablespoons grated orange peel*
     6 *eggs, separated*
     ½ *teaspoon cream of tartar*
        Orange Drizzle Frosting (see below)

Sift together first 4 ingredients into mixing bowl. Add oil, water, orange juice, peel, and egg yolks and beat until smooth. Beat egg whites and cream of tartar until mixture holds *very* stiff peaks (do not underbeat). Carefully fold in egg-yolk mixture.

Pour into ungreased 10-inch tube pan. Bake in slow oven (325° F.) for 60 to 70 minutes, or until cake tester inserted in middle comes out clean. Invert on wire rack until cold. Loosen cake from sides of pan and around tube with thin-bladed knife or spatula. Remove cake from pan. Spread Orange Drizzle Frosting over top.

ORANGE DRIZZLE FROSTING   ¾ cup

    ¼ *cup butter, softened*
    1 *tablespoon grated orange peel*
    ¼ *teaspoon salt*
    2 *cups sifted confectioners' sugar*
    2 *to 3 tablespoons hot orange juice or milk*

Beat together butter, orange peel, and salt. Stir in sugar and orange juice or milk. Spread frosting over top of cake, allowing it to drizzle naturally over edges and down sides of cake.

SPONGE CAKES

Savoy cake is the centuries-old and Continental name for what we know as sponge cake. It is believed that the savoy cake is a descendant of the even older meringue cake. Light and airy, it uses stiffly beaten eggs for leavening but no fat, insuring its delicate texture.

BASIC SPONGE CAKE
One 10-inch roll or two 9-inch layers

- ¾ cup sifted cake flour
- ¾ cup sugar
- ½ teaspoon salt
- 4 eggs, separated
- 2 tablespoons cold water
- 1½ teaspoons vanilla
- 1 teaspoon lemon juice
- ½ teaspoon cream of tartar

Sift together into bowl flour, ½ cup sugar, and salt. Beat together egg yolks, water, vanilla, and lemon juice. Add to dry ingredients and beat at medium speed until mixture is smooth. Beat egg whites and cream of tartar until white and foamy. Add remaining ¼ cup sugar gradually, 1 tablespoon at a time, beating at high speed until mixture is stiff and glossy. Carefully fold egg-yolk mixture into egg whites. Prepare as directed in one of the following two ways.

SPONGE-CAKE LAYERS
Pour batter into 2 ungreased 9-inch round layer pans. Bake in moderate oven (350° F.) for 15 minutes, or until cake tester inserted in center comes out clean. Turn cakes upside down on wire racks and let stand until cool. Remove cake layers from pans. Use for making Boston Cream Pie or Washington Pie or other favorite small two-layer sponge cakes.

SPONGE-CAKE ROLL
Grease a 15 × 10 × 1-inch jelly-roll pan, line with waxed paper, and butter paper. Spread batter evenly in prepared pan. Bake in moderate oven (350° F.) for 15 to 18 minutes, or until cake tester inserted in center comes out clean.

Sift confectioners' sugar over surface of a clean towel the size of the pan. Loosen edges of cake from pan and turn cake out on sugared towel. Peel paper off quickly. Trim off dry crisp edges of cake with sharp knife. Roll cake up loosely in towel, starting at a narrow side. Cool on a wire rack. Fill and frost as desired.

VARIATIONS
Jelly Roll: Unroll a cooled Sponge-Cake Roll carefully. Spread thick red raspberry or plum preserves, currant jelly, or orange marmalade to within 1 inch of all edges. Reroll cake. Wrap snugly, seam side down, in foil or plastic wrap and refrigerate until serving time. Unwrap roll and dust with confectioners' sugar. Slice and serve plain or with sweetened whipped cream. Yield: 8 to 10 servings.

Lemon Cake Roll: Spread unrolled Sponge-Cake Roll with Lemon Curd Filling (see index) or Lemon Filling (see index) and proceed as directed for Jelly Roll.

Strawberry or Raspberry Whipped Cream Roll: Spread unrolled Sponge-Cake Roll with 1 cup whipped cream sweetened with 2 tablespoons confectioners' sugar. Spread 1 cup sliced fresh strawberries or red raspberries evenly over cream and proceed as directed for Jelly Roll. Frost with additional sweetened whipped cream or dust with confectioners' sugar. Slice diagonally. Yield: 10 to 12 servings.

Washington Pie: Spread red raspberry preserves between cooled layers of Sponge Cake and sift confectioners' sugar lightly on top of cake. Cut in wedges.

Strawberry Cream Cake: Clean 1 pint strawberries. Save a few perfect berries for garnish. Slice remaining strawberries and chill. Whip 1½ cups cream. Fold in ¼ cup confectioners' sugar and berries. Spread between and on top of cooled Sponge-Cake Layers. Decorate with reserved berries. Serve at once or refrigerate until serving time.

BOSTON CREAM PIE
8 to 12 servings

Why is this cake called a pie? Legend has it that an inventive Bostonian, tired of traditional pastry crust as the basis for a cream filling, baked a sponge cake batter in a pie shell. Originally the layers were topped with a sprinkling of confectioners' sugar, but today a chocolate frosting is associated with this popular dessert.

1 *recipe Sponge-Cake Batter (see index)*

CREAM FILLING

⅓ *cup sugar*

3 *tablespoons flour*

¼ *teaspoon salt*

1 *cup milk or half and half*

1 *egg, beaten*

1 *teaspoon butter, softened*

1 *teaspoon vanilla*

FROSTING

1 *square (ounce) unsweetened chocolate*

2 *tablespoons butter*

¼ *teaspoon salt*

1¼ *cups sifted confectioners' sugar*

2 *tablespoons milk*

1 *teaspoon vanilla*

Prepare Sponge-Cake Batter according to directions and pour batter into 2 ungreased 9-inch round layer pans. Bake in moderate oven (350° F.) for 15 minutes, or until cake tester inserted in center comes out clean. Turn cakes upside down on wire racks until cool. Remove from pans.

Combine first 3 filling ingredients in small, heavy saucepan. Add milk or half and half gradually, beating until free of lumps. Cook over low heat, stirring constantly, until thickened. Stir 2 or 3 tablespoonfuls of hot mixture into beaten egg and pour into remaining hot mixture, stirring briskly. Add butter and vanilla and stir until mixture is lukewarm. Stir frequently until cool. Spread between cake layers.

Combine first three frosting ingredients in heavy saucepan over low heat to melt chocolate. Add remaining ingredients and stir until smooth. Spread frosting over top or center of a 9-inch round paper doily on cake top. Sift additional confectioners' sugar over doily and press down lightly with a spatula, being careful not to move doily. Carefully lift off doily. Cut in wedges.

CHEESECAKE

Cheesecake, nowadays a rival to apple pie as a favorite American dessert, has obscure origins. A simple form was probably made by the ancient Greeks, and cheesecakes are known to have been a popular sweet in Imperial Rome.

Early American versions of cheesecake were made with cottage or farmer cheese, but modern cooks prefer a richer cake made with cream cheese.

ELEGANT CHEESECAKE

One 9-inch cake

CRUST

   1½ *cups fine graham-cracker crumbs*

   ¼ *cup sifted confectioners' sugar*

   1 *teaspoon allspice or ½ teaspoon cinnamon and ¼ teaspoon each nutmeg and allspice*

   ⅓ *cup melted butter*

FILLING

   2 *(8-ounce) packages cream cheese, at room temperature*

   3 *eggs*

   ⅔ *cup sugar*

   2 *teaspoons vanilla*

   ¼ *teaspoon salt*

TOPPING

   1 *cup sour cream*

   ⅓ *cup sugar*

   1 *teaspoon vanilla*

   ⅛ *teaspoon salt*

   Sweetened fresh or defrosted frozen berries or sliced peaches (optional) or Melba Sauce (optional)

Combine crumbs, sugar, and spices. Mix in butter with a pastry blender until crumbs are evenly coated. Press crumbs evenly over bottom and 1½ inches up sides of a 9-inch spring-form pan.

Beat cream cheese until smooth. Add eggs, one at a time, beating well after each addition. Stir in sugar, vanilla, and salt. Pour into crust. Bake in moderate oven (350° F.) for 30 minutes, or until filling is set. Remove from oven. Increase oven temperature to 450° F.

Mix together sour cream, sugar, vanilla, and salt. Spread evenly over top of hot cheesecake. Return to oven for 5 to 7 minutes, or until sour cream topping sets. Cool in pan on rack, then chill. Serve plain or with fruit.

VARIATION

Cherries Jubilee Cheesecake: Follow above recipe but omit sour cream topping. Chill thoroughly. To prepare cherry topping, drain 1 (1-pound 14-ounce) can pitted dark sweet cherries and reserve 1 cup syrup. Combine 2 tablespoons *each* sugar and cornstarch and a pinch of salt in a small, heavy saucepan. Stir in reserved cherry syrup. Cook, stirring constantly, until sauce is thick and clear. Stir in 2 tablespoons brandy (optional) and 1 teaspoon lemon juice. Fold in drained cherries and cool. Spoon over cheesecake. Chill.

PINKY'S CHEDDAR CHEESECAKE

One 9-inch cake

Being a connoisseur of cheesecakes, I truly appreciate Pinky's memorable cheesecake made with Cheddar cheese.

CRUST

   2 *cups sifted flour*

   ⅛ *teaspoon salt*

   1 *cup confectioners' sugar*

   1 *cup butter, softened*

   1 *egg, slightly beaten*

FILLING

4 *(8-ounce) packages cream cheese, at room temperature*

1 *cup finely grated mild Cheddar cheese*

1¾ *cups sugar*

3 *tablespoons flour*

1 *teaspoon lemon juice*

1½ *teaspoons grated orange peel (optional)*

1 *teaspoon vanilla*

5 *eggs plus 2 egg yolks*

½ *cup heavy cream*

To prepare crust, combine flour, salt, and sugar in bowl. Cut butter into dry ingredients and blend until a smooth ball is formed. With a fork, stir in egg. Lightly grease a 9-inch spring-form pan. Using a knife, spread crust mixture to a depth of ¼ inch over bottom of pan.

Bake in a moderate oven (350° F.) for 10 minutes, or until light golden in color. When pan has cooled, "frost" or spread sides of pan with a ¼-inch layer of dough (do not bake). Place in refrigerator until ready to fill.

Prepare filling. In a large bowl, beat cheeses and sugar together until well blended and creamy. Add flour, lemon juice, orange peel, and vanilla. Beat at high speed just to blend. Add eggs and egg yolks, one at a time, beating just enough to blend thoroughly. Stir in cream and pour into prepared pan. Bake in very hot oven (450° F.) for 8 minutes. Reduce oven temperature to 250° F. and bake for 1 hour longer, or until set.

NOTE: *Any remaining crust mixture may be spread into an 8-inch square pan. Spoon ¼ to ⅓ cup strawberry or raspberry preserves over crust. Bake in moderate oven (350° F.) for 10 minutes. Cool for 5 to 7 minutes and cut into 1-inch squares.*

JAN'S DETERMINATION CAKE
One 10-inch cake

Recently a friend gave me a new cake recipe using some prepared mixes. My first tries were great successes. But then there was the time I was entertaining some unexpected out-of-town visitors and my cake baking became a near fiasco. Since I couldn't find the recipe, I had to work from memory. To my relief, the cake turned out to be a huge success, and I was rewarded for my determination.

1 *(18½-ounce) package yellow cake mix*

1 *(3¾-ounce) package instant vanilla pudding and pie-filling mix*

½ *cup cooking oil*

¾ *cup dark rum*

4 *eggs*

1 *cup chopped pecans*

¾ *cup sugar*

¼ *cup butter*

¼ *cup water*

1 *teaspoon lemon juice*

Combine cake mix, vanilla pudding mix, oil, ½ cup dark rum, and eggs in mixer bowl. Beat at a medium speed for 4 minutes, scraping down sides of bowl as necessary. Fold in pecans. Pour into greased and floured bundt or 10-inch tube pan. Bake in moderate oven (350° F.) for 45 minutes, or until done.

When cake is almost done, prepare syrup. Combine sugar, butter, water, and lemon juice in heavy saucepan. Bring to a boil slowly, stirring until sugar is dissolved. Remove from heat and stir in remaining ¼ cup dark rum.

Turn cake out onto foil or waxed paper. Let cake cool for 10 minutes, top side up. Using a skewer or long bamboo pick, make holes all over top of hot cake. Drizzle hot syrup over top of cake very slowly, being careful that too much syrup does not run into crack on top of cake. Bring foil up around cake and wrap securely. Cake may be served when completely cool or may be stored in an airtight cake container overnight.

RASPBERRY CAKE

One 13 × 9-inch cake

Raspberry lovers will especially enjoy this cake. Easy to prepare, it's the perfect dessert for drop-in company or impromptu picnics.

2 *cups sifted flour*

3 *teaspoons baking powder*

½ *teaspoon salt*

½ *cup butter or shortening, softened*

1 *cup sugar*

2 *eggs*

1 *cup liquid (frozen raspberry syrup and/or milk)*

1 *teaspoon vanilla*

1 *pint fresh red raspberries or 1 (10- to 12-ounce) package frozen red raspberries, thawed and drained*

Glaze (see next column)

Sift together first 3 ingredients. Cream butter or shortening, add sugar, and continue creaming until light and fluffy. Add eggs, one at a time, beating well after each addition. Add dry ingredients alternately with liquids and vanilla, a small amount at a time, starting and ending with dry ingredients.

Pour two-thirds of the batter into a greased 13 × 9 × 2-inch pan. Sprinkle raspberries over top and cover with remaining batter. Bake in moderate oven (375° F.) for 25 to 30 minutes. A cake tester inserted in center comes out clean when cake is done. Cool in pan for 10 minutes. Remove from pan and cool to lukewarm on wire rack. Frost with Glaze.

GLAZE

3 *tablespoons half and half or cream*

1 *tablespoon melted butter*

½ *teaspoon vanilla*

1½ *cups sifted confectioners' sugar*

Stir half and half or cream, butter, and vanilla into sugar and blend thoroughly. Spread over top of cake. Cool until glaze is firm.

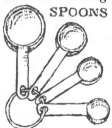

SPOONS

MRS. IOWA'S CHOCOLATE CAKE

One 13 × 9-inch cake

This cake is perfect for picnics, and the kids will enjoy it to the last morsel. The original recipe came from the southwestern United States, but I modified it and added my own touches. This is a standby I often prepared for television and personal appearances when I was Mrs. Iowa.

2 *cups sifted cake flour*

2 *cups sugar*

1 *teaspoon cinnamon (optional)*

½ *teaspoon salt*

1 *teaspoon instant coffee (optional)*

½ *cup butter*

½ *cup shortening*

1½ *squares (ounces) unsweetened chocolate*

1 *cup cold water*

3 *eggs, beaten*

1 *teaspoon vanilla*

½ *cup buttermilk*

1 *teaspoon baking soda*

Mrs. Iowa's Chocolate Frosting (see next column)

Sift together first 4 ingredients into large mixer bowl and stir in instant coffee. Combine butter, shortening, chocolate, and water in small, heavy saucepan and bring to a simmer, stirring until chocolate melts. Pour chocolate mixture over dry ingredients, blending thoroughly. Stir in eggs and vanilla. Mix together buttermilk and baking soda and stir into chocolate mixture, blending thoroughly.

Pour at once into greased and floured 13 × 9 × 2-inch pan. Bake in moderate oven (350° F.) for 35 minutes, or until cake tester inserted in center comes out clean. Cool cake in pan. Frost in pan.

MRS. IOWA'S CHOCOLATE FROSTING

½ *cup butter*

1½ *squares (ounces) unsweetened chocolate*

5 *tablespoons half and half or milk*

¼ *teaspoon salt*

1 *pound sifted confectioners' sugar (about 4½ cups)*

1½ *teaspoons vanilla*

½ *cup finely chopped pecans or walnuts (optional)*

Combine first 4 ingredients in heavy saucepan and melt butter and chocolate, stirring until smooth. Remove from heat and stir in sugar and vanilla, beating until smooth. Fold in nuts. Spread cake with warm frosting.

BROWNSTONE-FRONT CAKE
One 13 × 9-inch cake

Strictly an American invention, Brownstone-Front Cake enjoyed a great vogue in the late nineteenth century. Its rich dark-brown color was thought to resemble that of the façade of the brownstone, a popular architectural style in many metropolitan areas. The cake has retained popularity, although many of the rococo houses of the era have been torn down.

1 *cup boiling water*

2 *squares (ounces) unsweetened chocolate*

2½ *cups sifted cake flour*

1 *teaspoon baking powder*

1 *teaspoon baking soda*

½ *teaspoon salt*

½ *cup butter*

1½ *cups light brown sugar, firmly packed*

2 *teaspoons vanilla*

2 *eggs*

½ *cup buttermilk*

Mocha Frosting (see index)

Pour boiling water over chocolate and set aside while preparing cake batter. Sift together flour, baking powder, soda, and salt. Cream butter, add sugar gradually, and continue creaming until light and fluffy. Mix in vanilla. Beat in eggs, one at a time, beating well after each addition. Stir chocolate mixture, add buttermilk, and blend thoroughly. Add dry ingredients alternately with chocolate mixture, beginning and ending with dry ingredients. Stir until mixture is smooth.

Pour into greased 13 × 9 × 2-inch baking pan. Bake in moderate oven (350° F.) for 45 minutes, or until cake tester inserted in center comes out clean. Let stand in pan for 10 minutes, then remove from pan and transfer to wire rack to finish cooling. Frost top and sides with Mocha Frosting.

FRUITCAKES

Often called "great cakes," fruitcakes were generally baked at holiday time in Colonial America. Early ones were made with dried fruit, spices, and brandy and were then steamed or cooked over boiling water like a plum pudding. Many were frosted with a hard white sugar icing that helped to keep the cakes fresh and moist for weeks.

MONTICELLO WHITE FRUITCAKE

Two large loaf cakes, about 3 pounds each

3½ *cups sifted flour*

2 *teaspoons baking powder*

1½ *teaspoons salt*

3 *cups pecan halves, left whole*

2 *cups (1½-inch chunks) candied pineapple (any mixture of yellow, red, and green)*

2 *cups whole red candied cherries*

2 *cups dried apricots, cut in half*

1 *cup whole green candied cherries*

1 *cup chopped or diced mixed candied orange and lemon peel*

1½ *cups butter*

1½ *cups sugar*

3 *tablespoons grated fresh orange peel*

3 *teaspoons vanilla*

6 *eggs*

⅓ *cup brandy*

Sift together first 3 ingredients. Combine pecans and fruits in large bowl. Cream butter, add sugar gradually, and continue beating until light and fluffy. Add fresh orange peel and vanilla. Add eggs, one at a time, beating well after each addition. Add dry ingredients and brandy alternately, stirring until dry ingredients are moistened and mixture is smooth. Pour batter over fruit and nut mixture and blend thoroughly.

Pack batter evenly into 2 greased and foil-lined 9 × 5 × 3-inch loaf pans, smoothing tops. Bake in slow oven (275° F.) for 2 to 2¼ hours, or until cake tester inserted in center comes out clean. Cool in pan for 15 minutes, then remove from pan and transfer to wire racks to finish cooling.

To decorate and glaze fruitcakes: When cake is done, remove from oven and brush tops lightly with a melted fruit jelly. Decorate as desired with candied cherry halves, candied pineapple, pecan halves, or blanched almonds. Return to slow oven (275° F.) for 10 minutes. Brush tops lightly with melted jelly and return to oven for 15 minutes. Cool as directed above.

To store fruitcakes: Store in airtight container and refrigerate until ready to use. Unglazed fruitcakes may be wrapped in aluminum foil and stored in airtight container in refrigerator.

For a stronger brandy flavor: Drizzle 1 to 2 tablespoons brandy (or to taste) over top of cold unglazed cakes before wrapping. Repeat process 2 or 3 times if cakes are made 3 or 4 weeks before using, or wrap cakes in 2 or 3 layers of cheesecloth moistened with brandy.

Slicing fruitcake: Slicing is easy when the fruit used in the cake is left in large pieces and the baked cake is stored in refrigerator in an airtight container until serving time and sliced with a sharp, thin-bladed knife.

DARK FRUITCAKE

One 10-inch tube cake

   3 *cups pecan or walnut halves, left whole*

   3 *cups (1½-inch chunks) candied pineapple (any mixture of yellow, red, and green)*

   2 *cups whole red or green candied cherries*

   1 *(8-ounce) package pitted dates, cut in half*

1½ *cups golden seedless raisins*

   ½ *cup currants*

2¾ *cups sifted flour*

1½ *teaspoons baking powder*

1½ *teaspoons cinnamon*

   ½ *teaspoon each allspice, ground cloves, and nutmeg*

   ½ *teaspoon salt*

   ¼ *teaspoon baking soda*

   ¾ *cup shortening*

1½ *cups light brown sugar, firmly packed*

   4 *eggs*

   ½ *cup orange marmalade*

   ¼ *cup light molasses*

Grease a 10-inch tube pan, line with aluminum foil or brown paper, and grease again. Combine first 6 ingredients in large bowl. Sift together flour, baking powder, spices, salt, and baking soda. Cream shortening and sugar well. Add eggs, one at a time, beating well after each addition. Combine marmalade and molasses. Add sifted ingredients alternately with liquids to creamed mixture, beginning and ending with dry ingredients. Pour over fruits and nuts and mix.

Pour into prepared pan. Bake in very slow oven (275° F.) for about 3½ hours, or until cake tester inserted in center comes out clean. Cool in pan for 30 minutes. Turn out and remove foil or paper. Finish cooling right side up on wire rack. Decorate or glaze as directed for Monticello White Fruitcake.

FROSTINGS AND FILLINGS

WHITE SATIN FROSTING

Fills and frosts a three-layer 9-inch cake

   1 *cup sugar*

   ½ *cup water*

   ⅓ *cup light corn syrup*

   ⅛ *teaspoon cream of tartar*

   3 *egg whites*

   1 *teaspoon vanilla*

Combine first 4 ingredients in a heavy 3-quart saucepan. Bring syrup to 230° to 232° F. on a candy thermometer (syrup spins a thread 2 inches long when dropped from spoon or fork). Beat egg whites until they form stiff peaks. Pour syrup slowly in a fine stream into beaten egg whites, beating constantly at medium speed. Add vanilla and beat at high speed until mixture forms stiff peaks.

VARIATIONS

Ivory Satin Frosting: Substitute 1 cup light brown sugar, firmly packed, and use dark corn syrup.

Chocolate Swirl Frosting: Melt 2 squares (ounces) unsweetened chocolate. Cool slightly and fold carefully into White Satin Frosting or Old-Fashioned 7-Minute Frosting (see index) just until frosting is streaked with chocolate swirls. *Be careful not to overbeat.*

(see next page)

Coconut Marshmallow Frosting: Fold ¾ cup miniature marshmallow halves and ½ cup flaked or shredded coconut into White Satin Frosting or Old-Fashioned 7-Minute Frosting. (see index)

Lord Baltimore Cake Frosting: Prepare White Satin Frosting or Old-Fashioned 7-Minute Frosting (see index) and substitute ½ teaspoon *each* orange and lemon extract for vanilla. Fold in ¼ cup *each* chopped candied red cherries, blanched almonds, pecans, and macaroon crumbs (optional). Fills and frosts top and sides of two-layer 9-inch cake.

Mint Frosting: Tint White Satin Frosting or Old-Fashioned 7-Minute Frosting (see index) a pale green with green food coloring (optional). Substitute ½ teaspoon mint extract for ½ teaspoon vanilla and fold in ½ to ¾ cup crushed after-dinner mints.

Orange or Lemon Fluff Frosting: Prepare White Satin Frosting or Old-Fashioned 7-Minute Frosting (see index) and substitute ½ teaspoon orange lemon extract and 1 teaspoon grated orange or lemon peel for the vanilla. Tint an attractive pale yellow or orange with food coloring (optional).

Peppermint-Stick Frosting: Prepare White Satin Frosting or Old-Fashioned 7-Minute Frosting (see index) and substitute ½ teaspoon peppermint extract for vanilla. Tint frosting a delicate pink with red food coloring (optional) and fold in ⅓ cup crushed peppermint-stick candy. Garnish cake with additional crushed candy or chocolate curls.

Pistachio Frosting: Fold ½ teaspoon almond extract, green food coloring as needed to tint frosting an attractive pale-green color (optional), and ½ cup chopped toasted pistachio nuts into White Satin Frosting or Old-Fashioned 7-Minute Frosting (see index).

OLD-FASHIONED 7-MINUTE FROSTING

Fills and frosts top and sides of two-layer 8- or 9-inch cake

  1½ *cups sugar*
   ⅓ *cup water*
   2 *tablespoons light corn syrup*
   ⅛ *teaspoon salt*
   2 *egg whites*
   1 *teaspoon vanilla*

Combine all ingredients, except vanilla, in top of double boiler over boiling water. Beat rapidly with electric mixer for 5 to 7 minutes, or until mixture forms stiff peaks. Remove from heat and beat in vanilla.

CREAMY CHEESE FROSTING

Fills and frosts a three-layer 9-inch cake

   2 *(3-ounce) packages or ⅔ cup cream cheese, at room temperature*
   4 *teaspoons cream or milk (approximate)*
   2 *teaspoons vanilla*
   ¼ *teaspoon salt*
   1 *pound confectioners' sugar, sifted (about 4½ cups)*

Combine first 4 ingredients in beater bowl and beat at low speed until smooth. Blend in sugar gradually and continue beating until smooth and fluffy. Additional cream may be added, a few drops at a time, if needed to achieve spreading consistency.

CONFECTIONERS' SUGAR ICING

  1¼ *cups sifted confectioners' sugar*
   1 *tablespoon softened butter*
  1½ *tablespoons hot milk*

Blend sugar and butter with enough milk to make a smooth icing.

BUTTER CREAM FROSTING
Fills and frosts a two-layer 9-inch cake

½ cup softened butter

1 pound confectioners' sugar, sifted (about 4½ cups)

1 egg yolk

¼ teaspoon salt

2 teaspoons vanilla

2 tablespoons cream or milk (approximate)

Cream butter and blend in 1 cup sugar, egg yolk, salt, and vanilla. Add remaining sugar and 1 tablespoon cream or milk. Beat until smooth. Add remaining cream or milk as needed, a teaspoonful at a time, until a spreading consistency is obtained.

VARIATIONS

Mocha Frosting: Sift 2 tablespoons unsweetened cocoa with sugar. Substitute 2 tablespoons strong coffee for cream or milk. Omit vanilla. If additional liquid is needed to make frosting a good spreading consistency, stir in milk as needed, a teaspoonful at a time.

Lemon Cream Frosting: Substitute 2 teaspoons grated lemon peel for vanilla and lemon juice for cream or milk.

CARAMEL FROSTING
Fills and frosts top and sides of two-layer 9-inch cake

½ cup butter

¾ cup light brown sugar, firmly packed

⅓ cup half and half or cream

1½ teaspoons vanilla

¼ teaspoon salt

3½ to 4 cups sifted confectioners' sugar

Combine butter and brown sugar in heavy saucepan. Cook over moderate heat until mixture bubbles around edges of pan, then simmer slowly 1 minute. Transfer to a bowl and cool for 10 to 15 minutes. Stir in half and half

or cream, vanilla, and salt. Stir in confectioners' sugar, one-third at a time, adding sugar as needed to make frosting a spreading consistency. Spread on thoroughly cooled cake.

SMOOTH CHOCOLATE FROSTING
Fills and frosts top and sides of a two-layer 9-inch cake

½ cup softened butter

¾ cup sifted unsweetened cocoa

2 tablespoons light corn syrup

1 egg yolk

2 teaspoons vanilla

½ teaspoon salt

1 pound sifted confectioners' sugar (4½ cups)

¼ cup hot milk (approximate)

Combine first 6 ingredients and beat until very smooth and satiny. Stir in sugar and hot milk as needed, a small amount at a time, until very smooth and of spreading consistency.

GLOSSY CHOCOLATE FROSTING
Frosting for 26 to 28 cookies

1½ squares (ounces) unsweetened chocolate

1½ teaspoons softened butter

1 teaspoon corn syrup

1½ cups sifted confectioners' sugar

½ teaspoon salt

1 tablespoon very hot water

1 teaspoon vanilla

Combine chocolate, butter, and corn syrup in small, heavy saucepan. Melt chocolate over very low heat, stirring often. Pour into bowl and beat in sugar and salt until smooth. Stir in water and vanilla, cool to spreading consistency, and spread tops of cookies with a small amount of frosting. Cool until frosting is firm.

CHOCOLATE FROSTING
Fills and frosts a three-layer 9-inch cake

½ *cup butter, softened*
4 *cups sifted confectioners' sugar*
3 *squares (ounces) unsweetened chocolate, melted*
2 *egg yolks*
2 *teaspoons vanilla*
⅓ *cup half and half or cream*

Cream butter and ½ cup sugar. Add chocolate, egg yolks, and vanilla and beat thoroughly. Stir in remaining sugar and half and half or cream as needed to bring frosting to spreading consistency.

LEMON ORANGE FROSTING
Frosts top and sides of 4-layer or tube sponge cake or fills and frosts two-layer 8- or 9-inch cake

¼ *cup butter, softened*
1 *egg yolk*
1 *pound sifted confectioners' sugar (4½ cups)*
2 *teaspoons grated lemon peel*
2 *teaspoons grated orange peel*
¼ *teaspoon salt*
2 *tablespoons orange juice*
1½ *tablespoons lemon juice*

Beat together butter, egg yolk, 1 cup sugar, citrus peels, and salt. Beat in remaining sugar and fruit juices, a small amount at a time, until frosting is smooth and a proper spreading consistency.

CREAMY RUM FROSTING
Fills and frosts top and sides of three-layer 9-inch cake

¾ *cup butter, softened*
¼ *teaspoon salt*
1½ *pounds sifted confectioners' sugar (6½ to 7 cups)*
½ *cup light rum*

Cream butter and salt until very light and fluffy. Add sugar and rum alternately, beating constantly until smooth and a proper spreading consistency.

LEMON CURD FILLING
About 2 cups

⅓ *cup butter*
1 *cup sugar*
⅓ *cup lemon juice*
¼ *cup grated lemon peel*
¼ *teaspoon salt*
3 *eggs, beaten*

Melt butter in heavy saucepan. Add sugar gradually, stirring constantly until sugar dissolves. Stir in lemon juice, peel, and salt. Stir a small amount of hot mixture into eggs. Stir into hot mixture. Cook over low heat until mixture coats the spoon, stirring constantly. Cool, stirring occasionally.

APRICOT FILLING
Fills a two-layer 9-inch cake

1 *cup cooked, drained, dried apricots*
½ *cup sugar*
2 *tablespoons orange juice*
1 *tablespoon grated orange peel*
¼ *teaspoon salt*
¼ *cup chopped pecans or walnuts (optional)*

Sieve apricots or chop in blender. Combine first 5 ingredients in small, heavy saucepan over low heat and cook, stirring constantly, until sugar is dissolved and mixture is the consistency of marmalade. Cool and fold in nuts.

ORANGE FILLING
About 1¾ cups

    ¾ *cup sugar*
  3½ *tablespoons cornstarch*
    ¼ *teaspoon salt*
    ½ *cup water*
    ½ *cup orange juice*
    4 *egg yolks, beaten*
  1½ *tablespoons grated orange peel*
    2 *teaspoons butter*

Combine first 3 ingredients in heavy saucepan and stir in water and juice. Cook over low heat, stirring constantly, until clear and very thick. Remove from heat. Add half the orange mixture to egg yolks slowly, stirring briskly. Stir into remaining hot mixture. Return to heat and cook, stirring constantly, until thick. Stir in remaining ingredients. Cool.

KEY LIME CAKE FILLING
Fills a 4-layer cake

    1 *(14-ounce) can sweetened condensed milk*
    ½ *cup lime juice*
    1 *teaspoon grated lime peel*
    ⅛ *teaspoon salt*
       Few drops green food coloring (optional)

Combine and mix first 4 ingredients. Stir until mixture thickens. Add food coloring as desired to tint a pale green.

LEMON FILLING
About 1½ cups

    ⅔ *cup sugar*
  3½ *tablespoons cornstarch*
    ¼ *teaspoon salt*
    ⅔ *cup cold water*
    2 *to 4 egg yolks, beaten*
  1½ *tablespoons grated lemon peel*
    ¼ *cup lemon juice*
    1 *teaspoon butter*

Combine first 3 ingredients in heavy saucepan and stir in water. Cook over low heat, stirring constantly, until clear and very thick. Remove from heat. Add half the hot mixture to egg yolks very slowly, stirring briskly. Stir into remaining hot mixture. Return to heat and cook, stirring constantly, until thick and eggs are cooked. Stir in remaining ingredients. Cool.

CREAM FILLING FOR CAKES
About 3 cups filling

    ½ *cup sugar*
    ¼ *cup flour*
    ½ *teaspoon salt*
  2½ *cups milk*
    2 *eggs, beaten slightly*
    1 *tablespoon butter*
  1½ *teaspoons vanilla*

Combine first 3 ingredients in heavy saucepan. Add milk, stirring until smooth. Cook until thick and smooth, stirring constantly. Add about one-third of hot mixture to eggs in a fine stream, stirring constantly. Return to hot mixture. Cook, stirring constantly, for about 2 minutes. Remove from heat and stir in butter and vanilla. Chill thoroughly.

PIES

Pecan

SPOONS

GOOSEBERRY

PASTRY FOR UNBAKED PIE SHELL (9-inch)

1½ *cups sifted flour*

½ *teaspoon salt*

½ *cup shortening or butter*

¼ *cup very cold water (approximate)*

Sift together flour and salt into bowl. Cut in shortening or butter with pastry blender or two knives until mixture resembles coarse cornmeal. Sprinkle water evenly over surface, 1 tablespoonful at a time, mixing lightly with fork until particles hold together. Shape into a ball, wrap in waxed paper, and let stand at room temperature for 5 to 10 minutes.

On lightly floured board roll out into a circle ⅛ inch thick and 1½ inches larger in diameter than inverted 9-inch pie plate. Carefully fit crust into pie plate. Trim crust off 1 inch beyond edge of pie plate. Fold edge under and flute into a high standing edge. Bake as specified recipe directs.

VARIATION

Baked Pie Shell (9-inch): Prick deep holes close together on bottom and sides of crust, using a 4-tined dinner fork. Bake in very hot oven (450° F.) for 10 to 12 minutes, or until golden. Check crust after 5 minutes and prick any bubbles that have appeared. Cool on wire rack before filling.

PASTRY FOR DOUBLE-CRUST PIE (9-inch)

2 *cups sifted flour*

1 *teaspoon salt*

¾ *cup shortening*

5 *to 6 tablespoons very cold water (approximate)*

Sift together flour and salt into bowl. Cut in shortening with pastry blender or two knives until mixture resembles coarse cornmeal. Sprinkle water evenly over surface, 1 tablespoon at a time, mixing lightly with fork until particles hold together and leave sides of bowl. Shape into a ball and divide in half. Wrap each half with plastic film or waxed paper and let stand at room temperature for 5 to 10 minutes.

On a lightly floured board roll out half the dough into a circle ⅛ inch thick and 1¼ inches larger in diameter than inverted pie plate. Carefully fit crust into pie plate. Trim crust edge, leaving a ½-inch overhang. Pour filling into shell.

Roll out remaining dough into a circle ⅛ inch thick and 1 inch larger in diameter than top of inverted pie plate. Cut small designs or slits in center of crust for steam vents. Moisten edge of lower crust. Cover with top crust and press edges together. Trim crust ½ inch beyond edge of pie plate and press edges together to seal. Fold edges under bottom crust and flute with fingers or tines of a fork. Bake as directed for filling used.

VARIATIONS

Pastry for Lattice Pie (9-inch): Roll out pastry for top crust ⅛ inch thick into a rectangle 10 inches wide. Cut pastry lengthwise into strips ⅜ inch wide with sharp knife or pastry wheel. Fill lower crust as desired and moisten edges. Place strips over filling 1 inch apart crisscross fashion. Press crust together gently around edge. Cut off excess crust, leaving a ½-inch edge beyond rim. Fold overhanging pastry under rim and flute edge. Bake as specific recipe directs.

Pastry for Double-Crust Pie (10-inch):

2 *cups sifted flour*

Dash of salt

¾ *cup plus 1 tablespoon shortening*

4 *tablespoons cold water*

Sift together flour and salt. Cut in shortening with a pastry blender or two knives until mixture resembles coarse meal. Add water gradually, tossing lightly with a fork. Divide dough in half. Roll out one portion into a circle 12 inches in diameter and line a 10-inch pie plate. Roll out remaining portion into a circle 11 inches in diameter and reserve for top crust.

TART SHELLS

6 to 8 tart shells, depending on size of pan

Prepare Pastry for Unbaked Pie Shell (9-inch) *(see index)*. Roll out dough ⅛ inch thick on a lightly floured board. Invert a 3- or 3½-inch tart pan on crust and cut a circle 1 inch larger than pan and fit crust into pan.

If no tart pans are available, use 5-ounce custard cups or muffin pans. Cut rolled pastry into 5-inch circles and fit over inverted custard cups or muffin pans. Pinch crust together, making pleats in pastry so it will fit snugly.

Prick crust over sides and bottom of tart shell with tines of dinner fork. Place on baking sheet. Bake in very hot oven (450° F.) for 8 to 10 minutes, or until lightly browned. Cool thoroughly before removing from pans. Fill as desired.

GRAHAM-CRACKER CRUMB CRUST

One 9-inch pie crust

1½ *cups fine graham-cracker crumbs (18 to 20 crackers)*

⅓ *cup sugar*

¾ *teaspoon cinnamon*

⅛ *teaspoon ground nutmeg (optional)*

½ *cup butter, melted*

Combine first 4 ingredients. Add butter and blend thoroughly. Pack crumbs evenly over bottom and sides of a 9-inch pie plate, making a standing rim. Heat in moderate oven (350° F.) for 5 minutes, then chill.

VARIATION

Cookie Crumb Crust: Substitute 1½ cups fine vanilla, chocolate wafer, or gingersnap cookie crumbs for graham-cracker crumbs. Omit spices and reduce sugar to 3 tablespoons and melted butter to ⅓ cup.

TOASTED COCONUT PIE SHELL

One 9-inch pie shell

2 *(3½-ounce) cans flaked coconut (approximately 2½ cups)*

¼ *cup butter, melted*

Combine coconut and butter, mixing with a fork until coconut is evenly coated. Press mixture firmly and evenly over bottom and up sides of 9-inch pie plate. Bake in slow oven (300° F.) for 20 to 25 minutes, or until coconut is lightly toasted. Chill.

VANILLA COOKIE CRUST

One 9-inch pie crust

24 *brown-edge cookies or vanilla wafers*

¼ *cup butter, melted*

2 *tablespoons sugar*

Reserve 11 or 12 perfect cookies and trim a ¼-inch edge from one side of each so it can stand upright. Make fine crumbs of trimmings and remaining cookies. Blend together crumbs, butter, and sugar and pack over bottom of 9-inch pie plate. Stand reserved cookies, cut edge down, around edge of pie plate. Heat in moderate oven (350° F.) for 5 minutes, then chill.

PECAN CRUMB CRUST

One 9-inch pie crust

½ *cup pecans, halves or broken pieces*

1 *cup fine graham-cracker or vanilla wafer crumbs*

⅓ *cup butter, melted*

¼ *cup sugar*

Chop pecans very finely in blender or put through the fine blade of a grinder. Mix together nuts, crumbs, and sugar. Add butter, mixing well with pastry blender. Pack crumbs evenly over bottom and sides of 9-inch pie plate. Heat in moderate oven (350° F.) for 5 minutes, then chill.

MERINGUE PIE SHELL (For Angel Pies)

One 9-inch pie shell

4 *egg whites, at room temperature*

½ *teaspoon vanilla*

¼ *teaspoon cream of tartar*

¼ *teaspoon salt*

1 *cup sugar*

Beat together first 4 ingredients until white and foamy. Add sugar, 1 tablespoonful at a time, and continue beating until sugar is completely dissolved and egg whites are very stiff and glossy and form firm peaks. Pile egg-white mixture evenly over bottom and up sides of well-buttered 9-inch pie plate. If desired, meringue for the rim or edge may be put through the large rose tip of a pastry tube.

Bake in very slow oven (275° F.) for about 1 hour, or until shell is lightly browned and crisp. Turn heat off and cool in oven for 30 minutes. Finish cooling on wire rack away from drafts.

VARIATION

Pecan Meringue Pie Shell: Fold ½ cup finely chopped pecans into meringue just before spreading in pie plate.

BASIC 4-EGG MERINGUE

Generous topping for 9-inch pie

4 *egg whites*

¼ *teaspoon cream of tartar*

¼ *teaspoon lemon or orange extract or ½ teaspoon vanilla*

½ *cup sugar*

Combine first 3 ingredients in beater bowl and beat until egg whites are foamy. Add sugar gradually, 1 tablespoonful at a time, and beat until sugar is dissolved and whites are stiff, glossy, and hold soft peaks. Spread carefully over a hot or warm filling, sealing it securely to edges of crust.

Bake in moderate oven (375° F.) about 12 to 15 minutes, or until meringue is attractively browned. Cool on wire rack away from drafts.

VARIATION

Basic 3-Egg Meringue: Reduce egg whites to 3 and sugar to ⅓ cup. Yield: topping for 9-inch pie.

JEFF DAVIS PIE

One 9-inch pie

Visions of the old South and the tumultuous era of the 1860s come to mind with the mention of Jeff Davis Pie. One account of its origin relates that during the early days of the Civil War a merchant in the border state of Missouri entertained guests one Sunday and a special pie was served as dessert. The cook, a slave, when asked for its name, called it Jeff Davis Pie in loyalty to her master and his political beliefs.

1 *cup light brown sugar, firmly packed*

2 *tablespoons flour*

¼ *teaspoon salt*

1 *cup half and half*

4 *egg yolks*

1½ *teaspoons vanilla*

½ *cup butter, melted*

Unbaked Pie Shell (9-inch) (see index)

Basic 4-Egg Meringue (see index)

Combine first 3 ingredients. Beat together half and half, egg yolks, and vanilla. Beat in brown sugar mixture just until well mixed. Add butter slowly, beating constantly.

Pour into unbaked pie shell and bake in moderate oven (350° F.) for 30 minutes (filling will still be shaky). Prepare meringue and spread over top of pie, sealing meringue to edge of crust, and brown. Cool on wire rack.

GRETCHEN'S CREAMY APPLE PIE
One 9-inch pie

  5 *cups peeled, cored, sliced tart apples*
  Unbaked Pie Shell (9-inch) (see index)
  ¾ *cup heavy cream*
  ¾ *cup sugar*
  2 *tablespoons flour*
  1 *teaspoon cinnamon*

Arrange sliced apples in pie shell. Combine remaining ingredients, beating until very thick. Spread over apples, covering them completely. Bake in very hot oven (450° F.) for 10 minutes. Reduce oven temperature to 350° F. and bake 45 to 50 minutes longer, or until apples are tender and filling bubbling. Serve warm or cold, topped with ice cream or whipped cream.

BUTTERMILK MERINGUE PIE
One 9-inch pie

An old Southern favorite, Buttermilk Meringue is more like a custard than a cream pie. Some cooks flavor the filling with lemon and cinnamon, while others prefer bourbon and nutmeg.

  1 *cup sugar*
  3 *tablespoons flour*
  ¼ *teaspoon salt*
  2 *cups buttermilk*
  ¼ *cup butter, melted*
  3 *egg yolks*
  ½ *teaspoon lemon extract*
  Unbaked Pie Shell (9-inch) (see index)
  Basic 3-Egg Meringue (see index)

Combine first 3 ingredients. Mix together buttermilk, butter, egg yolks, and lemon extract. Add sugar mixture, blending thoroughly. Pour into unbaked pie shell.

Bake in hot oven (400° F.) for 30 to 35 minutes, or until filling has set and crust is a golden brown. Prepare meringue just before filling is set. Spread over top of pie, sealing it to edge of crust, and brown. Cool on wire rack.

VARIATION

Apricot Buttermilk Pie: Substitute 3 whole eggs, slightly beaten, for the 3 egg yolks and add ¼ teaspoon *each* cinnamon and nutmeg or mace to the buttermilk mixture.

Bake as directed above. Omit meringue and cool pie on wire rack.

To prepare apricot topping, drain 1 (1-pound) can apricot halves and reserve syrup. Combine ¼ cup syrup and 4 teaspoons cornstarch, stirring until smooth. Heat remaining syrup (about ¾ cup) and add cornstarch mixture, all at once. Cook, stirring constantly, until clear and thickened. Remove from heat and stir in ⅓ cup thick orange marmalade. Arrange apricot halves, cavity side down, on top of cooled buttermilk pie, cover with glaze, and cool.

MONTGOMERY PIE
(Lemon Cake Pie)

One 9-inch pie

A cake or a pie? One really can't be sure. The filling has the consistency of a cake batter baked in a pastry crust. Very popular in Pennsylvania Dutch country, it may be called Montgomery Pie for its place of origin in Montgomery County.

LEMON

1 *cup sugar*
⅓ *cup flour*
¼ *teaspoon salt*
4 *eggs, separated*
⅓ *cup lemon juice*
2 *teaspoons grated lemon peel*
1¼ *cups milk*
3 *tablespoons butter, melted*
Unbaked Pie Shell (9-inch) (see index)

Combine ¾ cup sugar, flour, and salt. Beat egg yolks well and stir in lemon juice and peel, milk, and butter. Stir in sugar mixture. Beat egg whites until foamy. Add remaining ¼ cup sugar, 1 tablespoonful at a time, and continue beating until stiff and glossy. Fold into egg-yolk mixture.

Bake pie shell with high fluted edge in hot oven (400° F.) for 5 to 7 minutes. Pour filling into crust and bake 10 minutes longer. Reduce heat to slow oven (325° F.) and continue baking for 20 minutes, or until filling is set. Cool before cutting.

SHOO-FLY PIE

One 9-inch pie

In the 1940s a popular tune, "Shoo-fly Pie and Apple Pandowdy," celebrated one of the favored desserts of Pennsylvania Dutch country. Probably descended from a German crumb cake, Shoo-fly Pie is made with a molasses-sweetened filling prepared without eggs or milk. The mixture is baked in a pie crust for good measure. A dry Shoo-fly Pie, containing less molasses, is served at breakfast and dunked in coffee. The "wet bottom" variety features extra molasses in the filling and is served as a dessert. The pie was christened, as legend goes, when a fastidious housewife found flies enjoying the molasses of a cooling pie and declared, "Shoo-fly."

2 *cups sifted flour*
1 *cup light brown sugar, firmly packed*
½ *teaspoon salt*
¼ *teaspoon cinnamon*
¾ *cup butter*
¾ *cup boiling water*
½ *cup light molasses*
¾ *teaspoon baking soda*
Unbaked Pie Shell (9-inch) (see index)
Vanilla ice cream (optional)

Combine first 4 ingredients in bowl. Cut in butter with pastry blender or two knives until mixture resembles fine crumbs. Combine boiling water and molasses and stir in baking soda (mixture will foam). Arrange alternate layers of crumb and molasses mixtures in pie shell, beginning and ending with crumb mixture.

Bake in moderate oven (375° F.) for 30 to 35 minutes, or until top and crust are browned and filling set. Cool. Serve plain or topped with vanilla ice cream.

Arrange apple slices neatly in prepared pie plate, mounding them slightly in center. Dot with butter and sprinkle with lemon juice. Top with crust, fluting edges as directed for double-crust or lattice pies. Brush top lightly with milk and sprinkle with small amount of sugar.

Bake in hot oven (400° F.) for 60 minutes, or until apples are tender. Cool to lukewarm on wire rack. Serve warm or cold, plain, or with wedges of cheese, whipped cream, or vanilla ice cream.

APPLE PIE

One 9-inch pie

John Chapman, better known as "Johnny Appleseed," certainly did his job well. Traveling throughout the Ohio wilderness, the itinerant preacher planted apple seeds everywhere he went. Today, apples and apple pie are all-American favorites. The following recipe is adapted from two that were popular during the latter half of the nineteenth century.

> *Pastry for Double-Crust Pie (9-inch) or Lattice Pie (see index)*

1¼ *cups sugar*

  3 *tablespoons flour*

  ½ *to 1 teaspoon cinnamon*

  ¼ *teaspoon nutmeg*

  ¼ *teaspoon salt*

  6 *cups peeled, cored, and thinly sliced tart cooking apples (about 2 pounds)*

  2 *tablespoons butter*

  1 *tablespoon lemon juice*

> *Milk (optional)*

> *Additional sugar (optional)*

> *Wedges of cheese, whipped cream, or vanilla ice cream (optional)*

Prepare crust and line a pie plate with pastry. Combine sugar, flour, spices, and salt. Add to apples and mix carefully to coat fruit.

SAVANNAH PECAN PIE

One 9-inch pie

Traditionally associated with the South, pecan pie is very rich and, happily, easy to prepare. Pecans have great nutritional value. Spanish explorers traveling through Texas during the 1500s reported that Indians ate pecans to ward off starvation.

  3 *eggs*

  ¾ *cup light brown sugar, firmly packed, or ¾ cup granulated sugar*

  2 *tablespoons flour*

  ½ *teaspoon salt*

  1 *cup dark corn syrup*

  2 *tablespoons melted butter*

1½ *teaspoons vanilla*

1¼ *cups pecan halves*

> *Unbaked Pie Shell (9-inch) (see index)*

> *Sweetened whipped cream (optional)*

Beat eggs lightly. Blend in sugar, flour, and salt and continue beating lightly. Stir in syrup, butter, and vanilla and fold in pecans. Pour into pie shell. Turn pecans rounded side up.

Bake in center of hot oven (400° F.) for 10 minutes. Reduce heat to slow (325° F.) and bake 35 to 40 minutes longer, or until pie crust is golden brown and filling firm. When pie is just the right color, cover with a tent of foil and finish baking. Cool. Serve plain or topped with whipped cream.

VARIATIONS

Bourbon Pecan Pie: Substitute 3 tablespoons bourbon for the vanilla.

Chocolate Pecan Pie: Melt 2 squares (ounces) unsweetened chocolate and add with butter.

Deep-South Pecan Pie: Substitute ½ cup light molasses and ½ cup dark corn syrup for the dark corn syrup.

Honey Pecan Pie: Use granulated sugar and substitute honey for dark corn syrup.

Southern Peanut Pie: Substitute 1¼ cups coarsely chopped salted peanuts for the pecans.

Texas Pecan Pie: Substitute coarsely chopped or broken pecans for pecan halves.

Walnut Pie: Substitute light corn syrup for dark, increase butter to ¼ cup, and use coarsely chopped English or black walnuts in place of the pecans.

PUMPKIN PIE

One 9-inch pie

A Thanksgiving favorite, Pumpkin Pie is an offshoot of an English custard pie with the addition of a readily available home-grown American product. Molasses was often used to sweeten pies when sugar was absent. On several occasions a Thanksgiving celebration was delayed many days while the inhabitants of New England towns awaited a shipment of molasses from the West Indies. Cousins to the Pumpkin Pie are squash and sweet potato pies. Their fillings are often sweeter and more delicate in flavor.

1½ *cups pumpkin, fresh or canned*
3 *eggs, beaten slightly*
1 *cup sugar*
1¼ *teaspoons cinnamon*
½ *teaspoon salt*
½ *teaspoon ginger*
½ *teaspoon nutmeg*
¼ *teaspoon ground cloves*
1⅔ *cups half and half*
Unbaked Pie Shell (9-inch) (see index)
Sweetened whipped cream (optional)

Combine first 9 ingredients in bowl. Stir slowly so air will not be incorporated. Pour into pie shell.

Bake in lower third of hot oven (425° F.) for 10 minutes. Reduce heat to moderate (350° F.) and continue baking for 30 to 35 minutes until set, or until a silver knife inserted in center comes out clean. Cool on wire rack. Top with whipped cream before serving.

VARIATIONS

Ginger Pumpkin Pie: Fold 2 tablespoons finely chopped preserved or candied ginger into pumpkin mixture before pouring into crust. Garnish whipped-cream topping with slivers of preserved or candied ginger.

Plantation Pumpkin Pie: Substitute ¾ cup half and half and ½ cup molasses for the half and half. Use ½ cup granulated and ½ cup light brown sugar, firmly packed, to replace granulated sugar. Garnish with whipped cream and chopped pecans.

Sweet Potato Pecan or Walnut Pie: Substitute 1¾ cups well-mashed cooked sweet potatoes, cooled, for pumpkin and fold ½ cup chopped pecans or walnuts and ¼ cup rum into mixture before pouring into crust. Serve slightly warm or cold, topped with whipped cream.

Squash Pie: Substitute defrosted frozen squash for pumpkin. If desired, substitute ¼ cup cognac or brandy for ¼ cup of the half and half. Garnish with whipped cream and a few chopped nuts.

KENTUCKY MOUNTAIN SKILLET PIE

6 servings

Long a favorite of Kentucky and southern Indiana cooks, skillet pie is an adaptation of the traditional apple pie. In pioneer days ingredients and utensils were often hard to come by, and cooks improvised with what was available. One of the most highly prized utensils was an iron skillet, which could be used for a variety of cooking or baking purposes.

   Pastry for Double-Crust Pie (9-inch) (see index)

1   cup sugar

1   tablespoon flour

1   teaspoon cinnamon

¼   teaspoon nutmeg

¼   teaspoon salt

6   cups peeled, cored, and sliced apples (about 2 pounds)

⅓   cup chopped pecans

⅓   cup seedless raisins or currants

1   tablespoon lemon juice

1   teaspoon grated lemon peel

3   tablespoons white wine (optional)

3   tablespoons butter

   Melted butter (optional)

   Spiced Milk (see index), sweetened whipped cream, or vanilla ice cream (optional)

   To prepare pastry for crust, on lightly floured board roll out pastry ¼ inch thick into a 14-inch square. Center crust over an 8-inch heavy skillet with heatproof handle and press over bottom and sides of skillet, allowing edges to hang evenly over edges of pan.
   Reserve 1 tablespoon sugar. Combine remaining sugar, flour, spices, and salt. Sprinkle over apples and mix thoroughly. Stir in pecans, raisins or currants, lemon juice, and peel. Sprinkle reserved sugar over crust. Spread apple mixture in even layer. Sprinkle

wine over apples and dot with butter. Fold edges of crust over apple mixture, overlapping edges. Brush top with melted butter.
   Bake in hot oven (400° F.) for 40 to 45 minutes, or until crust is lightly browned and apples tender. Serve warm, plain, or with Spiced Milk, whipped cream, or vanilla ice cream.

ALMOND.

CRAZY PIE

One 9-inch pie

Filled with apples, raisins, and almonds for a delightful flavor and crunch, Crazy Pie is an adaptation of a recipe popular in the 1930s.

   Pastry for Double-Crust Pie (9-inch) (see index)

4   cups peeled, cored, and thinly sliced apples

¾   cup seedless raisins

¼   cup blanched whole almonds, finely ground

1   cup sugar

1   tablespoon flour

2   eggs, beaten

¼   cup lemon juice

1   teaspoon grated lemon peel

2   tablespoons butter

   Cream or half and half (optional)

   Prepare crust and line a pie plate with pastry. Blend together next 5 ingredients until apples are evenly coated with sugar and flour. Mix in eggs, lemon juice, and peel. Spoon into prepared pie plate. Moisten edge of crust with cold water. Dot top of fruit mixture with butter and cover with top crust. Trim, seal, and flute edge. Brush crust with cream or half and half to glaze.

Bake in hot oven (400° F.) for 45 minutes, or until crust is nicely browned. Cool pie before cutting.

BLUEBERRY PIE
One 9-inch pie

Early New England settlers found an abundance of berries growing wild and soon incorporated them into their style of cookery, particularly their hearty pies. Blueberries, blackberries, black and red raspberries, boysenberries, loganberries, huckleberries, and elderberries all make great berry pies. Served warm or cool, a fresh berry pie is a delight to the palate.

Pastry for Double-Crust Pie (9-inch) (see index)

1 *tablespoon lemon juice*

4 *cups (2 pints) fresh blueberries, carefully washed and drained*

1 *cup sugar*

¼ *cup flour or 2 tablespoons quick-cooking tapioca*

¼ *teaspoon salt*

2 *tablespoons butter*

Milk, whipped cream, or ice cream (optional)

Prepare crust and line a pie plate with pastry. Sprinkle lemon juice over berries. Mix together sugar, flour or tapioca, and salt and sprinkle over berries, tossing lightly. Turn

into prepared pie plate. Dot with butter. Cover with top crust and flute edge as directed for double-crust or lattice pies.

Bake in hot oven (400° F.) for 45 to 50 minutes, or until crust is browned and juices bubble. Cool on wire rack. Serve slightly warm or cold with desired accompaniments.

LOG CABIN RHUBARB PIE
One 9-inch pie

A favorite of Midwesterners, rhubarb pie has the dubious distinction of also being called "pie-plant pie." Rhubarb's ready availability in colder climates made it a desirable choice as a pie filling.

Pastry for Double-Crust Pie (9-inch) (see index)

1¼ *cups sugar*

2½ *tablespoons quick-cooking tapioca or ¼ cup flour*

2 *teaspoons grated orange peel or 3 to 4 drops almond extract (optional)*

⅛ *teaspoon salt*

4 *cups diced fresh rhubarb*

2 *tablespoons butter*

Prepare crust and line a pie plate with pastry. Combine sugar, tapioca or flour, orange peel or almond extract, and salt. Add rhubarb, mixing carefully until rhubarb is evenly coated. Spoon into prepared pie plate. Dot with butter. Moisten edge of crust with cold water and cover with top crust. Trim, seal, and flute edges.

Bake in hot oven (400° F.) for 45 minutes, or until pastry is browned and filling thick and bubbly. Cool before cutting.

VARIATION

Strawberry Rhubarb Pie: Increase tapioca to 3 tablespoons or flour to ⅓ cup. Omit orange peel and add ¼ teaspoon nutmeg (optional). Substitute 1 cup halved, cleaned, and stemmed strawberries for 1 cup rhubarb. Top with Lattice Pie Crust (see index)

PLANTATION LEMON MERINGUE PIE

One 9-inch pie

I am unable to trace the origin of this, my favorite pie.

> 1½ *cups sugar*
> ⅓ *cup cornstarch*
> 2 *tablespoons flour*
> ¼ *teaspoon salt*
> 2 *cups warm water*
> 1 *tablespoon grated lemon peel*
> 2 *tablespoons butter*
> ½ *cup lemon juice*
> 4 *egg yolks*
> *Baked Pie Shell (9-inch), cooled (see index)*
> *Basic 4-Egg Meringue (see index)*

Combine first 4 ingredients in saucepan. Gradually stir in water and add lemon peel. Cook over moderate heat, stirring constantly, until mixture thickens, then simmer for 5 minutes. Stir in butter and lemon juice. Beat egg yolks well. Stir in ⅓ cup of hot lemon mixture, then stir egg mixture into remaining hot mixture. Pour into baked shell.

Bake in moderate oven (350° F.) for 10 minutes. Prepare meringue while pie is baking and spread carefully over hot filling, sealing it securely to edges of crust. Brown. Cool on wire rack away from drafts.

FUNERAL PIE (Raisin Pie)

One 9-inch pie

Traditionally served at funerals of Old Order Mennonites and Old Amish, raisin pie takes its unusual name from this custom.

> *Pastry for Double-Crust Pie (9-inch) (see index)*
> 2 *cups seedless raisins*
> 2 *cups water*
> 1 *cup sugar*
> 2 *tablespoons cornstarch*
> 1 *teaspoon cinnamon*
> ¼ *teaspoon ground cloves*
> ¼ *teaspoon salt*
> ¼ *cup lemon juice*
> 1 *teaspoon grated lemon peel*
> 2 *tablespoons butter*
> 2 *eggs, beaten*

Prepare crust and line a pie plate with pastry. Combine raisins and water in saucepan and simmer, uncovered, for 5 minutes. Combine sugar, cornstarch, spices, and salt. Stir into raisin mixture and cook, stirring constantly, until mixture thickens. Add lemon juice, peel, and butter. Pour over eggs slowly, beating constantly. Pour into prepared pie plate. Moisten edge of crust with cold water. Cover with top crust with slits in it. Trim, seal, and flute edges.

Bake in hot oven (400° F.) for 35 to 40 minutes, or until crust is nicely browned. Cool before cutting.

GLAZED STRAWBERRY PIE
One 9-inch pie

Growing abundantly in the wild, strawberries were utilized by the early Colonists in many ways, one of which was as a pie filling.

5 *cups firm fresh strawberries, washed and drained*

1 *cup sugar*

3 *tablespoons cornstarch*

Pinch of salt

¾ *cup water*

3 *tablespoons light corn syrup*

Red food coloring (optional)

Baked Pie Shell (9-inch) or Vanilla Cookie Crust (see index)

1½ *cups sweetened whipped cream*

Finely chopped pistachio nuts or mint sprigs (optional)

Crush 1 cup of the smaller, less perfect berries and reserve. Combine sugar, cornstarch, and salt and stir in water, corn syrup, and crushed berries. Cook over low heat, stirring constantly, until thickened. Tint a pretty strawberry color with a few drops of food coloring. Spread a small amount of sauce over bottom of crust. Arrange strawberries in shell and spoon remaining sauce over berries. Cool.

To serve, garnish with a border of whipped cream and pistachio nuts or a few mint sprigs.

REGAL MINCE PIE
One 9-inch pie

Pastry for Double-Crust Pie (9-inch) or Lattice Pie (see index)

3 *cups Homemade Mincemeat (see index)*

1 *cup peeled, finely chopped apples*

2 *tablespoons flour*

¼ *cup apple juice, cider, or syrup from watermelon or peach pickles*

2 *or 3 tablespoons brandy or rum (optional)*

Hard Sauce or Brandy Sauce (see index)

Prepare crust and line pie plate with pastry. Combine remaining ingredients and spoon into prepared pie plate. Top with crust and flute edges as directed for double-crust or lattice pies.

Bake in hot oven (400° F.) for 40 to 45 minutes, or until crust is browned. Serve slightly warm with Hard Sauce or Brandy Sauce.

HOOSIER CREAM PIE

One 9-inch pie

The thought of a velvety cream pie always makes my mouth water. Cream pies have been popular throughout the country, and farm women, who had all the ingredients on hand, became experts at making these delicate and delicious concoctions.

¾ cup sugar

¼ cup cornstarch

½ teaspoon salt

2½ cups milk or half and half

3 egg yolks, beaten slightly

2 tablespoons butter

2 teaspoons vanilla

Baked Pie Shell (9-inch) (see index)

Fresh fruit and whipped cream (optional)

Combine first 3 ingredients in heavy saucepan and stir in milk or half and half. Cook over low heat until thickened, stirring constantly. Simmer gently for 5 minutes and remove from heat. Beat one-third of the hot mixture into egg yolks, then stir into remaining hot mixture. Cook over low heat for 1 minute, stirring constantly. Remove from heat and stir in butter and vanilla. Cool for 10 minutes, stirring often.

Pour into baked pie shell and cool on wire rack. Serve plain or top with fresh fruit, such as raspberries or sliced peaches, and whipped cream.

VARIATIONS

Vanilla Meringue Pie: Top Hoosier Cream Pie with Basic 3-Egg Meringue (see index) made with ½ teaspoon vanilla. Brown.

Banana Cream Pie: Use 2 ripe bananas, peeled and sliced. Fill pie shell with alternate layers of partially cooled Hoosier Cream Pie filling and thin banana slices, starting and ending with filling. Chill and garnish with sweetened whipped cream or top with Basic 3-Egg Meringue (see index) and brown.

Chocolate Meringue Pie: Increase sugar to 1 cup and add 3 squares (ounces) unsweetened chocolate to milk before cooking. Top with Basic 3-Egg Meringue (see index) and brown.

Coconut Cream Pie: Stir 1 cup flaked coconut into cream filling with butter and vanilla. Top with Basic 3-Egg Meringue (see index). Sprinkle ⅓ cup coconut over meringue and brown as directed for basic meringue.

RUM CREAM PIE

One 9-inch pie

Rum Cream Pie was first made in Colonial days by cooks who whipped the eggs and cream with hickory rods, for egg beaters did not come into existence until the late 1800s. It is still a favorite today, and the preparation is much easier.

¾ cup sugar

1 envelope unflavored gelatin

¼ teaspoon salt

4 eggs, separated

½ cup milk

¼ cup light or dark rum

1 teaspoon vanilla

1 cup heavy cream, whipped

Cookie Crumb Crust (see index)

Raspberry Sauce (optional—see index)

Additional whipped cream and chocolate curls (optional)

Combine ½ cup sugar, gelatin, and salt in heavy saucepan. Beat egg yolks slightly and add to saucepan with milk. Cook over low heat, stirring constantly, until gelatin melts and mixture coats the spoon. Stir in rum and vanilla. Chill until mixture starts to set, stirring occasionally.

Beat egg whites until foamy. Add remaining ¼ cup sugar, 1 tablespoonful at a time, and continue beating until stiff and glossy but not dry. Beat gelatin mixture well and carefully fold in egg whites and whipped cream. Spoon into pie shell and chill until firm. Serve with Raspberry Sauce or garnish with whipped cream and chocolate curls.

CHIFFON PIES

Legend credits the invention of Chiffon Pie to a baker named Monroe Boston Strauss in 1921. Needing a new item to promote his pastry shop, Strauss beat many egg whites into a fruit syrup until he had a fluff. His mother declared that it looked like a pile of chiffon. This same baker concocted the graham-cracker crust, as his "pile of chiffon" was too delicate for ordinary pastry.

LEMON CHIFFON PIE
One 9-inch pie

    1 *cup sugar*
    1 *envelope unflavored gelatin*
    ¼ *teaspoon salt*
    4 *large or 5 medium-sized eggs, separated*
    ½ *cup cold water*
    ½ *cup lemon juice*
    1 *tablespoon grated lemon peel*
       Baked Pie Shell (9-inch) or Graham-Cracker Crumb Crust (see index)
    1½ *cups sweetened whipped cream*
       Grated lemon peel, mint sprigs, or curled lemon slices (optional)

Combine ½ cup sugar, gelatin, and salt in heavy saucepan. Add egg yolks, water, and lemon juice. Cook, stirring constantly, until gelatin melts and mixture coats the spoon. Stir in lemon peel. Transfer to a bowl and chill until mixture starts to set, stirring occasionally. Beat egg whites until foamy. Add remaining ½ cup sugar, 1 tablespoonful at a time, and continue beating until stiff and glossy but not dry. Beat gelatin mixture well and carefully fold into egg-white mixture. Spoon into pie shell and chill until set. Top with whipped cream and garnish each serving as desired.

VARIATION

Luscious Lime Chiffon Pie: Substitute lime juice for lemon juice and 2 teaspoons grated lime peel for lemon peel. Garnish with a few flecks of grated lime peel or a curled lime slice.

DIAMOND HEAD CHIFFON PIE
One 9-inch pie

    ⅔ *cup sugar*
    2 *envelopes unflavored gelatin*
    ¼ *teaspoon salt*
    1 *cup water*
    1 *(13½-ounce) can crushed pineapple, undrained*
    1 *tablespoon grated orange peel*
       Few drops of yellow food coloring (optional)
    1 *cup heavy cream, whipped*
    ½ *cup flaked coconut*
       Toasted Coconut Pie Shell (see index)
       Additional whipped cream (optional)
    4 *canned pineapple slices, drained and halved (optional)*
       Mint sprigs (optional)

Combine first 3 ingredients in heavy saucepan and stir in water. Cook, stirring constantly, until sugar is dissolved and gelatin melted. Remove from heat. Stir in undrained crushed pineapple, orange peel, and food coloring as needed to tint a pale yellow. Chill until mixture begins to thicken. Fold in whipped cream and coconut. Spoon into pie shell and chill until set. Spoon an edge of whipped cream around edge of pie and garnish with half slices of pineapple and mint sprigs.

PUMPKIN CHIFFON PIE
One 9-inch pie

   ¾ cup sugar

   1 envelope unflavored gelatin

   1 teaspoon cinnamon

   ½ teaspoon nutmeg

   ½ teaspoon salt

   3 eggs, separated

   ½ cup milk

   1 cup pumpkin, fresh or canned

   ½ cup heavy cream, whipped

   Baked Pie Shell (9-inch) or Cookie Crumb
      Crust (see index)

   Additional sweetened whipped cream
      (optional)

Combine ½ cup sugar and next 4 ingredients in heavy saucepan. Beat egg yolks slightly and add to saucepan with milk. Cook over low heat, stirring constantly, until gelatin melts and mixture thickens slightly. Stir in pumpkin. Transfer to a bowl and chill until mixture starts to thicken.

Beat egg whites until foamy. Add remaining ¼ cup sugar, 1 tablespoonful at a time, and continue beating until stiff and glossy. Fold egg-white mixture, then whipped cream, into pumpkin mixture. Spoon into pie shell and chill until firm. Serve plain or garnish with a circle of whipped cream around edge of pie.

ANGEL PIES

Often called a kiss torte, these pies are useful as a make-in-advance dessert. Perhaps they are known as angel pies because the meringue crust and light filling give a suggestion of something airy and special.

LEMON ANGEL PIE (Kiss Torte)
One 9-inch pie

   4 egg yolks, beaten slightly

   ½ cup sugar

   ¼ cup lemon juice

   1 tablespoon grated lemon peel

   ⅛ teaspoon salt

   1 cup heavy cream, whipped

   Meringue Pie Shell (see index)

   Additional whipped cream (optional)

Combine first 5 ingredients in heavy saucepan. Cook over low heat just until thickened, stirring constantly. Chill, stirring often. Fold in whipped cream. Spoon into shell and chill for at least 6 hours or overnight. Garnish with whipped cream.

VARIATIONS

Lime Angel Pie: Substitute lime juice for lemon juice and 2 teaspoons grated lime peel for lemon peel.

Orange Angel Pie: Substitute undiluted defrosted frozen orange juice concentrate for lemon juice. Omit grated lemon peel and add 1 tablespoon lemon juice.

FLORIDA KEY LIME PIE
One 9-inch pie

Grown in the Florida Keys, key limes are smaller, juicier, and tarter than ordinary limes. When fully ripe the skin is lemon-colored and the fruit is green. Condensed milk became a major staple in many households after the Civil War. In Key West, Florida, it also became the inspiration for a new pie recipe, Key Lime.

> 3 *egg yolks*
> 2 *tablespoons sugar*
> 1 *(14-ounce) can sweetened condensed milk*
> ½ *cup lime juice*
> 1 *teaspoon grated lime peel*
> ¼ *teaspoon salt*
> *Few drops green food coloring (optional)*
> *Baked Pie Shell (9-inch) (see index)*
> *Basic 3-Egg Meringue (see index)*

Combine egg yolks and sugar, beating slightly. Add condensed milk, lime juice, peel, salt, and food coloring and stir until mixture thickens.

Pour into pie shell. Cover with meringue, sealing it securely to edges of crust. Bake in moderate oven (350° F.) for 15 to 18 minutes, or until meringue is browned. Cool.

CHOCOLATE ANGEL PIE
One 9-inch pie

> 4 *egg yolks, beaten*
> ½ *cup sugar*
> ⅓ *cup water*
> *Pinch of salt*
> 1 *(6-ounce) package semisweet chocolate bits*
> 1 *teaspoon vanilla*
> 1 *cup heavy cream, whipped*
> *Pecan Crumb Crust (see index)*
> *Additional whipped cream (optional)*
> *Chocolate curls, drained maraschino cherries, or finely chopped pecans (optional)*

Combine first 4 ingredients in heavy saucepan. Cook over low heat, stirring constantly, until thickened and mixture coats the spoon. Add chocolate bits and vanilla, stirring until chocolate melts. Chill, stirring often.

Fold in whipped cream. Spoon into pie shell and chill for at least 6 hours or overnight. Garnish with whipped cream and chocolate curls, maraschino cherry halves, or chopped pecans.

FRENCH SILK CHOCOLATE PIE
One 9-inch pie

Smooth as French silk, this calorie-laden pie was the *pièce de résistance* of many a dinner party during the 1950s. Sometimes called chocolate velvet pie, it gained fame nationally when it was promoted by a well-known food company as a contest winner.

> 1 *(6-ounce) package semisweet chocolate bits*
> ¾ *cup butter*
> 1 *cup sifted confectioners' sugar*
> 2 *teaspoons vanilla*
> ¼ *teaspoon salt*
> 3 *eggs*
> *Baked Pie Shell (9-inch) or Vanilla Cookie Crust (see index)*
> *Sweetened whipped cream (optional)*
> *Toasted slivered almonds or maraschino cherries (optional)*

Melt and cool chocolate, stirring often. Cream butter until light and fluffy. Add sugar, vanilla, and salt and beat with electric mixer at high speed for about 10 minutes, or until very light and fluffy. Add eggs, one at a time, beating about 3 minutes after each addition. Carefully and quickly fold in cooled chocolate.

Pour into pie shell *at once*. Chill for at least 6 hours or overnight. Garnish with whipped cream and almonds or cherries.

CHERRY PIE

"Cherry ripe, ripe, ripe, I cry.
Full and fair ones; come and buy;
If so be, you ask me where
They do grow, I answer, there,
Where my Julia's lips do smile;
There's the land, a cherry-isle."

These lyrical words of seventeenth-century En-
glish poet Robert Herrick described his lady love
and one of Europe's best-loved fruits. Cherries
have become equally popular in the United
States. Approximately 140,000 tons of fresh,
frozen, or canned cherries are consumed by
Americans yearly. Who has not heard of George
Washington's famous cherry tree?

DOOR COUNTY CHERRY PIE
One 9-inch pie

> *Pastry for Double-Crust Pie (9-inch) (see*
> *index)*

1⅓ *cups sugar*

⅓ *cup quick-cooking tapioca*

¼ *teaspoon salt*

3 *cups pitted sour cherries (about 1 quart)*

¼ *teaspoon almond extract (optional)*

2 *tablespoons butter*

> *Sweetened whipped cream or vanilla ice*
> *cream (optional)*

Prepare pastry and line pie plate with crust. Combine sugar, tapioca, and salt and stir in cherries. Pour into pie crust. Drizzle almond extract over cherries and dot with butter. Cover with top crust as directed for double-crust pie.

Bake in very hot oven (450° F.) for 15 minutes. Reduce oven temperature to 350° F. and bake 40 to 45 minutes longer, or until pastry is browned and filling is hot and bubbling. If crust browns too fast, cover with a sheet of aluminum foil. Cool. Serve plain or topped with whipped cream or ice cream.

VARIATIONS
For a thicker pie, increase sugar to 1½ cups, tapioca to ½ cup, and pitted sour cherries to 4 cups. Increase baking time at 350° F. to 50 or 55 minutes.

For a lattice pie, prepare as directed for thicker pie and substitute Pastry for Lattice Pie (9-inch) (see index).

CANNED CHERRY PIE

2 *(1-pound) cans pitted, sour, water-pack*
   cherries

1¼ *cups sugar*

⅓ *cup cornstarch*

¼ *teaspoon salt*

2 *tablespoons butter*

¼ *teaspoon almond extract (optional)*

> *Pastry for Double-Crust Pie (9-inch) (see*
> *index)*

> *Sweetened whipped cream or vanilla ice*
> *cream (optional)*

Drain cherries and reserve 1 cup liquid. Combine sugar, cornstarch, and salt in heavy saucepan. Add reserved cherry liquid gradually, stirring until smooth. Cook over moderate heat until thick and clear, stirring constantly. Remove from heat and add butter, cherries, and almond extract. Cool slightly. Pour into crust-lined pie plate, cover with top crust, and proceed as directed above.

PEACH PIE
One 9-inch pie

A favorite from Maine to California, Peach Pie has been enjoyed since Colonial days, when cooks turned English meat pies into American fruit pies.

> *Pastry for Double-Crust Pie (see index)*
> 5 *cups peeled, sliced fresh peaches (about 10 medium-sized or 4 large peaches)*
> 2 *teaspoons lemon juice*
> ¼ *teaspoon almond extract (optional)*
> ¾ *cup sugar*
> 3 *tablespoons quick-cooking tapioca or ¼ cup flour*
> ¼ *teaspoon cinnamon or nutmeg*
> ⅛ *teaspoon salt*
> 2 *tablespoons butter*
> *Sweetened whipped cream or ice cream (optional)*

Prepare pastry and line pie plate with crust. Combine peaches, lemon juice, and almond extract, mixing carefully. Combine sugar, tapioca or flour, cinnamon or nutmeg, and salt. Fold into peaches. Turn into crust and dot with butter. Cover with top crust as directed for double-crust or lattice pies.

Bake in hot oven (425° F.) for 45 minutes, or until crust is browned, peaches tender, and juice is hot and bubbly. If crust browns too fast, cover edge loosely with a strip of aluminum foil cut 2 or 3 inches wide. Cool on rack. Serve warm or cold, plain, or topped with whipped cream or ice cream.

VIRGINIA FRUIT CREAM TARTS
8 servings

During the past 200 years of American cooking, pies and tarts have retained much of their originality. A pie can be made of one or two crusts with various kinds of filling, while a tart is smaller in size and made of one crust, usually containing a fruit or cream filling.

> 2 *eggs*
> ½ *cup sugar*
> 3 *tablespoons cornstarch*
> ¼ *teaspoon salt*
> 2 *cups milk*
> 2 *teaspoons vanilla or 1 tablespoon kirsch or sherry*
> 8 *baked Tart Shells (3-inch) (see index)*
> 1½ *cups sweetened fresh or well-drained canned fruit (fresh berries, pineapple, peaches, apricot halves, cherries)*
> *Sweetened whipped cream (optional)*

Beat together first 4 ingredients in heavy saucepan. Stir in milk. Cook over low heat until mixture thickens, stirring constantly. Cool, stirring frequently. Stir in vanilla, kirsch, or sherry. Fill baked tart shells half full. Cover with fruit and top with a dollop of whipped cream.

COOKIES

OLD-FASHIONED SUGAR COOKIES

3½ to 4 dozen

2½ *cups flour*

1 *teaspoon baking powder*

½ *teaspoon baking soda*

½ *teaspoon salt*

¼ *teaspoon nutmeg (optional)*

¾ *cup butter*

¾ *cup sugar*

1 *egg*

1 *teaspoon vanilla*

¼ *cup milk*

Granulated or colored sugar or other decorations (optional)

Sift together first 5 ingredients into bowl and set aside. Cream butter until light and fluffy. Add sugar, egg, and vanilla and cream well. Add dry ingredients and milk, stirring until thoroughly blended. Wrap with foil, waxed paper, or plastic film, and chill in refrigerator for 2 or 3 hours. Roll out half the dough at a time on lightly floured surface to a ⅛-inch thickness. Cut into fancy shapes, using lightly floured cookie cutters.

Arrange cookies on an ungreased baking sheet. Bake in hot oven (400° F.) for 6 to 7 minutes. Cookies may be sprinkled lightly with granulated or colored sugar before baking, or baked cookies may be cooled, frosted, and decorated as desired.

CONFEDERATE PEANUT COOKIES

About 6 dozen cookies

What child has not grabbed for a fistful of peanut-butter cookies? Old favorites, they are an American, probably Southern, invention. Peanuts were first grown in South America and were brought to Europe by the Spaniards. From Europe, peanut cultivation spread to Africa, where it thrived. The African slaves who were transported to America introduced the peanut into Southern households.

1½ *cups sifted flour*

1 *teaspoon baking powder*

1 *teaspoon salt*

½ *cup softened butter*

¾ *cup light brown sugar, firmly packed*

1 *egg*

¼ *cup honey*

1½ *teaspoons vanilla*

1 *cup creamy or chunk-style peanut butter*

⅔ *cup finely chopped salted peanuts*

Sift together first 3 ingredients. Cream butter until soft. Add sugar, ¼ cup at a time, beating well after each addition. Mix in egg, honey, and vanilla. Stir in peanut butter, then sifted ingredients. Shape rounded teaspoonfuls of dough into balls. Dip tops in nuts and place, 2 inches apart, on a greased baking sheet. Flatten slightly. Bake in slow oven (325° F.) for 10 to 12 minutes. Cool in pan slightly, then transfer to wire rack to finish cooling.

VARIATION

Old-Fashioned Peanut-Butter Cookies: Omit nuts. Flatten balls crisscross fashion, using tines of a dinner fork dipped in flour.

DATE-OATMEAL DROP COOKIES
45 to 50 large or 8 dozen small cookies

When I was small I had great fun visiting my Aunt Effie's farm near Oswego, Illinois. My recollections include chasing chickens (which was forbidden) and robbing the huge cookie bin (also forbidden). Oatmeal cookies were usually baked at least once a week.

2½ *cups sifted flour*

1½ *teaspoons cinnamon*

1 *teaspoon baking powder*

1 *teaspoon baking soda*

1 *teaspoon salt*

½ *teaspoon ground cloves*

½ *teaspoon nutmeg*

¾ *cup shortening*

1¼ *cups light brown sugar, firmly packed*

2 *teaspoons vanilla*

2 *eggs*

2 *cups rolled oats (quick or regular)*

1 *cup milk*

1½ *cups chopped pitted dates*

½ *cup chopped nuts*

Sift together first 7 ingredients. Cream shortening, add sugar and vanilla, and cream thoroughly. Beat in eggs. Stir in dry ingredients, rolled oats, and milk alternately, stirring just until well mixed. Fold in dates and nuts. Drop by rounded tablespoonfuls or teaspoonfuls, 2½ inches apart, on a lightly greased baking sheet. Bake in moderate oven (375° F.) for 10 to 12 minutes for large cookies, 8 to 10 minutes for small ones. *Do not overbake.*

FROSTED CHOCOLATE DROPS OR RED DEVILS
26 to 28 thick cookies

Popular throughout the United States, these fat, soft cookies don't keep well, but they're such good eating they don't last long.

2¼ *cups sifted flour*

½ *teaspoon salt*

½ *teaspoon baking soda*

2 *squares (ounces) unsweetened chocolate*

½ *cup softened butter or shortening*

1 *cup light brown sugar, firmly packed*

1 *egg*

1½ *teaspoons vanilla*

⅔ *cup milk*

⅛ *teaspoon red food coloring (optional)*

Glossy Chocolate Frosting (see index)

Sift together first 3 ingredients. Melt chocolate and butter or shortening over low heat, then cool. Pour into mixing bowl and beat in sugar, egg, and vanilla. Combine milk and food coloring. Add dry ingredients and milk alternately to chocolate mixture, stirring after each addition only enough to moisten dry ingredients.

Spoon rounded tablespoonfuls of batter, 2 inches apart, onto a lightly greased baking sheet. Bake in moderate oven (375° F.) for 10 to 12 minutes. Test for doneness with wooden pick or cake tester. *Do not overbake.* Cool slightly, then frost cookie tops with Glossy Chocolate Frosting.

Variation

Black Walnut Chocolate Drops: Fold ½ cup chopped black walnuts into batter just before spooning onto baking sheet.

BENNE SEED WAFERS
About 50 large wafers

Benne, or sesame, seeds, from an East Indian herb, were brought to the United States by African slaves. According to legend, the seeds bring good luck to those who plant or eat them, so they were planted around the rows of cotton or scattered over the doorsteps of houses. Roasted, the seeds were used in the preparation of desserts and baked goods.

> ¾ *cup plus 1½ teaspoons softened butter*
> ¾ *cup benne (sesame) seeds*
> 1¼ *cups sifted flour*
> ¾ *teaspoon baking powder*
> ½ *teaspoon salt*
> 1½ *cups light brown sugar, firmly packed*
> 2 *eggs*
> 2 *teaspoons vanilla*

Melt 1½ teaspoons butter in heavy 10-inch skillet. Add benne seeds, stirring until seeds are lightly toasted, and cool. Sift together flour, baking powder, and salt. Cream ¾ cup butter, add sugar, eggs, and vanilla and cream well. Stir in dry ingredients and seeds.

Drop by level tablespoonfuls, 3 inches apart, onto a greased and floured baking sheet. Bake in slow oven (325° F.) for 10 to 15 minutes, or until lightly browned. Cool on sheet 1 minute, then transfer to wire rack to finish cooling.

JOE FROGGERS
About 3 dozen large cookies

Known in New England as Joe Froggers, these fat, soft molasses cookies were great favorites of early American fishermen. They were easy to eat and kept well in a pocket or knapsack.

> 2½ *cups sifted flour*
> 1½ *teaspoons ginger*
> 1 *teaspoon baking soda*
> 1 *teaspoon salt*
> ½ *teaspoon ground cloves*
> ½ *teaspoon nutmeg*
> ½ *cup shortening*
> 1 *cup sugar*
> 1 *cup light molasses*

Sift together first 6 ingredients. Cream shortening and sugar well and beat in molasses. Add dry ingredients and stir until thoroughly mixed. Wrap and chill dough thoroughly. Roll out half the dough at a time to a ¼-inch thickness on a lightly floured board. Cut with lightly floured 3-inch cookie cutter (keep remaining dough in refrigerator until ready to use).

Arrange cookies on lightly greased baking sheet and bake in moderate oven (350° F.) for 10 minutes, or until done. Cool on baking sheet for 1 or 2 minutes, or until set. Remove from baking sheet with wide spatula and cool on wire rack. Store in airtight container.

APRICOT COOKIE SLICES

3½ dozen slices

FILLING

    1 *(8-ounce) package (1¾ cups) dried apricots, quartered*

    1 *cup water*

    1 *cup sugar*

    1 *tablespoon grated orange or lemon peel*

    ⅓ *cup well-drained chopped maraschino cherries*

DOUGH

    4 *cups sifted flour*

    ⅓ *cup sugar*

    2 *teaspoons salt*

    1½ *cups softened butter*

    ¾ *cup orange juice*

    ¾ *cup sliced almonds*

    Half and half or milk

    Sugar

To prepare filling, combine apricots, water, and sugar in saucepan, cover, and simmer for 15 minutes. Uncover and cook, stirring, until excess liquid evaporates. Stir in orange or lemon peel and cherries and cool.

To prepare dough, sift together flour, sugar, and salt. Cut in butter with pastry blender until mixture resembles fine meal. Using a fork, stir in orange juice, a small amount at a time, until particles are evenly moistened. Divide dough into three equal parts. Roll out each into a 14 × 6-inch rectangle on a lightly floured board.

Place on an ungreased baking sheet. Spread one-third of the filling on each rectangle in a 3-inch band, lengthwise down center of dough. Sprinkle each with one-third of the almonds. Fold edges of dough up over filling. Brush dough with half and half or milk and sprinkle with sugar. Bake in hot oven (400° F.) for 18 to 20 minutes, or until done. Remove from pan, cool slightly, and with sharp knife cut into 1-inch slices.

SPICY FRUIT NUT DROPS

About 4½ dozen cookies

    1⅓ *cups sifted flour*

    1 *teaspoon salt*

    1 *teaspoon baking powder*

    ¾ *teaspoon cinnamon*

    ½ *teaspoon ground cloves*

    ½ *teaspoon allspice*

    ¼ *teaspoon nutmeg or mace*

    ½ *cup shortening*

    1 *cup light brown sugar, firmly packed*

    2 *eggs*

    1 *teaspoon grated lemon peel*

    2 *tablespoons milk*

    ¾ *cup chopped pecans or walnuts*

    1 *cup chopped mixed candied fruit*

    ½ *cup seedless raisins*

    ½ *cup currants*

Sift together first 7 ingredients. Cream shortening and sugar thoroughly. Add eggs, one at a time, beating well after each addition. Stir in lemon peel. Blend in dry ingredients and milk, mixing well. Fold in nuts and fruit. Refrigerate for 2 hours or overnight.

Drop rounded teaspoonfuls of batter, 2 inches apart, on a lightly greased baking sheet. Bake in moderate oven (350° F.) for 12 to 15 minutes, or until done. Transfer to wire rack to cool.

ALBANY CAKES
About 5 dozen cookies

Not really a cake but a cookie, Albany Cakes may have been named to honor the hostesses of Albany, New York. The recipe for this sour cream cookie is adapted from one appearing in a cookbook published in 1865.

3   *cups sifted flour*

¾   *teaspoon salt*

½   *teaspoon baking soda*

¼   *teaspoon mace*

½   *cup softened butter*

1   *cup sugar*

2   *teaspoons vanilla*

2   *eggs, beaten*

¾   *cup sour cream*

Additional sugar or cinnamon sugar

Sift together first 4 ingredients. Cream butter, sugar, and vanilla and beat in eggs. Stir in one-third of dry ingredients and sour cream at a time, mixing well after each addition. Wrap dough and chill for 2 hours or overnight. Roll out one-quarter of the dough at a time to a ¼-inch thickness on a lightly floured board. Cut with a 2½-inch round floured cookie cutter and sprinkle tops with sugar or cinnamon-sugar mixture.

Place cookies, 1½ inches apart, on an ungreased baking sheet. Bake in moderate oven (350° F.) for 10 minutes, or until very lightly browned. Remove from baking sheet and cool on wire rack.

NOTE: *To make cinnamon sugar, combine 2 tablespoons sugar and 1 teaspoon cinnamon.*

BLUEGRASS BOURBON BALLS
40 to 45 balls

Kentucky is known for its rolling hills, blue grass, and thoroughbred horses. It's also famous for whisky and good cooking, a combination that has produced this confection. Bluegrass Bourbon Balls have been especially popular at Christmas for over a hundred years.

2   *cups crushed vanilla wafers (about 60 wafers)*

1½   *cups sifted confectioners' sugar*

3   *tablespoons cocoa*

1½   *cups finely chopped pecans*

½   *cup bourbon whisky*

¼   *cup light corn syrup*

Granulated or confectioners' sugar or finely chopped pecans

Combine first 3 ingredients and stir in nuts. Mix whisky and syrup, stir into crumb mixture, and blend thoroughly. Shape rounded teaspoonfuls of mixture into compact balls. Roll in granulated or confectioners' sugar or finely chopped nuts twice. Place on a lightly buttered baking sheet and let stand, uncovered, in refrigerator for 2 hours to dry. Store in airtight container in cool place. If possible, store for 4 or 5 days before serving. These will keep for several weeks if wrapped tightly in foil and refrigerated.

VARIATION

Rum or Brandy Balls: Prepare as directed for **Bluegrass Bourbon Balls** and substitute rum or brandy for bourbon.

NOR'EASTER MOLASSES COOKIES

3½ dozen 3-inch cookies

Hearty molasses cookies have long been a favorite in New England. Molasses and rum were readily available, being shipped in large quantities from the West Indies to New England ports during the late seventeenth century.

> 3½ *cups sifted flour*
> 2 *teaspoons baking soda*
> 2 *teaspoons ginger*
> 1 *teaspoon cinnamon*
> ½ *teaspoon salt*
> ¾ *cup softened butter or shortening*
> ¾ *cup sugar*
> 2 *eggs*
> ¾ *cup light molasses*
> ½ *cup buttermilk or sour milk*
> 1 *cup seedless raisins*
> *Confectioners' sugar*

Sift together first 5 ingredients. Cream butter or shortening, add sugar and eggs, and continue creaming. Combine molasses and buttermilk or sour milk. Add dry ingredients and liquids alternately, one-third at a time, and stir just until dry ingredients are moistened after each addition. Fold in raisins. Chill for 1 hour before baking.

Drop slighly rounded tablespoonfuls of dough, 2 inches apart, on lightly greased baking sheet. Flatten with wet cloth wrapped over bottom of a glass and sprinkle with confectioners' sugar. Bake in moderate oven (375° F.) for 10 minutes, or until done. Transfer cookies to wire rack to cool.

OLD-FASHIONED SOUR CREAM COOKIES

3 dozen cookies

Sour cream cookies were concocted to use up old cream that had soured. Yesteryear's sour cream, actually cream skimmed from sour milk, bears little relation to today's commercial product.

> 2 *cups sifted flour*
> 1 *teaspoon baking powder*
> ½ *teaspoon baking soda*
> ½ *teaspoon salt*
> ½ *teaspoon nutmeg or mace*
> ½ *cup softened butter*
> 1 *cup light brown sugar, firmly packed, or granulated sugar*
> 1 *egg*
> 2 *teaspoons vanilla*
> ½ *cup sour cream*

Sift together first 5 ingredients. Cream butter and sugar until light and fluffy. Beat in egg and vanilla. Stir in sour cream, one-third at a time, and dry ingredients alternately, mixing well after each addition.

Drop slightly rounded tablespoonfuls of batter, 2 inches apart, on a greased baking sheet. Bake in moderate oven (375° F.) for 10 to 12 minutes, or until done. Transfer cookies to wire rack to cool.

VARIATIONS

Black Walnut or Pecan Drops: Fold ¾ cup chopped black walnuts or pecans into batter before spooning onto baking sheet.

Sour Cream Pinwheels: Increase flour to 2¼ cups. Chill dough for 30 minutes to 1 hour. Roll out half the dough at a time to ¼-inch thickness on a lightly floured board. Cut into 2½- to 3-inch rounds with floured cookie cutter. Place 2 inches apart on a greased baking sheet.

Bake plain or sprinkle tops with sugar, or brush with cream and sprinkle with a mixture of sugar and finely chopped nuts before baking. Bake in moderate oven (375° F.) for 8 to 10 minutes, or until lightly browned. When cooled, you may pipe concentric circles of your favorite chocolate icing onto cookies through writing tip of pastry tube. Yield: about 4½ to 5 dozen cookies.

PEPPER COOKIES
About 5 dozen cookies

Yes, we do mean pepper! Adapted from an old Scandinavian recipe, this cookie is thin, crisp, and the pepper is barely detectable but adds much in flavor.

    5   cups sifted flour
    1   teaspoon baking soda
 1¼   teaspoons cinnamon
 1¼   teaspoons ginger
    1   teaspoon ground cloves
   ½   teaspoon ground black pepper
    1   cup softened butter
    1   cup dark corn syrup
    1   cup sugar
    1   tablespoon cider vinegar
    2   eggs, beaten

Sift together first 6 ingredients. Combine butter, syrup, sugar, and vinegar in a saucepan and heat until butter melts. Cool and stir in dry ingredients and eggs, mixing well. Cover and refrigerate for 3 hours or overnight. Divide dough into 4 equal portions. Remove one portion of dough from refrigerator at a time and roll to ⅛-inch thickness on a lightly floured board. Cut into diamonds, rounds, or attractive shapes.

Arrange ¾ inch apart on a lightly greased baking sheet and bake in moderate oven (350° F.) for 7 or 8 minutes, or until done. Transfer cookies to wire rack to cool.

SNICKERDOODLES
5 dozen

 2½   cups sifted flour
    2   teaspoons baking powder
   ½   teaspoon salt
   ½   cup softened butter
   ½   cup shortening
 1⅓   cups light brown sugar, firmly packed
    2   eggs
    1   teaspoon vanilla
   ⅓   cup each currants and chopped nuts
   ¼   cup granulated sugar
    1   teaspoon cinnamon

Sift first 3 ingredients together. Cream butter, shortening, and brown sugar thoroughly and beat in eggs and vanilla. Add dry ingredients and mix well. Fold in ⅔ cup nuts or currants or a combination. Wrap dough in aluminum foil or plastic film and chill thoroughly (for about 30 minutes). Mix granulated sugar and cinnamon and reserve. Shape level tablespoonfuls of dough into balls. Roll balls in cinnamon-sugar mixture.

Place balls, 2 inches apart, on an ungreased baking sheet. Bake in moderate oven (375° F.) for 10 to 12 minutes, or until done. Transfer to wire rack to cool.

CAMPBELL-WHITTLESEY ORANGE COOKIES
About 2½ dozen cookies

Campbell-Whittlesey House in Rochester, N.Y., is an outstanding example of American architecture and design during the Empire period. Built in 1835 by Benjamin Campbell, a wealthy miller and merchant, the house was later bought by Frederick Whittlesey, a prominent judge and civil leader, and remained in his family for over eighty years. Now a museum, early American lunches are offered in the "old" kitchen. The following recipe is an adaptation of one used at the house.

> 1 cup sifted flour
> 1 teaspoon baking powder
> ½ teaspoon salt
> ½ cup softened butter
> ⅓ cup sugar
> 1 egg
> 4 teaspoons grated orange peel
> 3 tablespoons orange juice
> Confectioners' sugar (optional)

Sift together first 3 ingredients. Cream butter and sugar until light and creamy. Add egg and orange peel. Add dry ingredients and orange juice, stirring until blended. Refrigerate for 1 to 2 hours.

Drop level tablespoonfuls, 3 inches apart, on ungreased baking sheet. Bake in moderate oven (350° F.) for 10 to 12 minutes, or until lightly browned around edges. Cool on wire rack and sprinkle lightly with confectioners' sugar.

VARIATION
Campbell-Whittlesey Nut Cookies: Follow above recipe and fold ½ cup chopped hickory nuts, black walnuts, or pecans into batter after flour is added.

COCONUT BUTTER BALLS
About 3½ dozen balls

> ½ cup softened butter
> 2 tablespoons confectioners' sugar
> 1 teaspoon vanilla
> 1 teaspoon grated orange peel
> 1 cup sifted flour
> ¾ cup coconut
> Confectioners' sugar

Combine first 4 ingredients and cream until fluffy. Stir in flour and coconut. Chill in refrigerator for 10 minutes. Form dough into balls, using 1 rounded teaspoonful for each.

Place balls, 1 inch apart, on an ungreased baking sheet. Bake in moderate oven (350° F.) for 15 minutes, or until done. Transfer balls to wire rack to cool. Roll in confectioners' sugar while slightly warm.

BISCOCHITOS
About 5 dozen cookies

A Christmas tradition of many New Mexico families is the making of Biscochitos, rich butter cookies with a subtle brandy flavor. The name comes from the Mexican Indian word for biscuit or cookie.

> 2½ cups sifted flour
> 1½ teaspoons baking powder
> ½ teaspoon salt
> 1 cup softened butter or shortening
> ¾ cup sugar
> 1 teaspoon anise seeds
> 1 egg
> 2 tablespoons brandy, whisky, or water
> Cinnamon sugar (2 tablespoons sugar and 1 teaspoon cinnamon)

Sift together first 3 ingredients. Cream butter or shortening, sugar, and anise seeds thoroughly. Beat in egg. Stir in dry ingredients and liquid. Shape into a flat patty. Wrap dough and chill thoroughly. Roll out half the dough at a time on a lightly floured board to a ¼-inch thickness (keep remaining dough refrigerated). Cut into fancy shapes or 2-inch rounds with lightly floured cookie cutters.

Arrange on a very lightly greased baking sheet. Sprinkle generously with cinnamon sugar. Bake in moderate oven (350° F.) for 12 minutes, or until done. Cookies do not brown but are cream-colored. Cool on wire rack.

MACAROONS
20 to 22 macaroons

This crunchy confection is made of almond paste, sugar, and egg whites. Its origin is unknown, but some authorities believe it was invented in Italy in the sixteenth century and from there went to France, where it gained wide popularity. The early French settlers of New Orleans brought it to this country. Macaroons were probably named for the process of mashing the almonds.

- ½ *pound (1 cup) Almond Paste (see next column)*
- ⅔ *cup granulated sugar*
- ¼ *cup sifted confectioners' sugar*
- 2 *tablespoons flour*
- ⅛ *teaspoon salt*
- ½ *teaspoon almond extract*
- 3 *tablespoons egg white, unbeaten (approximate)*

Break Almond Paste into very small pieces. Mix in remaining ingredients, adding just enough egg white to make a very stiff mixture.

Drop heaping teaspoonfuls, 2 inches apart, onto ungreased brown wrapping paper or lightly greased aluminum foil on a baking sheet. Bake in slow oven (325° F.) for 18 to 20 minutes, or until set and lightly browned. Let stand for 1 or 2 minutes. Set paper on a damp cloth to loosen the macaroons for easy removal. Let stand 1 or 2 minutes and remove macaroons, using a spatula. Cool on wire rack.

VARIATION

Chocolate Macaroons: Increase granulated sugar to 1 cup and egg white to about ¼ cup. Add 2 squares (ounces) unsweetened chocolate, melted.

ALMOND PASTE   3 cups
- 1 *pound (3 ¼ cups) whole blanched almonds*
- 2 *cups sifted confectioners' sugar*
- ⅓ *cup egg whites, unbeaten*
- 2 *teaspoons almond extract*
- 1 *teaspoon vanilla*

Whiz almonds, a few at a time, in blender until *very* fine. Mix with confectioners' sugar. Add remaining ingredients and blend thoroughly. (Mixture will be very stiff.) Store in refrigerator in airtight container for *at least* 4 days before using. Use for making marzipan, confections, cookies, or pastries. Can be refrigerated for 1 to 2 weeks.

MADELEINES
About 4 dozen Madeleines

Perhaps an imaginative French pastry chef named these delightful tea cakes in honor of his lady love. Baked in special scalloped shells, Madeleines are pretty and very, very rich. A cross between a pound and a sponge cake, they are served in elegant restaurants throughout the United States.

Madeleine pans are available in gourmet specialty shops or in the houseware sections of large department stores. If unavailable, substitute small muffin pans (about ¼ inch deep).

  1 *cup sifted flour*
  ¼ *teaspoon salt*
  4 *eggs*
  1 *tablespoon brandy (optional)*
  1 *teaspoon vanilla*
  ¼ *teaspoon orange extract or ½ teaspoon finely grated orange peel*
  ⅔ *cup granulated sugar*
  ½ *cup butter, melted and cooled*
     Confectioners' sugar

Grease and flour pans for 4 dozen Madeleines. Sift flour and salt. Beat eggs, brandy, vanilla, and orange extract or peel until light and lemon-colored. Add sugar gradually, beating constantly until mixture is thick and fluffy. Carefully fold in flour mixture. Quickly fold in butter. Spoon into prepared pans *immediately,* filling about three-fourths full.

Bake *at once* in slow oven (325° F.) for 12 to 15 minutes, or until lightly browned. Let cool in pans for 2 to 3 minutes. Turn onto wire rack, shell side up, to cool. Just before serving, sprinkle with confectioners' sugar.

NOTE: *Batter must be baked immediately or the butter will settle and the Madeleines will be tough. Cut the recipe in half or quarters, according to the number of Madeleine pans available.*

FLORENTINES
32 cookies

Favorites in old Vienna, these delicate cookies are easy to make. They're rich, sweet, and so delicious.

  1 *cup very finely chopped blanched almonds*
  ⅔ *cup very finely chopped candied orange or lemon peel*
  ⅓ *cup sifted flour*
  ¼ *cup sugar*
  ¼ *teaspoon salt*
  ¾ *cup sweetened condensed milk*
  1 *egg, beaten*
  1 *teaspoon vanilla*
  ¼ *teaspoon orange extract*
  2 *(4-ounce) packages sweet baking chocolate*

Combine first 9 ingredients and blend thoroughly. Spoon by level tablespoonfuls onto a well-greased and floured baking sheet, spreading batter to make cookies 3½ inches in diameter. Make only 4 cookies at a time.

Bake in slow oven (325° F.) for 8 minutes, or until lightly browned around edges. Remove from baking sheet immediately and cool on wire rack. When all cookies are baked, melt chocolate and spread on bottom of cookies. Cool until chocolate is firm.

SPRITZ
About 8 dozen cookies

The Swedes invented this delectable cookie. Pronounced *spritsar* by the Scandinavians, this all-American favorite was brought here by the Swedish immigrants who settled in the lovely lake regions of Minnesota and Wisconsin.

2¼ cups sifted flour
½ teaspoon baking powder
½ teaspoon salt
1 cup softened butter
⅔ cup sugar
2 egg yolks
2 teaspoons vanilla or 1 teaspoon almond extract
Chopped red or green candied cherry (optional)

Sift together first 3 ingredients. Cream butter, add sugar gradually, and continue creaming until light and fluffy. Beat in egg yolks and flavoring. Stir in dry ingredients. Force dough through cookie press onto a cold ungreased baking sheet. Use tip desired for making ribbon, S, O, star, or other fancy-shaped cookies. Decorate tops with bits of red or green candied cherry.

Bake in moderate oven (375° F.) for 7 to 10 minutes, or until lightly browned. Bake cookies of the same shape together, since small, thin cookies bake faster than big, thick ones.

VARIATIONS
Spritz—with Fancy Tops: Brush tops of cookies lightly with slightly beaten egg whites and sprinkle sparingly with colored decorating sugars or candies, chocolate sprinkles, or chopped nuts before baking.

Almond Spritz: Reduce flour to 2 cups and omit baking powder. Substitute ½ cup confectioners' sugar for the ⅔ cup granulated sugar and use only almond extract. Stir in ¼ cup sieved, finely ground blanched almonds and 2 tablespoons brandy or rum. Shape and bake as directed above.

HOLIDAY CRESCENTS
5 to 5½ dozen cookies

Cookies of this type have long been popular at holiday time. The dough can be formed into many shapes and decorated with a variety of nuts.

1 cup softened butter
½ cup confectioners' sugar
1 tablespoon water
2 teaspoons vanilla
½ teaspoon salt
1¾ cups finely chopped pecans
2 cups sifted flour
Confectioners' sugar

Cream butter and ½ cup confectioners' sugar until light and fluffy. Beat in water, vanilla, and salt. Add nuts and mix well. Stir in flour, a small amount at a time, mixing well after each addition.

Shape rounded teaspoonfuls of dough into compact crescents, balls, or 2½-inch fingers. Arrange on an ungreased baking sheet and bake in slow oven (300° F.) for 12 to 15 minutes, or until very lightly browned. When cookies are slightly warm, sift confectioners' sugar over tops or roll each cookie in confectioners' sugar.

Store in cool place in an airtight container. To give cookies a fresh baked look after storage, sprinkle with additional confectioners' sugar just before serving.

VARIATIONS
Almond Crescents: Substitute ½ teaspoon almond extract for ½ teaspoon of the vanilla and very finely grated, chopped, or ground blanched almonds for pecans.

Sand Tarts: Reduce confectioners' sugar to ⅓ cup, sift 1 teaspoon baking powder with flour, and reduce nuts to 1 cup. Shape mixture into 1-inch balls, place on ungreased baking sheet, and flatten slightly with flat-bottomed glass. Bake as directed above and roll in confectioners' sugar when slightly warm.

Nut Variations: Substitute very finely chopped or ground macadamias, English or black walnuts, or unblanched hazelnuts for pecans.

PFEFFERNUESSE
About 4 dozen

Spicy, gingery Pfeffernuesse (pepper nuts) are a traditional holiday cookie with many German-American families. Introduced into America in the eighteenth century in the Pennsylvania Dutch and Moravian communities, "pepper nuts" were also popular with the German immigrants of the late 1800s. In early German settlements where a community oven was used, the dough was mixed at home and then taken to the bakery to be baked after the bread.

   3½ *cups sifted flour*
   1½ *teaspoons baking powder*
   1 *teaspoon cinnamon*
   ½ *teaspoon ground cloves*
   ½ *teaspoon allspice*
   ¼ *teaspoon nutmeg*
   ½ *teaspoon salt*
   ¼ *teaspoon ginger*
   ¼ *teaspoon cardamom*
   ¼ *teaspoon pepper*
   ¼ *teaspoon mace*
   3 *eggs*
   1 *cup light brown sugar, firmly packed*
   2 *tablespoons molasses*
   1 *teaspoon grated lemon peel*
   ½ *cup finely ground almonds*
   Brandy (optional)
   Pfeffernuesse Frosting (see next column)

Sift together first 11 ingredients. Beat eggs with electric beater at high speed for 2 minutes. Add sugar, molasses, and lemon peel and beat for 3 minutes. Put almonds through the fine blade of food chopper or whiz, a few at a time, in a blender. Stir dry ingredients and ground almonds into egg mixture, blending thoroughly. Roll level tablespoonfuls of dough into 1-inch balls. Moisten hands with water if dough becomes sticky. Place balls on lightly greased cookie sheets. Put a drop of brandy on center top of each cookie.

Bake in moderate oven (375° F.) for 12 minutes, or until golden in color. Cool on wire racks. When cookies have cooled, frost as directed below. Pfeffernuesse are best when allowed to age in an airtight container for 1½ to 2 weeks before serving.

PFEFFERNUESSE FROSTING

   3 *cups granulated sugar*
   Dash of cream of tartar
   1 *cup water*
   ⅛ *to* ¼ *teaspoon anise extract*
   2 *egg whites*
   1 *cup sifted confectioners' sugar*

Combine first 3 ingredients in saucepan and cook, stirring, until sugar is dissolved. Continue cooking until mixture forms a 2-inch thread when dropped from tip of spoon, or to a temperature of 235° F. Combine anise and egg whites and beat until stiff. Add hot syrup in a fine stream, beating constantly, until mixture thickens slightly.

Drop cookies in glaze to cover completely. Remove from glaze right side up on a fork, drain slightly, and place on a wire rack to finish draining. Roll cookies in sifted confectioners' sugar. Dry slightly and sift additional confectioners' sugar over tops.

GINGERBREAD MEN
14 to 16 6-inch Gingerbread Men

Appealing to children of all ages, whether six or sixty, Gingerbread Men have been a culinary delight since the Middle Ages. The great medieval fairs of Europe would not have been complete without gingerbread stalls. At holiday time gingerbread was baked in fanciful molds and decorated elaborately. Gingerbread men and women, six feet tall, were baked for St. Nicholas Day in Holland and Belgium. American colonists were also proud of their gingerbreads and interesting wooden molds. George Washington's mother was famous for her gingerbread and often served it to visitors.

2¼ *cups sifted flour*

1 *teaspoon baking powder*

½ *teaspoon salt*

1½ *teaspoons ginger*

1 *teaspoon cinnamon*

¾ *teaspoon ground cloves*

½ *teaspoon cardamom (optional)*

⅔ *cup softened butter or shortening*

½ *cup sugar*

½ *cup light molasses*

1 *egg*

1 *to 1½ teaspoons grated orange peel*

Confectioners' Sugar Icing (see index—optional)

Sift together first 7 ingredients. Cream together butter or shortening, sugar, and molasses. Beat in egg and orange peel. Add dry ingredients, mix well, and divide dough in half. Wrap dough with plastic film or aluminum foil and chill thoroughly for 2 hours or overnight.

To make Gingerbread Men, roll out dough about ¼ inch thick on lightly floured board. Cut with floured gingerbread-man cookie cutter. Place cookies on a lightly greased baking sheet and bake in moderate oven (350° F.) for 8 to 12 minutes, or until done. Decorate with Confectioners' Sugar Icing.

VARIATION

Swedish Christmas Cookies: Follow recipe for Gingerbread Men and add ½ teaspoon cardamom. Roll out dough ⅛ inch thick on lightly floured board. Cut into assorted fancy shapes (animals, angels, fluted circles, or diamonds).

Bake in moderate oven (350° F.) for 8 minutes. After cooling, decorate, if desired, with Confectioners' Sugar Icing put through a pastry tube. Yield: 5½ to 6 dozen cookies, depending on size and shape of cutters.

BOHEMIAN KOLACH COOKIES
3 dozen cookies

A cousin of the sweet yeast bun, *koláč*, Bohemian Kolach Cookies are perfect accompaniments for coffee or tea. Made of a rich cream-cheese dough, the cookies resemble small, white sugared squares with a sweetened filling of prunes, apricots, or poppy seeds. They're especially popular in the Midwest, where many good Bohemian cooks are found.

2 *cups sifted flour*

3 *tablespoons sugar*

2 *teaspoons baking powder*

½ *teaspoon salt*

1 *(8-ounce) package cream cheese, at room temperature*

1 *cup butter*

2 *eggs*

1 *teaspoon vanilla*

1 *to 1¼ cups thick apricot, prune, strawberry, raspberry, or cherry jam or preserves, or commercial poppyseed filling*

Confectioners' sugar

Sift together first 4 ingredients. Beat cream cheese and butter until creamy. Add eggs and vanilla, beating thoroughly. Stir in dry ingredients to make a stiff dough. Shape into a patty and wrap in plastic film or waxed paper. Chill for at least 2 hours. Roll out dough, one-third at a time, ¼ inch thick on lightly floured board. Cut into 2½-inch squares. Place a rounded teaspoonful of filling in center of each square. Bring the corners up over the center and press together.

Place on ungreased baking sheet and bake in moderate oven (375° F.) for about 15 minutes, or until lightly browned. Transfer to wire rack to cool. Sprinkle generously with confectioners' sugar while still warm.

MORAVIAN SPICE COOKIES

8 to 9 dozen cookies

In the Moravian town of Old Salem, North Carolina, spice cakes or cookies are still part of a Christmas tradition. The old recipes remain essentially unchanged, combining molasses, lard or shortening, and butter, flour, sugar, soda, spices, and possibly a little brandy. Some people use a heavy hand with the cloves to give these cookies a little "bite."

> 5 *cups sifted flour*
> 1 *tablespoon ginger*
> 1 *tablespoon cinnamon*
> 2 *teaspoons ground cloves*
> ½ *teaspoon salt*
> ½ *cup softened butter*
> ⅓ *cup shortening*
> 1 *cup light brown sugar, firmly packed*
> 1 *cup light or dark molasses*
> 1½ *teaspoons baking soda*
> ¼ *cup boiling water*
> *Confectioners' Sugar Icing (see index)*

Sift together first 5 ingredients. Cream butter and shortening until soft and fluffy. Add sugar, one-third at a time, beating well after each addition. Stir in molasses and one-third of dry ingredients. Dissolve baking soda in water and stir into batter. Stir in remaining dry ingredients, mixing with hands if necessary. Divide dough into four equal portions, cover with aluminum foil or plastic wrap, and refrigerate for several hours or overnight. Remove one package of dough at a time and roll out *very, very* thin on a well-floured board. Cut with round (2½- or 3-inch) or fancy cutters.

Place on a lightly greased baking sheet and bake in moderate oven (350° F.) for 6 to 8 minutes, or until edges begin to brown. *Do not overbake.* Run spatula under cookies to loosen and transfer to wire racks to cool. Serve plain or decorate with Confectioners' Sugar Icing.

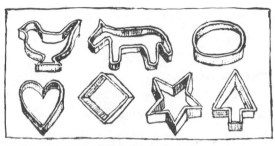

SCOTCH SHORTBREAD

4 dozen cookies

Known in Scotland for over three centuries, this biscuit-type cake is immensely popular today in the United States, especially in those states bordering Canada. It gets its name from the large amount of shortening or "shortness" used in the dough. Shortbread is served each Hogmanay, the Scottish New Year's Eve, often in the form of a large round biscuit with crimped edges.

> 2¼ *cups sifted flour*
> ¼ *teaspoon salt*
> 1 *cup softened butter*
> ½ *cup sugar*
> 1 *teaspoon vanilla*
> *Granulated or cinnamon sugar (optional)*
> *Confectioners' sugar (optional)*

Combine flour and salt. Cream butter, add sugar and vanilla, and cream well. Stir in dry ingredients. Knead a few times on very lightly floured board. Wrap dough in aluminum foil or plastic film and chill for at least 1 hour. Divide dough into two parts. Roll out ¼ inch thick and into a 9 × 6-inch rectangle on lightly floured board. Cut into 1½-inch squares, triangles, or small fancy shapes. Imprint center with a fancy design or points of dinner fork.

Place on an ungreased baking sheet. Cookies can be sprinkled with granulated or cinnamon sugar before baking or sprinkled with confectioners' sugar after baking, while still slightly warm. Bake in slow oven (325° F.) for 15 to 18 minutes, or until delicately browned on edges.

NOTE: *To make cinnamon sugar, combine 2 tablespoons sugar and 1 teaspoon cinnamon.*

VARIATIONS

Shortbread Rolls: Shape dough before chilling into three rolls and roll in chopped pecans or granulated sugar. Roll in waxed paper and refrigerate for 3 to 4 hours. Slice ¼ inch thick and bake as directed above.

Pecan Coffee Shortbread Bars: Substitute brown sugar, firmly packed, for granulated sugar and add ¾ teaspoon powdered instant coffee to butter when creaming. Roll out ½ inch thick and cut into 2 × ½-inch bars. Roll each bar in slightly beaten egg whites and roll in finely chopped nuts. Bake as directed above for 20 to 25 minutes.

Butterscotch Shortbread: Substitute light brown sugar, firmly packed, for granulated.

KOURABIEDES (GREEK BUTTER (Greek Butter Cakes)

3 dozen cookies

Made traditionally at Christmastime, these small, rich cookies trace their history back to the fourth century A.D. A clove placed in the center of each cookie symbolizes the spices brought to the Christ Child by the Wise Men. Kourabiedes are also served at weddings as a symbol of good luck.

> 2 *cups sifted flour*
> ½ *teaspoon salt*
> 1 *cup softened salted or sweet butter*
> ½ *cup sifted confectioners' sugar*
> 1 *tablespoon brandy or cognac*
> 1 *teaspoon vanilla*
> 3 *dozen whole cloves*
> *Confectioners' sugar*

Sift flour and salt together. Cream butter and sugar thoroughly. Mix in brandy or cognac and vanilla. Stir in dry ingredients, mixing well. Cover dough and chill for 30 minutes. Shape level tablespoonfuls of dough into small oval cakes about 2 inches long. Place

cakes, 1 inch apart, on an ungreased baking sheet. Stick the stem of a whole clove down in the center of each cake.

Bake in moderate oven (350° F.) for 10 to 12 minutes, or until a sandy color. Transfer cookies to wire rack. Sprinkle with confectioners' sugar while warm.

SHREWSBURY CAKES

About 7 dozen 2-inch cookies

Shrewsbury Cakes or biscuits originated in England. These thin, rich, crisp cookies delicately flavored with brandy, cinnamon, and mace are excellent served as a tea cake or as an accompaniment to fruit or ice cream. Don't include them in gift packages sent to friends or relatives as they crumble easily.

> 2½ *cups sifted flour*
> ½ *teaspoon salt*
> ½ *teaspoon cinnamon*
> ½ *teaspoon mace or nutmeg*
> ½ *cup softened butter*
> ¼ *cup shortening*
> ½ *cup sugar*
> 1 *egg*
> ¼ *cup brandy or white wine*

Sift together first 4 ingredients. Cream butter and shortening, add sugar gradually, and cream well. Beat in egg. Stir in dry ingredients and brandy or wine. Knead slightly and divide into two equal portions. Wrap dough and refrigerate for 2 hours or overnight. Roll out half the dough at a time to ⅛-inch thickness on a lightly floured board. Cut with floured 2-inch fluted round or fancy cookie cutter.

Place 1 inch apart on an ungreased baking sheet and bake in moderate oven (350° F.) for 8 to 10 minutes, or until a light ivory color. Remove from baking sheet and cool on wire rack.

TRILBYS

About 3½ dozen cookies

A fruit-filled cookie, very popular with Mid-western cooks at the turn of the nineteenth century, Trilbys are now generally made at holiday time. Probably raisin, apple butter, or fruit fillings were used at first, with more elaborate fillings developed later.

2½ *cups sifted flour*
¾ *teaspoon salt*
½ *teaspoon baking powder*
¼ *teaspoon baking soda*
½ *cup softened butter or shortening*
1 *cup sugar*
2 *eggs*
1½ *teaspoons vanilla*
½ *cup sour cream*
Filling (see next column) or thick preserves

Sift together first 4 ingredients. Cream butter or shortening, add sugar gradually, and continue creaming. Beat in eggs and vanilla. Add sour cream and dry ingredients alternately, a small amount at a time, stirring just until dry ingredients are moistened. Divide dough in half, wrap, and refrigerate for 2 hours or longer. Roll out dough, half at a time, ⅛ inch thick, on lightly floured board.

Cut with 2½-inch round fluted, plain, or fancy cookie cutter. In the center of half the cookies cut out a small design (circle, star, or crescent). Arrange undesigned cookies 1½ inches apart on lightly greased baking sheet. Spoon a rounded teaspoonful of fruit filling or preserves in center, spreading to within ¾ inch of all edges. Cover each with a designed cookie and crimp edges with fingers or tines of fork.

Bake in moderate oven (350° F.) for 12 to 15 minutes, or until edges are lightly browned. Remove from baking sheet and cool on wire rack.

MINCEMEAT FILLING   About 1½ cups

1 *(9-ounce) package condensed mincemeat, broken into small pieces*
¾ *cup water*
⅔ *cup sugar*
⅓ *cup chopped nuts (optional)*

Combine first 3 ingredients in heavy saucepan. Cook over low heat until thick, stirring constantly. Stir in nuts and cool.

APRICOT FILLING   About 1½ cups

1¼ *cups quartered dried apricots*
⅔ *cup water*
½ *cup sugar*
2 *teaspoons grated orange or lemon peel*

Combine ingredients in small saucepan. Cover and simmer slowly for 15 minutes. Uncover and cook, stirring constantly, until thickened, then cool.

DATE AND RAISIN FILLING   About 1½ cups

⅓ *cup sugar*
2 *teaspoons flour*
¼ *teaspoon salt*
⅔ *cup water*
⅔ *cup chopped pitted dates*
⅔ *cup chopped seedless raisins*
1½ *teaspoons grated lemon peel*
¼ *cup chopped nuts*

Combine first 3 ingredients in heavy saucepan and stir in water. Add fruits and lemon peel, mixing thoroughly. Cover and cook over very low heat until mixture begins to simmer. Uncover and cook, stirring constantly, until thickened. Fold in nuts and cool.

ROLLED LACE WAFERS

4½ dozen wafers

Some versions of this cookie orginated in France, while other versions came from Sweden. They are made with oats, nuts, or coconut. All are thin, lacy, and crisp, except on humid days.

   1 *cup sifted flour*
   1 *cup finely chopped pecans or walnuts*
  ¼ *teaspoon salt*
  ½ *cup light corn syrup*
  ½ *cup light brown sugar, firmly packed*
  ½ *cup butter*
   1 *teaspoon vanilla*

Blend flour, nuts, and salt. Combine syrup, sugar, and butter in heavy saucepan and bring to a full boil, stirring constantly. Remove from heat. Stir in flour-nut mixture and vanilla and continue stirring until thoroughly blended. Drop rounded teaspoonfuls of batter, about 4 inches apart, on greased baking sheet. Bake only 4 or 6 wafers at a time in moderate oven (350° F.) for 7 to 8 minutes, or until lightly browned around edges. Remove from oven and let stand for 1 to 2 minutes until cool enough to lift easily from baking sheet. Remove one wafer at a time and roll up around the handle of a wooden spoon, lacy side out. Cool on a wire rack covered with paper towels.

BROWNIES

One of the earliest brownie recipes appeared in the January 1914 issue of St. Nicholas Magazine. *Similar recipes are found in* The Boston Cooking School Cookbook *(1906) and* The Settlement Cookbook *(1901). Another early cookbook, published by Lowney's Chocolate Company in 1907, includes a recipe for Bangor Brownies, using brown sugar and chocolate.*

GOOEY MARBLED BROWNIES

About 16 squares

Cream cheese and sweet baking chocolate combine to produce a brownie that is rich and moist, with a distinct flavor.

  ⅔ *cup sifted flour*
  ½ *teaspoon baking powder*
  ½ *teaspoon salt*
   1 *(4-ounce) package sweet baking chocolate*
  ⅓ *cup butter*
   1 *(3-ounce) package cream cheese, at room temperature*
   1 *cup sugar*
   3 *eggs*
   2 *teaspoons vanilla*
  ⅔ *cup chopped pecans.*

Sift together first 3 ingredients. Combine chocolate and 3 tablespoons butter in heavy pan and melt chocolate over very low heat, stirring. Cool. Beat remaining butter and cream cheese thoroughly. Add ¼ cup sugar gradually, beating well after each addition. Add 1 egg, beat until fluffy, and set aside. Beat remaining 2 eggs, add remaining ¾ cup sugar and vanilla, and continue beating until very thick and fluffy. Stir in cooled chocolate and dry ingredients. Fold in pecans. Alternate spoonfuls of chocolate and cheese mixtures into greased and floured 9 × 9 × 2-inch pan. Using a knife, fold chocolate mixture over cheese mixture to marbleize batter. Bake in moderate oven (350° F.) for 45 minutes, or until done. Cool in pan for 5 minutes before removing. Finish cooling on wire rack and cut into squares. Store in plastic bag or aluminum foil in refrigerator.

REBEL PEANUT-BUTTER BROWNIES

About 24 brownies

According to Georgians, the peanut was a Southern secret until after the Civil War. Soldiers returning home brought peanuts with them, and the tasty nut soon gained a wide popularity in the North.

BROWNIES

> 1½ cups sifted flour
>
> 2 teaspoons baking powder
>
> ½ teaspoon salt
>
> ½ cup creamy peanut butter
>
> ½ cup butter
>
> 1½ cups light brown sugar, firmly packed
>
> 1 teaspoon vanilla
>
> 2 eggs
>
> ½ cup chopped salted peanuts

TOPPING

> ½ cup light brown sugar, firmly packed
>
> 3 tablespoons butter
>
> 1 tablespoon honey
>
> 1 tablespoon milk
>
> ¼ cup finely chopped salted peanuts

To prepare brownies, sift together first 3 ingredients. Cream peanut butter, butter, sugar, and vanilla thoroughly. Add eggs and beat until very light and fluffy. Add dry ingredients and stir until well blended. Fold in peanuts.

Spread batter in an even layer in greased 13 × 9 × 2-inch pan. Bake in moderate oven (350° F.) for 30 minutes, or until done. Cool in pan to lukewarm.

To prepare topping, combine sugar, butter, honey, and milk in saucepan. Bring to a boil, reduce heat, and cook slowly for about 5 minutes, stirring constantly. Remove from heat and stir in peanuts. Spread evenly over top of lukewarm brownies. Cool and cut into squares.

LINZER SQUARES

35 squares

An adaptation of the famous Austrian Linzer Torte, these rich and delicate tea cookies are traditionally filled with raspberry preserves. An apricot filling may be substituted.

> 3 cups sifted flour
>
> ⅔ cup sugar
>
> 1½ teaspoons baking powder
>
> 1 teaspoon cinnamon
>
> 1 cup softened butter
>
> 2 eggs, well beaten, plus 1 egg yolk
>
> ¼ cup milk
>
> 1 teaspoon grated lemon peel
>
> 1½ to 1¾ cups thick red raspberry or apricot preserves
>
> 1 tablespoon water
>
> ⅓ cup finely chopped pistachio nuts or pecans
>
> Confectioners' sugar

Sift together first 4 ingredients. Cut in butter with pastry blender until mixture resembles fine meal. Combine 2 eggs, milk, and lemon peel and add to flour mixture, mixing until dry particles are moistened. Divide dough into 2 portions, using two-thirds of dough in one and one-third in the other. Wrap each in foil or plastic film and chill. Roll the larger portion of dough on lightly floured board in a rectangle to fit a 15 × 10 × 1-inch jelly-roll pan. Place dough in pan and press up around edges, making a ½-inch rim. Spread preserves over crust. Roll remaining dough about ¼ inch thick. Using a sharp knife or fluted pastry wheel, cut in strips ½ inch wide. Lay strips over preserves diagonally in lattice pattern. Dough is very rich and hard to handle. If it breaks, just overlap the strip. Beat egg yolk and water and brush over lattice top. Sprinkle with nuts. Bake in moderate oven (350° F.) for 30 to 35 minutes, or until done. Cool. Sprinkle lightly with confectioners' sugar and cut into 2-inch squares.

LEMON BARS
24 bars

One of my favorite cookies for many years, Lemon Bars make a nice addition to any fancy confection tray. Tart but sweet, with a rich buttery crust, they keep well wrapped in foil or an airtight container. Mine have never been known to get from the pan to the cooling rack.

CRUST

> 1 *cup butter*
> ½ *cup sifted confectioners' sugar*
> 2 *cups sifted flour*

FILLING

> 4 *eggs*
> 2 *cups sugar*
> ¼ *cup sifted flour*
> 1 *teaspoon baking powder*
> ¼ *cup lemon juice*
> 3 *tablespoons grated lemon peel*

GLAZE

> 2 *cups sifted confectioners' sugar*
> 3 *tablespoons hot water*

To prepare crust, beat butter and sugar until creamy. Stir in flour until evenly blended. Spread evenly into an ungreased 13 × 9 × 2-inch baking pan. Bake in moderate oven (350° F.) for 15 minutes, or until lightly browned.

While crust is baking, prepare filling. Beat eggs and sugar until light and fluffy. Stir in remaining filling ingredients. Pour over hot crust. Return to oven and continue baking for 30 minutes, or until filling is set. Remove from oven and cool for 10 minutes.

Make a glaze by combining sugar and hot water, stirring until sugar is dissolved. Spread over top and finish cooling. Cut into bars, 3 × 1½ inches.

VARIATIONS

Orange Bars: Add 1 cup flaked coconut to crust mixture. Substitute orange juice and orange peel for lemon juice and peel.

Cherry Almond Bars: Add ½ cup *each* of finely chopped maraschino cherries and slivered almonds to crust mixture. Substitute ¼ cup milk and ½ teaspoon almond extract for lemon juice and peel.

CRUNCH-TOP APPLESAUCE BARS

30 to 36 bars

BATTER

   2 *cups sifted flour*

1½ *teaspoons cinnamon*

   1 *teaspoon baking soda*

   1 *teaspoon salt*

  ¼ *teaspoon nutmeg*

  ⅛ *teaspoon ground cloves*

  ½ *cup shortening or softened butter*

   1 *cup sugar*

   1 *teaspoon vanilla*

   1 *cup thick applesauce*

   1 *cup seedless raisins*

  ¼ *cup chopped nuts*

TOPPING

  ¼ *cup sugar*

   2 *tablespoons softened butter*

  ⅓ *cup crushed cereal flakes (corn, whole-wheat, or high-protein)*

  ⅓ *cup chopped nuts*

To prepare batter, sift together first 6 ingredients. Cream shortening or butter, sugar, and vanilla thoroughly. Stir in dry ingredients and applesauce. Fold in raisins and nuts. Spread in an even layer in a greased 13 × 9 × 2-inch pan.

To prepare topping, combine sugar and butter and stir in cereal and nuts. Sprinkle mixture evenly over batter. Bake in moderate oven (350° F.) for 25 to 30 minutes. Cool and cut into bars.

VARIATION

Nutty Applesauce Bars: Omit topping and sprinkle ½ cup chopped nuts over batter. Bake as directed above. Cool until slightly warm and sift confectioners' sugar over top. Cut into bars.

ENGLISH TOFFEE BARS

About 70 to 90 cookies

   2 *cups sifted flour*

   1 *teaspoon cinnamon*

  ¼ *teaspoon salt*

   1 *cup softened butter*

   1 *cup light brown sugar, firmly packed*

   1 *egg, separated*

   1 *teaspoon vanilla*

 12 *ounces dipping or sweet baking chocolate, melted*

  ¾ *cup chopped pecans*

Butter a 15 × 10 × 1-inch jelly-roll pan. Sift first 3 ingredients together. Cream butter, add sugar, and continue creaming until light and fluffy. Beat in egg yolk and vanilla. Stir dry ingredients into creamed mixture, a small amount at a time, beating well after each addition. Press mixture evenly into prepared pan. Brush top with slightly beaten egg white.

Bake in very slow oven (275° F.) for 35 to 40 minutes, or until lightly browned. Spread melted chocolate over top while still hot and sprinkle on nuts. Cut into squares or bars and cool on wire rack.

CANDIES

OLD-FASHIONED MOLASSES TAFFY

About 1¼ pounds

Molasses taffy is just as popular today as it was a century ago. Originating in Louisiana, where the first sugar refinery was established in 1791, the taffy with the "big stretch" has traveled from coast to coast. Sadly, taffy pulls, during which boys and girls with buttered hands would pull each piece of taffy until it was creamy and light, have disappeared.

  1 *cup granulated sugar*
  1 *cup light brown sugar, firmly packed*
  1 *cup light molasses*
  ½ *cup light corn syrup*
  ½ *cup water*
  ½ *teaspoon salt*
  ⅛ *teaspoon cream of tartar*
  ¼ *cup butter*
  ¼ *teaspoon baking soda*
  ½ *teaspoon vanilla*

Butter a 15 × 10 × 1-inch pan. Combine first 7 ingredients in large, heavy saucepan and cook, stirring, just until sugar dissolves. Cook until candy thermometer registers 270° F. (syrup separates into hard brittle threads in very cold water). Remove from heat and gently stir in butter, baking soda, and vanilla. Pour into prepared pan and let stand. As syrup cools, carefully fold edges of candy back over center every 15 to 20 minutes so candy will cool evenly. When cool enough to handle, butter fingers and gather candy into a ball. Pull and twist until it holds its shape and becomes a light bronze color. Twist and pull into long thin rope and cut into 1-inch lengths with buttered scissors. Cool thoroughly but do not refrigerate. Wrap each piece of taffy in waxed paper.

VARIATION

Black Walnut Molasses Taffy: Stir in 1 cup chopped black walnuts with butter.

OLD-FASHIONED SALT-WATER TAFFY

About 1¾ pounds

Taffy pulls and quilting bees are nostalgic memories of a quieter era when they provided entertainment for the hearty pioneers. Salt-water taffy is thought to be named from its early production near the seashore. Atlantic City, New Jersey, is famous for its boardwalk and its salt-water taffy.

  3 *cups granulated sugar*
  1½ *cups light corn syrup*
  1¼ *cups boiling water*
  1½ *teaspoons salt*
  3 *tablespoons butter*
  2 *teaspoons vanilla*

Butter a 15 × 10 × 1-inch pan. Combine first 4 ingredients in heavy saucepan and cook, stirring, just until sugar dissolves. Cook until candy thermometer registers 270° F. (syrup separates into hard brittle threads in very cold water). Remove from heat and gently stir in butter and vanilla. Pour into prepared pan and let stand. As syrup cools, fold edges of candy back over center every 15 or 20 minutes. When cool enough to handle, shape into a ball and pull and twist with buttered fingers until candy holds its shape and is white and shiny. Twist and pull into a long thin rope and cut into 1-inch lengths with buttered scissors. Cool thoroughly but do not refrigerate. Wrap each piece of taffy in waxed paper.

VARIATION

Peppermint, Wintergreen, or Cinnamon Taffy: Add a few drops of an appropriate food coloring (optional), omit vanilla, and flavor with oil of peppermint, wintergreen, or cinnamon.

VICTORIAN POPCORN BALLS
18 to 22 balls

A Victorian favorite, especially at Christmas-time, popcorn balls are now a children's party treat. For years a friend of mine has tucked homemade popcorn balls into Christmas packages before mailing. They were good "protectors" as well as tasty morsels.

    5 *quarts popped unsalted popcorn (free of "old maids")*

2½ *cups sugar*

 ¾ *cup light corn syrup*

 ½ *cup water*

 ⅔ *cup butter*

    2 *teaspoons salt*

 ⅛ *teaspoon cream of tartar*

    1 *teaspoon vanilla*

    Measure popcorn into large heavy pan and keep hot and crisp in very slow oven (250° F). Combine remaining ingredients, except vanilla, in heavy saucepan and cook until candy thermometer registers 295° to 300° F. (syrup separates into brittle threads in cold water). Remove from heat and carefully mix in vanilla. Pour syrup in a fine stream over popcorn, stirring with large buttered metal spoon to coat each kernel evenly. If possible, turn out onto clean buttered enamel- or formica-top table. Butter hands and *quickly* shape mixture into balls of desired size. Cool. Wrap each cold ball in small plastic bag and tie with red and green ribbon.

VARIATIONS

    Pastel Popcorn Balls: Tint syrup red or green with food coloring (optional) and, flavor syrup with peppermint extract instead of vanilla.

    Caramel-Flavored Popcorn Balls: Substitute 2½ cups light brown sugar, firmly packed, for granulated sugar and dark corn syrup for light syrup.

    Molasses Popcorn Balls: Substitute 1 cup light brown sugar, firmly packed, for 1 cup granulated sugar and light molasses for corn syrup. Omit vanilla.

    NOTE: *This recipe works better with two cooks and four hands.*

NEW ORLEANS PRALINES
30 to 36 pralines

According to legend, pralines were named for the French diplomat César du Plessis-Praslin, whose butler suggested that almonds be coated with sugar to prevent indigestion. Creole cooks adapted the idea, preparing a confection of native pecans and brown sugar.

    3 *cups sugar*

    1 *cup light cream*

 ¼ *teaspoon salt*

    2 *tablespoons butter*

    2 *teaspoons vanilla*

    2 *cups pecan halves*

    Combine 2 cups sugar, light cream, salt, and butter in large, heavy saucepan over low heat, stirring often. In a small, heavy saucepan melt remaining 1 cup sugar over low heat. Pour the melted sugar into hot sugar-cream mixture very slowly, stirring constantly. Cook until candy thermometer registers 236° F. (syrup forms a soft ball in cold water). Remove from heat and stir in vanilla and nuts. Beat or stir until mixture begins to thicken. Drop rounded teaspoonfuls onto aluminum foil or waxed paper. Allow to cool and set and remove from foil or paper.

OLD ENGLISH ALMOND TOFFEE

40 to 50 candies

> 2 *cups sugar*
> 1 *cup butter*
> ½ *cup half and half or cream*
> ¼ *cup light or dark corn syrup*
> ½ *teaspoon salt*
> 1½ *cups finely chopped toasted almonds*
> 2 *teaspoons vanilla*
> 1½ *(4-ounce) bars sweet baking chocolate or 6 (1-ounce) squares dipping chocolate, melted*

Butter a 13 × 9 × 2-inch baking pan thoroughly. Combine first 5 ingredients in large, heavy saucepan and bring to a gentle boil, stirring just until sugar dissolves. Cook, stirring often, until candy thermometer registers 280° F. (syrup separates into hard brittle threads in very cold water). Remove from heat and stir in 1 cup almonds. Return to heat and cook until thermometer registers 295° to 300° F. (syrup separates into brittle strings in cold water). Remove from heat and stir in vanilla. Pour at once into prepared pan, spreading evenly. Cool to lukewarm. Mark candy into serving pieces with buttered knife. Let stand until cold, then turn out onto baking sheet. Turn right side up, spread chocolate over candy, and sprinkle remaining ½ cup nuts evenly over top. Cool. Break or cut into serving pieces.

VARIATION

Pecan Toffee: Substitute chopped pecans for almonds.

CHOCOLATE CREAM CARAMELS

About 80 candies

Caramel candies are soft in texture and quite chewy. Various flavorings may be added, and they may be dipped in chocolate.

> 2 *cups sugar*
> 1 *cup half and half or light cream*
> 1 *cup butter*
> ¾ *cup light corn syrup*
> 3 *(1-ounce) squares unsweetened chocolate*
> ½ *teaspoon salt*
> ⅛ *teaspoon cream of tartar*
> 2 *teaspoons vanilla*

Butter a 9 × 9 × 2-inch pan. Combine first 7 ingredients in heavy saucepan and cook over low heat, stirring constantly, until sugar dissolves. Cook until candy thermometer registers 244° to 248° F. (syrup forms a firm ball in cold water). Remove from heat and stir in vanilla. Pour into prepared pan (do not scrape pan) and let stand until cool. Cut into ¾- or 1-inch squares. Turn out of pan onto a cold marble slab or baking sheet. Let stand to dry. Wrap each caramel in waxed paper.

VANILLA CREAM CARAMELS

About 2 pounds candy (80 pieces)

> 1 *cup light brown sugar, firmly packed*
> 1 *cup granulated sugar*
> ¼ *teaspoon salt*
> 2 *cups light corn syrup*
> ½ *cup butter*
> 1 *cup light cream or half and half*
> 1 *teaspoon vanilla*

Butter a 9 × 9 × 2-inch pan. Combine first 5 ingredients in large, heavy saucepan and cook until candy thermometer registers 245° F.

(syrup forms a firm ball in cold water). Stir in cream or half and half and continue cooking, stirring constantly, until mixture returns to the firm-ball stage (245° F.). Stirring is necessary, as the mixture scorches easily. Remove from heat and stir in vanilla. Pour at once into prepared pan. When cool, turn out onto aluminum foil and cut into ¾- to 1-inch squares. Wrap each caramel in waxed paper.

VARIATION

Vanilla Nut Caramels: Stir ½ to ¾ cup finely chopped black walnuts, pecans, or hickory nuts into caramel mixture with vanilla.

PEANUT BRITTLE

About 1½ pounds

A popular confection, especially at holiday time, this old recipe has a good crunchy peanut flavor. One tip: You must work fast.

1½ *cups sugar*
1 *cup light corn syrup*
⅓ *cup water*
¼ *teaspoon salt*
¼ *cup butter*
1½ *cups coarsely chopped salted peanuts*
1 *teaspoon baking soda (free of lumps)*
1 *teaspoon vanilla*

Butter 2 large baking sheets or 15 × 10 × 1-inch jelly-roll pans. Combine first 4 ingredients in heavy 3-quart saucepan and cook, stirring, until sugar melts. Cook until candy thermometer registers 270° to 280° F. (syrup separates into hard brittle threads in very cold water). Reduce heat, add butter and peanuts, and mix quickly. Continue cooking until syrup reaches the hard-crack stage (290° to 300° F.), syrup separates into brittle strings when dropped into cold water. Remove from heat and quickly stir in soda and vanilla. Pour at once into prepared pans, spreading very thin with buttered spatula. As the candy cools, stretch it as thin as possible. When cold, break into irregular serving pieces.

CHERRY NUT BRITTLE

About 1½ pounds

Brittles should be stored in airtight containers to retain freshness. If exposed to air, they often become sticky.

½ *cup* each *red and green candied cherry halves*
¾ *cup pecan halves*
¾ *cup whole blanched almonds*
¼ *cup walnut halves*
1¼ *cups sugar*
¾ *cup light corn syrup*
⅓ *cup water*
3 *tablespoons butter*
¼ *teaspoon salt*
Pinch of cream of tartar
1 *teaspoon vanilla or orange extract*

Butter a 15 × 10 × 1-inch jelly-roll pan or baking sheet. Mix together cherries and nuts and set aside. Combine sugar, syrup, water, butter, salt, and cream of tartar in heavy saucepan. Cook over moderate heat, stirring constantly, until sugar dissolves and candy thermometer registers 295° to 300° F. (syrup separates into brittle strings in cold water). Remove from heat and stir in vanilla or orange extract. Add fruit and nuts, stirring just until they are evenly coated with syrup. Turn mixture into prepared pan. Using 2 buttered forks, spread candy *quickly* and evenly into a thin layer or bite-sized pieces. Cool. Break into serving pieces if spread into a layer.

FUDGE

Fudge-making has been a popular pastime in the United States for almost 300 years. In bygone years many a cold winter's evening was spent concocting a delicious batch of hot fudge. Fudge is simpler and less time-consuming to prepare today, but still remains a favorite American confection.

DARK CHOCOLATE FUDGE
36 to 40 pieces

  1¼ *cups milk or half and half*

    4 *squares (ounces) unsweetened chocolate, broken into small pieces*

    3 *cups sugar*

  ¼ *cup light corn syrup*

  ½ *teaspoon salt*

  ¼ *cup butter*

    2 *teaspoons vanilla*

Butter a 9 × 9 × 2-inch pan. Cook milk and chocolate in heavy 3-quart saucepan, stirring constantly, until chocolate melts and mixture is smooth. Blend in sugar, syrup, and salt, stirring until sugar dissolves. Cook until candy thermometer registers 234° to 236° F. (syrup forms a soft ball in cold water). Remove from heat and add butter and vanilla. Set saucepan in cold water and cool to lukewarm (110° F.) without stirring. Beat vigorously until candy holds its shape and begins to lose its gloss. Pour at once into prepared pan and spread quickly into even layer. Cool and cut into squares.

VARIATIONS
Favorite Chocolate Fudge: Reduce chocolate to 2 squares (ounces).

Chocolate Nut Fudge: Stir 1 cup pecan halves or coarsely chopped English or black walnuts or hickory nuts into fudge with vanilla.

Marshmallow Fudge: Stir 1 cup miniature marshmallows into fudge with vanilla.

Christmas Fudge: Stir in ⅓ cup *each* red candied cherry halves and chopped candied pineapple and ½ cup pecan halves into fudge with vanilla.

Brown-Sugar Fudge: Substitute 3 cups light brown sugar, firmly packed, for granulated sugar and reduce vanilla to 1 teaspoon.

JEWELED WHITE SATIN FUDGE
50 to 60 pieces

    4 *cups sugar*

  ½ *cup light corn syrup*

  ½ *cup butter*

    1 *cup half and half or cream*

  ½ *cup water*

    1 *teaspoon salt*

  ½ *cup marshmallow cream*

    2 *teaspoons vanilla or 1 teaspoon orange extract or rum flavoring*

  ½ *cup* each *red and green candied cherry quarters*

  ½ *cup pecan halves*

Butter a 9 × 9 × 2-inch pan. Cook first 6 ingredients in heavy saucepan, stirring constantly, until sugar dissolves. Cook rapidly, stirring several times, until candy thermometer registers 238° F. (syrup forms a soft ball in cold water). Remove from heat. Set pan in cold water and cool to lukewarm (110° F.) without stirring. Add marshmallow cream and flavoring. Beat until mixture starts to stiffen. Stir in fruit and nuts and beat until mixture starts to lose its gloss. Spread in an even layer in prepared pan. Cool and cut into squares.

DIVINITY
About 40 candies

Divinity is a confection of the fudge family, though no one remembers who first made it or how it was named. Possibly someone exclaimed, "It's divine!" after the first bite.

2½ *cups sugar*

⅔ *cup light corn syrup*

½ *cup water*

2 *egg whites*

¼ *teaspoon salt*

½ *cup chopped pecans or walnuts*

¼ *cup each chopped red cherries, chopped green candied cherries, and candied pineapple*

1½ *teaspoons vanilla*

Candied cherry halves (optional)

Combine first 3 ingredients in heavy saucepan and cook slowly, stirring constantly, until syrup comes to a boil. Beat egg whites and salt until foamy. Pour 2 tablespoons of boiling syrup in a fine stream over egg whites, beating constantly. Cook remaining syrup to soft-ball stage (234° F.). Pour half the syrup in a fine stream into beaten egg whites, beating constantly. Cook remaining syrup to soft-crack stage (272° F.), or until syrup separates into hard brittle threads in very cold water. Pour syrup in a fine stream over egg-white mixture, beating constantly until beater leaves its impression in mixture. Quickly stir in remaining ingredients. Beat until mixture starts to lose its gloss. Drop heaping teaspoonfuls onto waxed paper, twirling spoon to form an attractive peak. If Divinity becomes too stiff to shape nicely, add a few drops of very hot water. Top each candy with a candied cherry half.

VARIATIONS

Cherry Coconut Divinity: Omit nuts and use ¾ cup flaked coconut and ¼ cup chopped candied cherries instead of the fruit specified. Top each candy with a candied cherry half.

Christmas Divinity: Substitute ¾ cup chopped mixed candied fruit for red and green cherries and pineapple.

Divinity Fudge Squares: Pour any of the above candies into a buttered 9 × 9 × 2-inch pan instead of spooning into individual pieces. Cool until firm and cut into squares. Yield: 25 to 36 pieces.

Maple-Nut Divinity: Substitute 2½ cups light brown sugar, firmly packed, for granulated and 1 teaspoon maple flavoring for vanilla. Omit fruit and increase nuts to ¾ cup.

Pecan Divinity: Omit candied cherries and pineapple and increase pecans to 1¼ cups. Top each piece of candy with a pecan half.

CANDIED ORANGE PEEL
About 1¼ pounds

This is easy to prepare—even kids can make it—and the eating is great.

6 *large thick-skinned oranges*

2 *cups sugar*

1 *cup water*

½ *cup light corn syrup*

⅛ *teaspoon salt*

Yellow food coloring (optional)

Additional sugar

Melted dipping or sweet baking chocolate (optional)

Remove the zest (thin outside peel) from oranges in quarters or sixths and cut into thin strips (¼ to ⅓ inch wide) with a sharp knife. Place in heavy saucepan and cover with cold water. Bring to a boil and simmer for 10 minutes. Drain and repeat process 4 times. Combine sugar, water, syrup, salt, and a few drops of coloring in another heavy saucepan, heat to a simmer, and add well-drained peel. Boil gently until syrup is thick and peel is translucent. Spread peel out on wire rack over jelly-roll pan, foil, or waxed paper to drain and cool. Roll strips of peel, a few at a time, in sugar and dip ends of cooled peel in melted chocolate. Let stand for 24 hours to dry. Store in airtight container.

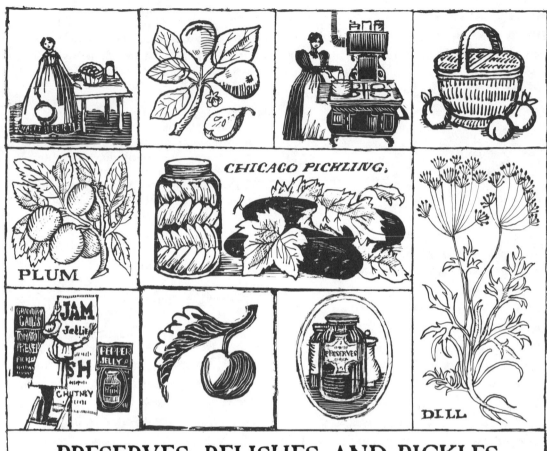

PRESERVES, RELISHES, AND PICKLES

PEACH JAM
About 8 ½-pint jars

- 3¾ *pounds ripe peaches (approximate)*
- 2 *(1-inch) squares lemon peel, cut into thin strips (no white)*
- 7 *cups sugar*
- 2 *tablespoons lemon juice*
- ¼ *teaspoon ground cloves*
- ¼ *teaspoon cinnamon*
- ¼ *teaspoon allspice*
- ½ *(6-ounce) bottle liquid pectin*

Peel, pit, and slice peaches. Whiz peaches, 1 cup at a time, in blender until finely chopped. Stop motor and stir down as necessary. Process lemon peel with first cup of peaches. Repeat as needed to obtain 4¼ cups chopped fruit.

Pour fruit into large saucepan. Stir in sugar, lemon juice, and spices. Quickly bring to full rolling boil, stirring constantly, until bubbles form over surface. Boil hard 1 minute, stirring constantly. Remove from heat and stir in pectin. Skim foam from surface, if necessary. Ladle into hot, sterilized jars to within ½ inch of top. Seal and process in Boiling-Water Bath for 5 minutes.

BOILING-WATER BATH

Processing is the name given to cooking covered jars in a covered bath of boiling water, with the water completely covering the jars. Adjust jar covers as manufacturer suggests and place filled jars on a rack in a kettle containing boiling water to a depth of one or two inches over tops of glass jars (do not pour boiling water directly over tops of glass jars). Cover the kettle and begin to count processing time specified in recipe. Add additional boiling water, if necessary, to keep jars covered. Remove jars immediately when processing time is over, tighten seals if necessary, and set upright on wire rack, a few inches apart, to cool.

SPICED BLUEBERRY JAM
About 4½ cups

- 3 *cups fully ripe blueberries, washed, drained, and mashed well (2¼ cups mashed)*
- 1 *tablespoon lemon juice*
- 2 *teaspoons grated lemon peel*
- 3½ *cups sugar*
- ¼ *teaspoon cinnamon*
- ¼ *teaspoon ground cloves*
- ½ *(6-ounce) bottle liquid fruit pectin*

Combine all ingredients, except pectin, in a large saucepan and mix thoroughly. Bring to a full rolling boil and boil hard for 1 minute, stirring constantly. Remove from heat and immediately stir in fruit pectin. Skim off foam with metal spoon. Stir and skim for 5 minutes, or until slightly cooled and fruit is not floating. Pour into sterilized jars and seal with hot paraffin.

RHUBARB-STRAWBERRY JAM
7 or 8 ½-pint jars

- 1 *pound red-stalked rhubarb*
- ¼ *cup water*
- 1½ *quarts fully ripe strawberries (about 2½ cups crushed)*
- 6½ *cups sugar*
- ½ *(6-ounce) bottle liquid pectin*

Wash rhubarb but do not peel and slice thin or chop. Combine rhubarb and water in saucepan, cover, and simmer until rhubarb is tender, about 1 minute. Makes 1 cup cooked. Wash and stem strawberries and crush.

Measure fruits into large kettle and stir in sugar. Bring to a full rolling boil with bubbles over entire surface and boil hard for 1 minute, stirring constantly. Remove from heat and stir in pectin. Skim. Ladle into hot, sterilized ½-pint jars, seal, and process in Boiling-Water Bath (see index) for 5 minutes.

FROZEN STRAWBERRY JAM

4½ pints

Frozen jams and jellies are newcomers, but they have caught on fast. Easy to prepare, they have a very fresh-fruit flavor and can be stored in a freezer for several months.

> 4 *cups (1 quart) fully ripe strawberries (2 cups crushed)*
> 4 *cups sugar*
> ¾ *cup water*
> 1 *package powdered fruit pectin*

Use only perfect, fully ripe berries. Crush berries or whiz in blender 1 cup at a time until finely chopped. Measure 2 cups crushed berries into bowl. Add sugar, blend thoroughly, and let stand for 10 minutes.

Combine water and pectin in saucepan, bring to a boil, and boil for 1 minute, stirring constantly. Mix into fruit and continue stirring for 3 minutes. Ladle at once into ½-pint glass or plastic freezer containers that have been scalded and drained. Cover and let stand at room temperature for 1 hour, then refrigerate until mixture jells, about 24 hours. Label, date, and freeze for up to 6 months.

VARIATION

Frozen Red Raspberry or Blackberry Jam: Use 6 cups (1½ quarts) washed, fresh, fully ripe red raspberries or blackberries and crush as needed to make 3 cups. Increase sugar to 5¼ cups. Yield: 6½ pints.

QUICK-MADE FROZEN STRAWBERRY JAM

4½ pints

> 2 *(10- or 12-ounce) packages frozen sliced and sweetened strawberries, partially defrosted and cut into 1-inch cubes*
> 3 *cups sugar*
> 1 *package powdered fruit pectin*
> 1 *cup cold water*

Whiz strawberries 1 cup at a time in blender until finely chopped. Pour into mixing bowl and stir in sugar. Let stand at room temperature for 20 to 25 minutes, stirring frequently.

Combine powdered pectin and water in saucepan, bring to a boil, and boil rapidly for 1 minute, stirring constantly. Remove from heat and add strawberry mixture, stirring constantly for 5 minutes. Pour into ½-pint glass or plastic freezer containers that have been scalded and drained. Cover and let stand at room temperature for 1 hour, then refrigerate until mixture jells, about 24 hours. Label, date, and freeze for up to 6 months.

GRAPE JELLY

8 or 9 ½-pint glasses

> 3½ *pounds ripe Concord grapes*
> 1 *cup water*
> 1 *package powdered pectin*
> 7 *cups sugar*

Pick over, wash, and stem grapes. Place in large, heavy saucepan and crush with potato masher. Add water and bring to a boil. Reduce heat and simmer for 10 minutes. Put fruit in damp jelly bag, hang it, and squeeze out juice (the clearest jelly comes from juice that drips through bag without squeezing). Let juice stand overnight in cool place in covered container. Strain through a double thickness of damp cheesecloth to remove tartrate crystals in jelly.

Measure 5 cups grape juice into large, heavy saucepan and stir in pectin. Place over high heat and bring to a full rolling boil, stirring constantly. Stir in sugar, bring to full rolling boil, and boil hard for 1 minute, stirring constantly. Remove from heat and skim off foam quickly. Pour into hot sterilized jelly glasses and seal at once with hot paraffin.

WINE JELLY

About 4 6-ounce jars

A favorite in the wine country of California, Wine Jelly can now easily be made by homemakers throughout the United States.

3 *cups sugar*

2 *cups Burgundy, sherry, claret, or favorite fruit wine*

½ *(6-ounce) bottle liquid pectin*

Combine sugar and wine in large saucepan. Cook until mixture is just below the boiling point, stirring constantly. Cook 5 minutes longer, stirring until sugar dissolves. *Do not boil*. Remove from heat and stir in pectin at once. Skim off foam, if necessary. Pour into hot sterilized jars and seal with hot paraffin.

SOUTHERN GREEN PEPPER JELLY

12 or 13 ½-pint jars

4 *large green peppers*

13 *small hot peppers*

⅓ *cup water*

5 *pounds sugar*

3 *cups white vinegar*

2 *(6-ounce) bottles pectin*

6 *to 8 drops green food coloring (optional)*

Wash the peppers, cut out the stems, and remove the seeds. Put green peppers, hot peppers, and water into blender and pureé. Dissolve sugar in vinegar in large saucepan. Add peppers, bring to the boiling point, and boil for 5 minutes. Remove from heat and skim top. Add pectin and coloring, stirring well. Pour into sterilized jars and seal.

BRANDIED SWEET CHERRIES

12 ½-pints

3 *pounds large Bing or sweet cherries, washed and pitted*

3 *pounds sugar*

Brandy

Combine cherries and sugar in large, heavy saucepan, cover, and let stand for 2 hours. Uncover, stir, and bring to a boil. Lower heat and cook slowly until cherries are barely tender, then remove from syrup.

Cook syrup until slightly thickened, then measure. Return syrup to pan, bring to a boil, and add cherries. Stir in ¼ cup brandy for each cup syrup. Ladle into hot sterilized ½-pint jars. Clean rims and seal.

CRIST'S CITRON PRESERVES

4 to 5 pints

Crist's Citron Preserves is an old Virginia recipe that has been handed down from generation to generation.

4 *pounds citron, cut in small pieces*

16 *cups (1 gallon) cold water*

1 *tablespoon salt*

4 *tablespoons sugar*

1 *lemon, thinly sliced*

1 *teaspoon ground ginger or cloves (or ½ teaspoon each)*

1 *teaspoon cinnamon*

Place citron in a 4-quart kettle and add 8 cups cold water and salt. Let stand for 1 hour, then drain thoroughly. Return to kettle and add remaining 8 cups cold water. Bring to a boil and boil for 10 minutes. Remove from heat and drain thoroughly, reserving 1 cup citron water for syrup. Add sugar, lemon, and spices to the reserved 1 cup citron water. Pour over citron and again bring to a boil. Lower heat and simmer until mixture is the consistency of honey. Pour into sterilized jars and seal.

GRANDMA GAUL'S TOMATO PRESERVES

8 cups

    5 *pounds fully ripe tomatoes, peeled and cored*

    4 *pounds sugar*

    2 *lemons, thinly sliced*

    ⅛ *teaspoon salt*

    3 *sticks cinnamon, broken*

    1 *tablespoon whole cloves*

Cut a slice from the top of each tomato, press tomato to drain juice and part of seeds, and discard juice and seeds. Chop tomatoes coarsely (makes about 9 cups chopped tomato). Mix together chopped tomato, sugar, lemon, and salt in very large heavy kettle or Dutch oven. Mix well. Tie spices in cheesecloth bag and add to tomato mixture. Bring to a boil, stirring constantly. Reduce heat to very low and cook, uncovered, stirring as needed, for 45 to 50 minutes, or until mixture thickens and threads from tip of spoon. Remove spice bag. Remove mixture from heat and stir and skim for 5 minutes or until slightly cooled. Seal with paraffin in ½-pint hot sterilized jars.

FINE SPICES

SPICY FRESH ITALIAN OR PRUNE PLUM CONSERVE

9 or 10 ½-pint jars

    4 *cups coarsely chopped or ground unpeeled fresh Italian or prune plums*

    6 *cups sugar*

    ¾ *teaspoon cinnamon*

    ¾ *teaspoon ground cloves*

    ½ *teaspoon allspice*

    ½ *cup vinegar or lemon juice*

    ½ *(6-ounce) bottle liquid pectin*

Combine all the ingredients, except pectin, in large, heavy saucepan and quickly bring to a rolling boil, stirring often. Boil hard for 1 minute, stirring constantly. Remove from heat and immediately stir in pectin. Stir and skim at frequent intervals for 5 minutes. Seal in hot sterilized ½-pint jars.

PLUM

ORANGE-PLUM CONSERVE

7 or 8 ½-pint jars

    1 *large orange*

    1 *lemon*

    5 *cups sugar*

    3 *pounds (36 or 40) fresh Italian or prune plums, washed, pitted, and quartered*

    ½ *teaspoon allspice*

    ½ *teaspoon ground cloves*

    1 *cup coarsely chopped pecans*

Cut orange and lemon in half and extract juice. Remove as much white pulp from peel as possible and cut peel into very thin strips, 1 inch long. Pour orange and lemon juices and sugar over plums and mix. Let stand for 2 hours.

Combine all ingredients except nuts in large saucepan, blending thoroughly. Cook over low heat, stirring often, until thickened. Add warmed pecans during last few minutes of cooking. Ladle into hot sterilized jars and seal.

AMBER CITRUS MARMALADE
3 to 4 ½-pint jars

Peel of ½ grapefruit (¾ cup)
Peel of 1 orange (¾ cup)
Peel of 1 lemon (⅓ cup)
1 quart cold water
Pulp of 1 grapefruit
Pulp of 4 medium-sized oranges
⅓ cup lemon juice
2 cups boiling water
3 cups sugar

Cut peels into very thin strips, 1 inch long, and combine with water in saucepan. Simmer, covered, until peel is tender, about 30 minutes, and drain. Remove seeds and white membrane from peeled fruit and dice.

To prepare marmalade, combine cooked peel, diced fruit, lemon juice, and boiling water. Add sugar and blend thoroughly. Quickly bring to a boil and cook until mixture is thick and reaches 220° F. on a candy or jelly thermometer, about 20 minutes. Remove from heat, skim, and ladle into hot sterilized ½-pint jars, filling jars to within ½ inch from top. Seal and process in Boiling-Water Bath (see index) for 5 minutes.

HOMEMADE MINCEMEAT
About 5½ quarts

Mincemeat was created as a means of preserving meat and was served as a main dish. As time passed, the amount of meat in the mincemeat decreased and the amount of fruit increased. Fruit mincemeat used as a filling for a dessert pie is an American invention.

In old England, a superstition arose whereby eating a Christmas pie on each day between Christmas and Twelfth Night would bring luck for the coming year. In Henry VIII's time, these pies were baked in enormous rectangles to represent the Christ Child's manger. The spices used in the preparation represented the gifts of the Wise Men. During Puritan times, such extravagant Christmas pies were denounced as symbols of "popery." Those who did prepare them used smaller round pans and changed the name to "minc'd pyes."

4 pounds peeled, cored, and quartered apples (about 5 cups)
1½ pounds boiled lean beef, cut in chunks
½ pound beef suet, cut in chunks
1 pound (3 cups) seedless raisins
1 pound (3 cups) golden raisins
½ pound candied citron, cut in strips
½ pound candied lemon peel, cut in strips
½ pound candied orange peel, cut in strips
¾ pound (2½ cups) currants
2 cups apple cider or apple juice
1½ cups brandy, apple juice, cider, or beef stock
¾ cup cider or red wine vinegar
½ cup light molasses
⅓ cup lemon or orange juice
¼ cup grated lemon or orange peel
3 cups light brown sugar, firmly packed
1 cup granulated sugar
3 tablespoons cinnamon
1 tablespoon allspice
1 tablespoon nutmeg
1 tablespoon ground cloves
2 teaspoons salt

Put first 8 ingredients through the coarse blade of a food chopper. Transfer to a large mixing bowl or pan. Mix in currants, liquids, and grated peel. Combine sugar, spices, and salt, add to fruit, and mix thoroughly. Pack into freezer containers and freeze until ready to use.

NOTE: *Do not freeze for more than two months.*

SHENANDOAH EASY APPLE BUTTER

11 pints

Apple butter is as American as apple pie.

    6 *pounds tart cooking apples, peeled, cored, and sliced (about 5 quarts sliced)*

    4 *cups sweet cider or water*

    5 *cups sugar*

1½ *to 2 teaspoons cinnamon*

    ½ *to 1 teaspoon ground cloves*

    ½ *to 1 teaspoon allspice*

Combine apples and cider or water in large, heavy Dutch oven or saucepan and simmer gently, covered, just until apples are tender. Press apples through sieve or food mill or whiz in blender, a small amount at a time, just until smooth. Turn apple mixture into large, heavy roasting pan or saucepan. Combine sugar and spices and stir into apples. Bring to a boil, stirring occasionally. Place, uncovered, in slow oven (325° F.) for about 1½ hours, or until apple butter is a rich amber color and very thick. Stir every 15 to 20 minutes. Pour into hot sterilized ½-pint or pint canning jars, leaving ¼-inch head space. Seal and process in Boiling-Water Bath (see index) for 10 minutes.

NOTE: *If the apples used fail to produce an amber-colored apple butter, stir in just a few drops of food coloring, if desired.*

PICKLED CRAB APPLES

3 to 4 pints

    2 *quarts firm ripe crab apples*

    4 *(1-inch) pieces stick cinnamon*

    2 *teaspoons whole cloves*

1½ *teaspoons whole allspice*

    4 *cups sugar*

    2 *cups cider vinegar*

1½ *cups water*

Wash apples and leave 1 inch of stems intact. Tie spices in a cheesecloth bag. Combine sugar, vinegar, and water in large, heavy saucepan and bring to a boil, stirring until sugar is dissolved. Add spice bag and boil for 5 minutes.

Add apples to the pan, 1 layer at a time, and heat very slowly to keep skins from breaking. Simmer gently until apples are just tender, pushing apples under surface of syrup frequently (skins on about half will break). Drain spice bag and remove from syrup. Carefully transfer apples to hot sterilized pint jars. Fill jars with syrup to within ½ inch of top. Seal and process in Boiling-Water Bath (see index) for 15 minutes.

NOTE: *Early-season crab apples are best for this recipe.*

SPICED WINTER PEARS

6 to 8 servings

    3 *cups water*

    2 *cups sugar*

    1 *cup light corn syrup*

    2 *tablespoons lemon or orange juice*

    1 *teaspoon shredded lemon or orange peel*

    6 *whole cloves*

    2 *cinnamon sticks*

    ¼ *teaspoon salt*

    6 *or 8 slightly underripe winter pears (Bosc or Anjou)*

Whipped cream (optional)

Combine first 8 ingredients in a large saucepan or Dutch oven and bring syrup to a boil. While syrup is heating, peel pears, leaving stems on. Drop pears in cold water to which a small amount of additional lemon juice is added to keep pears from darkening. Add pears to syrup, cover, and maintain syrup at a gentle boil so pears will turn or roll in syrup.

Remove pears from syrup when tender, 20 to 25 minutes. Let pears stand upright while cooling, basting often with syrup. Serve plain or topped with whipped cream.

SAUERKRAUT RELISH
6 to 8 servings

Sauerkraut is typically German, and a salad or relish is one of the "seven sours and seven sweets" often served in Pennsylvania Dutch or German homes.

   1 *(1-pound 11-ounce) can sauerkraut*
   1 *cup diced green pepper*
   1 *cup diced celery*
   ¾ *cup chopped onion*
   ¼ *cup diced pimiento*
1¼ *cups sugar*
   ½ *cup vinegar*
   ¼ *cup water*
   1 *teaspoon salt*

Drain sauerkraut, rinse with cold water, and drain thoroughly. Combine sauerkraut and next 4 ingredients in bowl. Combine remaining ingredients, stirring to dissolve sugar. Pour over vegetables and mix. Cover and chill for 4 hours or overnight.

PEPPER RELISH
5 to 6 ½-pint jars

First cousin of the famous Philadelphia pepper relish, a Pennsylvania Dutch creation, this provides a tangy accompaniment to meats.

   1 *tablespoon mixed pickling spices (optional)*
   6 *medium-sized red sweet peppers, finely chopped (1 pint)*
   6 *medium-sized green peppers, finely chopped (1 pint)*
   4 *cups finely chopped onions*
   4 *cups vinegar*
   1 *cup sugar*
   4 *teaspoons salt*

Tie pickling spices in a cheesecloth bag. Combine the ingredients in large kettle and bring to a boil. Cook 45 minutes, or until slightly thickened, stirring. Remove spice bag.

Pack boiling hot relish into hot sterilized ½-pint jars, filling to within ½ inch of top. Adjust lids. Seal and process in Boiling-Water Bath (see index) for 5 minutes after water returns to boiling point.

COUNTRY CORN RELISH
1½ quarts

   1 *tablespoon cornstarch*
   1 *teaspoon turmeric*
   1 *cup plus 1 tablespoon vinegar*
   2 *green peppers, seeded and diced*
   2 *sweet red peppers, seeded and diced*
   2 *large tomatoes, peeled and diced*
   1 *large cucumber, peeled and diced*
   ½ *pound white onions, diced*
   2 *ears fresh corn, cut from cob*
   4 *stalks celery, diced*
1¼ *cups sugar*
   ¼ *teaspoon mustard seed*

In large kettle or pot, blend cornstarch and turmeric with small amount of vinegar. Add remaining vinegar and mix in all the other ingredients. Bring to a boil, then reduce heat and simmer, uncovered, for 50 to 60 minutes, or until thick. Pour into hot sterilized jars and seal.

NOTE: *Relish may also be cooled and poured into refrigerator or freezer containers. Refrigerate for immediate use or freeze for future serving.*

BREAD AND BUTTER PICKLES
6 to 8 pints

  30 *medium cucumbers, unpeeled*
  10 *to 12 medium onions, peeled*
  ½ *cup salt*
  5 *cups white vinegar*
  4 *cups sugar*
  2 *tablespoons celery seed*
  2 *tablespoons ginger*
  2 *tablespoons white mustard seed*
  1 *tablespoon turmeric*

Slice cucumbers and onions thinly. Place in a glass bowl and sprinkle with salt. Let stand for 1 hour, then drain. Combine remaining ingredients in large kettle, bring to a boil and boil for 10 minutes. Add cucumbers and onions and return to a boil. Spoon into sterilized pint jars and seal. Cool.

HOMEMADE DILL PICKLES
7 quarts

  17 *to 18 pounds cucumbers, 3 to 5 inches long*
  2 *to 3 gallons (8 to 12 quarts) water combined with 1 ½ to 2 ¼ cups salt (5% brine)*
  6 *cups vinegar*
  ¾ *cup salt*
  ¼ *cup sugar*
  9 *cups (2 ¼ quarts) water*
  2 *tablespoons whole mixed pickling spices*
  14 *teaspoons whole mustard seed*
  7 *to 14 garlic cloves (optional)*
  21 *heads fresh or dried dill or 7 tablespoons dill seed*

Scrub cucumbers thoroughly, rinse, and drain. Cover pickles with 5% brine, let stand overnight, and then drain. Combine vinegar, ¾ cup salt, sugar, and 9 cups water in large saucepan. Tie pickling spices in cheesecloth and add to vinegar mixture. Bring to a boil.

Pack cucumbers in 7 hot sterilized quart jars. To each jar add 2 teaspoons mustard seed, 1 or 2 cloves of garlic, 3 heads of dill or 1 tablespoon dill seed. Add boiling liquid to within ½ inch of top of jar. Seal and process in Boiling-Water Bath (see index) for 20 minutes.

NOTE: *The proportion of brine is ¾ cup salt for each gallon (4 quarts) of water.*

DILLED GREEN BEANS
7 pints

  4 *pounds whole green beans*
  5 *cups vinegar*
  5 *cups water*
  ½ *cup salt*
  1¾ *teaspoons crushed hot red pepper*
  3½ *teaspoons whole mustard seed*
  3½ *teaspoons dill seed*
  7 *small cloves garlic*

Wash beans thoroughly and drain. Cut into lengths to fit pint jars. Combine vinegar, water, and salt and bring to a boil. Pack beans in 7 hot sterilized pint jars. Add to each jar ¼ teaspoon red pepper, ½ teaspoon mustard seed, ½ teaspoon dill seed, and 1 clove garlic. Pour in boiling liquid, filling jars to within ½ inch of top. Seal and process in Boiling-Water Bath (see index) for 5 minutes after water comes to a boil.

FATHER'S FAVORITE BEET RELISH

1⅔ cups

Beet relish is delicious served with beef or pork roast, corned beef, ham or cold cuts.

    3   *tablespoons cider or tarragon vinegar*
    2   *tablespoons prepared horseradish*
    2   *tablespoons sugar*
    2   *teaspoons finely chopped onion*
    ½   *teaspoon salt*
        Dash of pepper
    1   *(1-pound) jar sliced canned beets,
        drained and coarsely ground or finely
        chopped (1⅔ cups)*

Blend together first 6 ingredients. Add to beets and mix thoroughly. Pack into a covered container and refrigerate for 1 to 2 days.

TOMATO TART

7 pints

Delicious as an accompaniment to turkey or ham, Tomato Tart is an old Scottish recipe that has been given a Southern accent.

    7   *pounds ripe tomatoes, peeled and finely
        chopped*
    7   *large apples, peeled and finely chopped*
    2   *large onions, finely chopped*
    1   *pint cider vinegar*
    3   *pounds brown sugar*
    1   *tablespoon salt*
    1   *teaspoon red pepper*
    2   *ounces whole mixed pickling spices, tied
        in cheesecloth*

Combine all ingredients in 4-quart kettle and bring to a boil. Reduce heat and simmer for 1½ to 2 hours, or until slightly thickened. Remove spice bag. Pour into sterilized jars and seal.

FARM-STYLE CHILI SAUCE

8 ½-pint jars

Commercial chili sauce is available throughout the United States today, but a good homemade chili sauce still tastes the best.

    5   *pounds ripe tomatoes, peeled, cored, and
        cut into small wedges*
    1½ *medium-sized onions, halved and sliced*
    1½ *medium-sized green peppers, cleaned
        and cut into 1-inch squares*
    2   *teaspoons whole cloves*
    1   *teaspoon whole allspice*
    1   *teaspoon mustard seed*
    1   *teaspoon celery seed*
    2   *cinnamon sticks, broken*
    1¼ *cups cider vinegar*
    1¼ *cups sugar*
    3   *teaspoons salt*
    1   *teaspoon paprika*
    ¼   *teaspoon white pepper*
    2   *dashes hot pepper sauce*

Coarsely chop tomatoes, onions, and green pepper in blender, a small amount at a time, and turn into a large saucepan or Dutch oven. Bring to boil, stirring constantly. Cook over low heat about 30 minutes, stirring occasionally.

Transfer to a slow oven (325° F.) and cook for 1½ hours, stirring several times. Tie whole spices and seeds in cheesecloth bag and add to tomato mixture. Stir in vinegar, sugar, salt, paprika, white pepper, and hot pepper sauce. Return to oven and continue cooking, uncovered, for about 1½ hours, or until mixture thickens or is cooked down to about one-third the original volume. Remove spice bag. Ladle into sterilized jars and seal.

NOTE: *Ground spices, ½ teaspoon each ground cloves and mustard and ¾ teaspoon each ground allspice and cinnamon, may be substituted for whole cloves and allspice, seeds, and cinnamon sticks. Add to vinegar mixture.*

GINGERY CHUTNEY

6 pints

>   12 *bananas, peeled and diced*
>   2 *pounds white onions, peeled and finely grated*
>   1 *pound dates, peeled and chopped*
>   2 *cups vinegar*
>   2 *cups molasses*
>   ½ *pound crystallized ginger, chopped*
>   1 *tablespoon salt*
>   2 *to 3 teaspoons curry powder*
>   ⅛ *to ¼ teaspoon ground ginger*

Combine bananas, onions, dates, and vinegar in 4-quart saucepan. Simmer for 20 minutes. Blend in remaining ingredients. Cook over low heat for 30 minutes. Spoon into 6 sterilized pint jars and seal.

MARTHA'S WATERMELON-RIND PICKLES

4 to 5 pints

>   3 *quarts prepared watermelon rind (6 to 8 pounds watermelon rind)*
>   3 *quarts plus 3 cups water*
>   ¾ *cup salt*
>   2 *quarts ice cubes*
>   48 *(about 1 tablespoon) whole cloves*
>   ½ *tablespoon whole allspice*
>   6 *(1-inch) pieces stick cinnamon*
>   9 *cups sugar*
>   3 *cups cider or white vinegar*
>   1 *lemon, thinly sliced, with seeds removed*

To prepare the rind, cut away all of the outside green and pink edges from melon and cut into 1-inch squares or fancy shapes. Measure and place in large ceramic or glass bowl. Combine 3 quarts water and salt, stirring to dissolve salt, pour over watermelon rind, and spread ice cubes over top. Let stand for 5 or 6 hours, drain, and rinse in cold water. Place in large kettle, cover with cold water, and cook just until tender, about 10 minutes (do not overcook). Drain.

Tie whole spices in cheesecloth bag and combine with sugar, vinegar, and 3 cups water. Bring to a boil and boil 5 minutes, stirring to dissolve sugar. Pour over watermelon and lemon slices, cover, and let stand overnight. Heat watermelon in syrup until boiling and cook until rind is translucent, about 10 minutes.

Pack hot pickles loosely into hot sterilized pint jars. To each jar add 1 piece of stick cinnamon from spice bag. Cover with boiling syrup to within ½ inch of top. Seal and process in Boiling-Water Bath (see index) for 5 minutes after water returns to a boil.

PICKLED PEACHES

7 pints

>   6 *cups sugar*
>   4 *cups cider vinegar*
>   7 *(1-inch) pieces stick cinnamon*
>   1 *tablespoon whole cloves*
>   8 *pounds firm whole peaches*

Combine first 4 ingredients in large, heavy saucepan. Bring to a boil and simmer gently for 15 to 20 minutes. Wash peaches and dip each in boiling water for 1 minute. Quickly rinse in cold water and peel. To prevent discoloring, drop peaches in salty cold-water mixture (to 1 gallon of cold water add 2 tablespoons each salt and vinegar). Add enough drained peaches to boiling syrup to fill 2 to 4 pints at a time. Cook peaches just until tender, 6 to 8 minutes, depending on size. Transfer peaches to hot sterilized pint jars. Add 1 piece of cinnamon and 2 or 3 whole cloves to each jar. Fill jar with boiling syrup to within ½ inch of top. Wipe off rims of jars and seal. Process in Boiling-Water Bath (see index) for 20 minutes.

POTABLES

TEA POT

100% PURE SPRING WATER

HOPS

CAFÉ BRÛLOT

4 to 6 servings

An Acadian specialty, Café Brûlot is strong black coffee laced with brandy and spices and served flaming.

6 *lumps sugar*
1 *cup brandy*
4 *cups (1 quart) very strong hot coffee*
6 *whole cloves*
1 *(2- to 3-inch) stick cinnamon*
Vanilla bean (1-inch)
3 *(½-inch) squares orange peel*

Soak 1 lump sugar in brandy, remove, and reserve. Add remaining 5 lumps sugar to brandy. Pour coffee into chafing dish over direct heat. Stir in cloves, cinnamon, vanilla bean, and orange peel. Add brandy. Place reserved brandy-soaked lump of sugar on serving ladle and ignite. Add flaming cube of sugar to Café Brûlot and serve at once in demitasse cups.

VIENNESE COFFEE

6 servings

¾ *cup cream*
4 *teaspoons confectioners' sugar*
¾ *teaspoon vanilla*
6 *(4-inch) cinnamon sticks*
5 *cups extra-strong hot coffee*
½ *teaspoon grated orange peel*

Combine first 3 ingredients in bowl and beat until stiff. Place a cinnamon stick in each cup and fill with coffee. Spoon whipped cream on top and garnish with orange peel. Serve at once.

IRISH COFFEE

6 servings

I tasted my first and my most memorable Irish Coffee in my favorite city, San Francisco, while dining at the Buena Vista restaurant, a Victorian delight dating back to the latter part of the nineteenth century.

6 *teaspoons sugar*
4 *to 6 cups strong hot coffee**
6 *(1½-ounce) jiggers Irish whisky*
Softly whipped cream

Warm glasses (goblets, cups, or mugs). Hold bowl of metal spoon near bottom of serving glass, pour hot water into spoon and then into glass. Empty glass and repeat. Add 1 teaspoon sugar to each glass. Fill glasses one-fourth full with coffee. Stir until sugar dissolves. Add a jigger of whisky to each glass and fill glass to within 1 inch of top with coffee. Top with softly whipped cream. Do not stir. Serve at once.

*Depending on size of goblet, cup, or mug.

MEXICAN CHOCOLATE

4 to 6 servings

¼ *cup sugar*
¼ *cup unsweetened cocoa*
½ *teaspoon cinnamon*
Pinch of salt
4 *cups milk*
¼ *cup half and half*
½ *teaspoon vanilla*

Mix together first 4 ingredients. Heat 1 cup milk and add to dry ingredients, beating with electric or rotary beater until smooth. Add remaining milk, heat, and add half and half and vanilla. Heat and beat until frothy.

MOTHER'S BEST SWEDISH COFFEE

10 6-ounce cups

  1 *egg, slightly beaten*
  1 *eggshell*
 20 *level tablespoons coffee*
 10 *coffee cups (6 ounces each) cold water*

Combine egg, eggshell, and coffee together in bowl and mix well. Put mixture in center of large cheesecloth bag and secure tightly. Pour water into 10- to 12-cup coffeepot. Add coffee bag, cover, and brew over low heat for 5 to 8 minutes. Remove coffee bag and keep coffee hot over low heat until serving time.

This coffee may also be made in an electric percolator by using a coffee filter in the basket. Place the filter in the basket and add the coffee-egg mixture. Place the brewing dial on strong. Brew as directed by manufacturer. If coffee is too mild, pour 1 cup of freshly brewed coffee over grounds several times until desired strength is achieved.

NOTE: *The Pan American Coffee Bureau recommends 2 level tablespoonfuls of coffee for 6 ounces of water. Decrease to 1 tablespoon per 6 ounces water for a milder brew.*

SPICED CIDER

8 punch-cup servings

New Englanders have always been partial to their apple cider. Many Colonists, including women and children, would start their day with a mug of cider—not the sweet, bland fruit juice but the hard stuff that varied in strength from mild to very strong.

  4 *cups (1 quart) apple cider*
 ¼ *cup brown sugar, firmly packed*
  8 *whole cloves*
  4 *whole allspice*
  2 *(3-inch) sticks cinnamon*
Dash of salt
Thin lemon slices

Combine first 6 ingredients in heavy saucepan and bring to a boil, stirring until sugar is dissolved. Simmer for 5 minutes. Cool. Cover and refrigerate for several hours, then strain. Serve cold or reheat. Garnish each mug with a lemon slice.

HOT RUM CIDER

4 servings

  2 *cups apple cider*
  4 *teaspoons light brown sugar*
  2 *tablespoons butter*
 ½ *cup light rum*
  4 *(4-inch) sticks cinnamon*

Combine first 3 ingredients in heavy saucepan and heat but do not boil. Pour 2 tablespoons rum into each warmed cup and fill with hot cider mixture. Add a cinnamon stick to each cup as a stirrer.

HOT MULLED PORT

12 to 15 punch-cup servings

  2 *cups water*
  1 *tablespoon brown sugar*
  2 *teaspoons grated lemon peel*
  2 *(2- or 3-inch) sticks cinnamon, broken into ½-inch lengths*
  8 *whole cloves*
 ¼ *teaspoon ground ginger*
  1 *cup orange juice*
 ½ *cup lemon juice*
  1 *(⁴/₅-quart) bottle port*

Combine first 6 ingredients in saucepan and bring to a boil. Cover, remove from heat, and let stand for 30 minutes, then strain. Strain orange and lemon juices into spice mixture. Stir in port and heat but do not boil. Serve steaming hot in mugs.

MULLED WINE PUNCH

9 to 12 servings

Mulled Wine Punch is served at the annual Victorian Christmas exhibit at the Wilton Heritage Museum in the Sloan-Raymond-Fitch House in Wilton, Connecticut.

⅓ *cup sugar*

½ *cup water*

1½ *(2- or 3-inch) sticks cinnamon*

18 *whole cloves*

2 *cups unsweetened pineapple juice*

1 *cup strained orange juice*

3½ *cups Burgundy or claret wine*

1 *lemon, thinly sliced*

Heat first 4 ingredients in saucepan for 5 minutes and strain. Add fruit juices and heat slowly.. Add wine and heat but do not boil. Ladle into small mugs or punch cups and top each with a lemon slice.

TOM AND JERRY

6 8-ounce servings

3 *eggs, separated*

Grated nutmeg

½ *cup confectioners' sugar*

½ *cup Jamaican rum*

¾ *cup brandy or bourbon whisky*

Hot milk or boiling water

Beat egg yolks until thick and lemon-colored. Add ½ teaspoon nutmeg and ¼ cup sugar gradually, beating constantly until very thick. Beat egg whites until frothy. Gradually add remaining ¼ cup sugar and continue beating until stiff. Fold egg whites into egg-yolk mixture. Stir in rum, cover, and refrigerate for several hours.

To serve, turn egg mixture into small punch bowl. Spoon an equal amount of mixture into each warmed mug. Add 3 tablespoons of brandy or bourbon and fill mug with hot milk or boiling water. Stir and sprinkle with nutmeg.

CHAMPAGNE PUNCH

About 30 punch-cup servings

2 *(6-ounce) cans frozen lemonade concentrate*

Ice water

¼ *cup cognac*

¼ *cup Cointreau*

1 *tray ice cubes*

1 *(⁴/₅-quart) bottle champagne, chilled*

1 *pint fresh strawberries, washed, hulled, and halved lengthwise*

In large chilled punch bowl, combine lemonade and ice water as directed on can label. Add cognac and Cointreau and mix thoroughly. Just before serving, add ice cubes and champagne and float strawberries on top.

EGGNOGS

Rich eggnogs were served in the Colonial South at Christmas and New Year's. An English drink, eggnog was originally made with ale (the word nog *defines a strong ale). It has been Americanized to include bourbon, rum, brandy, or cider in place of the nog.*

GEORGE WASHINGTON'S CHRISTMAS NOG
About 4 quarts

> 2 *cups brandy*
> 1 *cup rye whisky*
> ½ *cup Jamaican rum*
> ½ *cup dry sherry*
> 12 *eggs, separated*
> ¾ *cup sugar*
> 4 *cups milk*
> 4 *cups half and half or cream*

Combine first 4 ingredients. Beat egg yolks, add sugar gradually, and beat until light and lemon-colored. Add 1 cup liquor mixture, a drop at a time, beating slowly. Add remaining liquor gradually, beating slowly. Stir in milk and half and half or cream. Beat egg whites until they form soft peaks and fold into egg-yolk mixture. Chill.

PLANTATION EGGNOG
15 4-ounce servings

> 6 *eggs, separated*
> ⅔ *cup superfine sugar*
> 1¼ *cups bourbon whisky*
> ⅓ *cup cognac*
> 1¼ *cups half and half*
> 2 *cups heavy cream*
> *Grated nutmeg*

Beat yolks until light and lemon-colored. Add sugar gradually, beating constantly, until thick and fluffy. Stir in bourbon, cognac, and half and half. Chill for several hours, or until very cold. Beat egg whites until they form stiff peaks. Whip cream in large bowl. Fold egg whites and whipped cream into yolk mixture and pour into a large punch bowl. Sprinkle with grated nutmeg. Serve in punch cups.

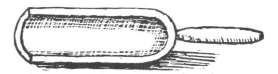

SYLLABUB
12 to 16 servings

Related to eggnog but made with wine instead of hard liquor, Syllabub is traditionally served at Christmas in England. Its name is derived from the wine that came from Sillery in the Champagne region of France and "bub," an Elizabethan slang term for a bubbly drink. Anne Boleyn may have referred to it as "silly bubbles." The drink was supposed to have been served with a great froth.

> *Peel of 1 lemon*
> ⅓ *cup lemon juice*
> 1½ *cups sweet white wine*
> 1½ *cups Madeira*
> 1¼ *cups superfine sugar (or to taste)*
> ¼ *teaspoon grated nutmeg or mace*
> 4 *cups (1 quart) chilled cream*

Wash lemon and peel off outer rind in a spiral. Combine peel and next 5 ingredients in bowl, stirring until sugar is dissolved. Cover and chill for several hours. Remove lemon peel. At serving time, beat cream until it forms soft peaks. Turn into large shallow serving bowl. Gradually whisk in wine mixture. When top of bowl is covered with froth, skim off and spoon·froth into tall serving glasses. Continue beating and skimming off froth. Serve with fruit or pound cake, cookies, or salted nuts.

WASSAIL BOWL (Vodka)

18 4-ounce servings

Whole cloves

3 *small oranges, washed and dried*

2 *quarts (8 cups) apple juice*

¼ *cup lemon juice*

5 *(2-inch) pieces cinnamon sticks*

1 *cup vodka*

¼ *cup brandy*

Insert cloves ½ inch apart in unpeeled oranges. Place in shallow pan and bake, uncovered, in moderate oven (350° F.) for 25 minutes. Heat apple juice to a simmer and stir in lemon juice, cinnamon sticks, and oranges. Cover and cook over very low heat for 30 minutes. Remove from heat and gently stir in vodka and brandy. Pour into punch bowl or large chafing dish over hot-water bath. Serve warm.

WASSAIL BOWL

12 4-ounce servings

6 *lady apples or small red apples*

3 *tablespoons water*

2 *whole cloves*

2 *whole allspice*

2 *cardamom seeds, coarsely broken*

1 *(3-inch) stick cinnamon, broken into ½-inch pieces*

1 *(28-ounce) bottle ginger ale*

½ *teaspoon ground nutmeg*

1 *cup sugar*

2 *cups dry sherry*

3 *eggs, separated*

Place apples in a shallow baking pan, add water, and cover with aluminum foil. Bake in moderate oven (350° F.) for 15 minutes, or until appleas are tender but hold their shape. Remove apples from the pan carefully and reserve.

Tie whole spices in a small double-thick cheesecloth bag. Combine half the ginger ale, nutmeg, and spice bag in saucepan, and simmer gently for 10 minutes. Remove the spice bag. Stir in remaining ginger ale, sugar, and sherry. Heat slowly, but do not boil. Beat egg whites until they form stiff peaks. Beat egg yolks in separate bowl and fold in whites. Slowly whisk or stir in hot ginger-ale mixture until smooth. Pour mixture into large punch bowl carefully and float apples on top. Serve in warmed mugs or punch cups.

NOTE: *Washed and polished fresh apples are a bit more attractive and may be substituted for cooked ones, if preferred.*

MARBELLA SANGRIA

12 to 15 4-ounce servings

Sangria, the fruity wine punch traditionally served in Spain and Mexico, is a specialty of the Meson del Garbanza in Marbella, Spain, owned by Edward Saxe.

1 ⁴/₅ *quart red Burgundy wine*

3 *ounces cognac*

2 *ounces banana liqueur*

2 *ounces Triple Sec*

2 *ounces light rum*

2 *ounces peach or pineapple brandy*

1 *lime, thinly sliced*

1 *orange, thinly sliced*

1 *lemon, thinly sliced*

1 *apple, diced*

1 *banana, peeled and diced*

12 *fresh strawberries, halved*

½ *fresh pineapple, cut in chunks*

13 *to 20 ounces club soda (½ to ¾ large bottle)*

Combine wine and liqueurs in a 2½- to 3-quart pitcher. Add fruit and chill for 1 hour to blend flavors. Add soda to taste and ice just before serving. Spoon a small amount of fruit into each serving glass and pour in Sangria.

KAHLUA
About 10 servings

Here is a home-brew recipe for the popular Mexican coffee liqueur, Kahlua.

    3 *cups water*
    4 *cups sugar*
    ¾ *cup freeze-dried coffee*
    1 *quart (4 cups) 100-proof vodka*
    1½ *vanilla beans*

Bring water to boiling point. Remove from heat and add sugar and coffee, stirring until dissolved. Cool completely. Add vodka. Use 3 sterile screw-top wine bottles. Drop ½ vanilla bean into each bottle, then add coffee–vodka mixture. Store for 3 weeks in cool, dark place, turning bottles periodically.

VARIATION
Kahlua Ice: Pour 1 tablespoon Kahlua into blender container. Add ¼ cup crushed ice and 1 scoop French vanilla ice cream. Cover and whiz. Serve at once or freeze.

ROSTAFINSKI'S POLISH TANGERINE LIQUEUR
A Rostafinski family recipe of long standing, tangerine liqueur becomes more delicious as it ages.

    15 *tangerines, unpeeled*
    2 *quarts grain alcohol*
    4 *pounds sugar*
    1 *quart water*

Place tangerines in large crock and cover with grain alcohol. Let stand in a cool, dark place for 4 days. Filter liquid through cheesecloth into large kettle and discard residue.

Add sugar and water to filtered tangerine–alcohol liquid and bring to a boil over high heat. Remove from heat immediately and pour into sterilized bottles. Cork and seal. Age *at least* three months.

ICED MEXICAN CHOCOLATE
4 servings

    1 *cup chocolate syrup*
    1 *cup cold strong coffee*
    2 *cups chilled milk*
    Crushed ice
    4 *(4-inch) cinnamon sticks*

Combine chocolate syrup and coffee. Add to milk gradually, mixing thoroughly. Fill glasses half full with crushed ice. Pour chocolate milk over ice and stir gently. Place a cinnamon stick in each glass.

NELL'S LEMON CHILLERS
(Old-Fashioned Lemonade)
10 to 12 servings

    1½ *cups sugar*
    1 *cup water*
    Grated peel of 2 lemons
    1½ *cups fresh-squeezed lemon juice*
    Crushed ice
    Thin lemon slices
    Ice water
    Mint sprigs
    Maraschino cherries

Combine first 3 ingredients in saucepan, bring to a boil, and simmer for 5 minutes. Strain and chill. Stir in lemon juice. Pour into a covered jar and refrigerate until ready to use.

To serve, fill tall glass with crushed ice and 2 lemon slices. Add ¼ cup lemon concentrate and fill with ice water, mixing gently. Garnish each glass with a mint sprig and a maraschino cherry.

ON DISTILLING YOUR OWN "MOONSHINE" SWEET MASH CORN LIKKER

Approximately 1½ gallons of corn likker

First you take one bushel of good-quality corn and grind it up real fine into "corn grit," or "chop." (In the old days the member of the family with the stoutest arms would be put to work for this process.) Empty the corn into a container—a good oak barrel is best—and scald it down with boiling water until the mixture becomes soupy. Allow to steep for an hour or so, then add one gallon of ground rye meal and one quart of homemade malt.* Let rest for a couple of hours, then stir down the rye and malt. In another hour or two add half a gallon of warm water and stir like crazy to agitate the mash.

*Homemade malt is made from germinated grain. It is usually made from barley, but corn or rye can be used. The grain is soaked in water and kept damp until it begins to sprout. When the shoots are one or two inches long, spread them out in a warm place to dry. Grind when completely dried. Mixed with the corn grit and rye meal, the malt converts starch into sugar, which the yeast then turns into alcohol. Commercial distillers malt is available.

Next, dissolve four packages of dry yeast in one pint of lukewarm water and let rise for one hour. Empty the yeast mixture into the mash (which has cooled to "body heat" temperature, as moonshiners call it) and stir gently until thoroughly mixed. Cover the entire surface of the mash with a one-half-inch-thick layer of malt called the "cap." The cap floats and welds itself together, sealing off the air and sealing in the yeast action.

The mash, or "wort," is now ready for fermentation. Set the barrel in a warm place because exposure to direct sunlight will bring

CORN

about the quickest results. The mash mixture described here should ferment in three to four days if kept at a temperature of 65° to 75° while exposed to the sun. Actually the mash will ferment anywhere at room temperature—it just takes a little longer.

When fermentation begins, you will be able to see air bubbles and agitation in the mash. The appearance of large bubbles known as "snowballs" indicates that the fermentation cycle is nearly complete. When all bubbling and agitation cease, the mash is ready for distillation. At this stage, the liquid is called "still

100% PURE SPRING WATER

beer" because it tastes like a non-effervescent beer and has an alcoholic content of 4% to 5%.

Pour the still beer into a large, well-made copper still and start the fire. Distillation is the process of getting rid of vapor and condensing the purified product back to liquid. Both alcohol and water vaporize when heated—but this happens at different temperatures (alcohol at 172° and water at 212°). To separate the alcohol from the water, the temperature of the mash should remain constantly between these two boiling points, or at about 190°. The cooking must be watched carefully. Keep the fire gentle and steady because water vapor will build up or the mash will scorch if overheated. Stir constantly.

When the mash begins to steam, cover the still with a cap, which should then be plastered with a thick flour paste to prevent leakage. The cap arm or tube is connected to a copper coil known as a "worm." This rests in a large container of cool water which, in turn, has a trough coming from a stream or other cool water source so that the "jacket" or "cooler barrel" stays at a temperature of about 55°.

As the pressure builds, the vapor pushes through the worm. To avoid "blowing the cap" and being scalded, the still cap should be heavily weighted. The condensed vapor, as it emerges from the coil, has several names for the different stages. The first dribbles are "singlings" or "foreshot," the thin steady liquid stream is "low wine," and the end of the run is called the "tailings."

When the tailings are through, wash out the still and begin the distillation process (or

"doubling") again. This increases the alcohol content, clears out additional impurities, and improves the taste. The timing of all these steps depends on your fire, which must be very steady throughout. The proof of the likker can be varied by mixing some of the low-wine stage with the "doubling." The average mix aimed for is 100 proof. The leftover spent mash (or "slop") is used as hog feed.

Following the above directions faithfully, you will have about 1½ gallons of real old-fashioned white lightning. WARNING: The law of the land permits production of spirits for home comsumption only. "Moonshiners" suspected of selling homemade likker are subject to prosecution—and jail.

Traditional Menus

The dishes in the following menus
may be located in the book
by consulting the index.

NEW YEAR'S DAY BUFFET

Champagne Punch or Spiced Cider

Steak Tartare   Liver Sausage Pâté in Aspic
Caviar Crown   Brandied Meat Balls   White House Shrimp
Marinated Brussels Sprouts

Seafood Bisque   Oyster Stew

Baked Ham in Crust   Beef Burgundy

Hopping John

Avocado Ring with Fruits   Aspic Spectacular

Down East Cranberry Nut Bread   Tillamook Cheese Bread
Crescent Rolls

Chocolate Mint Torte   Tipsy Parson or Squire Cake

Candied Orange Peel   Cherry Nut Brittle

MARDI GRAS BRUNCH

Embassy Frosted Pâté   Pork Tenderloin   Hot Mardi Gras Spread
Served in the French Manner

Quiche à la Jeanette

Palmetto Deviled Crab   Royal Street Chicken Livers   Shrimp
and Mushrooms   New Orleans

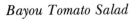

Bayou Tomato Salad

Rosé or Red Wine

Brioche   Sally Lunn Bread

Pickled Peaches   Martha's Watermelon-Rind Pickle

New Orleans Flaming Bananas   Strawberries with Grand Marnier
French Quarter Doughnuts

Café Brûlot

ST. PATRICK'S DAY SUPPER

Hot Rum Cider

Irish Pot Roast   Lamb Stew with Dill

Mrs. Howard's Baked Cabbage   Carrot Pudding
New Potatoes

Irish Soda Bread

Baked Custard   Feathery Pound Cake   Hot Fudge Sauce
Irish Coffee

GARDEN WEEK BUFFET

Miniature Piroshki   *Cheese Straws*   *Crab Dabs*

Creamy Chicken and Broccoli Bake   *Brandied Tenderloin Flambé with Brandied Peaches*

Parker House Rolls   *Butter Curls*

Cucumber Mousse   *Cranberry-Orange Mold*

Mae's Tidewater Cake   *Sour Cream Pound Cake*   *Chocolate Fantasy Cake*
Jan's Determination Cake

Champagne   *Coffee*   *Divinity*   *Nuts*

BACKYARD FOURTH OF JULY PICNIC

Deviled Eggs

Southern-Fried Chicken, Virginia Style   *Oven-Baked Herb Chicken*
Quilters' Potato Salad
Midwestern Baked Beans
Roasted Corn on the Cob

Vegetable Medley Marinade   *Picnic Coleslaw*

Muffin Gems   *Father's Favorite*   *Dakota Rolls*
Beet Relish

Old-Fashioned Vanilla Ice Cream with Strawberries
Mrs. Iowa's Chocolate Cake

Lemon Chillers (Old-Fashioned Lemonade)

THANKSGIVING DINNER

Mulled Wine Punch

Tiny Meat Tarts   Ham and Cheese Ball

Roast Turkey with Virginia or Chestnut Stuffing

Orange-Glazed Sweet Potatoes
Williamsburg Creamed Onions
Fresh Peas with Mint

Cranberry Sauce   Assorted Relishes, Jellies, and Preserves
Perfection Salad with Tangy Cooked Salad Dressing

Colonial Brown Bread   Cloverleaf Rolls

Ginger Pumpkin Pie   Regal Mince Pie

Old English Almond Toffee

PLANTATION CHRISTMAS DINNER

George Washington's Christmas Nog   Wassail Bowl

Angels on Horseback
Benne Seed Wafers

Iced Tomato Bisque

Jewel Glazed Holiday Ham   Smithfield Ham
Sweet-Potato Soufflé
Asparagus Casserole Imperial
Mount Vernon Salad

Baking Powder Biscuits   Virginia Spoon Bread

Burgundy

Plum Pudding with Brandy Sauce or Hard Sauce   Christmas Ambrosia
Monticello White Fruit Cake

Index